GW00854380

LIST OF MAPS

INVITATION TO THE READERS

In researching this book, I have come across many wonderful establishments, the best of which I have included here. However, I'm sure that many of you will also come across appealing hotels, inns, restaurants, guest houses, shops, and attractions. Please don't keep them to yourself. Share your experiences. If you want to comment on places that have been covered in this edition that have changed for the worse, share those, too. You can address your letters to:

Rena Bulkin
Frommer's Orlando '95
c/o Macmillan Travel
15 Columbus Circle
New York, NY 10023

A DISCLAIMER

Readers are advised that prices fluctuate in the course of time, and travel information changes under the impact of the varied and volatile factors that affect the travel industry. The author and the publisher cannot be held responsible for the experiences of the reader while traveling. Readers are invited to write to the publisher with ideas, comments, and suggestions for future editions.

SAFETY ADVISORY

Whenever you're traveling in an unfamiliar city or country, stay alert. Be aware of your immediate surroundings. Wear a moneybelt and keep a close eye on your possessions. Be particularly careful with cameras, purses, and wallets—all favorite targets of thieves and pickpockets.

INTRODUCING ORLANDO

Orlando was a sleepy Southern town ringed with sparkling lakes, pine forests, and citrus groves until Walt Disney waved his pixie-dusted paintbrush over 43 square miles of swampland and turned it into a Magic Kingdom. He literally "animated" the area, sparking an unprecedented building boom, as hotels, restaurants, and scores of additional attractions arose to take advantage of the tourist traffic Disney had generated.

The world's most famous mouse changed central Florida forever. Though the citrus industry still exists here, orange groves have largely given way to high-rise apartment complexes, vast hotels and resorts, and shopping malls. Many national firms have relocated their headquarters to this thriving sunbelt region, and it has also become one of the fastest-growing high-technology centers in the country. Recently, *Newsweek* named Orlando one of the 10 best U.S. cities in which to live and work.

For travelers, Orlando represents a vacation from stressful reality to a gossamer world of make-believe—one where there are parades every day and fireworks every night. Forget all your problems but one: How are you possibly going to cram so many attractions into one short vacation?

1. HISTORY

It would almost seem that the history of Orlando could be condensed into two terse sentences. 1. There were orange groves. 2. Walt Disney

IN THE WORDS OF WALT DISNEY

"I only hope we never lose sight of one thing . . . that it was all started by a mouse."

came. There is, however, considerably more juice to be squeezed from the story. The modern metropolis of Orlando began as a rough-and-tumble Florida frontier town.

DATELINE

- **1513** Spanish explorer Ponce de León, in search of the fabled Fountain of Youth, discovers and names Florida.
- **1817–18** The First Seminole War. Aligned with refugee Creeks from Georgia, native Apalachees, and runaway slaves, the Seminoles battle Andrew Jackson's troops while Florida is still a Spanish territory.
- **1821** After centuries of European struggle for supremacy in the New World, Spain cedes the territory of Florida to the United States.
- **1835–42** Resistance to white settlement results in the Second Seminole War. Many Native Americans migrate south to central Florida.
- **1843** Mosquito County is renamed Orange County.
- **1845** Florida becomes the 27th state in the Union.
- **1856** Orlando becomes the official *(continues)*

SETTLERS VS. SEMINOLES: THE ROAD TO STATEHOOD

Florida history dates back to 1513—more than a century before the Pilgrims landed at Plymouth Rock—when Ponce de León, in search of the fabled "fountain of youth," spied the beaches and lush greenery of Florida's Atlantic coast. He named it La Florida—"the Flowery Land." After years of alternating Spanish, French, and British rule, the territory was ceded (by Spain) to the United States in 1821. Lost in the international shuffle were the Seminoles, who, after migrating from Georgia and the Carolinas in the late 18th century to settle on some of Florida's richest farmlands, were viewed by the Americans as an obstacle to white settlement. After a series of compromise treaties that left both sides dissatisfied, the federal government threw down the final gauntlet with the Indian Removal Act of 1830, stipulating that all eastern tribes be removed to reservations west of the Mississippi. This cruel edict sparked the Second Seminole War (1835–42). At a treaty conference at Payne's Landing in 1832, a young warrior named Osceola strode up to the bargaining table, slammed his knife into the papers on it, and pointing to the quivering blade, proclaimed, "The only treaty I will ever make is this!"

Guerrilla warfare thwarted the U.S. army's attempt to remove the Seminoles for almost eight years, during which time many of the resisters drifted south into the interior of central Florida. In what is today the Orlando area—on a small triangular parcel of land formed by Lake Gatlin, Lake Gem Mary, and Lake Jennie Jewell—the Americans built Fort Gatlin in 1838 to offer protection to pioneer homesteaders. The fort, sited near an ancient oak tree where followers of Osceola frequently met to discuss strategies, was the scene of many skirmishes. The Seminoles kept up a fierce rebellion until 1842, when, undefeated, they accepted a treaty whereby their remaining numbers (about 300) were given land and left in peace. The same year, the Armed Occupation Act offered 160 acres to any pioneers willing to settle here for a minimum of five years. The land was fertile, wild turkeys and deer abounded in the woods, grazing for cattle was equally plentiful, and dozens of lakes provided fish and watering for livestock. In 1843, what had been Mosquito County was more invitingly renamed Orange County. And with the Seminoles more or less out of the way (though sporadic cattle rustling and bloody uprisings still occurred), the Territorial General Legislature petitioned Congress for statehood. On March 3, 1845, Pres. John Tyler signed a bill making Florida the 27th state in the Union.

Settlements and statehood notwithstanding, at the middle of the 19th century the Orlando area (named Jernigan for one of its first settler families) was comprised largely of pristine lakes and pine-forested wilderness. There were no roads, and you could ride all day (if you could find a trail) without meeting a soul. The Jernigans successfully raised cattle, and their home and stockade, which was granted a post office in 1850, became a waystop for travelers and the seat of future development. Farmers and cattle ranchers were drawn to the area's verdant grasslands. Before long a sawmill went up (on the site of today's Orlando Public Library) and a trading post was opened. Other merchants followed as farms and ranches—which would grow to vast agricultural dynasties—were carved out of the wilderness. In 1856, the boundaries of Orange County were revised, and, thanks to the manipulations of resident James Gamble Speer, a member of the Indian Removal Commission, Fort Gatlin (Jernigan) became its official seat. How the fledgling town came to be named Orlando is a matter of some speculation. Some say Speer renamed the town after a dearly loved friend, while other sources say he named it after one of his favorite Shakespearean characters from *As You Like It*. But the most

DATELINE

seat of Orange County.

- **1861** Florida secedes from the Union. The demise of slavery sounds the death knell for the area's burgeoning cotton industry.
- **1870** Cattle ranching and citrus growing replace cotton as the bulwark of Orlando's economy.
- **1875** Orlando is officially incorporated as a municipality under state law.
- **1880** The South Florida Railroad facilitates the expansion of Orlando's agricultural markets.
- **1884** Fire rages out of control, destroying much of Orlando's fledgling business district.
- **1894–95** Freezing temperatures destroy two years of citrus crops and wreck orchards. Many growers lose everything.
- **1910–25** A land boom hits Florida. Fortunes are made overnight.
- **1926** The land boom goes bust. Fortunes are lost overnight.
- **1929** An invasion of Mediterranean fruit flies devastates Orlando's citrus in-

(continues)

DATELINE

dustry. Its ruined economy is capped by the stock market crash.

• **1939–45** World War II revives Orlando's ailing economy. The city becomes "Florida's Air Capital."

• **1955** Nearby Cape Canaveral becomes a focal point for the space program.

• **1964** Walt Disney begins surreptitiously buying up central Florida farmland, purchasing more than 28,000 acres at a cost of nearly $5.5 million.

• **1965** Disney announces his plan to build the world's most spectacular theme park in Orlando.

• **1968** Kennedy Space Center becomes the launch site for American manned space missions.

• **1971** The Magic Kingdom opens its gates.

• **1972** A new one-day attendance mark is set on December 27, when 72,328 people visit the Magic Kingdom. It will be broken almost every year thereafter.

(continues)

accepted version is that the town was named for prominent plantation owner Orlando Reeves (or Rees), who died in battle with the Seminoles in 1835. The site where he was buried on the shores of Lake Eola came to be known as "Orlando's Grave." Speer is reported to have said, "This place is often spoken of as 'Orlando's Grave.' Let's drop the word "grave" and let the county seat be called Orlando."

THE 1860s: CIVIL WAR/CATTLE WARS

Throughout the early 1860s, cotton plantations and cattle ranches became the hallmarks of central Florida. Orlando was ringed by a vast cotton empire. Log cabins went up along the lakes, and the pioneers eked out a somewhat lonely existence separated from each other by miles of farmland. But there were troubles brewing in the 31-state nation that would soon devastate Orlando's planters. The institution of slavery was a major issue of the day. In his 1858 debate with Stephen Douglas, Abraham Lincoln declared, "This government cannot endure permanently half slave and half free." A year later it was obvious that only a war would resolve the issue. In 1861, Florida became the third state to secede from the Union, and the modest progress it had achieved came to a standstill. The Stars and Bars flew from every flagpole, and local men enlisted in the Confederate army, leaving the fledgling town in poverty. A Federal blockade made it difficult to obtain necessities, and many slaves fled. In 1866, the Confederate troops of Florida surrendered, the remaining slaves were freed, and a ragtag group of defeated soldiers returned to Orlando. They found a dying cotton industry, unable to function without slave labor or transport to markets. In 1868 Florida was readmitted into the Union.

Its untended cotton fields having gone to seed, Orlando now concentrated on cattle ranching, a business plagued by heavy taxation on herds by the occupation government and one that ushered in an era of lawlessness and violence. Cattle rustling, widely practiced, generated vicious feuds, clogging courtroom calendars and igniting long-running hostilities between warring parties. Like frontier cattle towns out west, post-Civil War Orlando was short on civilized behavior; gunfights, brawls, and murders were commonplace. But as the 1860s drew to a close, large herd owners from other parts of the state moved into the area and began organizing the industry in a less chaotic fashion. Branding and penning greatly reduced rustling, though it never totally eliminated the problem; even a century later soaring beef prices brought on a rash of cattle thievery as late as 1973!

AN ORANGE TREE GROWS IN ORLANDO

In the 1870s, articles in national magazines began luring large numbers of Americans to central Florida with promises of arable land and a warm climate. In Orlando, public roads, schools, and churches appeared to serve the newcomers, many of whom replanted defunct cotton fields with citrus groves. Orlando was officially incorporated under state law in 1875, setting up definitive boundaries, a city government complete with a mayor, laws and ordinances, a city hall, a jail, and other adjuncts of a municipality. New settlers poured in from all over the country, businesses flourished, and by the end of the year, the town had its first newspaper, the *Orange County Reporter*. The first locomotive of the South Florida Railroad chugged into town in 1880, representing a major step toward growth and prosperity and sparking a building and land boom—the first of many. Orlando got sidewalks and its first bank in 1883—the same year the town voted itself "dry" in hopes of averting the fistfights and brawls that ensued when cowboys crowded into local saloons every Saturday night for rowdy R&R. For many years the city continued to vote itself alternately wet and dry, but in actuality, it made very little difference. Legal or not, liquor was always readily available.

DATELINE

- **1973** Shamū ventures into Orlando waters. Sea World opens.
- **1979** Mickey Mouse welcomes the Magic Kingdom's 100-millionth visitor, 8-year-old Kurt Miller from Kingsville, Maryland.
- **1982** Epcot opens to the public with vast hoopla. Participating celebrities include everyone from Richard Nixon to George Steinbrenner.
- **1984** Donald Duck's 50th birthday is celebrated with a special parade down Main Street that includes 50 live Peking ducks.
- **1988** Walt Disney World celebrates Mickey Mouse's 60th birthday. A special parade *does not* include 50 live mice!
- **1989** WDW launches Disney-MGM Studios Theme Park (offering a behind-the-scenes look at Tinseltown), Typhoon Lagoon (a 56-acre water theme park), and Pleasure Island (an adult nightclub theme park).
- **1990** Universal Studios opens, offer-

(continues)

DATELINE

ing visitors thrilling
encounters with
E. T. and King Kong.
• **1993** Sea World
continues a major
expansion. And Uni-
versal Studios un-
leashes the
fearsome *Jaws*.

FIRE & ICE

In January of 1884, a grocery fire that started at 4am wiped out blocks of businesses, including the offices of the *Orange County Reporter*. But 19th-century Orlando was a bit like a Frank Capra movie. The town rallied round, providing a new location for the paper and presenting its publisher, Mahlon Gore, with $1,200 in cash to help defray losses and $300 in new subscriptions. The paper not only survived but flourished. And the city, realizing the need, created its first fire brigade. By August of 1884, a census revealed that the population had grown to 1,666. That same year 600,000 boxes of oranges were shipped from Florida to points north—most of those boxes originating in Orlando. By 1885, Orlando was a viable town boasting as many as 50 businesses. It was dubbed the "Phenomenal City" after a South Florida Railroad booklet called the city's growth "phenomenal." Which is not to say it was New York. Razorback hogs roamed the streets, and alligator wrestling was a main form of entertainment.

Disaster struck a week after Christmas in 1894, when the temperature plummeted to an unseasonal 24 degrees. Water pipes burst, and orange blossoms froze, blackened, and died. The freeze continued for three days, wrecking the citrus crop for the year. Karl H. Abbott, son of the owner of the San Juan Hotel, where northern buyers met to bid on citrus crops, later described the pandemonium that broke out as the thermometer began dipping shortly after noon:

". . . The buyers hurriedly left the lunch tables and went out of doors to view the weather. The big thermometer in front of the hotel indicated unusual cold. By 2:00 p.m. the San Juan was in an uproar. Prices had dropped to 'no sale.' Commission merchants were frantically trying to get out of options and heated debates and fist fights started in the lobby . . . About nine that night a fine looking grey haired gentleman in a black coat and Stetson hat walked up the street in front of the hotel and looked at the thermometer, groaned 'Oh my God!' and shot himself through the head . . ."

Many grove owners went bust, and those who remained were hit with a second devastating freeze the following year. Tens of thousands of trees died in the killing frost. Small growers were wiped out, but large conglomerates that could afford to buy up their properties at bargain prices and wait for new groves to mature assured the survival of the industry.

SPECULATION FEVER: GOOD DEALS, BAD DEALS . . .

As Orlando entered the 20th century, citrus and agriculture had surpassed cattle ranching as the mainstay of the local economy. Stray cows no longer had to be shooed from the railway tracks. Streets were being paved and electricity and telephone service installed. The population at the turn of the century was 2,481. In 1902, the city passed its first automobile laws, which included an in-town speed limit of five miles per hour. In 1904, the city flooded. And in 1905 it suffered a drought that ended—miraculously or coincidentally—on a day when all faiths united at the local First Baptist Church to pray for rain. By 1910, prosperity had returned, and Orlando, with a population of nearly 4,000, was becoming a tourism and convention center. World War I brought further industrial growth and a real estate boom, not just to Orlando but to all of Florida. Millions of immigrants, speculators, and builders descended on the state in search of a quick buck. As land speculation reached a fever pitch, and property was bought and resold almost overnight, many citrus groves gave way to urbanization. Preeminent Orlando builder and promoter Carl Dann described the action thusly: "It finally became nothing more than a gambling machine, each man buying on a shoestring, betting dollars a bigger fool would come along and buy his option."

Quite suddenly, the bubble burst. A July 1926 issue of the *Nation* provided the obituary for the Florida land boom: "The world's greatest poker game, played with lots instead of chips, is over. And the players are now . . . paying up." Construction slowed to a trickle, and many newcomers who had arrived in Florida to jump on the bandwagon returned to their homes in the north. Though Orlando was not quite as hard hit as Miami—scene of the greediest land grabs—some belt-tightening was in order. The city even managed to build a municipal airport in 1928. Then came a Mediterranean fruit fly infestation that crippled the citrus industry. Hundreds of thousands of acres of land in quarantined areas had to be cleared of fruit and vast quantities of boxed fruit destroyed. The 1929 stock market crash that precipitated the Great Depression seemed almost an afterthought to Florida's ruined economy.

. . . AND NEW DEALS

Pres. Franklin D. Roosevelt's New Deal helped the state climb back on its feet. The Works Progress Administration (WPA) put 40,000 unemployed Floridians back to work—work that included hundreds of public projects in Orlando. Of these, the most important was the expansion and resurfacing of the city's airport. By 1936, the tourist trade had revived somewhat, construction was up once again, and the state began attracting a broader range of visitors than ever before. But the event that finally lifted Florida—and the nation—out of the depression was World War II.

Orlando had weathered the Great Depression. Now it prepared for war with the construction of army bases, housing for servicemen, and training facilities. Almost all new business was geared toward defense. Enlisted men poured into the city, and the airport was again enlarged and equipped with barracks, a military hospital, administration buildings, and mess halls. By 1944, Orlando had a second airport and was known as "Florida's Air Capital"—home to major aircraft and aviation-parts-manufacturing factories. Thousands of U.S. serv-

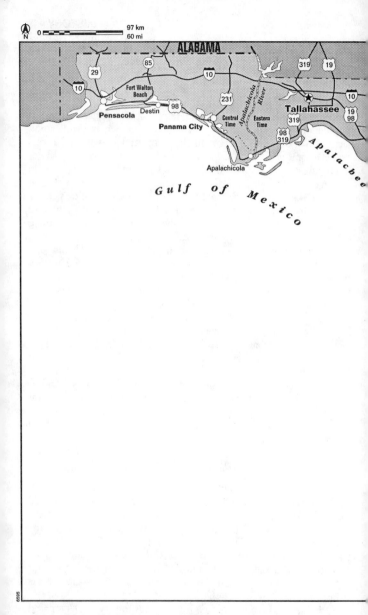

icemen did part of their hitch in Orlando, and when the war ended, many returned to settle there.

POSTWAR PROSPERITY

By 1950, Orlando—with a population of 51,826—was the financial and transportation hub of central Florida. The city shared the bullish

FLORIDA

GEORGIA

Amelia Island

Jacksonville
Lake City
Jacksonville Beach

St. Augustine
St. Augustine
Beach

Gainesville

Ocala
National
Forest
Ocala
De Land

Daytona Beach

Cedar
Key
Homosassa
Springs

Tarpon Springs

Orlando
Bee Line
Expwy.

NASA-Kennedy
Space Center

Cape
Canaveral
Merritt Island

Kissimmee

Tampa Lakeland
Clearwater
Winter
Haven

Melbourne

St.
Petersburg

Tampa
Bay

Bradenton

Sarasota

Vero Beach

Fort Pierce

Jensen Beach

Lake
Okeechobee

Riviera Beach
West Palm
Palm Beach
Beach

Captiva Island

Cape
Coral

Caloosahatchee River

Fort Myers

Big Cypress
Swamp

Everglade Pkwy.
(Alligator Alley)

Delray Beach
Boca Raton
Pompano
Beach

Fort Lauderdale
Dania
Hollywood

Sanibel Island

Naples

Big Cypress
National
Preserve

Miami
Beach

Marco
Island

Everglades City

Ten
Thousand
Islands

Everglades
National
Park

Homestead

Miami

Biscayne
Bay

Flamingo

Florida Bay

Key Largo

Florida Keys
Long Key
Marathon

Key West

Atlantic Ocean

Suwannee River

St. Johns River

Florida's Turnpike

Kissimmee River

economy of the 1950s with the rest of the nation. In the face of the cold war, the Orlando air force base remained and grew, funneling millions of dollars into the local economy. Florida's population increased by a whopping 78.7% during the decade—making it America's 10th most-populous state—and tourists came in droves, nearly 4.5 million in 1950 alone. One reason for the influx was the advent of the air conditioner, which made life in Florida infinitely more pleasant. Also fueling Orlando's economy was a brand-new industry arriving in nearby Cape Canaveral in 1955—the government-run space program. Cape Canaveral became NASA's headquarters for the Apollo rocket program that eventually blasted Neil Armstrong heavenward toward his famous "giant leap." During the same decade, the Glenn L. Martin Company (later Martin Marietta), builder of the Matador Missile, purchased 10 square miles for a plant site four miles south of Orlando. Its advent sparked further industrial growth, and property values soared. More than 60 new industries located in the area in 1959 alone. But even the most optimistic Orlando boosters could not foresee the glorious future that was the city's ultimate destiny.

THE DISNEY DECADES

In 1964, Walt Disney began secretly buying up millions of dollars worth of central Florida farmland. As vast areas of land were purchased in lots of 5,000 acres here, 20,000 there—at remarkably high prices—rumors flew as to who needed so much land and had so much money to acquire it. Some thought it was Howard Hughes; others, the space program. Speculation was rife almost to the very day, November 15, 1965 ("D" Day for Orlando), when Disney himself arrived in town and announced his plans to build the world's most spectacular theme park ("bigger and better than Disneyland"). In a two-year construction effort, Disney employed 9,000 people. Land speculation reached unprecedented heights, as hotel chains and restaurateurs grabbed up property near the proposed parks. Mere swampland sold for millions. Total cost of the project by its October 1971 opening was $400 million. Mickey Mouse personally led the first visitor into the Magic Kingdom, and numerous celebrities— everyone from Bob Hope to Julie Andrews—took part in the opening ceremonies. In Walt Disney World's first two years, the attraction drew 20 million visitors and employed 13,000 people. The sleepy citrus-growing town of Orlando had become the "Action Center of Florida" and the fastest-growing city in the state. A 1972 referendum revitalized downtown Orlando. Additional attractions multiplied faster than fruit flies, and hundreds of firms relocated their businesses in the area. Sea World, a major theme park, came to town in 1973. Walt Disney World has continued to grow and expand, adding Epcot in 1982 and Disney-MGM Studios in 1989, along with water parks, over a dozen "official" resorts, a shopping/restaurant village, campgrounds, a vast array of recreational facilities, and several other adjuncts thoroughly described farther on in this book. Universal Studios, which also continues to expand, opened in 1990.

In the 1990s, Orlando enjoys the best overall business climate in the state. In addition to tourism, its dynamic economy thrives on diverse industry, thousands of technology-related companies, and agriculture. The only remnant of Orlando's slow-paced pre-Disney southern image is its down-home friendliness. This burgeoning sunbelt metropolis looks forward to the future with unbounded optimism.

2. FAMOUS ORLANDOANS

Walter Elias [Walt] Disney (1901–66). Animation impresario Walt Disney created world-famous cartoon characters Mickey Mouse, Donald Duck, Pluto, and Goofy, among many others. His first full-length cartoon feature was *Snow White and the Seven Dwarfs* (1938). In 1955 he built the 250-acre Disneyland Park in Anaheim, California, which became one of the major tourist attractions in the United States. Many of his plans were realized after his death—among them Orlando's Magic Kingdom, Epcot, and Disney-MGM Studios Theme Park.

Donald Duck (b. 1934). Member of a prominent thespian family (which includes nephews Huey, Dewey, and Louie, billionaire Uncle Scrooge, and Grandma Duck), Donald has starred in more than 170 cartoons and movies since his 1930s debut as an extra in *The Wise Little Hen*. As recorded in Disney archives, "he bellowed and strutted his way into that production until, bit part or no, he was practically the star of the piece." Though Disney directors have always liked working with the superbly gifted "mad mallard," his career has been somewhat hindered by his terrible temper—most notably his public tantrums when Mickey got his own television show, "The Mickey Mouse Club," in the 1950s. The bellicose duck's most memorable line of dialogue, "Wanna fight?" is said to have inspired Clint Eastwood's "Make my day."

Christian [Buddy] Ebsen (b. 1908). American actor and dancer specializing in countrified characters. He played second fiddle to Fess Parker in the Davy Crockett movies and was a lead character in the television series "The Beverly Hillbillies." At 64 he became Barnaby Jones. Ebsen has appeared in many movies, including *Breakfast at Tiffany's*.

Michael Dammann Eisner (b. 1942). Chairman and CEO of the entire Walt Disney Company since 1984. Though his father made him read for two hours each day before watching TV, Eisner started climbing the corporate ladder in the programming departments of CBS, NBC, and ABC. Prior to taking over the helm at Disney, Eisner was president and CEO of Paramount Pictures. In his first decade at the firm, Eisner revitalized Disney's motion picture, television, and theme park operations; opened Disney-MGM Studios Theme Park; moved into commercial television, magazines, and book publishing; and expanded to Europe with Euro Disney.

Goofy (b. 1932). Goofy first appeared along with Mickey Mouse in a cartoon called *Mickey's Revue*. Though his original name was Dippy Dawg, which later evolved into Dippy the Goof, and finally, Goofy, there has been, over the years, an ongoing controversy as to exactly what kind of animal he is. The claim of Disney representatives that he is supposed to be a human being has never been adequately substantiated. And Goofy himself fueled speculation when he answered a reporter's question about his species in 1992 with the words "Gawrsh! I dunno." Tabloid rumors notwithstanding, this dumb but likable toon is the living embodiment of Murphy's Law—whatever can go wrong will go wrong. But he continues to laugh ("hyuk, hyuk") in the face of adversity.

Mahlon Gore (1837–1917). Editor and proprietor of the *Orange County Reporter,* businessman, and tireless city booster, Gore came to Orlando from Iowa in 1880 when, he later reported, there were only "200 inhabitants, three stores, a livery stable, and a saloon." Today an Orlando avenue bears his name.

Mickey Mouse (b. 1928). A prominent Orlando resident since 1971, Mickey also maintains a home in Anaheim, California. Star of more than 120 cartoons and movies, he made his film debut the year of his birth in *Steamboat Willie*. His significant other, Minnie Mouse (no relation), also appeared in the film. Mickey's dad almost named him Mortimer, but his mom (Mrs. Disney) persuaded her husband that Mortimer was too pompous a moniker for a mouse and suggested Mickey. Mickey considers the 1940s, when he starred in *Fantasia,* as his "Golden Decade." And he's especially proud that during World War II his name was used as the password of Allied forces on D-Day. Having reached the age of retirement, Mickey has no plans to stop working. "Better to wear out than rust out," says the still teenlike toon.

James Gamble Speer (1820–93). A prominent early settler, Judge Speer took a leading role in securing the county seat for Orlando. He is also credited with naming the city. Today an Orlando avenue is named in his honor.

Jacob Summerlin (1820–93). Dubbed "King of the Crackers" and "Cattle King of Florida," Summerlin was the first child born in the new state—in a fort where his parents had sought refuge from Seminole attack. He organized Florida cattle owners to supply the Confederate army with beef during the Civil War, engaged in blockade-running, financed free public schools, built Orlando's first luxury hotel, and donated his property for parkland around Lake Eola.

IN THE WORDS OF WALT DISNEY

"Why be a governor or a senator when you can be king of Disneyland?"

"You can dream, create, design, and build the most wonderful place in the world . . . but it required people to make the dream a reality."

Joe Tinker   (1880–1948). Florida building developer, former star shortstop of the Chicago Cubs, and manager of the Cincinnati Reds, Tinker created a baseball team for Orlando that won the 1921 Florida State League championship. He also convinced the Cincinnati Reds to sign a three-year contract to play in Orlando at the new $15,000 Tinker Field completed in 1923—a ballpark larger than the New York Yankee Field. Tinker was immortalized in Franklin P. Adams' verse *Baseball's Sad Lexicon,* better known as "Tinker to Evers to Chance."

W. W. Yothers   (1879–1971). An entomologist who worked for a quarter of a century in the Orlando area, Yothers is credited with stopping the Mediterranean fruit fly epidemic of 1929–30 and helping control diseases that threatened the citrus industry.

CHAPTER 2

PLANNING A TRIP TO ORLANDO

I n attraction-rich Orlando, advance planning is the sure key to optimum enjoyment. In addition to the information below, see Chapters 5 (accommodations) and 7 (attractions) for "how-to" hints.

1. INFORMATION & MONEY

As soon as you know you're going to Orlando, write or call the **Orlando/Orange County Convention & Visitors Bureau,** 8445 International Dr. (in the Mercado Shopping Village), Orlando, FL 32819 (tel. 407/363-5871). The bureau can answer all your questions and will be happy to send you maps, brochures (including the informative *Official Visitors Guide,* the *Area Guide* to local restaurants, and the *Official Accommodations Guide),* and the "Magicard," good for discounts of 10% to 50% on accommodations, attractions, car rentals, and more.

For general information about Walt Disney World—and a copy of the informative *Walt Disney World Vacation Guide*—write or call the **Walt Disney World Co.,** Box 10,000, Lake Buena Vista, FL 32830-1000 (tel. 407/824-4321).

Also contact the **Kissimmee–St. Cloud Convention & Visitors Bureau,** 1925 U.S. 192 (P.O. Box 422007), Kissimmee, FL 34742-2007 (tel. 407/847-5000, or toll free 800/327-9159). They'll send maps, brochures, discount books, and the *Kissimmee–St. Cloud Vacation Guide,* which details the area's accommodations and attractions.

WHAT THINGS COST IN ORLANDO U.S. $

Taxi from airport to WDW area	38.00
Bus from airport to WDW area (adult fare)	23.00
Local telephone call	.25
Double room at Disney's Grand Floridian Beach Resort (very expensive)	230.00–325.00
Double room at Marriott's Orlando World Center (expensive)	149.00–189.00
Double room at Disney's Port Orleans Resort (moderate)	89.00–121.00
Double room at Disney's All-Star Music Resort (inexpensive)	69.00–79.00
Double room at Ramada Ltd., Kissimmee (budget)	27.95–45.00
Seven-course prix-fixe dinner for one at Victoria & Albert's, not including tip or wine (very expensive)	80.00
Three-course dinner at L'Originale Alfredo di Roma, in the Italy pavilion of Epcot, not including tip or wine (expensive)	30.00
All-you-can-eat buffet dinner at Akershus, in the Norway pavilion of Epcot, not including tip or wine (inexpensive)	17.25
Bottle of beer (restaurant)	2.25
Coca-Cola (restaurant)	.95
Cup of coffee	1.25
Roll of ASA 100 Kodacolor film, 36 exposures purchased at Walt Disney World	7.37
Adult Four-Day Value Pass admission to Walt Disney World	132.00
Four-Day Value Pass admission to Walt Disney World for children 3–9	103.50
Adult one-day admission to Sea World	32.95
One-day admission to Sea World for children 3–9	28.95
Adult one-day admission to Universal Studios	35.00
One-day admission to Universal Studios for children 3–9	28.00

2. WHEN TO GO — CLIMATE & EVENTS

WHEN TO GO

Orlando is essentially a theme park destination, and its busiest seasons are whenever kids are out of school—summer (early June to about August 20), holiday weekends, Christmas season (mid-December to mid-January), and Easter. Obviously, the whole experience is more enjoyable when the crowds are thinnest and the weather most temperate. Hotel rooms are also lower priced off-season. Best times: the week after Labor Day until Thanksgiving, the week after Thanksgiving until mid-December, and the six weeks before and after school spring vacations. Worst time: summer, when crowds are very large and weather oppressively hot and humid. I probably shouldn't say this, but I would pull the kids out of school for a few days around an off-season weekend to avoid long lines.

Central Florida Average Temperatures

	Jan	Feb	Mar	Apr	May	June	July	Aug	Sept	Oct	Nov	Dec
High F°	71.7	72.9	78.3	83.6	88.3	90.6	91.7	91.6	89.7	84.4	78.2	73.1
C°	22.0	22.7	25.7	28.7	31.3	32.5	33.2	33.1	32.0	29.1	25.7	22.8
Low F°	49.3	50.0	55.3	60.3	66.2	71.2	73.0	73.4	72.5	65.4	56.8	50.9
C°	9.6	10.0	12.5	15.7	19.0	21.8	22.7	23.0	22.5	18.6	13.8	10.5

ORLANDO CALENDAR OF EVENTS

JANUARY

✪ **FLORIDA CITRUS BOWL CLASSIC** This annual college football game, featuring two of the year's top national teams, usually plays to a full house.
Where: The Florida Citrus Bowl Stadium. 1610 W. Church St., at Tampa Street. **When:** New Year's Day. **How:** Call 407/849-2020 for information, 407/839-3900 for tickets. Tickets go on sale late October/early November. Tickets are $30.

☐ **Scottish Highland Games.** Featuring Scottish dancing, caber tossing, antique British car shows, dog shows, bagpipe playing, and food and crafts vendors, this two-day event takes place during the last weekend of the month at the Central Florida Fairgrounds, 4603 W. Colonial Dr., between Mercy and Pine Hills roads. Tickets are $8 for adults, $3 for children 6 to 12, under 6 free. Call 407/422-8226 for details.

☐ **Walt Disney World Marathon.** This 26.2-mile marathon winding through the resort and theme park areas is open to all comers, including the physically challenged. There is a $50 entry fee, which is included in room price with some Disney resort packages. Call 407/824-4321 for details.

FEBRUARY

✪ *SILVER SPURS RODEO A major event on the professional circuit, this is one of the top 20 PRCA rodeos in the nation, featuring professional cowboys and cowgirls in a wide variety of competitions—calf roping, bull and bronc riding, barrel racing, and more. The Silver Spurs Quadrille performs their famous dance on horseback.*

Where: At the Silver Spurs Arena, 1875 E. Irlo Bronson Memorial Hwy. (U.S. 192) in Kissimmee. When: On the third weekend in February. How: Call 407/847-5000 for details, 407/67-RODEO for tickets. All seats are $12.

☐ **Kissimmee Valley Livestock Show and Osceola County Fair.** This down-home-style county fair—complete with agricultural exhibits, livestock judging, rides, and crafts—takes place for six days during the third week of the month at the Kissimmee Valley Agricultural Center, 1901 E. Irlo Bronson Memorial Hwy. (U.S. 192), next to the Silver Spurs Arena. Admission is $3 for adults, $1 for children 4 to 12, under 4 free. Midway rides are extra. Call 407/846-6046 for details.

☐ **Mardi Gras Celebration at Pleasure Island,** Walt Disney World. This rollicking Mardi Gras revel is a street party with food, drink, costumes, and entertainment. Admission includes all food and drinks. Call 407/824-4321 for details.

MARCH

☐ **Houston Astros Spring Training.** Training begins in late February and there are games from March through early April at Osceola County Stadium, 1000 Bill Beck Blvd., in Kissimmee. Tickets are $7 to $8. Call 407/933-2520 for details and tickets.

☐ **Kissimmee Bluegrass Festival.** Bluegrass and gospel entertainers from all over the country, including the Lewis Family, perform at this four-day festival beginning the first weekend of the month. It takes place at the Silver Spurs Arena, 1875 E. Irlo Bronson Memorial Hwy. (U.S. 192). Tickets are $10 to $17. Multi-day packages are available. Call toll free 800/473-7773 for details.

☐ **Central Florida Fair.** During 11 days in early March, the fair features rides, entertainers, 4-H and Future Farmers of America exhibits, livestock exhibits, a monkey show, and food booths. The Orange County District School Science and Engineering Fair takes place here at the same time. At the Central Florida Fairgrounds, 4603 W. Colonial Dr., between Mercy and Pine Hills roads. Tickets cost $5 for adults, $2 for children 6 to 10, under 6 free. Call 407/295-3247 for details.

☐ **Nestle Invitational.** Arnold Palmer hosts this seven-day, mid-month PGA Tour event at the Bay Hill Club, 9000 Bay Hill Blvd. Daily admission is $28, week-long admission $50. Call 407/876-2888 for details.

☐ **Spring Flower Festival.** More than 88,000 brightly colored bedding plants, including yellow pansies, violet and orange impatiens, and red and pink begonias, create beautiful floral topiaries shaped as butterflies, birds, and animals. At Cypress Gardens, FL 540 at Cypress Gardens Boulevard, in Winter Haven. Entry included with park admission. Call 813/324-2111 for details.

☐ **Sidewalk Art Festival.** This major arts festival in Winter Park, drawing artists and artisans from all over North America, takes place along Park Avenue. Third weekend in March. Call 407/623-3234 or 407/644-8281 for details.

APRIL

☐ **Orlando Cubs Baseball Season.** The Chicago Cubs farm team plays at Tinker Field, 287 Tampa Ave. South, from April through early September. Admission is $3 to $5. Call 407/872-7593 for details.

☐ **Easter Sunrise Service.** An interdenominational service, with music, is presented at the Atlantis Theatre at Sea World, 7007 Sea World Dr. It is hosted by a well-known person each year, most recently Elizabeth Dole. Admission is free. Call 407/351-3600 for details.

☐ **Easter Sunday,** Walt Disney World. The holiday is celebrated with an old-fashioned Easter Parade. All areas of the park open early and stay open late during the Easter season. Call 407/824-4321 for details.

JUNE

☐ **Walt Disney World Wine Festival.** More than 60 wineries from all over the United States participate. Events include wine tastings, seminars, food, and celebrity-chef cooking demonstrations at the Disney Village Marketplace. Call 407/827-7200 or 407/824-4321 for details.

☐ **Walt Disney World All-American College Orchestra and College Band.** The best collegiate musical talent in the country performs at Epcot and the Magic Kingdom throughout the month. Call 407/824-4321 for details.

JULY

☐ **Independence Day.** Walt Disney World's Star-Spangled Spectacular brings bands, singers, dancers, and unbelievable fireworks displays to all the Disney parks. Call 407/824-4321 for details. **Sea World,** 7007 Sea World Dr., also features a dazzling laser/fireworks spectacular. Call 407/351-3600 for details.

✪ *SILVER SPURS RODEO* Big-time rodeo returns to Kissimmee (see details above in February listings).
   Where: At the Silver Spurs Arena, 1875 E. Irlo Bronson Memorial Hwy. (U.S. 192) in Kissimmee. *When:* On a weekend in early July. *How:* Call 847-5000 for details, 407/67-RODEO for tickets. All seats are $10. Children 12 and under pay half price.

SEPTEMBER

✪ *NIGHTS OF JOY* The Magic Kingdom is closed down for a festival of contemporary Christian music featuring top artists.
   When: Over two weekends, selected annually. *How:* This is a very popular event; obtain tickets early. Admission is about $25 to $30 per night. Exclusive use of Magic Kingdom attractions is included. Call 407/824-4321 for details.

OCTOBER

☐ **Florida State Air Fair.** Sponsored by the Rotary Club of Kissimmee, this is one of the biggest air shows in the southeast, featuring aerobatics, static displays, wing walking, and jet and piston aircraft demonstration teams. On a selected weekend in October each year. At the Kissimmee Municipal Airport, 301 N. Dyer Blvd. Tickets are $10 for adults, $7 for children 7 to 17, under 7 free. Call 407/933-8922 for details.

☐ **Halloween Horror Nights.** Universal Studios, 1000 Universal Studios Plaza, off Kirkman Road, transforms its studios and attractions for a gigantic "spooktacular" nighttime Halloween party during several long weekends prior to Halloween. Attractions include a haunted sound stage, a psychopath maze, special shows, and hundreds of ghouls and goblins roaming the studio streets terrifying the populace. Special admission is charged. Call 407/363-8000 for details.

☐ **Walt Disney World Oldsmobile Golf Classic.** Top PGA tour players compete for a total purse of $1 million at WDW golf courses. The event is preceded by the world's largest golf tournament, the Oldsmobile Scramble, on the same courses. Admission for Scramble is free. For the Golf Classic, daily ticket prices range from $8 to $15. Call 407/824-4321 for details.

☐ **Walt Disney World Village Boat Show.** Central Florida's largest in-the-water boat show featuring the best of new watercraft takes place at the Village Marketplace over a three-day weekend early in the month. Call 407/824-4321 for details.

NOVEMBER

☐ **Annual Chrysanthemum Festival.** A month-long event featuring displays of over two million multicolored mums—in flower beds, "blooming" gazebos, poodle baskets, and bonsais. At Cypress Gardens, FL 540 at Cypress Gardens Boulevard, in Winter Haven. Entry included with park admission. Call 813/324-2111 for details.

☐ **Walt Disney World Festival of the Masters.** One of the largest art shows in the south takes place at the Village Marketplace for three days including the second weekend of November. It features top artists, photographers, and craftspeople, winners of juried shows throughout the country. No admission. Call 407/824-4321 for details.

☐ **Walt Disney World Doll and Teddy Bear Convention.** The top doll and teddy bear designers from around the world travel to WDW to meet with enthusiasts and collectors. Special editions and one-of-a-kind auctions highlight the event, which takes place in a selected Disney resort and throughout the parks. Call 407/824-4321 or 407/560-7232 for details.

☐ **Walt Disney World Jolly Holidays Dinner Shows.** Late November through mid-December, all-you-can-eat dinner shows are offered at the Contemporary Resort's Fantasia Ballroom. A cast of over 100 Disney characters, singers, and dancers performs in a delightful old-fashioned Christmas extravaganza. Call 407/W-DISNEY for details and ticket prices.

☐ **Magic Basketball.** Shaquille O'Neal and his teammates on the Orlando Magic do battle against visiting teams between October and April at the Orlando Arena, 600 W. Amelia St. Ticket prices range from about $17 to $45. Call 407/896-2442 for details, 407/839-3900 for tickets.

DECEMBER

☐ **Annual Poinsettia Festival.** A spectacular floral showcase of more than 40,000 red, white, and pink poinsettias (including topiary reindeer). From early December through mid-January at Cypress Gardens, FL 540 at Cypress Gardens Boulevard, in Winter Haven. Entry included with park admission. Call 813/324-2111 for details.

☐ **Florida Citrus Sports Half-Marathon and Hooter's 5K Run.** This annual race, early in December, takes place in downtown Orlando, beginning at Church Street Market, 200 S. Orange Ave. It begins at 8am. Anyone can participate. An entry fee is charged. The event kicks off the Citrus Bowl season. Call 407/423-2476 for information.

☐ **Walt Disney World Christmas Festivities.** For the holiday season, Main Street is lavishly decked out with lights and holly, and visitors are greeted by carolers. An 80-foot tree is illuminated by thousands of colored lights. Epcot and MGM Studios also offer special embellishments and entertainments throughout the holiday season, as do all Disney resorts. Holiday highlights include: **Mickey's Very Merry Christmas Party,** an after-dark ticketed event weekends at the Magic Kingdom with a traditional Christmas parade and a breathtaking fireworks display. Admission price includes free cookies and cocoa and a souvenir photo. The **Glory and Pageantry of Christmas** at the Walt Disney Village Marketplace, including several shows nightly, tells the story of the birth of Jesus. Admission is free. The **Candle-light Procession,** along Main Street at the Magic Kingdom, features thousands of candleholding carolers walking darkened streets. There's storytelling as well.

Call 407/824-4321 for details about all of the above—and more, 407/W-DISNEY to inquire about hotel/events packages.

☐ **Walt Disney World New Year's Eve Celebration.** The **Magic Kingdom** is open until 2am for a massive fireworks exhibition. Other New Year's festivities in the WDW parks include: a big bash at **Pleasure Island** featuring music headliners, a special *Hoop-Dee-Doo Musical Revue* show, and guest performances by well-known musical groups at **Disney-MGM Studios.** Call 407/824-4321 for details.

☐ **Sea World Holiday Events.** Sea World, 7007 Sea World Dr., features a special Shamu and a luau show called *Christmas in Hawaii.* The 400-foot sky tower is lit like a Christmas tree nightly. Call 407/351-3600 for details.

☐ **The Citrus Bowl Parade.** On December 31, lavish floats—including some from Disney and Sea World—join with local high school bands for a nationally televised parade beginning at 1pm. Reserved seats in the bleachers are $12. Call 407/423-2476 for details.

☐ **New Year's Citrus Eve.** The official New Year's Eve celebration of the Florida Citrus Bowl takes place at Sea World, 7007 Sea World Dr. Events include headliner concerts (featuring artists such as Miami Sound Machine, Lee Greenwood, and Tanya Tucker), a laser and fireworks spectacular, a countdown to midnight, and special shows throughout the park. Admission is charged. Call 407/351-3600 for details.

3. WHAT TO PACK

The most important aspect of a traveler's wardrobe is comfort. It can get very unpleasant trekking around theme parks in the hot Florida sun if your feet hurt or your clothing is too warm. Most of the year, the ideal Orlando ensemble is sneakers, shorts, and a T-shirt—in other words, the least amount of clothing you can wear in public without causing a commotion. You might, however, wish to pack jeans and a light jacket for the occasional cooler day. Since interior spaces are always frigidly air-conditioned—even at indoor theme park attractions—carry a sweater if you tend to feel chilly. And a fold-up umbrella is always a good idea, even in Florida. If you don't ever use it, so much the better.

Packing evening wear is optional, though I do suggest that men pack at least one jacket and women one evening outfit for dinners at upscale establishments. However, even at better Orlando restaurants, not everyone dresses up. Especially casual are restaurants at the Disney parks, where most of the clientele is a come-as-you-are crowd, having spent the day on rides.

One thing I like to pack is a 100-watt light bulb, especially if I'm staying at an inexpensive hotel where bedside lamps seldom provide adequate wattage for reading. You don't need to pack a travel iron. Almost all hotels these days provide irons at the front desk, albeit usually with those tiny boards that make ironing even more hateful than usual. Find out if your hotel offers hairdryers before you pack one. And, finally, don't forget sunscreen.

---

4. TIPS FOR THE DISABLED, SENIORS, SINGLES, STUDENTS & FAMILIES

FOR THE DISABLED   Write or call **The Florida Department of Commerce,** Division of Tourism, Visitor Services, 107 W. Gaines St., Suite 501D, Tallahassee, FL 32399-2000 (tel. 904/487-1462), for a free copy of the *Physically Challenged Guide to Florida.* It offers valuable information on accessibility at tourist facilities throughout the state.

An Orlando-based organization called **Friends of the Family,** 7380 Sand Lake Rd., Orlando, FL 32819 (tel. 407/352-5209, or toll free 800/945-2045), provides help with transportation, accommodations, medical care, and other aspects of travel for the disabled. They can also refer you to travel agents who offer packages tailored to the disabled.

At Walt Disney World: WDW does everything possible to facilitate disabled guests. Its many services are detailed in the *Guidebook for Guests with Disabilities.* To obtain a copy prior to your visit, write Guest Letters, P.O. Box 10,040, Lake Buena Vista, FL 32830-0040, or call 407/824-4321. Also call that number for answers to any questions regarding special needs. Some examples of Disney services: Almost all Disney resorts have handicap rooms;

there are braille directories inside the Magic Kingdom in front of the Main Street train station and in a gazebo in front of the Crystal Palace restaurant; there are special parking lots at all three parks; complimentary guided-tour audio cassette tapes and recorders are available at Guest Services to assist visually impaired guests; personal translator units are available to amplify the audio at selected Epcot attractions (inquire at Earth Station); and wheelchairs can be rented at all of the Disney parks. For information about Telecommunications Devices for the Deaf (TDDs) call 407/827-5141.

Some nationwide resources: Mobility International USA, P.O. Box 10767, Eugene, OR 97440 (tel. 503/343-1284), offering accessibility information and has many interesting travel programs for the disabled. They also publish a quarterly newsletter called *Over the Rainbow* ($10 per year to subscribe). Help is also available from the **Travel Information Service** (tel. 215/456-9603) and the **Society for the Advancement of Travel for the Handicapped** (SATH), 347 Fifth Ave., Suite 610, New York, NY 10016 (tel. 212/447-7284). **Evergreen Travel Service,** 4114 198th St. SW, Suite 13, Lynnwood, WA 98036 (tel. 206/776-1184, or toll free 800/435-2288), offers tours designed for the visually impaired, the elderly, and the physically or mentally disabled.

Recommended books: A publisher called Twin Peaks Press, Box 129, Vancouver, WA 98666 (tel. 206/694-2462, or toll free 800/637-2256 for orders only), specializes in books for the disabled. Write for their *Disability Bookshop Catalog,* enclosing $3.

Amtrak (tel. toll free 800/USA-RAIL) provides redcap service, wheelchair assistance, and special seats with 72 hours' notice. The disabled are also entitled to a 25% discount on one-way regular coach fares. Disabled children ages 2 to 15 can also get a 50% discount on already discounted one-way disabled adult fares. Documentation from a doctor or an ID card proving your disability is required. Amtrak also provides wheelchair-accessible sleeping accommodations on long-distance trains, and service dogs are permissible and travel free of charge. Write for a free booklet called *Amtrak's America* from Amtrak Distribution Center, P.O. Box 7717, Itasca, IL 60143, which has a chapter detailing services for passengers with disabilities.

Greyhound (tel. toll free 800/752-4841) allows a disabled person to travel with a companion for a single fare and, if you call 48 hours in advance, they will arrange help along the way.

FOR SENIORS   Always carry some form of photo ID so that you can take advantage of discounts wherever they're offered. And it never hurts to ask.

If you haven't already done so, consider joining the **American Association of Retired Persons** (AARP), 601 E St. NW, Washington, DC 20049 (tel. 202/434-2277). Annual membership costs $8 per person or per couple. You must be at least 50 to join. Membership entitles you to many discounts. Write to Purchase Privilege Program, AARP Fulfillment, 601 E St. NW, Washington,

DC 20049, to receive AARP's Purchase Privilege brochure—a free list of hotels, motels, and car-rental firms nationwide that offer discounts to AARP members. **AARP Travel Experience** from American Express (tel. toll free 800/927-0111 for tours, 800/745-4567 for cruises) arranges a wide array of discounted cruises and group tours for members.

Elderhostel is a national organization that offers low-priced educational programs for people over 60 (your spouse or companion must be at least 50). Programs are generally a week long, and prices average about $315 per person, including room, board, and classes. For information on programs in central Florida call or write Elderhostel headquarters, 75 Federal St., Boston, MA 02110-1941 (tel. 617/426-8056), and ask for a free catalog.

Saga International Holidays, 222 Berkeley St., Boston, MA 02116 (tel. toll free 800/343-0273), offers group tours designed for travelers over 60.

Amtrak (tel. toll free 800/USA-RAIL) offers a 15% discount off the lowest available coach fare (with certain travel restrictions) to people 62 or over.

Greyhound also offers discounted fares for senior citizens. Call your local Greyhound office for details.

FOR SINGLE TRAVELERS The main problem for single travelers is meeting up with other singles. In Orlando, the ultimate family destination, this can be difficult. Best nightlife choices for meeting up with others are **Church Street Station** (in downtown Orlando) and **Pleasure Island** (see details on both, and other clubs, in Chapter 9).

Outdoor group activities—such as hiking, cycling, or fishing trips, are also good ways to meet people. Check the Friday "Calendar" section of the *Orlando Sentinel* for suggestions.

You can also meet up with others by taking a four-hour group tour of Epcot or the Magic Kingdom (cost is $5; inquire at Guest Relations or call 407/560-6233).

Want a fellow traveler? Contact **Travel Companion,** P.O. Box P-833, Amityville, NY 11701-0833 (tel. 516/454-0880), an organization that matches up single travelers with compatible partners. For a fee, you'll be listed in and receive the organization's newsletter, which provides a list of potential companions (you can request same sex or opposite sex).

FOR STUDENTS The key to securing discounts is valid student ID. Be sure to carry such and keep your eyes open for special student prices.

FOR FAMILIES No city in the world is more geared to family travel than Orlando. In addition to its theme parks, recreational facilities provide abundant opportunities for family fun. Every restaurant in town has a low-priced children's menu, and many hotels maintain children's activity centers (see details in Chapter 5). A few general suggestions to make traveling with kids easier:

Get the Kids Involved Let them, if they're old enough, write to the tourist offices for information and color brochures. If you're driving, give them a map on which they can outline the route. Let them help decide your sightseeing itinerary.

Packing Although your home may be toddler-proof, hotel accommodations are not. Bring blank plugs to cover outlets and whatever else is necessary.

En Route Carry a few simple games to relieve the tedium of traveling. A few snacks will also help and save money. If you're using public transportation (Amtrak, airlines, bus) always inquire about discounted fares for children.

Accommodations Children under 12, and in many cases even older, stay free in their parents' rooms in most hotels. Look for establishments that have pools and other recreational facilities (see "Frommer's Cool for Kids: Hotels" in Chapter 5).

Ground Rules Set up ground rules before leaving home about issues such as bedtime and spending money on souvenirs.

Publications Contact **Travel With Your Children (TWYCH),** 45 W. 18th St., New York, NY 10011 (tel. 212/206-0688), to subscribe to the *Family Travel Times,* a newsletter about traveling with children. It's packed with useful information, and readers can call in for advice during certain periods each week.

---

5. GETTING THERE

BY PLANE

Serving over 21 million passengers each year, **Orlando International Airport** (tel. 407/825-2001), 25 miles from Walt Disney World, is a thoroughly modern and user-friendly facility with pleasant restaurants, shops, a 450-room on-premises Hyatt Regency Hotel, and centrally located information kiosks. In public areas, trees and plants flourish under a lofty skylight ceiling. **Delta,** the official airline of Walt Disney World, has the most flights—over 25%—into Orlando International Airport. It offers service from 200 cities and has a Fantastic Flyer program for kids. Other carriers include Aero Costa Rica, Aeropostal, Air Jamaica, All Nippon Airways, America West, American, American Trans Air, British Airways, ComAir, Continental, Icelandair, KLM, Kiwi, LTU, Leisure Air, Mexicana, Northwest, Spirit, Transbrasil, TWA, United, USAir, Valvejet, and Virgin Atlantic.

Since advance-purchase fares are almost always the lowest available, it's a good idea to book your flight as far in advance as possible. Advance-purchase fares can be as much as 75% lower than fares booked the last minute!

FROMMER'S SMART TRAVELER:
AIRFARES

1. Call *all* the airlines that serve your destination—and check ads in the travel section of the *New York Times* or other big-city newspaper—to find the best fare.
2. Try to make your reservation 30 days in advance to take advantage of the lowest fares.
3. Keep checking fares as your departure date nears; airlines would rather fill a seat than have it fly empty, so they may cut fares dramatically in the days just before a flight leaves.
4. Investigate the cost of charter flights.
5. Avoid high-season travel, especially holidays. You can often get lower fares if you're willing to take midweek flights, too.
6. Always ask for the lowest fare, not just a discount fare.
7. Consider money-saving packages such as Delta's Dream Vacations.

When you call to reserve your flight, also inquire about money-saving packages. **Delta Dream Vacations,** in several price ranges, include: round-trip air transport; accommodations (state and hotel room tax/baggage gratuities included); an air-conditioned intermediate rental car with unlimited mileage or round-trip airport transfer; a "Magic Passport" that provides unlimited admission to all WDW parks for the length of your stay; one breakfast (which can be a character breakfast); and entry into a selected theme park one hour before regular opening time. Since the packages utilize Walt Disney World Resorts, you get all the advantages accruing to guests at these properties (see Chapter 5 for details). If you put all of those components together on your own, the cost would be much, much higher. Delta also has Orlando packages for which WDW tickets are optional. For details, call toll free 800/872-7786 or consult your local travel agent. *Note:* Though it also offers packages using non-WDW accommodations, Delta is the only airline authorized to use Disney resorts in its packages.

BY TRAIN

Amtrak trains (tel. toll free 800/USA-RAIL) pull into stations at 1400 Sligh Blvd., between Columbia and Miller streets in downtown Orlando (about 23 miles from Walt Disney World), and 316 Pleasant St., at the corner of Dakin Avenue and Thurman Street in Kissimmee (about 15 miles from Walt Disney World).

A limited number of seats on each train are set aside for discount fares, and the sooner you reserve, the greater the savings. Many people reserve fares months in advance, so the minute you know the dates of your trip, make your reservations. There may be some restrictions on travel dates for discounted fares, mostly around very busy holiday times.

To inquire about Amtrak's money-saving packages—including hotel accommodations, car rentals, tours, etc., with your train fare—call toll free 800/321-8684.

AMTRAK'S AUTO TRAIN Amtrak's Auto Train offers the convenience of having a car in Florida without driving it there. The Auto Train begins in Lorton, Virginia—about a four-hour drive from New York, two hours from Philadelphia—and ends up at Sanford, Florida, about 23 miles northeast of Orlando. Once again, reserve early for the lowest fares. The Auto Train departs Lorton and Sanford at 4:30pm daily, arriving at its destination at 9am the next morning. *Note:* You have to arrive one or two hours before departure time so they can board your car. Call toll free 800/USA-RAIL for details.

BY BUS

Greyhound buses connect the entire country with Orlando. They pull into a terminal at 555 N. Magruder Blvd. (John Young Parkway), between West Colonial Drive and Winter Garden Road, a few miles west of downtown Orlando (tel. 407/292-3422), or in Kissimmee at 16 N. Orlando Ave., between Emmett and Mabbette streets, about 14 miles from Walt Disney World (tel. 407/292-3440). There is van

---

IT'S BETTER WITH THE BAHAMAS

Premier Cruise Lines (the Big Red Boat) offers three- and four-night luxury ocean cruises to the Bahamas (Nassau and Port Lucaya) in conjunction with three- or four-day Orlando theme-park vacations. Cruises depart from and return to Port Canaveral, 45 minutes from Walt Disney World. You can add the island segment before or after your stay in Orlando. Participating hotels include Disney resorts. Ships are equipped with swimming pools, Jacuzzis, health clubs, jogging tracks, movie theaters, beauty salons, casinos, bar/lounges, video-game arcades, shops, and nightclubs. Looney Tunes characters (Bugs Bunny, Porky Pig, Daffy Duck) are your on-board hosts. Package price includes all meals on board ship, a rental car with unlimited mileage for seven days, round-trip airfare to/from Orlando, and admission to varied attractions. Rates depend on stateroom and hotel category and the season you're traveling. Call toll free 800/473-3262 for details.

transport from the Kissimmee terminal to most area hotels and motels. From Orlando, a taxi ($25 to $30 to Walt Disney area hotels) is the only viable option. Greyhound's fare structure tends to be complex, but the good news is that when you call to make a reservation, the agent will always give you the lowest-fare options. Once again, advance-purchase fares booked three to 21 days prior to travel represent vast savings. Check your phone book for a local Greyhound listing or call toll free 800/231-2222.

BY CAR

Orlando is 436 miles from Atlanta, 1,312 miles from Boston, 1,120 miles from Chicago, 1,009 miles from Cleveland, 1,170 miles from Dallas, 1,114 miles from Detroit, 1,105 miles from New York City, and 1,261 miles from Toronto.

From Atlanta take I-75 south to the Florida Turnpike to I-4 west. From Boston, New York, and other points northeast, take I-95 south to I-4 west. From Chicago take I-65 south to Nashville, then I-24 south to I-75 south to the Florida Turnpike to I-4 west. From Cleveland take I-77 south to Columbia, South Carolina, then I-26 east to I-95 south to I-4 west. From Dallas take I-20 east to I-49 south to I-10 east to I-75 south to the Florida Turnpike to I-4 west. From Detroit take I-75 south to the Florida Turnpike to I-4 west. From Toronto take Canadian Route 401 south to Queen Elizabeth Way south to I-90 (New York State Thruway) east to I-87 (New York State Thruway) south to I-95 over the George Washington Bridge, and continue south on I-95 to I-4 west. AAA and some other automobile club members can call local offices for maps and optimum driving directions.

CHAPTER 3

FOR FOREIGN VISITORS

Although American fads and fashions have spread across Europe and other parts of the world so that America may seem like familiar territory before your arrival, there are still many peculiarities and uniquely American situations that any foreign visitor will encounter.

1. PREPARING FOR YOUR TRIP

ENTRY REQUIREMENTS

DOCUMENT REGULATIONS   Canadian citizens may enter the United States without visas; they need only proof of residence.

Citizens of the U.K., New Zealand, Japan, and most western European countries traveling on valid passports may not need a visa for fewer than 90 days of holiday or business travel to the United States, providing that they hold a round-trip or return ticket and enter the United States on an airline or cruise line participating in the visa waiver program.

(Note that citizens of these visa-exempt countries who first enter the United States may then visit Mexico, Canada, Bermuda, and/or the Caribbean islands and then reenter the States, by any mode of transportation, without needing a visa. Further information is available from any U.S. embassy or consulate.)

Citizens of countries other than those stipulated above, including citizens of Australia, must have two documents: a valid **passport,** with an expiration date at least six months later than the scheduled end of the visit to the United States; and a **tourist visa,** available without charge from the nearest U.S. consulate. To obtain a visa, the traveler must submit a completed application form (either in person or by mail) with a 1½-inch square photo and demonstrate binding ties to a residence abroad.

Usually you can obtain a visa at once or within 24 hours, but it may take longer during the summer rush from June to August. If you cannot go in person, contact the nearest U.S. embassy or consulate for directions on applying by mail. Your travel agent or airline office may also be able to provide you with visa applications and instructions. The U.S. consulate or embassy that issues your visa will determine whether you will be issued a multiple- or single-entry visa and any restrictions regarding the length of your stay.

MEDICAL REQUIREMENTS   No inoculations are needed to enter the United States unless you are coming from, or have stopped over in, areas known to be suffering from epidemics, particularly cholera or yellow fever.

If you have a disease requiring treatment with medications containing narcotics or drugs requiring a syringe, carry a valid signed prescription from your physician to allay any suspicions that you are smuggling drugs.

CUSTOMS REQUIREMENTS   Every adult visitor may bring in free of duty: one liter of wine or hard liquor; 200 cigarettes or 100 cigars (but no cigars from Cuba) or three pounds of smoking tobacco; $100 worth of gifts. These exemptions are offered to travelers who spend at least 72 hours in the United States and who have not claimed them within the preceding six months. It is altogether forbidden to bring into the country foodstuffs (particularly cheese, fruit, cooked meats, and canned goods) and plants (vegetables, seeds, tropical plants, and so on). Foreign tourists may bring in or take out up to $10,000 in U.S. or foreign currency with no formalities; larger sums must be declared to Customs on entering or leaving.

INSURANCE

There is no national health system in the United States. Because the cost of medical care is extremely high, we strongly advise every traveler to secure health coverage before setting out.

You may want to take out a comprehensive travel policy that covers (for a relatively low premium) sickness or injury costs (medical, surgical, and hospital); loss or theft of your baggage; trip-cancellation costs; guarantee of bail in case you are arrested; and costs of accident, repatriation, or death. Such packages (for example, "Europe Assistance" in Europe) are sold by automobile clubs at attractive rates, as well as by insurance companies and travel agencies.

MONEY

CURRENCY & EXCHANGE   The U.S. monetary system has a decimal base: one American **dollar ($1)** = 100 **cents** (100¢)

Dollar bills commonly come in $1 ("a buck"), $5, $10, $20, $50, and $100 denominations (the last two are not welcome when paying for small purchases and are not accepted in taxis or at subway ticket booths). There are also $2 bills (seldom encountered).

There are six denominations of coins: 1¢ (one cent or "penny"),

5¢ (five cents or "a nickel"), 10¢ (ten cents or "a dime"), 25¢ (twenty-five cents or "a quarter"), 50¢ (fifty cents or "a half dollar"), and the rare $1 piece.

TRAVELER'S CHECKS   Traveler's checks denominated in U.S. dollars are readily accepted at most hotels, motels, restaurants, and large stores. But the best place to change traveler's checks is at a bank. Do not bring traveler's checks denominated in other currencies.

CREDIT CARDS   The method of payment most widely used is the credit card: Visa (BarclayCard in Britain), MasterCard (EuroCard in Europe, Access in Britain, Chargex in Canada), American Express, Diners Club, Discover, and Carte Blanche. You can save yourself trouble by using "plastic money" rather than cash or traveler's checks in most hotels, motels, restaurants, and retail stores (a growing number of food and liquor stores now accept credit cards). You must have a credit card to rent a car. It can also be used as proof of identity (often carrying more weight than a passport), or as a "cash card," enabling you to draw money from banks that accept them.

Note: The "foreign-exchange bureaus" so common in Europe are rare even at airports in the United States, and nonexistent outside major cities. Try to avoid having to change foreign money, or traveler's checks denominated other than in U.S. dollars, at a small-town bank, or even a branch in a big city; in fact, leave any currency other than U.S. dollars at home—it may prove more nuisance to you than it's worth.

SAFETY

GENERAL   While tourist areas are generally safe, crime is on the increase everywhere, and U.S. urban areas tend to be less safe than those in Europe or Japan. Visitors should always stay alert. This is particularly true of large U.S. cities. It is wise to ask the city's or area's tourist office if you're in doubt about which neighborhoods are safe. Avoid deserted areas, especially at night. Don't go into any city park at night unless there is an event that attracts crowds—for example, New York City's concerts in the parks. Generally speaking, you can feel safe in areas where there are many people, and many open establishments.

Avoid carrying valuables with you on the street, and don't display expensive cameras or electronic equipment. Hold on to your pocketbook, and place your billfold in an inside pocket. In theaters, restaurants, and other public places, keep your possessions in sight.

Remember also that hotels are open to the public, and in a large hotel, security may not be able to screen everyone entering. Always lock your room door—don't assume that once inside your hotel you are automatically safe and no longer need be aware of your surroundings.

DRIVING   Safety while driving is particularly important. Question your rental agency about personal safety, or ask for a brochure of traveler safety tips when you pick up your car. Obtain written directions, or a map with the route marked in red, from the agency showing how to get to your destination. And, if possible, arrive and depart during daylight hours.

Recently more and more crime has involved cars and drivers. If you drive off a highway into a doubtful neighborhood, leave the area as quickly as possible. If you have an accident, even on the highway, stay in your car with the doors locked until you assess the situation or until the police arrive. If you are bumped from behind on the street or are involved in a minor accident with no injuries and the situation appears to be suspicious, motion to the other driver to follow you. *Never* get out of your car in such situations. You can also keep a pre-made sign in your car which reads: PLEASE FOLLOW THIS VEHICLE TO REPORT THE ACCIDENT. Show the sign to the other driver and go directly to the nearest police precinct, well-lighted service station, or all-night store.

If you see someone on the road who indicates a need for help, do *not* stop. Take note of the location, drive on to a well-lighted area, and telephone the police by dialing 911.

Park in well-lighted, well-traveled areas if possible. Always keep your car doors locked, whether attended or unattended. Look around you before you get out of your car, and never leave any packages or valuables in sight. If someone attempts to rob you or steal your car, do *not* try to resist the thief/carjacker—report the incident to the police department immediately.

You may wish to contact the local tourist information bureau in your destination before you arrive. They may be able to provide you with a safety brochure.

2. GETTING TO & AROUND THE U.S.

Travelers from overseas can take advantage of the **APEX (Advance Purchase Excursion) fares** offered by all the major U.S. and European carriers. Aside from these, attractive values are offered by **Icelandair** on flights from Luxembourg to New York and by **Virgin Atlantic Airways** from London to New York/Newark.

British Airways (tel. 081/897-4000 from within the U.K.) offers direct flights from London to Miami and Orlando, as does **Virgin Atlantic** (tel. 02/937-47747 from within the U.K.). Canadian readers might book flights with **Air Canada** (tel. toll free 800/776-3000), which offers service from Toronto and Montréal to Miami and Tampa.

Some large American airlines (for example, TWA, American Airlines, Northwest, United, and Delta) offer travelers on their transatlantic or transpacific flights special discount tickets under the name **Visit USA,** allowing travel between any U.S. destinations at minimum rates. They are not on sale in the United States, and must, therefore, be purchased before you leave your foreign point of departure. This system is the best, easiest, and fastest way to see the United States at low cost. You should obtain information well in advance from your travel agent or the office of the airline concerned, since the conditions attached to these discount tickets can be changed without advance notice.

The visitor arriving by air, no matter what the port of entry, should cultivate patience and resignation before setting foot on U.S. soil. Getting through Immigration control may take as long as two hours on some days, especially summer weekends. Add the time it takes to clear Customs and you'll see that you should make very generous allowance for delay in planning connections between international and domestic flights—an average of two to three hours at least.

In contrast, travelers arriving by car or by rail from Canada will find border-crossing formalities streamlined to the vanishing point. And air travelers from Canada, Bermuda, and some places in the Caribbean can sometimes go through Customs and Immigration at the point of departure, which is much quicker and less painful.

International visitors can also buy a **USA Railpass,** good for 15 or 30 days of unlimited travel on Amtrak. The pass is available through many foreign travel agents. Prices in 1994 for a 15-day pass were $208 off-peak, $308 peak; a 30-day pass cost $309 off-peak, $389 peak. (With a foreign passport, you can also buy passes at some Amtrak offices in the United States, including locations in San Francisco, Los Angeles, Chicago, New York, Miami, Boston, and Washington, D.C.) Reservations are generally required and should be made for each part of your trip as early as possible.

Visitors should also be aware of the limitations of long-distance rail travel in the United States. With a few notable exceptions (for instance, the Northeast Corridor line between Boston and Washington, D.C.), service is rarely up to European standards: Delays are common, routes are limited and often infrequently served, and fares are rarely significantly lower than discount airfares. Thus, cross-country train travel should be approached with caution.

The cheapest way to travel the United States is by bus. Greyhound, the nation's nationwide bus line, offers an **Ameripass** for unlimited travel for 7 days (for $250), 15 days (for $350), and 30 days (for $450). Bus travel in the United States can be both slow and uncomfortable, so this option is not for everyone.

For further information about travel to Florida, see "Getting There" in Chapter 2.

FAST FOR THE FOREIGN TRAVELER

Automobile Organizations Auto clubs will supply maps, suggested routes, guidebooks, accident and bail-bond insurance, and emergency road service. The major auto club in the United States, with 955 offices nationwide, is the **American Automobile Association (AAA).** Members of some foreign auto clubs have reciprocal arrangements with the AAA and enjoy its services at no charge. If you belong to an auto club, inquire about AAA reciprocity before you leave. The AAA can provide you with an International Driving Permit validating your foreign license. You may be able to join the AAA even if you are not a member of a reciprocal club. To inquire, call toll free 800/336-4357. In addition, some automobile rental agencies now provide these services, so you should inquire about their availability when you rent your car.

Automobile Rentals   To rent a car you need a major credit card. A valid driver's license is required, and you usually need to be at least 25. Some companies do rent to younger people but add a daily surcharge. Be sure to return your car with the same amount of gas you started out with; rental companies charge excessive prices for gasoline. All the major car-rental companies are represented in Florida (see "Getting Around" in Chapter 4).

Business Hours   Banks are open weekdays from 9am to 3 or 4pm, although there's 24-hour access to the automatic tellers (ATMs) at most banks and other outlets. Generally, offices are open weekdays from 9am to 5pm. Stores are open six days a week, with many open on Sunday, too; department stores usually stay open until 9pm at least one day a week.

Climate   See "When to Go" in Chapter 2.

Currency   See "Money" in "Preparing for Your Trip," above.

Currency Exchange   You will find currency-exchange services at the Orlando International Airport and at other major airports with international service. Elsewhere, they may be quite difficult to come by. In New York, a very reliable choice is Thomas Cook Currency Services, Inc., which has been in business since 1841 and offers a wide range of services. They also sell commission-free foreign and U.S. traveler's checks, drafts, and wire transfers; they also do check collections (including Eurochecks). Their rates are competitive and service excellent. They maintain several offices in New York City (tel. for the Fifth Avenue office is 212/757-6915), at the JFK Airport International Arrivals Terminal (tel. 718/656-8444), and at La Guardia Airport in the Delta Terminal (tel. 718/533-0784).

Drinking Laws   See "Liquor Laws" in "Fast Facts: Orlando" in Chapter 4.

Electricity   The United States uses 110–120 volts, 60 cycles, compared to 220–240 volts, 50 cycles, as in most of Europe. In addition to a 100-volt converter, small appliances of non-American manufacture, such as hairdryers or shavers, will require a plug adapter, with two flat, parallel pins.

Embassies and Consulates   All embassies are located in the national capital, Washington, D.C.; some consulates are located in major cities, and most nations have a mission to the United Nations in New York City. Foreign visitors can obtain telephone numbers for their embassies and consulates by calling "Information" in Washington, D.C. (tel. 202/555-1212).

The Canadian consulate closest to Orlando is at 200 S. Biscayne Blvd., Suite 1600, Miami, FL 33131 (tel. 305/579-1600). There's a British consulate located at 1001 S. Bayshore Dr., Miami, FL 33131 (tel. 305/374-1522).

Emergencies   Call **911** to report a fire, call the police, or get an ambulance.

Gasoline (Petrol)   One U.S. gallon equals 3.75 liters, while 1.2 U.S. gallons equals one imperial gallon. You'll notice there are several grades (and price levels) of gasoline available at most gas stations. And you'll also notice that their names change from company to company. The unleaded ones with the highest octane are the most expensive (most rental cars take the least expensive "regular" unleaded) and leaded gas is the least expensive, but only older cars can take this any more, so check if you're not sure.

Holidays   On the following legal national holidays, banks, government offices, post offices, and many stores, restaurants, and museums are closed:

January 1 (New Year's Day)
Third Monday in January (Martin Luther King Day)
Third Monday in February (Presidents Day, Washington's Birthday)
Last Monday in May (Memorial Day)
July 4 (Independence Day)
First Monday in September (Labor Day)
Second Monday in October (Columbus Day)
November 11 (Veteran's Day/Armistice Day)
Last Thursday in November (Thanksgiving Day)
December 25 (Christmas).

Finally, the Tuesday following the first Monday in November is Election Day, and is a legal holiday in presidential-election years.

Languages   Major hotels may have multilingual employees. Unless your language is very obscure, they can usually supply a translator on request. Especially in southern Florida, many people are fluent in Spanish.

Legal Aid   The foreign tourist, unless positively identified as a member of the Mafia or of a drug ring, will probably never become involved with the American legal system. If you are pulled up for a minor infraction (for example, of the highway code, such as speeding), never attempt to pay the fine directly to a police officer; you may wind up arrested on the much more serious charge of attempted bribery. Pay fines by mail, or directly into the hands of the clerk of the court. If accused of a more serious offense, it's wise to say and do nothing before consulting a lawyer. Under U.S. law, an arrested person is allowed one telephone call to a party of his or her choice. Call your embassy or consulate.

Mail   If you want your mail to follow you on your vacation and you aren't sure of your address, your mail can be sent to you, in your name, c/o General Delivery at the main post office of the city or region where you expect to be. The addressee must pick it up in person and produce proof of identity (driver's license, credit card, passport, etc.).

Generally to be found at intersections, mailboxes are blue with a red-and-white stripe and carry the inscription U.S. MAIL. If your mail is addressed to a U.S. destination, don't forget to add the five-figure postal code, or ZIP (Zone Improvement Plan) Code, after the two-letter abbreviation of the state to which the mail is addressed (CA for California, FL for Florida, NY for New York, and so on).

Newspapers and Magazines National newspapers include the *New York Times, USA Today,* and the *Wall Street Journal.* National news weeklies include *Newsweek, Time,* and *U.S. News & World Report.* All over Florida, you'll be able to purchase the *Miami Herald,* one of the most highly respected dailies in the country. The local newspaper is the *Orlando Sentinel,* and there's a monthly city magazine called *Orlando.*

Radio and Television Audiovisual media, with four coast-to-coast networks—ABC, CBS, NBC, and Fox—joined in recent years by the Public Broadcasting System (PBS) and the cable network CNN, play a major part in American life. In big cities, televiewers have a choice of about a dozen channels (including the UHF channels), most of them transmitting 24 hours a day, without counting the pay-TV channels showing recent movies or sports events. All options are usually indicated on your hotel TV set. You'll also find a wide choice of local radio stations, each broadcasting particular kinds of talk shows and/or music—classical, country, jazz, pop, gospel—punctuated by news broadcasts and frequent commercials.

Safety See "Safety" in "Preparing for Your Trip," above.

Taxes In the United States there is no VAT (Value-Added Tax) or other indirect tax at a national level. Every state, and each city in it, has the right to levy its own local tax on all purchases, including hotel and restaurant checks, airline tickets, and so on. In Florida, sales tax is 6%. Hotel tax in Orlando is 10%, in Kissimmee 11%.

Telephone, Telegraph, and Telex The telephone system in the United States is run by private corporations, so rates, especially for long distance service, can vary widely—even on calls made from public telephones. Local calls in the United States usually cost 25¢.

Generally, hotel surcharges on long-distance and local calls are astronomical. You are usually better off using a public pay telephone, which you will find clearly marked in most public buildings and private establishments as well as on the street. Outside metropolitan areas, public telephones are more difficult to find. Stores and gas stations are your best bet.

Most **long-distance** and **international calls** can be dialed directly from any phone. For calls to Canada and other parts of the United States, dial 1 followed by the area code and the seven-digit number. For international calls, dial 011 followed by the country code, city code, and the telephone number of the person you wish to call.

For **reversed-charge or collect calls,** and for **person-to-person calls,** dial 0 (zero, *not* the letter "O") followed by the area code and number you want; an operator will then come on the line, and you should specify that you are calling collect, or person-to-person, or both. If your operator-assisted call is international, ask for the overseas operator.

For local **directory assistance** ("information"), dial 411; for **long-distance information,** dial 1, then the appropriate area code and 555-1212.

Like the telephone system, **telegraph** and **telex** services are provided by private corporations like ITT, MCI, and above all, Western Union, the most important. You can bring your telegram in to the nearest Western Union office (there are hundreds across the country), or dictate it over the phone (a toll-free call, 800/325-6000). You can also telegraph money, or have it telegraphed to you, very quickly over the Western Union system.

Telephone Directory There are two kinds of telephone directories available to you. The general directory is the so-called **white pages,** in which private and business subscribers are listed in alphabetical order. The inside front cover lists the emergency number for police, fire, and ambulance, and other vital numbers (like the Coast Guard, poison-control center, crime-victims hotline, and so on). The first few pages are devoted to community-service numbers, including a guide to long-distance and international calling, complete with country codes and area codes.

The second directory, printed on yellow paper (hence its name, *yellow pages*), lists all local services, businesses, and industries by type of activity, with an index at the back. The listings cover not only such obvious items as automobile repairs by make of car, or drugstores (pharmacies), often by geographical location, but also restaurants by type of cuisine and geographical location, bookstores by special subject and/or language, places of worship by religious denomination, and other information that the tourist might otherwise not readily find. The yellow pages also include city plans or detailed area maps, often showing postal ZIP Codes and public transportation routes.

Time The United States is divided into four time zones (six, if Alaska and Hawaii are included). From east to west, these are: eastern standard time (EST), central standard time (CST), mountain standard time (MST), Pacific standard time (PST), Alaska standard time (AST), and Hawaii standard time (HST). Always keep changing time zones in mind if you are traveling (or even telephoning) long distances in the United States. For example, noon in New York City (EST) is 11am in Chicago (CST), 10am in Denver (MST), 9am in Los Angeles (PST), 8am in Anchorage (AST), and 7am in Honolulu (HST).

Most of Florida observes eastern standard time, though the western part of the Panhandle region is on central standard time (its

clocks are set an hour earlier). Daylight saving time is in effect from
the last Sunday in April through the last Saturday in October
(actually, the change is made at 2am on Sunday) except in Arizona,
Hawaii, part of Indiana, and Puerto Rico. Daylight saving time moves
the clock one hour ahead of standard time.

Tipping   This is part of the American way of life, on the
principle that you must expect to pay for any service you get. Here are
some rules of thumb:

Bartenders: 10% to 15%.
Bellhops: at least 50¢ per piece; $2 to $3 for a lot of baggage.
Cab drivers: 15% of the fare.
Cafeterias, fast-food restaurants: no tip.
Chambermaids: $1 a day.
Checkroom attendants (restaurants, theaters): $1 per garment.
Cinemas, movies, theaters: no tip.
Doormen (hotels or restaurants): not obligatory.
Gas-station attendants: no tip.
Hairdressers: 15% to 20%.
Redcaps (airport and railroad station): at least 50¢ per piece, $2 to
    $3 for a lot of baggage.
Restaurants, nightclubs: 15% to 20% of the check.
Sleeping-car porters: $2 to $3 per night to your attendant.
Valet parking attendants: $1.

Toilets   Foreign visitors often complain that public toilets are
hard to find in most U.S. cities. True, there are none on the streets,
but the visitor can usually find one in a bar, restaurant, hotel,
museum, department store, or service station—and it will probably
be clean (although the last-mentioned sometimes leaves much to be
desired). Note, however, a growing practice in some restaurants and
bars of displaying a notice that "toilets are for the use of patrons
only." You can ignore this sign, or better yet, avoid arguments by
paying for a cup of coffee or soft drink, which will qualify you as a
patron. The cleanliness of toilets at railroad stations and bus depots
may be more open to question, and some public places are equipped
with pay toilets, which require you to insert one or more coins into a
slot on the door before it will open.

THE AMERICAN SYSTEM OF MEASUREMENTS

LENGTH

1 inch (in.)	=	2.54cm			
1 foot (ft.)	=	12 in.	=	30.48cm	=	.305m

1 yard	=	3 ft.	=	.915m
1 mile (mi.)	=	5,280 ft.	=	1.609km

To convert miles to kilometers, multiply the number of miles by 1.61 (for example, 50 mi. × 1.61 = 80.5km). Note that this conversion can be used to convert speeds from miles per hour (m.p.h.) to kilometers per hour (km/h).

To convert kilometers to miles, multiply the number of kilometers by .62 (for example, 25km × .62 = 15.5 mi.). Note that this same conversion can be used to convert speeds from kilometers per hour to miles per hour.

CAPACITY

1 fluid ounce (fl. oz.)	=	.03 liter		
1 pint	=	16 fl. oz.	=	.47 liters
1 quart	=	2 pints	=	.94 liters
1 gallon (gal.)	=	4 quarts	=	3.79 liters
	=	.83 Imperial gal.		

To convert U.S. gallons to liters, multiply the number of gallons by 3.79 (example, 12 gal. × 3.79 = 45.58 liters).

To convert U.S. gallons to Imperial gallons, multiply the number of U.S. gallons by .83 (example, 12 U.S. gal. × .83 = 9.95 Imperial gal.).

To convert liters to U.S. gallons, multiply the number of liters by .26 (example, 50 liters × .26 = 13 U.S. gal.).

To convert Imperial gallons to U.S. gallons, multiply the number of Imperial gallons by 1.2 (example, 8 Imperial gal. × 1.2 = 9.6 U.S. gal.).

WEIGHT

1 ounce (oz.)	=	28.35 grams				
1 pound (lb.)	=	16 oz.	=	453.6 grams	=	.45 kilograms
1 ton	=	2,000 lb.			=	907 kilograms
	=	.91 metric ton				

To convert pounds to kilograms, multiply the number of pounds by .45 (example, 90 lb. × .45 = 40.5kg).

To convert kilograms to pounds, multiply the number of kilos by 2.2 (example, 75kg × 2.2 = 165 lb.).

AREA

1 acre	=	.41 hectare		
1 square mile (sq. mi.)	=	640 acres	=	259 hectares
	=	2.6km^2		

To convert acres to hectares, multiply the number of acres by .41 (example, 40 acres × .41 = 16.4ha).

To convert square miles to square kilometers, multiply the number of square miles by 2.6 (example, 80 sq. mi. × 2.6 = 208km^2).

To convert hectares to acres, multiply the number of hectares by 2.47 (example, 20ha × 2.47 = 49.4 acres).

To convert square kilometers to square miles, multiply the number of square kilometers by .39 (example, 150km² × .39 = 58.5 sq. mi.).

TEMPERATURE

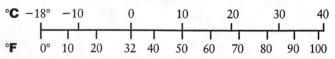

To convert degrees Fahrenheit to degrees Celsius, subtract 32 from °F, multiply by 5, then divide by 9 (example, 85°F − 32 × 5/9 = 29.4°C).

To convert degrees Celsius to degrees Fahrenheit, multiply °C by 9, divide by 5, and add 32 (example, 20°C × 9/5 + 32 = 68°F).

GETTING TO KNOW ORLANDO

Many Orlando visitors never venture beyond the Disney World area, except perhaps to Sea World and Universal Studios, which are close by. For those who do, almost all area hotels offer transportation to the airport and city attractions.

1. ORIENTATION

ARRIVING

BY PLANE **Orlando International Airport** is 25 miles from Walt Disney World. **Mears Transportation Group** (tel. 407/423-5566) buses ply the route from the airport (board outside baggage claim) to all Disney resorts and official hotels as well as most other area properties. Their comfortable, air-conditioned shuttle vans operate around the clock, departing every 15 to 25 minutes in either direction. Rates vary with your destination. Round-trip cost for adults is $19 between the airport and downtown Orlando or International Drive, $23 for Walt Disney World/Lake Buena Vista, $35 for Kissimmee/Hwy. 192. Children ages 4 to 11 pay $14, $17, and $28, respectively. Children 3 and under ride free. *Note:* It's always a good idea to ask about transportation options between the airport and your hotel when you make your reservations, or, if you're planning to rent a car, for driving directions from the airport.

BY TRAIN From the **Orlando Amtrak station,** you can catch **LYNX** bus no. 34, which departs weekdays at least once an hour between 10:25am and 5:25pm (weekends take bus nos. 7 or 11 from the stop at the corner of Orange and Columbia avenues, two blocks away). All trips involve a transfer at the downtown bus station—not too much of a hassle because the bus will usually be right there when you arrive. This connecting bus (no. 8) makes stops about every 1½ blocks along International Drive, culminating at Sea World where you can get a taxi ($17 to $20) to Walt Disney World–area hotels. For further details about bus transportation from the Orlando Amtrak station call 407/841-8240. A taxi from the Orlando Amtrak station to Walt Disney World–area hotels is $30 to $35. From the Kissimmee Amtrak station a taxi ($20 to $25 to WDW-area hotels) is your only option.

BY BUS   Van transport is available from the **Kissimmee Grey-hound station** to most area hotels and motels. Call 407/847-3911 for details.

TOURIST INFORMATION

Contact the **Orlando/Orange County Convention & Visitors Bureau,** 8445 International Dr. (in the Mercado Shopping Village), Orlando, FL 32819 (tel. 407/363-5871). They can answer all your questions and will be happy to send you maps, brochures (including the informative *Official Visitors Guide,* the *Area Guide* to local restaurants, and the *Official Accommodations Guide*), and the "Magicard," good for discounts of 10% to 50% on accommodations, attractions, car rentals, and more. Discount tickets to attractions other than Disney parks are sold on the premises, and the multilingual staff can also make dining reservations and hotel referrals. The bureau is open daily except Christmas from 8am to 8pm.

For general information about Walt Disney World—and a copy of the informative *Walt Disney World Vacation Guide*—write or call the **Walt Disney World Co.,** Box 10,000, Lake Buena Vista, FL 32830-1000 (tel. 407/824-4321).

If you're driving, you can stop at a Walt Disney World information facility in Ocala, Florida, at the intersection of I-75 and FL 200, about 90 miles north of Orlando. Here you can purchase tickets and Mickey ears, get help planning your park itinerary, and make hotel reservations.

And at the Orlando International Airport, arriving passengers can stroll over to **Greetings from Walt Disney World Resort** (tel. 825-2301), a shop and information center on the third floor in the main lobby just behind the Northwest counter. This facility sells WDW park tickets, makes dinner show and hotel reservations at Disney properties, and provides brochures and assistance. Open daily from 7am to 10pm.

Radio: Upon entering WDW grounds you can tune your radio to 1030 AM when you're approaching the Magic Kingdom, 810 AM when approaching Epcot. Tune to 900 AM when departing either area. TVs in all Disney resorts and official Disney hotels also have park information stations.

Also contact the **Kissimmee–St. Cloud Convention & Visitors Bureau,** 1925 U.S. 192 (P.O. Box 422007), Kissimmee, FL 34742-2007 (tel. 407/847-5000, or toll free 800/327-9159). They'll send maps, brochures, discount books, and the *Kissimmee–St. Cloud Vacation Guide,* which details the area's accommodations and attractions.

CITY LAYOUT

Orlando's major artery is I-4, which runs diagonally across the state from Tampa to Daytona Beach. Exits from I-4 take you to Walt Disney World, Sea World, International Drive, U.S. 192, Kissimmee, Lake Buena Vista, Church Street Station, downtown Orlando, and

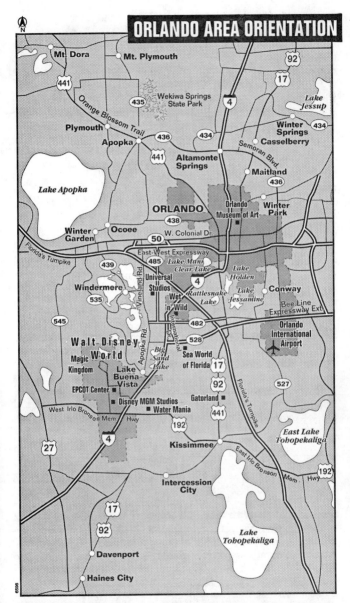

ORLANDO AREA ORIENTATION

Winter Park. The Florida Turnpike crosses I-4 and links up with I-75 to the north. U.S. 192, a major east-west artery, stretches from Kissimmee (along a major motel strip) to U.S. 27, crossing I-4 near the Walt Disney World entrance road. Farther north, a toll road called the Beeline Expressway (FL 528) goes east from I-4 past Orlando International Airport to Cape Canaveral. Walt Disney World property is bounded roughly by I-4 and FL 535 to the east (the latter also north), World Drive (the entrance road) to the west, and U.S. 192 to the south. Epcot Center Drive (Hwy. 536/the south end of International Drive) and Buena Vista Drive cut across the complex in a more-or-less east-west direction; the two roads cross at Bonnet Creek Parkway. Excellent highways and explicit signage make it very easy to find your way around. *Note:* The Disney parks are actually much closer to Kissimmee than to downtown Orlando.

NEIGHBORHOODS IN BRIEF

Walt Disney World   A city unto itself, WDW sprawls over more than 26,000 acres containing theme parks, resorts, hotels, shops, restaurants, and recreational facilities galore. Copious details below.

Lake Buena Vista   This area centers on a hotel village/marketplace owned and operated by Walt Disney World on the eastern edge of Disney property. However, though Disney owns all the real estate, many of the hotels, and some shops and restaurants here, are independently owned. Lake Buena Vista is a charming area of manicured lawns and verdant thoroughfares with traffic islands shaded by towering oak trees.

International Drive   This is another attractive area extending 7 to 10 miles north of the Disney parks between FL 535 and the Florida Turnpike. It, too, centers—for a long way—on a wide thoroughfare with a tree-shaded traffic island. It contains numerous hotels, restaurants, shopping centers, and the Orange County Convention Center, and offers easy access to Sea World and Universal Studios. *Note:* Locally, this road is always referred to as I-Drive.

Kissimmee   South of the Disney parks, Kissimmee centers on U.S. 192/Irlo Bronson Memorial Highway—a strip as archetypical of American cities as Main Street. U.S. 192 is lined with budget motels, lesser attractions, and every fast-food restaurant you can name.

Downtown Orlando   Reached via I-4 east, this burgeoning sunbelt metropolis is 17 miles northeast of Walt Disney World. Though many tourists never venture downtown, it does have a number of attractions, including noteworthy nightlife.

2. GETTING AROUND

In a city that thrives on its visitor attractions, you won't find it difficult to get around. All hotels offer transport to and from theme parks and other tourist destinations. It's not difficult getting places, but it can be expensive. If you don't have a car, one way to avoid many transportation costs is to stay at a Disney resort or official hotel.

BY BUS

Disney resorts and official hotels offer unlimited complimentary transportation via bus, monorail, ferry, and water taxi to all three parks from two hours prior to opening until two hours after closing; also to Disney Village Marketplace, Typhoon Lagoon, Pleasure Island, Fort Wilderness, and other Disney resorts. Disney properties offer transportation to other area attractions as well, though it's not complimentary. Almost all area hotels and motels also offer transportation to Walt Disney World and other attractions, but it can be pricey.

Mears Transportation Group (tel. 407/423-5566) operates buses to all major attractions, including Cypress Gardens, Kennedy Space Center, Universal Studios, Sea World, Busch Gardens (in Tampa), and Church Street Station, among others. Call for details.

BY TAXI

Taxis line up in front of major hotels, and at smaller properties the front desk will be happy to call you a cab. Or call **Yellow Cab** (tel. 699-9999). Charge is $2.45 for the first mile, $1.40 per mile thereafter.

BY CAR

Though you can get to and around Walt Disney World and other major attractions here without a car, it is always handy to have one. All the major car-rental companies are represented here and maintain desks at the airport. Some handy phone numbers: **Alamo** (tel. toll free 800/327-9633), **Avis** (tel. toll free 800/331-1212), **Budget** (tel. toll free 800/527-0700), **Dollar** (tel. toll free 800/800-4000), **Hertz** (tel. toll free 800/654-3131), **National** (tel. toll free 800/227-7368), and **Thrifty** (tel. toll free 800/367-2277).

FAST FACTS: ORLANDO

Ambulances See "Emergencies," below.
Area Code The area code for Orlando is 407.
Babysitters In this child-oriented town almost every hotel provides babysitting services, and several Disney properties have marvelous child-care facilities with counselor-supervised activity programs on the premises. Disney properties use KinderCare sitters (tel. 827-5444), so you can be sure they've been very carefully checked out. If you're not staying at a Disney accommodation, you can call them on your own. Rates for in-room service are: $8 per hour for one child, $9 per hour for two children, $11 per hour for three children, $14 per hour for four children. There is a four-hour minimum, the first half hour of which is travel time for the sitter. Twenty-four-hour advance notice is required.

Car Maintenance Walt Disney World operates an on-premises Car Care Center on Floridian Way near the Magic Kingdom Auto Plaza (tel. 824-4813). Its service garage is open weekdays from 7am to 6pm, and the facility also offers emergency road service and gas during park operating hours.

Car Rentals See "Getting Around," above in this chapter.

Climate See "When to Go," in Chapter 2.

Convention Center The Orange County Convention/Civic Center is located at 9800 International Dr. (tel. 407/345-9800).

Crime See "Safety," below.

Doctors and Dentists Inquire at your hotel desk. Or call Dental Referral Service (tel. 628-4363); they can tell you the nearest dentist who meets your needs. Phones are manned from 5:30am to 6pm daily. Check the yellow pages for 24-hour emergency services.

Disney has first-aid centers in all three major parks. There's also a very good 24-hour service in the area called HouseMed (tel. 648-9234). HouseMed doctors—who can dispense medication—make "house calls" to all area hotels. HouseMed also operates the Medi-Clinic, a walk-in medical facility (not for emergencies) at the intersection of I-4 and Hwy. 192 open daily from 9am to 9pm (same phone). Call for directions from your hotel. See also "Hospital Emergency Wards" and "Pharmacies," below.

Emergencies Dial 911 to contact the police or fire department or to call an ambulance.

Florist Floral and fruit arrangements can be delivered anywhere on Walt Disney World Resort property by calling 824-3505 between 8am and 8pm.

Hairdressers Many hotels have on-premises hairdressers. If yours doesn't, check out the better hotel listings in Chapter 5 to find one.

Hospital Emergency Wards Sand Lake Hospital, 9400 Turkey Lake Rd., is about two miles south of Sand Lake Road (tel. 351-8550). Take Exit 27A (Sea World exit) off I-4, make a left at the stop sign at the end of the exit ramp, and bear right onto Turkey Lake Road; the hospital is ahead on your left.

Kennels All of the major theme parks offer animal-boarding facilities at reasonable fees. At Walt Disney World, there are kennels at Fort Wilderness, Epcot, the Magic Kingdom, and Disney-MGM Studios. If you're traveling with a pet, don't leave it in the car—even with a window cracked—while you enjoy the park. Many pets have perished this way in the hot Florida sun.

Kosher Food It can be arranged at restaurants at Disney parks and resorts with 24 hours' advance notice. Call 560-6233.

Liquor Laws Minimum drinking age is 21. *Note:* No liquor is served in the Magic Kingdom at Walt Disney World; however, drinks are available at the other parks.

Lockers You can rent lockers at all of the Disney parks. Most other theme parks also offer this service. Inquire at Guest Relations.

Lost Children Every theme park has a designated spot for parents to meet up with lost children. Find out where it is when you enter any park and instruct your children to ask park personnel to take them there if they are lost. Young children should have name tags.

Newspapers and Magazines   The *Orlando Sentinel* is the major local newspaper, but you can also purchase papers of major cities (most notably the *New York Times*) in most hotel gift shops. Also informative is a city magazine called *Orlando*.

Pharmacies   Walgreen Drug Store, 1003 W. Vine St. (Hwy. 192), just east of Bermuda Avenue (tel. 847-5252), operates a 24-hour pharmacy. They can deliver to hotels for a charge ($10 from 7am to 5pm, $15 at all other times).

Photography   Two-hour film processing is available at all three major Disney parks. Look for the PHOTO EXPRESS sign. You can also buy film and rent or buy 35mm, disc, and video cameras in all three parks.

Poison Control Center   Call 897-1940, a 24-hour emergency hotline.

Post Office   The main post office in Lake Buena Vista is at 12541 FL 535 near TGI Friday's in the Crossroads Shopping Center (tel. 828-2606). It's open Monday through Friday from 9am to 4pm, Saturday from 9am to noon.

Religious Services   Hotel desks invariably keep a list of local churches and synagogues. You can also check the yellow pages.

Safety   Whenever you're traveling in an unfamiliar city, stay alert. Be aware of your immediate surroundings. It's a good idea to keep your valuables in a safety-deposit box (inquire at the front desk), though some hotels nowadays are equipped with in-room safes. Do keep a close eye on your valuables when you're in a public place—restaurant, theater, even airport terminal. And don't leave valuables in your car, even in the trunk.

Taxes   Hotel tax in Orlando is 10%, in Kissimmee 11%, both of those rates include a state sales tax (6%) that is charged on all goods except most grocery store items and medicines.

Time   Call 646-3131 for the correct time and temperature.

Tourist Information   See "Orientation," above.

Travel Information   The Delta Air Lines Travel Desk at Disney's Contemporary Resort (on the ground floor of the Tower) provides information on buses, airline reservations, rental cars, and tours to other central Florida attractions.

Weather   Call 851-7510 for a weather recording.

ORLANDO ACCOMMODATIONS

You'll find a wealth of hotel options in the Walt Disney World area. Stunningly landscaped multifacility resorts are the rule, but there's something to suit every taste and pocketbook. Do, of course, reserve as far in advance as possible—the minute you've decided on the dates of your trip.

In some hotel listings below, I've mentioned concierge levels. If you're not familiar with this concept, it involves a "hotel within a hotel" where guests enjoy a luxurious private lounge (usually with spectacular views) that is the setting for complimentary continental breakfast, hot and cold hors d'oeuvres at cocktail hour, and late-night cordials and pastries. Rooms are usually on high floors and room decor upgraded. Guests are cosseted with special services (private registration and checkout, a personal concierge, nightly bed turndown) and amenities (upgraded toiletries, bathroom scales, terry robes, hairdryers). Ask for specifics when you reserve.

Also mentioned under "Facilities" in some cases are counselor-supervised child-care/activity centers. Very popular in Orlando, these are marvelous, creatively run facilities where kids enjoy Disney movies, video games, arts and crafts, storytelling, puppet shows, indoor and outdoor activities, and much more. Some centers provide meals and/or have beds where a child can go to sleep while you're out on the town. Check individual hotel listings for these facilities and call to find out exactly what is offered.

Note: If you don't have a car, before reserving a room, be sure to ask the price of hotel shuttle buses to and from Walt Disney World parks and other area attractions you plan to visit. Compute these charges—which can be as high as $12 per person per day—in determining hotel price value. All Disney-owned properties and Disney "official" hotels offer complimentary transportation to and from WDW parks (see details below).

All Kissimmee hotels listed below can be booked by calling the **Kissimmee–St. Cloud Convention & Visitors Bureau's** toll-free number: 800/333-KISS.

Also consider using the services of an Orlando-based organization called **Check-In** (tel. 407/895-1050, or toll free 800/237-1033; fax

407/895-5521). A central booking agency, it has listings for hundreds of condos, resorts, hotels, villas, and luxurious private homes in all price ranges. A minimum stay of three nights is required. Check-In doesn't accept credit cards, but it does take personal checks. There's no fee for the service.

HOW TO READ THE LISTINGS The hotels listed below are first divided by location, then by price category alphabetically within a given district. All of the properties listed offer easy access to the Walt Disney World parks and other nearby major attractions.

Hotels listed in the **budget** category are those charging $50 or less for a double room. Those with rates ranging from $50 to $80 are rated **inexpensive** (don't blame me, I didn't invent inflation), $80 to $150 rooms make up the **moderate** category, $150 to $225 I've listed as **expensive,** and anything above that ranks as **very expensive.** Any extras included in the rates (for example, breakfast or other meals) are listed for each property. *Note:* Categories are approximate, because hotel rates do vary considerably, depending on whether you visit in peak or off-seasons.

1. DISNEY PROPERTIES & "OFFICIAL" HOTELS

Described below are the 14 Disney-owned properties (hotels, resorts, villas, wilderness homes, and campsites) and 9 privately owned properties designated as "official" hotels. All are within the Walt Disney World complex.

In addition to location (they all offer close proximity to the parks), there are a number of advantages to staying at a Disney property or official hotel, especially the former. At all Disney resorts and official hotels these include:

- Unlimited complimentary transportation via bus, monorail, ferry, and water taxi to and from all three parks from two hours prior to opening until two hours after closing. Unlimited complimentary transport is also provided to and from Disney Village Marketplace, Typhoon Lagoon, Pleasure Island, Fort Wilderness, and other Disney resorts. Three properties—the Polynesian, Contemporary, and Grand Floridian—are stops on the monorail. This free transport can save a lot of money you'd otherwise have to spend on a rental car or expensive hotel shuttle buses. It also means you're guaranteed admission to all parks, even during peak times when parking lots sometimes fill up.
- Special four- and five-day admission passes to WDW parks (see ticket information in Chapter 7 for details).
- Reduced-price children's menus in almost all restaurants.
- Character breakfasts and/or dinners at many restaurants.
- TVs equipped with the Disney channel and Walt Disney World information stations.

- A guest services desk where you can purchase tickets to all WDW theme parks and attractions and obtain general information.
- Use of—and in some cases complimentary transport to—the five Disney-owned golf courses and preferred tee times at them (these can be booked up to 30 days in advance).
- Access to most recreational facilities at other Disney resorts.
- Service by the Mears airport shuttle.

Additional perks at Disney-owned hotels, resorts, villas, and campgrounds—as well as at the Walt Disney World Swan and Dolphin, but not at other official hotels—include the following:

- You can make dining and show reservations—including for Epcot restaurants—on the premises or in advance via the concierge.
- Charge privileges at restaurants and shops throughout Walt Disney World.
- Early admission, prior to public opening, to the Magic Kingdom on specific days (except at the Dolphin).
- On-premises National Car Rental desk.

WALT DISNEY WORLD CENTRAL RESERVATIONS OFFICE To reserve a room at Disney hotels, resorts, and villas; official hotels; or Fort Wilderness homes and campsites, contact: the **Central Reservations Office,** P.O. Box 10,100, Lake Buena Vista, FL 32830-0100 (tel. 407/W-DISNEY), open seven days a week between the hours of 8:30am and 10pm. Have your dates and credit card ready when you call.

CRO can recommend accommodations that will suit your specific needs as to price, location (perhaps you wish to be closest to Epcot, Magic Kingdom, or Disney-MGM Studios), and facilities such as counselor-supervised child-care centers, a pool large enough for lap swimming, a state-of-the-art health club, on-premises golf or tennis (or other recreational facilities), a kitchen, and so on.

Be sure to inquire about their numerous package plans, which include meals, tickets, recreation, and other features. The right package plan can save you money and time (more of your vacation is planned in advance), and a comprehensive plan is helpful in computing the cost of your vacation in advance.

CRO can also give you information about various park ticket options and make dinner show reservations for you at the *Hoop-Dee-Doo Musical Revue* or the *Polynesian Luau Dinner Show* when you book your room.

OTHER SOURCES FOR PACKAGES In addition to the CRO, there are other sources for Disney packages. **Delta** is the official airline of Walt Disney World and the only airline permitted to use Disney resorts and campgrounds in its packages. Delta offers accommodations in different price ranges at your choice of the Caribbean Beach, Dolphin, Swan, Yacht Club, Beach Club, Port Orleans, Dixie Landings, Disney Village, Vacation Club, Polynesian, Contemporary,

Grand Floridian, All-Star Sports, All-Star Music, Wilderness Lodge, and Fort Wilderness resorts. At this writing, four-night midweek packages, including round-trip airfare, accommodations, a rental car with unlimited mileage or round-trip airport transfer, unlimited admission to all WDW parks, and much more, begin at $629 per person. For details call toll free 800/872-7786. **American Express Vacations** is also officially authorized to use Disney properties in its packages. For details call toll free 800/241-1700. Most hotels listed below also offer packages; inquire when you call. And finally, check with your travel agent.

DISNEY RESORTS IN THE WORKS Disney resorts have proven so successful that the company is expanding its accommodations offerings. Coming soon are the following:

The **Walt Disney World Boardwalk,** themed after plush seaside resorts of the 1920s and 1930s, will offer 375 luxurious rooms and 525 villas on 45 acres along the shores of Lake Crescent near Epcot. Two- to four-story buildings with shingled rooftops will surround private courtyards and New England–style gardens; a quarter-mile boardwalk on the premises will feature two dozen shops and restaurants; and facilities will include a sports bar, 1920s-style dance club, two dinner theaters, two waterside restaurants, a carnival-themed swimming pool with a roller-coaster slide, and a 15,000-square-foot conference center designed to resemble a New England town hall.

The moderately priced 1,980-room **Disney's Coronado Springs Resort** will be themed after the American Southwest. Its four- and five-story hacienda-like buildings will have terra-cotta tile roofs and palm-shaded courtyards. The property will encompass a major 95,000-square-foot convention center and the largest ballroom in the Southeast. Additional facilities will include a white-sand beach, boat rentals, and four swimming pools.

Shades of Green on Walt Disney World Resort will be a 288-room accommodation for vacationing military personnel from all branches of the armed forces. It will replace the current Disney Inn.

Disney's Mediterranean Resort, a deluxe 1,000-room property on the Seven Seas Lagoon, will be right on the monorail line. Designed to evoke the sunny resorts of the Greek Islands, it will provide a luxurious new convention facility and a marina.

And, finally, the 575-room **Disney's Wilderness Junction Resort** will be a rustic log-sided hotel in the Fort Wilderness woods at the end of a nature trail.

DISNEY RESORTS

VERY EXPENSIVE

DISNEY'S BEACH CLUB RESORT, 1800 Epcot Resorts Blvd., off Buena Vista Dr. (P.O. Box 10,100), Lake Buena Vista, FL 32830-0100. Tel. 407/W-DISNEY or

934-8000. Fax 407/354-1866. 584 rms, 24 suites. A/C MINIBAR TV TEL

$ Rates: $210–$290 single or double, depending on view and season. Extra person $15. Children under 18 free. Inquire about packages. AE, MC, V. **Parking:** Free self- and valet parking.

With its pristinely white-trimmed sky blue exterior, palm-fringed entranceway, sandy beach, and manicured gardens, the Beach Club evokes a luxurious Victorian Cape Cod resort. The sun-dappled lobby, done up in beachy pastels, has rose-toned sandstone tile flooring strewn with shell- and flower-motif rugs and upholstered wicker and rattan furnishings amid big potted palms. Charming rooms, furnished in bleached woods, are decorated in seafoam green with peach and coral accents. Wall sconces are seahorse-shaped, and beach umbrellas, seashells, and ocean waves adorn bedspreads, verdigris iron headboards, and a decorative frieze. Some rooms have widow's walk balconies. Amenities include ceiling fans, extra phones in the bath, remote-control cable TVs, AM/FM alarm-clock radios, safes, and game tables. *Note:* The Beach Club is within walking distance of Epcot.

Dining/Entertainment   Ariel's, named for the *Little Mermaid* character and open for dinner nightly, is an exquisite seafood restaurant awash in sea green, peach, and coral. Overlooking Stormalong Bay, it has whimsical fish mobiles overhead and a prismed 3,000-gallon tropical aquarium. You'll feel like you're dining in an underwater kingdom. Fresh seafood entrées are complemented by an extensive award-winning wine list. Wines are also highlighted at the adjoining **Martha's Vineyard Lounge,** where international selections are offered by the glass. Ideal for family dining is the **Cape May Cafe,** serving buffet character breakfasts hosted by Admiral Goofy and authentic New England clambake buffet dinners in a charming dining room adorned with colorful furled beach umbrellas, sand sculpture displays, and croquet mallets. The **Rip Tide Lounge,** off the lobby, features an array of California wines, wine coolers, and frosty concoctions. **Beaches & Cream,** adjoining the video-game arcade and central to both the Yacht and Beach clubs, looks like an old-fashioned ice-cream parlor, complete with oldies-stocked Wurlitzer jukebox and marble pedestal tables; light fare, plus sundaes, floats, and shakes are featured. Also central to both properties, adjacent to Stormalong Bay, is **Hurricane Hanna's Grill,** for light fare, ice-cream sundaes, and specialty drinks.

Services   24-hour room service, babysitting, guest services desk, complimentary daily newspaper, boat transport to MGM theme park.

Facilities   Large secluded swimming pool, Jacuzzi, quarter-mile white sandy beach, boat rentals (paddle boats, sailboats, miniature speedboats, rowboats, pontoons, canopy boats), two hard-surface night-lit tennis courts, state-of-the-art health club (including indoor whirlpool, sauna, and steam), massage, volleyball/croquet/bocci ball courts, two-mile jogging trail, coin-op washers/

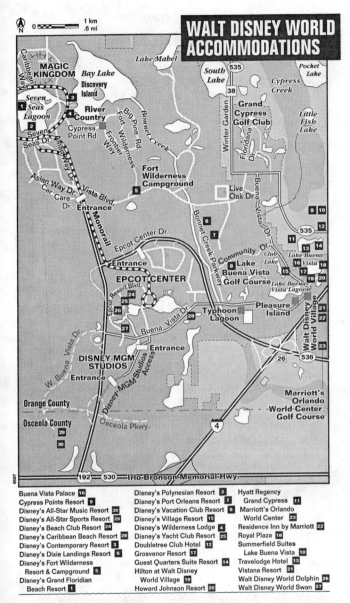

WALT DISNEY WORLD ACCOMMODATIONS

1 km
.6 mi

N

MAGIC KINGDOM

Lake Mabel

Bay Lake

Discovery Island

South Lake 535

38

Pocket Lake

Cypress Creek

Grand Cypress Golf Club

Little Fish Lake

Seven Seas Lagoon

River Country

Cypress Point Rd.

Big Pine Rd.

Fort Wilderness Way

Bonnet Creek

Winter Garden

Floridana Dr.

9 10

Seven Seas Dr.

Asian Way Dr.

Car Care Dr.

Entrance

Vista Blvd.

Monorail

Fort Wilderness Campground

Live Oak Dr.

Buena Vista Dr.

535 12

11 14

13

Epcot Center Dr.

Bonnet Creek Parkway

Community Dr.

Club Lake

Lake Buena Vista

16

15

18

19 20

Entrance

EPCOT CENTER

Epcot Resort Blvd.

24

25

26

27

Lake Buena Vista Golf Course

Lake Buena Vista Lagoon

Pleasure Island

21

22

W. Buena Vista Dr.

Buena Vista Dr.

28

Typhoon Lagoon

23

Entrance

DISNEY-MGM STUDIOS

Disney-MGM Studios Access

Entrance

26 536

Orange County

Osceola County

Osceola Pkwy.

29

30

Marriott's Orlando World-Center Golf Course

4

192 530 Irlo-Bronson-Memorial-Hwy.

Buena Vista Palace 16	Disney's Polynesian Resort 2	Hyatt Regency
Cypress Pointe Resort 9	Disney's Port Orleans Resort 7	Grand Cypress 11
Disney's All-Star Music Resort 30	Disney's Vacation Club Resort 8	Marriott's Orlando
Disney's All-Star Sports Resort 29	Disney's Village Resort 15	World Center 23
Disney's Beach Club Resort 24	Disney's Wilderness Lodge 4	Residence Inn by Marriott 22
Disney's Caribbean Beach Resort 28	Disney's Yacht Club Resort 25	Royal Plaza 18
Disney's Contemporary Resort 3	Doubletree Club Hotel 12	Summerfield Suites
Disney's Dixie Landings Resort 6	Grosvenor Resort 17	Lake Buena Vista 10
Disney's Fort Wilderness	Guest Quarters Suite Resort 14	Travelodge Hotel 13
Resort & Campground 5	Hilton at Walt Disney	Vistana Resort 21
Disney's Grand Floridian	World Village 19	Walt Disney World Dolphin 26
Beach Resort 1	Howard Johnson Resort 20	Walt Disney World Swan 27

dryers, full service unisex hair salon, shops (Disneyana, gifts, nautical/beach/resort wear, sundries), full business center, car-rental desk, large video-game arcade, Sandcastle Club (a counselor-supervised child-care/activity center). Stormalong Bay—a 790,000-gallon free-form swimming pool-cum-waterpark—sprawls over three acres between the Yacht and Beach clubs and flows into the lake; it includes a 150-foot serpentine water slide, a smaller slide for little kids, whirling waters, bubbling jets, shallow wading areas, and a sand strip.

DISNEY'S GRAND FLORIDIAN BEACH RESORT, 4401 Floridian Way, right near the Magic Kingdom (P.O. Box 10,100), Lake Buena Vista, FL 32830-0100. Tel. 407/ W-DISNEY or 824-3000. Fax 407/354-1866. 878 rms, 26 suites. A/C MINIBAR TV TEL

$ Rates: $230–$325 single or double, depending on view and season; $410–$440 concierge floors; $500–$1,450 suite. Extra person $15. Children under 18 free. Inquire about packages. AE, MC, V. **Parking:** Free self- and valet parking.

The Grand Floridian is magnificent from the moment you step into its opulent five-story lobby under triple-domed stained-glass skylights. The lacy white wrought-iron balustrades, plush furnishings amid potted palms, glittering chandeliers, white birdcage elevators, and Chinese Chippendale aviary housing Australian parrots are all reminiscent of a bygone era of luxury and leisure. A pianist entertains during afternoon tea, and an orchestra plays big-band music every evening from 5 to 10:30pm. Sunny rooms, some with dormer windows, are decorated in muted greens and pinks and furnished with Victorian-style convertible sofas and bleached oak two-poster beds made up with lovely floral-chintz spreads. In-room amenities include remote-control cable TVs, safes, AM/FM alarm-clock radios, and plantation-style ceiling fans. In the bath, you'll find a cosmetic mirror, extra phone, hairdryer, and terry robe. And private latticed balconies or verandas overlook formal gardens, the pool, or a 200-acre lagoon. Concierge-level guests enjoy private lounges and a library, upgraded furnishings and amenities, concierge services, complimentary buffet breakfast and evening refreshments.

Dining/Entertainment Victoria & Albert's, Orlando's finest restaurant, is described at length in Chapter 6. The lovely **Grand Floridian Cafe,** with elegantly draped Palladian windows overlooking formal gardens, serves American fare from 7am to 11pm daily; southern specialties such as battered fried catfish are featured. The festive exposition-themed **1900 Park Fare**—setting for buffet character breakfasts and dinners—is decorated with turn-of-the-century carved wooden carousel animals, antique toys, and murals of carnivals and circuses. An 1880s French fairground organ provides merry-go-round music. Entered via a Victorian rotunda, **Flagler's** has a 19th-century garden ambience. At dinner, the fare is northern Italian, and a strolling guitarist entertains. Weekends, the restaurant is used for buffet breakfasts. The gazebolike **Narcoossee's,** with fans suspended from a high cedar ceiling, overlooks the lagoon near the boat landing. Grilled meats and seafood are prepared in an exhibition kitchen. Open for lunch and dinner daily. The 24-hour **Gasparilla Grill,** adjoining the video-game arcade, proffers sandwiches, snacks, and ice cream, as well as continental breakfasts to Nintendo noshers. Cozily intimate, and very Victorian, **Mizner's Lounge** offers an international selection of ports, brandies, and appetizers. The light and airy **Garden View Lounge** off the lobby is the setting for ultra-elegant afternoon teas complete with crumpets and scones with Devonshire cream, nut breads, and finger sandwiches; evenings champagne cocktails are a specialty. And frozen drinks and snacks are available from the octagonal **Summerhouse Pool Bar.**

Services 24-hour room service, nightly turndown with Belgian chocolates, babysitting, on-premises monorail, boat transport to Magic Kingdom and Polynesian Resort, gratis trolley transport around property, shoeshine, massage, guest services desk, complimentary daily newspaper.

Facilities Large swimming pool, children's wading pool, whirlpool, two night-lit clay tennis courts, boat rental (canopy boats, catamarans, Sunfish and cabin sailboats, Water Sprites), waterskiing, croquet, volleyball, children's playground, jogging trails, fishing excursions, white-sand beach, full business center, full service unisex hair salon, car-rental desk, coin-op washers/dryers, shops (men's and women's resort fashions, upscale gifts/Victorian reproductions, designer Disney wear/Disneyana), extensive state-of-the-art health club, video-game arcade, organized children's activities in summer and peak seasons, the Mouseketeer Clubhouse (a counselor-supervised child-care/activity center).

DISNEY'S POLYNESIAN RESORT, 1600 Seven Seas Dr., just below the Magic Kingdom (P.O. Box 10,100), Lake Buena Vista, FL 32830-0100. Tel. 407/W-DISNEY or 824-2000. Fax 407/354-1866. 841 rms, 12 suites. A/C TV TEL
$ Rates: $195–$268 single or double, depending on view and season; $290–$310 concierge floors; $342–$1,050 suite. Extra person $15. Children under 18 free. Inquire about packages. AE, MC, V. **Parking:** Free self- and valet parking.

Designed to complement Adventureland in the Magic Kingdom, the 25-acre Polynesian is fronted by lush tropical foliage, waterfalls, palms, and koi ponds. At night lava-rock walkways are illuminated by flaming torchiers. A private white-sand beach—dotted with canvas cabanas, hammocks, umbrella tables, and large swings—looks out on a 200-acre lagoon. And the skylit lobby is a virtual rain forest of ferns, orchids, and hibiscus, with colorful resident macaws, bamboo rafters over the registration desk, and a rushing waterfall cascading into a stream stocked with goldfish. Large, beautiful rooms—most with balconies or patios—have canopied beds made up with gorgeous batik spreads, daybed sofas strewn with batik pillows, bamboo and rattan furnishings, and walls hung with Gauguin prints. All overlook tropical gardens or the lagoon. In-room amenities include AM/FM alarm-clock radios, remote-control cable TVs, and wood-bladed ceiling fans. Concierge-level guests enjoy a stunning private lounge (setting for complimentary continental breakfasts and afternoon snacks), nightly turndown, services of a private concierge, and upgraded amenities.

Dining/Entertainment The French Polynesian–themed

Papeete Bay Verandah is the setting for Minnie's Menehune Character Breakfast (a daily buffet featuring Minnie and other Disney characters). It also serves à la carte Polynesian dinners (enhanced by a three-piece island band and dancer). The exotic **Tambu Lounge,** specializing in Polynesian drinks and appetizers (pupu platters, etc.), plus nightly piano-bar music, adjoins. The **Coral Isle Cafe**—done up in seafoam green, with big planters of tropical foliage and flowers in straw baskets—serves American fare from 7am to 11pm. **Captain Cook's Snack Bar,** a classic ice-cream parlor, features an array of snack fare and a make-your-own-sundae bar. **Tangaroa Terrace**—a sunny plant-filled tropical dining room—serves à la carte and buffet breakfasts daily. **Luau Cove** is the setting for Mickey's Tropical Luau (a Polynesian character show for children that takes place daily at 4:30pm) and the Polynesian Luau Dinner Show at 6:45 and 9:30pm (details in Chapter 9). **Snack Isle,** adjoining the video-game arcade, serves light fare (pizza, burgers, nachos). And the **Barefoot Pool Bar**—also featuring island drinks and light fare—has a beautiful setting on the beach overlooking the lagoon. A pianist entertains on the second floor of the lobby nightly.

Services   Room service from 6:30am to 1am, babysitting, on-premises monorail, boat transport (to Magic Kingdom, Discovery Island, Fort Wilderness, and River Country), guest services desk, complimentary daily newspaper.

Facilities   Two swimming pools (one of them immense, with waterfalls, grottoes, and a water slide), children's wading pool, boat rental (canopy boats, paddle boats, pontoons, float boats, Sunfish, sailboats, Water Sprites), volleyball, children's playground, 1.5-mile jogging trail, fishing excursions, unisex hair salon, coin-op washers/dryers, car-rental desk, shops (liquor/snack fare, Disneyana, resort wear for the entire family, sundries), large video-game arcade, the Neverland Club (a Peter Pan–themed counselor-supervised child-care/activity center).

DISNEY'S YACHT CLUB RESORT, 1700 Epcot Resorts Blvd., off Buena Vista Dr. (P.O. Box 10,100), Lake Buena Vista, FL 32830-0100. Tel. 407/W-DISNEY or 934-7000. Fax 407/354-1866. 625 rms, 10 suites. A/C MINIBAR TV TEL

$ Rates: $210–$290 single or double, depending on view and season; $350–$390 concierge level. Extra person $15. Children under 18 free. Inquire about packages. AE, MC, V. **Parking:** Free self- and valet parking.

Legend has it that the ship of world traveler Old Stormalong went aground on a lagoon here, and the area was so beautiful, he decided to forsake adventuring and settle down. And beautiful it is. The Yacht Club shares a 25-acre lake, facilities, and gorgeous landscaping with the adjacent Beach Club (details above). Grounds are planted with Japanese elms, Bradford pear trees, magnolias, crape myrtles, and lush tropical foliage; and gardenias and roses bloom in charming brick courtyards. The main five-story oyster-gray clapboard building evokes a luxurious turn-of-the-century New England yacht club. It's entered via a magnificent lobby, furnished with plush tufted-leather wing chairs and sofas amid potted palms in Chinese porcelain pots. Persian and nautically themed rugs are strewn on highly polished parquet oak floors.

The nautical theme carries over to very inviting rooms, decorated in snappy blue and white, with brass sconces and ship lights, nautically themed headboards, maps and paintings of ship's captains on the walls, and crisp floral-chintz drapes, valances, and bed ruffles. French doors open onto porches or balconies. Amenities include ceiling fans, extra phones in the bath, remote-control cable TVs (with volume control in the dressing room area), AM/FM alarm-clock radios, safes, and game tables. The fifth floor is a concierge level, where guests enjoy a delightful private lounge—setting for gratis continental breakfasts, 3pm cookies, wine/cheese/hors d'oeuvres spreads at 5pm, and late-night international coffees and petit fours. Rooms are equipped with upgraded amenities (scales, terry robes, hairdryers, and more), and guests enjoy the services of a private concierge.

Dining/Entertainment The plush **Yachtsman Steakhouse,** open for dinner nightly, features an exhibition kitchen where select cuts of steak, chops, and fresh seafood are grilled over oak and hickory. The decor is woody, with knotty-pine flooring, paneling, and overhead beams. Elegantly appointed tables are lit by shaded lamps. The nautically themed **Yacht Club Galley**—with porthole windows and displays of knots and boating hardware—is the resort's comfortable family restaurant, offering American regional fare at all meals. **Crew's Cup Lounge,** its pine-paneled walls hung with Ivy League rowing-team memorabilia, serves up light fare and frosted mugs of international ales and beers; sporting events are aired on the TV. The cozy **Ale and Compass Lounge,** a lobby bar with working fireplace, features specialty coffees and cocktails. The seasonal **Sip Ahoy Snack Bar** serves the secluded pool. And a brass quartet entertains nightly on the mezzanine level. (See also Beach Club restaurants and bars, above.)

Services 24-hour room service, babysitting, guest services desk, complimentary daily newspaper, boat transport to Disney-MGM theme park, tram transport to Epcot.

Facilities Yacht Club facilities are identical to those of the Beach Club (details above).

EXPENSIVE

DISNEY'S CONTEMPORARY RESORT, 4600 N. World Dr. (P.O. Box 10,100), Lake Buena Vista, FL 32830-0100. Tel. 407/W-DISNEY or 824-1000. Fax 407/354-1866. 1,036 rms, 17 suites. A/C TV TEL

$ **Rates:** $195–$235 single or double, $250–$270 tower room.

IN THE WORDS OF WALT DISNEY

"My operations are based on experience, thoughtful observation, and warm fellowship with my neighbors at home and around the world."

Extra person $15. Children under 17 free. Inquire about packages. AE, MC, V. **Parking:** Free self- and valet parking.

When it opened in 1971 to complement the Magic Kingdom's futuristic Tomorrowland, the Contemporary's aesthetic was cutting-edge. Today its dramatic angular planes, free-form furnishings, and abstract paintings appear, rather charmingly, retro-modern. The property—centering on a sleek 15-story, A-frame Tower flanked by two Garden Wings—occupies 26 acres bounded by a natural lake and the Disney-made Seven Seas Lagoon. Kids are thrilled that the monorail whizzes right through the hotel. Rooms are quite nice, decorated in shades of tan with splashes of color. Furnishings (bleached woods with ebony accents) and lighting fixtures are art deco, there are ceiling fans overhead, and walls display cheerful Matisse prints. In-room amenities include AM/FM alarm-clock radios, remote-control cable TVs, two phones, and safes. The 14th floor of the Tower comprises a concierge level where guests enjoy a more sumptuous decor, plus upgraded amenities (hairdryers, live plants, toiletries) and services (nightly turndown, concierge). They also have balconies and a private lake-view lounge—the setting for complimentary breakfast buffets, hot and cold hors d'oeuvres with beer and wine every afternoon, and late-night cordials and petit fours.

Dining/Entertainment   The **Concourse Grill,** a large coffee shop, serves breakfast, lunch, and dinner daily. The adjacent **Contemporary Cafe** features all-you-can-eat prime rib/shrimp buffet dinners and morning character breakfasts. The **Outer Rim,** a glass-walled bar/lounge offering stunning views of vast Bay Lake, features piano bar and other live entertainment evenings, including sporting events aired on a large-screen TV in the bar area. Coffees spiked with liqueurs, malt scotches, grappas, and other specialty drinks are featured. A no-frills **cafeteria** adjoining the video-game arcade on the first floor serves light fare; next to it is a children's theater where Disney movies are shown nightly. And in peak season the **Sand Bar** dispenses specialty drinks poolside.

Services   24-hour room service; guest services desk; daily newspaper delivery to rooms; babysitting; boat transport to Discovery Island, Fort Wilderness, and River Country; direct monorail link to the Polynesian.

Facilities   Two swimming pools; children's wading pool; white-sand beach with volleyball court, shuffleboard, boat rentals (paddleboats, Water Sprites, canopy boats, motorized craft, waterskiing equipment); full-service unisex hair salon; six night-lit hard-surface tennis courts (lessons available); shops (tennis pro shop, food/wines/liquors, gifts, Disneyana, resort wear); Delta Air Lines desk; car-rental desk; coin-op washers/dryers; full business center; extensive health club; sauna/massage/tanning rooms; vast 24-hour video-game arcade; the Mouseketeer Clubhouse (a counselor-supervised child-care/activity center).

DISNEY'S VACATION CLUB RESORT, 1510 North Cove Rd., off Community Dr. (P.O. Box 10,100), Lake Buena Vista, FL 32830-0100. Tel. 407/W-DISNEY or 827-7700. Fax 407/354-1866. 709 villas. A/C TV TEL

$ Rates: $190–$205 deluxe room; $240–$260 one-bedroom vacation home; $345–$365 two-bedroom vacation home; $755 three-bedroom Grand Villa. Rates are for any number of people. Range reflects high and low seasons. Inquire about packages. AE, MC, V. **Parking:** Free self-parking.

Its architecture evocative of Key West at the turn of the century, the Vacation Club is a time-share property. If you're interested in purchasing a vacation villa here, they'll be happy to give you a presentation. For nonowners, however, this is just like any other luxurious Disney resort; you rent accommodations when not in use by owners. The 156-acre property is beautifully landscaped. Tree-lined brick walkways are edged by white picket fences, palms sway softly in the breeze, shorebirds swoop lazily over lagoons, and the air is scented with honeysuckle. The lobby includes a library with plush armchairs facing a massive oak fireplace and floor-to-ceiling book-shelves stocked with works of Key West authors, most notably Hemingway. Accommodations, in two- and three-story tin-roofed clapboard buildings painted in pale pastels, offer lovely water, woodland, or fairway views. Architecture reflects the themed period with Victorian gingerbread trim and Queen Anne scalloped shingles.

Gorgeous residential-style accommodations offer home-away-from-home comfort, with fully equipped kitchens and furnished patios and amenities including bedroom ceiling fans, full laundry rooms (washers/dryers/ironing boards/irons), large-screen remote-control cable TVs with VCRs in the living room (smaller sets in bedrooms), phones in each bedroom and living room, and AM/FM alarm-clock radios in all bedrooms. Many units contain whirlpool tubs in the master suite, and Grand Villas have stereo systems. *Note:* Deluxe rooms do not offer kitchens, patios, VCRs, or laundry rooms.

Dining/Entertainment Olivia's Cafe—a pleasant plant-filled dining room, its pale yellow walls hung with 19th-century Key West photographs and memorabilia—serves all meals; it offers al fresco seating on a patio overlooking the Trumbo Canal. At the **Gurgling Suitcase** pool bar (its name refers to liquor smuggling from Havana during Prohibition) you can sit out and watch the sunset while sipping a piña colada. Light fare and beverages are also served at the poolside **Turtle Shack.** And **Good's Food To Go** offers take-out sandwiches and light fare.

Services   Babysitting, guest services desk, ferry service to Disney Village Marketplace and Pleasure Island, gratis bus transport around property, food shopping for a minimal charge.

Facilities   Two hard-surface night-lit tennis courts, white-sand play area, boardwalk, four swimming pools, whirlpool, kiddie pool, bicycle rental, car-rental, boat rentals (paddleboats, rowboats, float boats, canopy boats), children's playground, extensive health club, sauna, shuffleboard, horseshoes, volleyball, complimentary use of washers/dryers, general store (groceries, resort wear, gifts, Disneyana, sundries), small video-game arcade. The Community Hall, a recreation center, shows Disney movies nightly and offers activities such as Monday-night football, Ping-Pong tournaments, bingo, Pictionary, and arts and crafts for adults and children.

DISNEY'S VILLAGE RESORT, 1901 Buena Vista Dr., adjacent to the Disney Village Marketplace (P.O. Box 10,100), Lake Buena Vista, FL 32830-0100. Tel. 407/W-DISNEY or 827-1100. Fax 407/354-1866. 324 suites. A/C TV TEL

$ Rates: $335–$355 Treehouse Villa (for up to 6 people); $355–$375 2-bedroom Fairway unit (for up to 8 people); $185–$200 Club Suite (for up to 5 people); $250–$270 1-bedroom Vacation Villa (for up to 4 people); $300–$320 2-bedroom Vacation Villa (for up to 6 people); $750 2-bedroom Grand Vista home; $825 3-bedroom Grand Vista home. Range reflects view and season. Inquire about packages. AE, MC, V. **Parking:** Free self-parking.

Sprawled over 265 arcadian acres of lakes, woodlands, and streams, the Village Resort is a great choice for golfers and families. Peacocks roam the grounds, and your accommodations might overlook a verdant golf course, gurgling river, or a forest of towering pines, magnolias, cypress, and live oaks draped with Spanish moss. Octagonal **Treehouse Villas,** elevated on stilts, have large outdoor patios and balconies amid the treetops. Decorated in earth tones, with knotty-pine furnishings, beamed ceilings, and windows all around, these rustic two-story lodgings offer fully equipped kitchens, dining areas, full living rooms, three bedrooms, and two baths. Amenities include remote-control cable TVs and phones on each floor and AM/FM alarm-clock radios in all bedrooms. Similarly equipped two-bedroom **Fairway Villas,** just off the golf course, are elegant ski-lodgey cedar town houses with rough-hewn slanted pine paneling (upstairs units have beamed cathedral ceilings). The most inexpensive accommodations are one-bedroom **Club Suites.** Bordering a lake, they're attractively decorated in forest green, rust, and tan, with cathedral ceilings, pine furnishings, and Ralph Lauren–look striped and plaid fabrics. They have kitchenettes (with microwave ovens, sinks, and small refrigerators) and balconies or porches. One- and two-bedroom **Vacation Villas** are in two-story town houses. Big picture windows overlook woodlands or waterways, and Early American bleached pine furnishings include spool beds and two-posters made up with pretty fabric spreads. All have country kitchens, dining areas, large living rooms with convertible sofas, and patios. And for total luxury there are two- and three-bedroom **Grand Vista homes** that sleep six to eight people. They're beautiful residential accommodations with full kitchens, two big screened porches (one set up for dining), upscale furnishings, marble whirlpool tubs in the bath, and homey touches such as live plants, shelves of books, and objets d'art. Each has its own electric golf cart, bicycles, and barbecue grill. Grand Vista guests also enjoy special services, such as nightly bed turndown and daily newspaper delivery.

Dining/Entertainment   Disney Village Marketplace restaurants are adjacent.

Services   Room service from 7am to 11pm, babysitting, guest services desk, gratis bus transport around property, gratis grocery delivery from the Gourmet Pantry (meat, poultry, fresh vegetables, and more).

Facilities   18-hole, par-72 championship golf course, three hard-surface night-lit tennis courts, golf/tennis pro shops, electric cart rentals, six swimming pools, five whirlpool spas, kiddie pool, bicycle rental, eight miles of bike trails, boat rentals (Water Sprites, mini-speedboats, float boats, canopy boats), health club, seven children's playgrounds, 3.4-mile jogging course with 32 exercise stations, car-rental desk, coin-op washers/dryers, outdoor barbecue grills and picnic tables scattered throughout property, two video-game arcades. A footbridge connects to Disney's Village Marketplace.

DISNEY'S WILDERNESS LODGE, 901 Timberline Dr., on the southwest shore of Bay Lake just east of the Magic Kingdom (P.O. Box 10,100), Lake Buena Vista, FL 32830-0100. Tel. 407/W-DISNEY or 824-3200. Fax 407/354-1866. 697 rms, 25 junior suites, 6 suites. A/C TV TEL

$ Rates: $149–$195 single or double, depending on view and season; $250–$270 junior suite; $480–$580 suite. Extra person $15. Children under 18 free. Inquire about packages. AE, MC, V.

Parking: Free self- and valet parking.

Evocative of rustic turn-of-the-century national park lodges, this new 56-acre Disney resort (opened in the spring of 1994) is surrounded by towering oak and pine forests. Its imposing lobby, supported by 55-foot bundled lodgepole-pine columns, centers on a massive floor-to-ceiling stone fireplace flanked by vast eagle- and raven-motif totem poles; replicas of Yellowstone fossils are embedded into its rocks. Natural light filters in via high dormer windows, and a geothermal spring flows under a picture-window wall into Silver Creek, which itself empties into beautiful 340-acre Bay Lake. Outside, "volcanic" meadow landscaping is punctuated by bubbling craters, babbling brooks, a cascading waterfall, and spewing geysers.

Guest rooms—off hallways with Native American–motif carpeting and buffalo-themed lighting fixtures—are decorated in muted shades of forest green, with reddish mahogany woodwork and

FROMMER'S SMART TRAVELER: HOTELS

1. Especially if you don't have a car, choose a hotel that offers complimentary transportation to and from Walt Disney World parks.
2. Ask about packages. Almost all Orlando area hotels offer money-saving packages including special features such as meals, golf fees, parking, shows, and park tickets.
3. Bargain with the reservations clerk. An unoccupied room nets a hotel zero dollars, and any reasonable offer is better than that. This works best off-season, and even then on the afternoon of your arrival, when the desk knows there will be empty rooms. Disney-owned and official hotels, however, will not make these kinds of deals.
4. Ask about special discounts for students, senior citizens, AAA members, corporate, or military personnel.
5. Book as far in advance as possible to insure optimum choices.

coffee-hued walls, the latter adorned with tribal friezes and landscape paintings of the northwest. Equipped with remote-control cable TVs, AM/FM alarm-clock radios, ceiling fans, and safes, they have patios or balconies overlooking the lake or meadow. Some have one queen bed and bunk beds—a convenient configuration for families. Junior suites offer living rooms with queen-size sleeper sofas, wet bars, and small refrigerators. Public areas include porches, reading rooms, and other intimate spaces.

Dining/Entertainment: Artist's Point (named for a scenic vista in Yellowstone Park), with large windows overlooking Bay Lake and dramatic western landscape murals adorning interior walls, specializes in hickory-, oak-, and mesquite-grilled steak, seafood, and wild game; open for all meals, it also has lakeside terrace seating for al fresco dining. Trappers and explorers who led the country's westward expansion are honored in the adjoining **Territory Lounge.** The cheerful **Whispering Canyon Cafe,** with its cowboy silhouette cutouts and brightly colored upholstery, serves coffee-shop fare at breakfast and dinner. The fly-fishing–themed **Roaring Fork,** adjacent to the video-game arcade, serves snack fare around the clock. And the **Trout Pass Bar** provides light fare and drinks poolside. Five-minute geyser shows take place in the meadow periodically throughout the day, and nightly electric water pageants can be viewed from the shores of Bay Lake.

Services: Room service, guest services desk, babysitting, Mears airport shuttle, boat transport to Magic Kingdom, free bus transport around the property.

Facilities: Immense swimming pool seemingly excavated out of rocks, kiddie pool with water slide, hot and cold spa pools, boat rentals (canoes, paddleboats, Water Sprites, pontoons), children's playground/recreation area, bicycle rental, two-mile jogging/bike trail with exercise stations, large video-game arcade, gift shop, Cub's Den (a counselor-supervised activity center for children 3–12).

MODERATE

DISNEY'S CARIBBEAN BEACH RESORT, 900 Cayman Way, off Buena Vista Dr. (P.O. Box 10,100), Lake Buena Vista, FL 32830-0100. Tel. 407/W-DISNEY or 934-3400. Fax 407/354-1866. 2,112 rms. A/C MINIBAR TV TEL

$ Rates: $89–$119 single or double. Extra person $12. Children under 17 free. Inquire about packages. AE, MC, V. **Parking:** Free self-parking.

Opened in 1988, the Caribbean Beach occupies 200 palm-fringed acres stunningly landscaped with lush tropical foliage. Upon registering in the Custom House lobby—where potted palms and overhead fans set the island mood—guests are issued helpful informational "passports." Accommodations surround a large, duck-filled lake in five "villages," each with metal-roofed stucco buildings architecturally evocative of Jamaica, Aruba, Martinique, Trinidad, or Barbados. They're painted in bright tropical hues. Buildings in the Jamaica section, for instance, are canary yellow, with muted blue roofing and shutters, and white Queen Anne–style trim. Room interiors are charming, utilizing pleasing color schemes such as dusty rose and mint. All have attractive oak furnishings with pineapple motifs, and exquisite floral-print cotton-chintz bedspreads. In-room amenities include coffee makers, ceiling fans, and remote-control cable TVs. All rooms have verandas, many of them overlooking the lake. In addition, 16 beautifully landscaped public courtyards furnished with umbrella tables dot the property.

Dining/Entertainment The festive **Farmers Market Food Court**—a garden setting with trellises and brightly colored Chinese kites overhead—has counters offering diverse fare: fresh-baked pastries, pizza, fajitas, chicken teriyaki, and more. The nautically themed **Captain's Tavern** specializes in crab legs, fresh fish, and prime rib. And **Banana Cabana**—featuring light snacks and frozen tropical drinks—serves the main pool.

Services Room service (pizza delivery only) from 4pm to midnight, guest services desk, babysitting, complimentary shuttle around grounds.

Facilities Video-game arcade, shops (gift/Disneyana/resort wear shop, snacks/sundries, Caribbean straw market), boat rentals (sailboats, runabouts, toobies, float boats, canopy boats, paddleboats, canoes), bicycle rental, car-rental, coin-op washers/dryers in each village. The main swimming pool, in a central area called Old Port Royale, replicates a Spanish-style Caribbean fort with pirate's cannons and stone walls. It has a water slide, kiddie pool, and whirlpool. In addition, there are nice-sized pools, children's playgrounds, and lakefront white-sand beaches in each village. A 1.4-mile promenade—popular for walking, jogging, and bicycling—circles the lake. An arched wooden bridge leads to Parrot Cay Island where there is a short nature trail, an aviary of tropical birds, a picnic area, and a playground.

DISNEY'S DIXIE LANDINGS RESORT, 1251 Dixie Dr., off Bonnet Creek Pkwy. (P.O. Box 10,100), Lake Buena Vista, FL 32830-0100. Tel. 407/W-DISNEY or 934-6000. Fax 407/934-5777. 2,048 rms. A/C TV TEL

$ Rates: $89–$121 for up to four in a room. Children under 18 free. Inquire about packages. AE, MC, V. **Parking:** Free self-parking.

Nestled on the banks of the Disney-made Sassagoula River and dotted with bayous, Dixie Landings shares its magnificently landscaped 325-acre site with the Port Orleans Resort, described below. Themed after the Louisiana countryside, it is divided into "parishes" with accommodations housed in stately colonnaded plantation homes (fronted by brick courtyards and manicured lawns with vine-covered trellises) or rustic Cajun-style dwellings (set amid bayous and stands of towering cypress and pine). Rooms in the former are elegantly decorated in Federalist blue and gold, with brass-trimmed maple furnishings, swagged draperies, and gilt-framed botanical prints on cream walls. Cajun rooms, on the other hand, feature bed frames made of bent branches, patchwork quilts, and calico-print drapes. In-room amenities throughout include remote-control cable TVs, ceiling fans, double sinks in the bath, and AM/FM alarm-clock radios. Many accommodations offer river views. As at all Disney resorts, the attention to thematic detail is notable. Low-decibel Cajun music wafts from speakers concealed in the shrubbery, foliage pressed into winding cement pathways create lovely fossillike designs, and the main lobby has a steamboat-company theme with a Victorian shiplike interior and a registration area designed to look like booths for booking ocean-liner passage.

Dining/Entertainment   **Boatwright's Dining Hall** is patterned after a 19th-century boat-building factory, with the wooden hull of a Louisiana fishing boat suspended from a very high beamed ceiling and peach stucco walls hung with antique boat-building tools. Bare oak tables are set with shop-rag napkins and condiments in toolboxes. Cajun fare is served at breakfast and dinner. **Colonel's Cotton Mill,** a food court, occupies a rustic setting under a 50-foot, massively beamed pine ceiling. The room centers on a cotton press powered by a gigantic water wheel. Fare runs the gamut from Tex-Mex to pizza and pasta. **Muddy Rivers,** a poolside bar in a ramshackle structure, serves drinks and light fare; it has a very pleasant shaded porch cooled by ceiling fans. Off the lobby, the **Cotton Co-op** lounge—with its beautiful pressed-

ⓕ FROMMER'S COOL FOR KIDS: HOTELS

All Disney Properties and "Official" Hotels
(see pp. 49 to 80) The many advantages for kids include proximity to Walt Disney World parks, complimentary transportation between hotels and the parks, and reduced-price children's menus and Disney character appearances in hotel restaurants. Extensive facilities might include lakefront beaches, boating, waterskiing, bike rentals, playgrounds, video-game arcades, swimming pools with waterfalls and slides, and/or organized children's activities. See listings for details.

Disney's Fort Wilderness Resort and Campground *(see p. 68)* All of the above and more is offered here—plus you get to go camping.

Residence Inns *(see pp. 84 and 92)* Residence Inns not only have swimming pools, children's playgrounds, and other recreational facilities, but accommodations with fully equipped kitchens—a potential money-saver when traveling with family. Rates include breakfast. The Meadow Creek Drive Residence Inn *(see p. 84)* has an extensive recreation department offering free children's activities. The Lake Cecile property *(see p. 92)* has on-premises barbecue grills and picnic tables and offers boating and waterskiing on a scenic lake.

Holiday Inn Sunspree Resort Lake Buena Vista *(see p. 88)* This hotel has a special check-in desk for kids and on-premises mascots to welcome them. Rooms are equipped with kitchenettes, but it doesn't cost much to feed your family here. Kids under 12 eat free in their own restaurant where movies and cartoons are shown. Numerous organized children's activities are free.

Holiday Inn Maingate East *(see p. 90)* The inn offers children's facilities identical to its Lake Buena Vista counterpart.

copper ceiling and plush leather couches before a blazing fireplace—is designed to suggest a cotton-trading commodity house. Monday-night football games are aired on a large-screen TV here, and Tuesday through Saturday comedians and singers entertain. *Note:* Bars here offer kiddie cocktails with names like Br'er Rabbit.

Services Room service (pizza delivery only), guest services desk, babysitting; boat transport to Port Orleans, Village Marketplace, and Pleasure Island.

Facilities Six large swimming pools, coin-op washers, dryers, children's playground, vast video-game arcade, bicycle rental, car-rental desk, boat rentals (paddleboats, rowboats, float boats, canopy boats), 1.7-mile riverfront jogging/biking path, Fulton's General Store (gifts, Disneyana, resort wear, snacks, sundries). Ol' Man Island, a woodsy 3½-acre recreation area, centers on an ancient live oak tree with a 78-foot branch spread. On it are an immense rustically themed free-form pool with waterfalls cascading from a broken bridge and a water slide entered via a pump house, a playground, children's wading pool, spa, sun deck, and fishin' hole (rent bait and poles and angle for catfish and bass).

DISNEY'S PORT ORLEANS RESORT, 2201 Orleans Dr., off Bonnet Creek Pkwy. (P.O. Box 10,100), Lake Buena Vista, FL 32830-0100. Tel. 407/W-DISNEY or 934-5000. Fax 407/934-5353. 1,008 rms. A/C TV TEL

$ Rates: $89–$121 for up to four in a room. Children under 18 free. Inquire about packages. AE, MC, V. **Parking:** Free self-parking.

This beautiful resort, themed after turn-of-the-century New Orleans, shares a site on the banks of the "mighty" Sassagoula River, with Dixie Landings, described above. (Sassagoula is the Native American name for the Mississippi.) The charming glass-walled lobby under a vaulted ceiling replicates a New Orleans mint; guests register at old-fashioned bank teller windows. Cheerful three-story buildings, painted in variegated pastels with shuttered windows and lacy wrought-iron balconies, house lovely rooms. Decorated in mocha, rust, and teal, they have pretty cherrywood furnishings, swagged draperies, art nouveau sconces, and walls hung with gilt-framed botanical prints and family photographs. Baths are equipped with double pedestal sinks (not to mention Mickey Mouse logo toiletries and toilet paper), a handsome armoire conceals your remote-control cable TV, and in-room amenities include ceiling fans and AM/FM alarm-clock radios. Accommodations buildings are fronted by lovely flower gardens (each unique to suggest individual lawns) opening onto fountained courtyards. And landscaping throughout the property is a delight, with stately oaks, formal boxwood hedges, azaleas, and fragrant jasmine.

Dining/Entertainment The very New Orleansy **Bonfamille's Café,** enclosing a fountained courtyard, has exposed-brick walls hung with paintings of the French Quarter and big baskets of flowering plants suspended from ceiling beams. Dixieland jazz is played softly. It's open for breakfast (come by for beignets and café au lait) and dinner, the latter featuring Créole specialties such as seafood jambalaya and po'boy sandwiches. At the festive **Sassagoula Floatworks and Food Factory,** its ceiling festooned with whimsical Mardi Gras parade float props—oversized masks, court jester mannequins, and saxophones looped with swags of colorful fabric—food court vendors serve up pizza, pasta, Créole specialties, spit-roasted chicken, and more from 6am to midnight daily. **Scat Cat's Club,** a cocktail lounge off the lobby, features family-oriented live entertainment (rock, country, New Orleans jazz, sing-alongs). And the poolside **Mardi Grog's** offers cool and fruity libations and light snacks.

Services   Room service (pizza delivery only) from noon to midnight, guest services desk, babysitting; boat transport to Dixie Landings, Village Marketplace, and Pleasure Island.

Facilities   Olympic-size Doubloon Lagoon swimming pool, which is surmounted by an enormous sea serpent–shaped water slide (an "alligator jazz band" plays in a pink clamshell near the pool), whirlpool, children's wading pool, coin-op washers/dryers, vast video-game arcade, bicycle rental, car-rental desk, boat rentals (paddleboats, rowboats, float boats, canopy boats), 1.7-mile river-front jogging/biking path, shop (gifts, Disneyana, resort wear, snacks, sundries).

INEXPENSIVE

DISNEY'S ALL-STAR MUSIC RESORT, 3499 W. Buena Vista Dr., at World Dr. and Osceola Pkwy. (P.O. Box 10,100), Lake Buena Vista, FL 32830-0100. Tel. 407/ W-DISNEY or 939-6000. Fax 407/354-1866. 1,920 rms. A/C TV TEL

$ Rates: $69–$79 single or double, depending on view and season. Extra person $8. Children under 18 free. Inquire about packages. AE, MC, V. **Parking:** Free self-parking.

Nestled among pristine pine forests southwest of MGM studios, this brand-new Disney property—part of a 246-acre complex that also includes the adjacent All-Star Sports Resort (see below)—offers numerous facilities and visitor perks at low prices. Partially opened in the fall of 1994, and scheduled to be completed in the spring of 1995, its 10 buildings are musically themed around country, jazz, rock, calypso, or Broadway show tunes, with oversized "icons" in public areas such as three-story cowboy boots, conga drum–shaped stair-ways, and a walk-through neon-lit jukebox. Small ponds dot the property, and building courtyards are attractively landscaped in appropriate themes (New Orleans–style gardens in the jazz section, a wildflower-filled meadow in the country-western area, and so on). Attractive rooms, with ecru walls and red-accented blue carpets, have musically themed bedspreads, paintings, and wall friezes. They're equipped with remote-control cable TVs, AM/FM alarm-clock radios, and safes.

Dining/Entertainment: The cheerful **Intermission Food Court,** adorned with music paraphernalia and memorabilia, has stations for barbecue, pizza, pastas, fresh-baked muffins and pastries, sandwiches, salads, and more; it's open for all meals. The adjoining **Singing Spirits Bar** serves both the food court and the pool area.

Services: Room service (pizza delivery only), babysitting, guest services desk, Mears airport shuttle.

Facilities: Two large swimming pools (one grand piano–shaped, the other guitar-shaped), kiddie pool, themed children's playground, jogging trail, coin-op washers/dryers, large retail shop (Disneyana, gifts, resort wear, sundries; music videos are shown on monitors over the registers), car-rental desk, vast state-of-the-art video-game arcade.

DISNEY'S ALL-STAR SPORTS RESORT, 3499 W. Buena Vista Dr., at World Dr. and Osceola Pkwy. (P.O. Box 10,100), Lake Buena Vista, FL 32830-0100. Tel. 407/ W-DISNEY or 939-5000. Fax 407/354-1866. 1,920 rms. A/C TV TEL

$ Rates: $69–$79 single or double, depending on view and season. Extra person $8. Children under 18 free. Inquire about packages. AE, MC, V. **Parking:** Free self-parking.

Adjacent to and sharing facilities with the above-listed All-Star Music Resort, this 82-acre sports-themed section of Disney's exciting new economy complex opened in May of 1994. Lobby walls are covered with sports memorabilia, and rooms are housed in 10 T-shaped buildings with football, baseball, basketball, tennis, and surfing themes. For instance, the turquoise surf buildings have waves along their rooflines, surfboards mounted on exterior walls, and a courtyard encompassing a swimming pool. And the basketball buildings surround a landscaped version of a basketball court, with "teams" and a "referee" represented by palm trees. Public-area "icons" include oversized lifeguard-shack and tennis-can stairways, four-story football helmets and whistles, a baseball scoreboard, and a tennis umpire chair. Cheerful rooms, with coffee-colored walls and painted dark green furniture, feature sports action–motif bedspreads, paintings, and wall friezes. They're equipped with remote-control cable TVs, AM/FM alarm-clock radios, and safes.

Dining/Entertainment: The **End Zone Food Court,** filled with sports memorabilia, has stations for barbecue, pizza, pastas, fresh-baked muffins and pastries, sandwiches, salads, and more. The adjoining **Team Spirits** bar also serves both the food court and the pool area.

Services: Room service (pizza delivery only), babysitting, guest services desk, Mears airport shuttle.

Facilities: Two large swimming pools (one with a surfing theme and two 38-foot shark fins, the other shaped like a baseball diamond with an "outfield" sun deck); kiddie pool, themed children's playground, jogging trail, coin-op washers/dryers, large ice-rink-themed shop (Disneyana, gifts, resort wear, sundries; sporting events are broadcast on monitors over the registers), car-rental desk, vast state-of-the-art video-game arcade.

A DISNEY CAMPGROUND

DISNEY'S FORT WILDERNESS RESORT AND CAMP- GROUND, 3520 N. Fort Wilderness Trail (P.O. Box 10,100), Lake Buena Vista, FL 32830-0100. Tel. 407/

W-DISNEY or 824-2900. Fax 407/354-1866. 784 campsites, 408 wilderness homes. AC TV

$ Rates: $35–$52 campsite per night (range depends on season, number of people, location, size, and extent of hookup); $180–$195 wilderness home. Inquire about packages. AE, MC, V.

Parking: Free self-parking at your campsite or wilderness home.

This woodsy 780-acre camping resort—shaded by towering pines and cypress trees and crossed by fish-filled streams, lakes, and canals—makes an ideal venue for family vacations. Secluded campsites (most of them set up for tent campers, the others for trailers), offer 110/220-volt outlets, barbecue grills, picnic tables, and children's play areas. Another option here are wilderness homes—rustic one-bedroom cabins with piney interiors. Accommodating two adults and up to four children, these have cozy living rooms with Murphy beds, baths, fully equipped eat-in kitchens, and on-premises telephones, picnic tables, and barbecue grills. Amenities include remote-control cable TVs (with WDW information channels) and AM/FM alarm-clock radios. Guests here enjoy a lot of extras, including extensive recreational facilities and a nightly campfire program hosted by Chip 'n' Dale and featuring Disney movies, cartoons, and sing-alongs.

Dining/Entertainment **Trails End,** in Pioneer Hall, has a rustic setting, with log beams and wagon-wheel chandeliers overhead and mounted moose antlers and steer hides adorning the walls. It's open for cafeteria-style breakfasts, lunches, and dinners daily (some noteworthy buffets here) and late-night pizza, with live entertainment (country and folk music) during the evening meal. Adjoining it is **Crockett's Tavern,** a cozy full-service restaurant with red-and-white-checkered tablecloths, walls covered with Davy Crockett memorabilia, even a stuffed "bar." It features Texas fare (fajitas, steaks, barbecued chicken and ribs) at dinner, after which you can "set" a while on rocking chairs out on the front porch. There's also a snack bar in the **Meadow Recreation Complex** adjacent to the video-game arcade, another near the beach. During summer months, guests enjoy a dazzling electrical water pageant from the beach here nightly at 9:45pm. And the rambunctious *Hoop-Dee-Doo Musical Revue* takes place in **Pioneer Hall** nightly (details in Chapter 9).

Services Guest services desk, babysitting; boat transport to Discovery Island, Magic Kingdom, and Contemporary Resort.

Facilities Comfort station in each campground area (with restrooms, private showers, ice machines, telephones, and laundry rooms), two large swimming pools, white-sand beach, Circle D Ranch horseback riding (trail rides), petting farm, pony rides, fishing, three sand volleyball courts, ball fields, tetherball, shuffleboard, bike rentals, boat rentals (canoes, paddleboats, Water Sprites, pontoons), 1.5-mile nature trail, 1.5-mile jogging path, two 18-hole championship golf courses, two night-lit hard-surface tennis courts, shops (camping supplies, groceries, propane gas, beer and wine, Disneyana), kennel, car-rental desk, two video-game arcades.

LAKE BUENA VISTA/OFFICIAL HOTELS

These properties, designated "official" WDW hotels, are located on and around Hotel Plaza Boulevard, a delightful thoroughfare with a wide traffic island shaded by lofty oaks. Guests at the below-listed hotels enjoy many privileges (see above). And the location is a big plus—close to the Disney parks and within walking distance of Disney Village Marketplace and Crossroads shops and restaurants as well as Pleasure Island nightlife.

Note: In addition to the addresses and toll-free phone numbers provided in each listing below, you can also make reservations at any of these official hotels through the Central Reservations Office, P.O. Box 10,100, Lake Buena Vista, FL 32830-0100 (tel. 407/W-DISNEY).

EXPENSIVE

BUENA VISTA PALACE, 1900 Buena Vista Dr., just north of Hotel Plaza Blvd., Lake Buena Vista, FL 32830. Tel. 407/827-2727, or toll free 800/327-2990. Fax 407/827-6034. 898 rms, 130 suites. A/C MINIBAR TV TEL

$ Rates: $130–$235 single or double; $219–$250 Crown Level; $245–$290 one-bedroom suite, $390–$455 two-bedroom suite. Range reflects view and season. Extra person $15. Children under 18 stay free. Inquire about packages. AE, CB, DC, MC, Optima, V. **Parking:** Free self-parking, valet parking $6 per night.

This 27-acre waterfront resort in Walt Disney World Village flies the flags of all Epcot countries at its entrance. Accommodations, in four handsome cream stucco towers with gleaming mirrored balconies, are decorated in earth tones (rust, tan, green, ecru), with dark oak furnishings. All but a few have balconies or patios, many of them overlooking Lake Buena Vista. Amenities include remote-control cable TVs (with Spectravision movie options), AM/FM alarm-clock radios, safes, bedroom and bath phones (the former a Mickey Mouse phone), and ceiling fans. Luxurious residential-style one- and two-bedroom suites—with living rooms, dining rooms, private balconies or patios, minibars, microwave ovens, and refrigerators—are housed in a peach stucco, art deco building with aqua trim on the property's Recreation Island; it connects to a tower building via tropically landscaped walkways. And Crown rooms on the 10th floor comprise a concierge level where guests enjoy larger rooms, hairdryers, and the services of a concierge. A plush private lounge, which offers a magnificent panorama of Disney World, is the setting for complimentary continental breakfasts, afternoon cocktails with hot and cold hors d'oeuvres, and evening cordials with petit fours.

Dining/Entertainment **Arthur's 27,** offering panoramic views of Walt Disney World parks from its 27th-floor location, is the hotel's elegant premier restaurant, serving haute-cuisine dinners enhanced by selections from an award-winning wine cellar. A meal here might begin with beluga caviar served with vodka, and continue with an entrée of breast of Barbary duck laced with tamarind, orange, and dark rum. An adjoining lounge offers live jazz and piano-bar entertainment, dancing, hors d'oeuvres, and, of course, the view. The rustic Australian-themed **Outback Restaurant,** with rough-hewn paneling and a three-story indoor waterfall, specializes in steak, prime rib, lobster, and fresh seafood—not to mention kangaroo!—grilled over an open pit. An Australian storyteller entertains during dinner. Minnie, Goofy, and Pluto host Sunday-morning (four times a week in summer) buffet breakfasts in the Mediterranean-style **Watercress Cafe,** a cheerful plant-filled eatery with paintings of parrots and flamingos on peach stucco walls and large windows overlooking Lake Buena Vista. Open from 6am to midnight daily, it specializes in Florida cuisine. The 24-hour **Watercress Bake Shop,** for incredible desserts, croissants, muffins, and Häagen-Dazs ice-cream sundaes adjoins. The festive **Laughing Kookaburra Good Time Bar** boasts a selection of 99 beers and offers happy hour international hors d'oeuvre buffets and live bands for dancing nightly. The gazebo-style **Lobby Lounge** in the atrium serves cocktails, premium wines by the glass, gourmet teas and coffees, and pastries; come by for piano-bar entertainment evenings. The **Recreation Island Pool Snack Bar** serves light fare and tropical drinks to sunbathers. And **Courtyard Pastries and Pizza,** an outdoor ice-cream parlor/snack bar serves breakfast and light fare (pizza, subs, deli sandwiches, and pastries) at umbrella tables on a fountained plaza where the WDW shuttle buses pull up.

Services 24-hour room service, babysitting, 24-hour guest services desk (sells tickets to WDW parks and all other nearby attractions), complimentary newspaper at guest services, shoeshine/shoe repair, nightly bed turndown.

Facilities Two large swimming pools, whirlpool, children's wading pool, three night-lit hard-surface tennis courts, gratis transportation to WDW golf courses, boat rental at nearby Disney Village Marina (mini-speedboats, paddleboats, pontoons, canoes), three-mile jogging path, volleyball, horseshoes, children's playground, car-rental desk, full-service unisex beauty salon, massage, full business center, fully equipped health club, sauna, shops (men's and women's resort wear, video-camera rental, Disneyana, gifts/sundries), coin-op washers/dryers, large video-game arcade, oversize speakerphone phone booths for family or group calls, Kids Stuff (a counselor-supervised child-care center, open summer and high season only).

HILTON AT WALT DISNEY WORLD VILLAGE, 1751 Hotel Plaza Blvd., just east of Buena Vista Dr., Lake Buena Vista, FL 32830. Tel. 407/827-4000, or toll free 800/782-4414. Fax 407/827-6380. 787 rms, 27 suites. A/C MINIBAR TV TEL

$ Rates: $119–$245 single or double. Tower rooms $40 additional. Range reflects season. Extra person $20. Children of any age stay free in parents' room. Inquire about packages and weekend rates. AE, CB, DC, DISC, ER, JCB, MC, V. **Parking:** Free self-parking, valet parking $6 per night.

Heralded by a palm-fringed circular driveway leading up to an imposing waterfall and fountain, the Hilton occupies 23 beautifully landscaped acres including two large lakes. Accommodations, in a vast 10-story main building with a plant-filled skylit lobby, are done up in soft earth tones with teal/mauve accents and splashy floral-print bedspreads. Amenities include remote-control cable TVs with HBO and Spectravision movie options, AM/FM alarm-clock radios, and phones with two lines. The ninth and 10th floors comprise The Towers, a concierge level with a gorgeous lake-view lounge. Perks for Tower guests include complimentary bottled water, bathroom scales, terry robes, upgraded toiletries, coffee makers, private registration and checkout, and nightly turndown. Complimentary continental breakfast, light snacks throughout the day, and cocktail hour hot and cold hors d'oeuvres are served in the lounge.

Dining/Entertainment The **Florida Fin Factory,** a seafood restaurant, has an adjoining bar/lounge and raw bar. **Benihana Japanese Steakhouse**—a stunning dining room decorated with beautiful Japanese art and three aquariums of tropical fish—features teppanyaki dinners nightly; you can also enjoy appetizers such as calamari tempura, and/or tropical drinks, in the adjoining lounge. Etched-glass carnival scenes, fairground murals, and striped awnings set the theme of **County Fair,** a cheerful coffee shop serving à la carte breakfasts, lunches, and dinners. The adjoining **County Fair Buffeteria** sets out a lavish buffet at breakfast. And the **County Fair Terrace,** with umbrella tables on a brick patio under a bright yellow canopy, offers light al fresco breakfasts and lunches while you wait for the shuttle bus to WDW. **Rum Largo Poolside Cafe & Bar** provides snack/lunch fare and exotic tropical drinks to sunbathers. Cozy and elegant, **John T's Plantation Bar** off the lobby evokes the antebellum South. It features light fare, exotic tropical drinks, and nighttime entertainment for dancing; major sporting events are aired on a large-screen TV. Kids love the **Old Fashioned Soda Shoppe** for pizzas, burgers, hot dogs, not to mention malts, shakes, and sundaes; it even has video games. And a cedar gazebo is the scene of frequent live poolside entertainment.

Services Room service from 6:30am to 1am, babysitting, concierge on duty from 7am to 10pm (sells tickets and arranges transport to all other nearby attractions/airport; WDW tickets available at Walt Disney World men's shop on the lobby level), nightly bed turndown on request.

Facilities Two very large swimming pools, two-tiered whirlpool in tropical/rock garden setting, children's spray pool, two night-lit hard-surface tennis courts, golf privileges at—and gratis transportation to—WDW courses, boat rental at nearby Disney Village Marina (mini-speedboats, paddleboats, pontoons, canoes), volleyball, water volleyball, badminton, children's playground, car-rental desk, full-service unisex beauty salon, full business center, fully equipped health club, sauna, shops (WDW men's and women's resort wear, jewelry, gifts/sundries, Disneyana), coin-op washers/dryers, large high-tech video-game arcade, Vacation Station Kids Hotel (a counselor-supervised child-care center).

MODERATE

GROSVENOR RESORT, 1850 Hotel Plaza Blvd., just east of Buena Vista Dr., Lake Buena Vista, FL 32830. Tel. 407/828-4444, or toll free 800/624-4109. Fax 407/828-8192. 625 rms, 5 suites. A/C TV TEL

$ Rates: $99–$160 for up to four people in a room. Range depends on view and season. Inquire about packages. AE, CB, DC, DISC, ER, JCB, MC, Optima, V. **Parking:** Free self-parking, valet parking $5 per night.

The British colonial–themed Grosvenor, on 13 beautifully landscaped lakeside acres, centers on a 19-story peach stucco building fronted by towering palms. Recently renovated guest rooms have been attractively decorated in seafoam green or muted blue color schemes with splashy print bedspreads, light oak furnishings, and marble-topped desks. Walls are adorned with decorative friezes and pleasant paintings of tropical resorts. Amenities include remote-control cable TVs with VCRs (movie tapes can be rented), AM/FM alarm-clock radios, coffee makers (tea and coffee supplied), safes, and hairdryers.

Dining/Entertainment The rather elegant **Baskervilles Restaurant,** on the mezzanine, displays 19th-century Sherlock Holmes book illustrations on its walls and even has a Sherlock Holmes museum—and a re-creation of his Baker Street headquarters—on the premises. Windowed walls overlook the lake. Saturday nights, Baskervilles is the scene of mystery dinner theater productions. The restaurant also features buffet breakfasts and dinners (including a character breakfast every Tuesday, Thursday, and Saturday morning, and a character dinner every Wednesday night). A la carte American/continental selections are also an option at all meals. **Moriarty's Pub,** offering live entertainment in high season and a pool table, adjoins. **Crumpets Cafe,** a food court, is open 24 hours. **Barnacles Pool Bar** serves tropical drinks and light fare. And at **Cricket's Lounge,** off the lobby, sporting events are aired on a large-screen TV.

Services Room service from 7am to midnight, babysitting, guest services from 7am to 10pm (sells tickets and arranges transport to all nearby attractions; WDW park tickets are available at the Disney shop), stocked minibar on request, gratis newspaper delivered to your room daily on request.

Facilities Two swimming pools (one of them quite large), whirlpool, children's wading pool, two hard-surface night-lit tennis courts, exercise room, boat rental at nearby Disney Village Marina (mini-speedboats, paddleboats, pontoons, canoes), children's playground, lawn games (shuffleboard, volleyball, basketball, handball, horseshoes), car-rental desk, coin-op washers/dryers, shops (gifts/ sundries, Disneyana), video-game arcade.

GUEST QUARTERS SUITE RESORT, 2305 Hotel Plaza Blvd., just west of Apopka-Vineland Rd./FL 535, Lake Buena Vista, FL 32830. Tel. 407/934-1000, or toll free 800/424-2900. Fax 407/934-1008. 229 suites. A/C TV TEL

$ Rates: $139–$195 for one or two people in a one-bedroom suite. Extra person $20. Children under 18 free. Range depends on view and season. $250–$395 two-bedroom suite. Inquire about packages and rates including breakfast. AE, CB, DC, DISC, JCB, MC, V. **Parking:** Free self-parking.

Entered via a small skylit atrium lobby with a large aviary of tropical birds, this seven-story all-suite hotel is a great choice for families. Children have their own check-in desk where they receive a free gift. Large one-bedroom suites (643 square feet)—which can sleep up to six people—are delightfully decorated in teal, mauve, and peach, utilizing light wood furnishings and pretty floral-print fabrics. They include a full living room with a convertible sofa, dining area, and a separate bedroom. Among your in-room amenities are a wet bar, refrigerator, coffee maker (gratis coffee and tea supplied), microwave oven, remote-control cable TVs with pay-movie options in the living room and bedroom, a smaller black-and-white TV in the bath, two phones, an alarm-clock, AM/FM radio, and a hairdryer.

Dining/Entertainment **Parrot Patch,** a tropically themed restaurant, serves American fare at all meals. There's a special children's dining area, and, at lunch, you can sit outside at umbrella tables. A bar/lounge adjoins. A **pool bar** serves the same menu as Parrot Patch. **Scoops & Games** is an ice-cream parlor-cum-video-game arcade off the pool area.

Services Room service from 6:30am to 11pm, babysitting, guest services desk (sells tickets to WDW parks and all other nearby attractions; also arranges transport to latter).

Facilities Large heated swimming pool, whirlpool, children's wading pool with fountain, two night-lit hard surface tennis courts, boat rental at nearby Disney Village Marina (mini speedboats, paddleboats, pontoons, canoes), jogging path, volleyball, children's playground, car-rental desk, exercise room, shops (gifts/ sundries, Disneyana, full grocery store), coin-op washers/dryers, video-game arcade.

HOWARD JOHNSON RESORT, 1805 Hotel Plaza Blvd., between Buena Vista Dr. and Apopka-Vineland Rd./FL 535, Lake Buena Vista, FL 32830. Tel. 407/828-8888, or toll free 800/223-9930. Fax 407/827-4623. 321 rms, 2 suites. A/C TV TEL

$ Rates: $85–$145 single or double, depending on view and season. Inquire about packages. AE, CB, DC, DISC, JCB, MC, Optima, V. **Parking:** Free self-parking.

Entered via an imposing atrium lobby with a lofty stained-glass skylight, this HoJo recently underwent a $2.1 million renovation. Public areas were upgraded and rooms refurbished and redecorated in a teal and peach color scheme. Most have balconies. Amenities include remote-control cable TVs and VCRs (movie tapes can be rented) and in-room safes; refrigerators are available on request.

Dining/Entertainment A **Howard Johnson's Restaurant** on the premises has a pleasant coffee-shop atmosphere; it's open from 6am to midnight daily for American fare and all 28 ice cream flavors. The **Lobby Lounge,** which has an indoor waterfall, is open nightly for cocktails and also serves an inexpensive continental breakfast during high season. And the **Sidewalk Cafe** serves light fare and drinks poolside.

Services Room service from 7am to 10pm, babysitting, guest services desk (sells tickets and arranges transport to all nearby attractions; WDW park tickets are available at an on-premises shop), complimentary transport to/from all WDW parks.

Facilities Two swimming pools (one is vaguely shaped like Mickey Mouse), whirlpool, children's wading pool, boat rental at nearby Disney Village Marina (mini-speedboats, paddleboats, pontoons, canoes), children's playground, car-rental desk, exercise room, shops (men's and women's resort wear, Disneyana, gifts/sundries), coin-op washers/dryers, large video-game arcade.

ROYAL PLAZA, 1905 Hotel Plaza Blvd., between Buena Vista Dr. and Apopka-Vineland Rd./FL 535, Lake Buena Vista, FL 32830. Tel. 407/828-2828, or toll free 800/248-7890. Fax 407/827-6338. 386 rms, 10 suites. A/C TV TEL

$ Rates: $97–$197 for up to four people in a room; $304–$550 suite. Range depends on view and season. Inquire about packages. AE, Barclaycard, CB, DC, DISC, ER, JCB, MC, Optima, V.
   Parking: Free self- and valet parking.

As we go to press, the 17-story Royal Plaza is completing a multimillion-dollar renovation and upgrade—adding two executive floors and a concierge level, and refurbishing all accommodations and public areas. Rooms are freshly decorated in teal, peach, and periwinkle, with grasspaper-covered walls and bright print bedspreads. You can watch Magic Kingdom fireworks from your furnished balcony. And amenities include remote-control cable TVs and VCRs (movie tapes can be rented), AM/FM alarm-clock radios, safes, and Mickey Mouse phones; refrigerators are available on request, and deluxe rooms have wet bars. Two of the suites here are unique; they were decorated, respectively, by Barbara Mandrell and Burt Reynolds, who supplied family photographs, platinum records/ acting awards, and other personal memorabilia for display.

Dining/Entertainment A new upscale restaurant and lounge, plus a lobby bar, are in the works at this writing. The **Giraffe Lounge,** a lively disco, plays high-energy music for dancing nightly. It also features complimentary happy hour buffets. And a **pool bar** is open in season.

Services Room service from 6am to midnight, babysitting, guest services (sells tickets and arranges transport to all nearby attractions; WDW park tickets are available at the Disney shop).

Facilities Large L-shaped swimming pool, whirlpool, four hard-surface night-lit tennis courts, boat rental at nearby Disney Village Marina (mini-speedboats, paddleboats, pontoons, canoes), children's playground, sauna, fitness center, shuffleboard, Ping-Pong, car-rental desk, overnight film developing, video-camera rental, unisex hair salon, coin-op washers/dryers, shops (gifts/sundries, Disneyana, men's and women's resort wear), video-game arcade.

TRAVELODGE HOTEL, 2000 Hotel Plaza Blvd., between Buena Vista Dr. and Apopka-Vineland Rd./FL 535, Lake Buena Vista, FL 32830. Tel. 407/828-2424, or toll free 800/348-3765. Fax 407/828-8933. 321 rms, 4 suites. A/C MINIBAR TV TEL

$ Rates: $99–$169 for up to four people in a room. Range depends on room size and season. Inquire about packages. AE, CB, DC, DISC, ER, JCB, MC, Optima, V. **Parking:** Free self-parking.

This 12-acre lakefront property is spiffy and immaculate, with rooms and public areas more upscale than you might expect at a Travelodge. This is the company's flagship hotel. Designed to evoke a Barbados plantation manor house, it has a Caribbean resort ambience with tropical foliage and colorful floral-print fabrics and carpeting. Rooms are particularly inviting, decorated in muted peach and beige with light-bleached wood furnishings. Walls are adorned with floral friezes and lovely framed botanical prints. All accommodations have furnished balconies, many of them overlooking Lake Buena Vista. Corner king rooms with chaise longues and convertible sofas are especially desirable. Amenities include remote-control cable TVs with Spectravision movie options, AM/FM alarm-clock radios, coffee makers (tea and coffee supplied), and hairdryers. Free local phone calls and in-room safes are a plus.

Dining/Entertainment Traders, with a wall of windows overlooking a densely wooded area, is open for breakfast and dinner, the latter featuring steak and seafood; a screened-in, plant-filled terrace adjoins. The **Flamingo Cove Lounge,** a cocktail bar featuring espresso and cappuccino drinks spiked with liqueurs, also has screened outdoor seating. The **Parakeet Cafe,** a casual self-service eatery evocative of a Paris bistro, is open from 7am to midnight for pizza, croissant sandwiches, and salads. And on the 18th floor, **Toppers,** a beautiful nightclub with windows all around, offers magnificent views of Lake Buena Vista and beyond. It's a great vantage point for watching nightly laser shows and fireworks. A DJ or live band plays Top 40s dance music.

Services Room service from 7am to midnight, babysitting, guest services (sells tickets and arranges transport to all nearby attractions; WDW park tickets are available at the Disney shop), gratis newspaper delivered to your room weekdays.

Facilities Large swimming pool, children's wading pool,

boat rental at nearby Disney Village Marina (mini-speedboats, paddleboats, pontoons, canoes), children's playground, car-rental desk, coin-op washers/dryers, shops (gifts/sundries, groceries and liquor, Disneyana), video-game arcade.

THE DOLPHIN & THE SWAN

The Dolphin and Swan, both within walking distance of Epcot, occupy some kind of middle ground between Disney properties and official hotels. They offer almost all the perks of Disney-owned properties, such as advance reservations at WDW restaurants and shows, including Epcot establishments, via the hotel concierge. Both are also distinctive for Michael Graves's fantastical architectural style, which people tend to adore or detest.

VERY EXPENSIVE

WALT DISNEY WORLD DOLPHIN, 1500 Epcot Resorts Blvd., off Buena Vista Dr., Lake Buena Vista, FL 32830-2653. Tel. 407/934-4000, or toll free 800/227-1500. Fax 407/934-4099. 1,370 rms, 140 suites. A/C MINIBAR TV TEL

$ Rates: $220–$335 single or double, depending on view and season; $310–$365 Dolphin Towers floors; $450–$2,400 suite. Extra person $15. Up to 2 children under 18 free. Inquire about packages. AE, CB, DC, DISC, ER, JCB, MC, V. **Parking:** Free self-parking, valet parking $7.

Designed by whimsical architect Michael Graves, the Dolphin, a Sheraton-operated hotel overlooking Crescent Lake, has a beachy coral and turquoise facade centered on a 27-story pyramid. This triangular tower is flanked by two 11-story wings painted with giant banana leaves and crowned by 56-foot twin dolphin sculptures. Graves dubs his more-Disneyesque-than-Disney creations "entertainment architecture." Close to a dozen cascading fountains on the property range from a seven-dolphin extravaganza at the entrance to waters rushing across rock-faced grottoes in a fiber-optic "starlit" foyer.

There are thousands of works of art in public areas. In the rooms, pastel-hued walls are hung with prints by Picasso, Matisse, Hockney, and other artists, and painted wood furnishings are stenciled with palm trees and pineapples. Amenities include remote-control cable TVs with HBO and pay-movie options, AM/FM alarm-clock radios, desk and bedside phones, safes, coffee makers, hairdryers, and irons/ironing boards. Floors 12 to 20 comprise the Dolphin Towers, a concierge level where guests are greeted with chilled champagne and enjoy complimentary continental breakfast, cocktail-hour hors d'oeuvres, and late-night desserts in a private lounge. Other Towers perks include a private concierge, express check-in/checkout, upgraded bath amenities, and terry robes.

Dining/Entertainment **Sum Chows,** the hotel's elegant signature restaurant, serves haute-cuisine Chinese, Japanese,

Vietnamese, and Thai dinners. At the exuberantly Italian **Ristorante Carnevale**—its walls hung with Venetian festival masks and Pierrot hats—strolling musicians, jugglers, and magicians entertain diners. Classic Italian fare is served at dinner; Sunday mornings Carnevale hosts a character brunch. Both the restaurant and its adjoining lounge have floor-to-ceiling windows overlooking Crescent Lake. **Harry's Safari Bar & Grille** is jungle-themed, with paintings of banana leaves and palm trees on the walls and a menagerie of stuffed tigers, elephants, and giraffes in residence (some are seated at tables). Open for dinner nightly, its menu highlights steak and fresh Florida seafood entrées. In the adjoining piano bar/lounge a baby gorilla tickles the ivories. The delightful **Coral Cafe,** with reef-motif carpeting and big wooden "fishmobiles" suspended overhead, serves à la carte American fare throughout the day as well as breakfast and dinner buffets. The **Dolphin Fountain Ice Cream & Snack Shop** is an old-fashioned malt shop, complete with oldies-stocked Wurlitzer jukebox. The waitstaff dances in the aisles en route to serving burgers and banana splits. **Tubbi Checkers,** a modernistic 24-hour cafeteria adjoining the video-game arcade, offers snack fare. **Copa Banana,** with tables shaped like citrus slices and a 50-foot-long banana-shaped bar, is open until 2am nightly for dancing (a DJ provides music) and karaoke; there are pool tables in an adjoining room. A pianist entertains every afternoon in the **Lobby Lounge,** a simpatico setting for tropical drinks, liqueurs, and coffee-liqueur drinks, among other tempting libations. And at the **Cabana Bar & Grill** light fare and frozen tropical drinks are brought to you poolside by servers on roller skates.

Services   24-hour room service, tram to Epcot, water launch transport to Disney-MGM Studios, concierge, guest services desk (sells tickets and arranges transport to all nearby attractions), Japanese tour desk, babysitting, complimentary daily newspaper.

Facilities   (See also facilities at the Swan, below.) Water volleyball, boat rentals (paddleboats, sailboats, Windsurfers, electric cruise boats), eight hard-surface night-lit tennis courts, tennis pro shop, fully equipped Body by Jake health club (including sauna, whirlpool, massage, personal training, aerobics classes, body wraps), two beach volleyball courts, three-mile jogging trail, coin-op washers/dryers, full service unisex hair salon, shops (Disneyana, jewelry, upscale gifts, resort wear, gourmet candy, sundries, pool accessories, groceries), full business center, car-rental desk, Delta Air Lines desk, large video-game arcade, Camp Dolphin (a counselor-supervised children's activity center, open daily. A free-form rock-sculpted grotto pool—with waterfalls, a water slide, rope bridge, and three secluded whirlpools—sprawls over two acres between the Dolphin and the adjoining Swan. Both properties also share a white sandy beach on Crescent Lake.

WALT DISNEY WORLD SWAN, 1200 Epcot Resorts Blvd., off Buena Vista Dr., Lake Buena Vista, FL 32830-2653.

Tel. 407/934-3000, or toll free 800/248-SWAN or 800/228-3000. Fax 407/934-4499. 694 rms, 64 suites. A/C MINIBAR TV TEL

$ Rates: $245–$305 single or double, depending on view and season; $335–$360 concierge floors; $360–$1,650 suite. Extra person $25. Children under 18 free. Inquire about packages. AE, CB, DC, DISC, ER, JCB, MC, V. **Parking:** Free self-parking, valet parking $7.

Operated by Westin Hotels & Resorts, this 12-story aquamarine and adobe-peach hotel—its rooftop flanked by 45-foot swan statues and seashell fountains—is adjacent to, and shares a lakeside beach and facilities with, the above-mentioned Dolphin. The hotels are connected by a canopied walkway. Here Michael Graves has created a festive interior replete with numerous swan fountains, sea horse-motif chandeliers, hallway walls painted with beach scenes, and striped room doors evocative of cabanas. Luxurious accommodations, decorated in cheerful pastels (peach, teal, yellow, and coral), have Drexel Heritage furnishings stenciled with parrots and pineapples, swan- and palm-tree motif lamps, and walls hung with prints by Matisse, Cézanne, and other artists. In-room amenities include remote-control cable TVs with HBO and pay-movie options, AM/FM alarm-clock radios, desk and bedside phones, safes, and baths with double sinks. King-bedded rooms have pullout sleeper sofas. The 11th and 12th floors comprise the Royal Beach Club, a concierge level offering a private lounge for complimentary extended continental breakfast, afternoon hot hors d'oeuvres, and evening cocktails. Guests on these floors also enjoy extra amenities including services of a personal concierge, nightly turndown, express check-in/checkout, upgraded toiletries, terry robes, hairdryers, and bathroom phones.

Dining/Entertainment The casually elegant Italian-*moderne* **Palio** is themed on a horse race that takes place each year in Siena. A mural evokes Tuscany, patterned flags of competing *contradas* (counties) are suspended overhead, and specially designed Villeroy & Boch china mirrors the flag motifs. Large windows overlook scenic canals, and strolling musicians entertain while you dine. The menu features classic Italian cuisine, and an exhibition kitchen affords an appetizing view of pizzas being placed in a wood-fired brick oven. Open for dinner nightly. Under a lofty dome, the **Garden Grove Cafe**—with striped canvas awnings, a terra-cotta fountain, and tall palms in clay pots—is a light and airy setting for casual dining, including twice-weekly character breakfasts and Thursday-night character dinners. Evenings the Grove becomes a steakhouse; weather permitting, it offers poolside umbrella tables for outdoor dining, and in the morning, a traditional Japanese breakfast is an option. The handsome **Kimono's,** with bamboo beams overhead, highly polished oak floors, and teak-paneled walls, serves a wide selection of sushi along with Japanese beers and fine American and European wines; open from 4pm daily, it becomes a karaoke bar after 8:30pm. The fanciful **Lobby Court Lounge,** with painted wooden monkeys hanging from streetlamps, features gourmet coffees, desserts, and specialty cocktails afternoons and evenings. And the **Splash Grill** serves frozen tropical fruit drinks and light fare (including full breakfasts) poolside.

Services   24-hour room service, babysitting, complimentary tram to Epcot, water launch transport to Disney-MGM Studios, guest services desk, concierge, nightly bed turndown with chocolate mint, complimentary daily newspaper.

Facilities   (See also facilities at the Dolphin, above.) Olympic-size lap pool, children's wading pool, fully equipped health club with sauna and massage therapy, full business center, car-rental desk, unisex hair salon, children's playground, shops (gifts, Disneyana, resort wear, sundries), video-game arcade, Camp Swan (a counselor-supervised child-care/activity center).

---

2. OTHER LAKE BUENA VISTA AREA HOTELS

All of the below-listed are within a few minutes' drive of WDW parks.

VERY EXPENSIVE

HYATT REGENCY GRAND CYPRESS/VILLAS OF GRAND CYPRESS, 1 Grand Cypress Blvd., off FL 535, Orlando, FL 32836. Tel. 407/239-1234, or toll free 800/233-1234. Fax 407/239-3800. For villas tel. 407/239-4700, or toll free 800/835-7377. Fax 407/239-7219. 676 rms, 74 suites, 146 villas. A/C MINIBAR TV TEL

$ Rates: $185–$325 for up to five people in a room; $350–$420 Regency Club; $150–$1,120 villa. Range reflects room size, view, and season. Inquire about packages. AE, CB, DC, DISC, ER, JCB, MC, V. **Parking:** Free self-parking, valet parking $7 per night.

This dazzling multifacility resort is in a class by itself. The lushly tropical plantings of the atrium lobby comprise a small rain forest with stone-bedded streams and live birds in brass cages. Outside, the Hyatt's gardeners have created an Edenic 1,500-acre botanic garden, dotted with babbling brooks, beautiful flower beds, charming outdoor sculpture, and rock gardens ablaze with bougainvillea and hibiscus. Colorful sailboats and swans glide serenely on 21-acre Lake Windsong. Thousands of palms sway in the breeze; dogwood, trumpet trees, and crape myrtle bloom in season; and native oaks, pines, and cypresses create canopies of shade.

Accommodations are deluxe, with grasspaper wall coverings and teal carpeting complemented by lovely cotton chintz bedspreads and curtains. Oak armoires house remote-control cable TVs with Spectravision movie options. Amenities include AM/FM alarm-clock radios, ceiling fans, safes, and, in the bath, hairdryers, cotton robes, bathroom scales, and fine toiletries. Three floors comprise the

Regency Club, a concierge level with a gorgeous lake-view lounge—setting for complimentary continental breakfasts, afternoon cocktails with hot and cold hors d'oeuvres, and late-night cordials and specialty drinks; beer, wine, coffee, champagne, and cookies are available in interim hours. Regency Club guests also enjoy free use of bikes, boats, and the health club; nightly turndown with a rose and chocolate; two newspapers delivered to their rooms daily; and complimentary fax service, among other perks.

And especially luxurious are one- to four-bedroom Mediterranean-style Villas of Grand Cypress accommodations, with fully equipped kitchens, patios, living rooms, and dining rooms. Many have working fireplaces and whirlpool bathtubs. Large picture windows overlook the golf course. Villa guests enjoy deluxe services and amenities.

Dining/Entertainment The Key West–themed **Hemingway's** serves steaks and Florida seafood at lunch and dinner. A bar/lounge adjoins. The **Cascade Grill,** down a brass spiral staircase, centers on a 35-foot sculpture of a bronze mermaid backed by a waterfall. American fare is served at all meals. **La Coquina,** with exquisitely appointed tables amid potted palms and splashing fountains, has a wall of two-story windows overlooking Lake Windsong. It serves French regional fare at dinner nightly; a harpist entertains. The gardenlike **Palm Cafe,** a self-service buffeteria with both indoor seating and umbrella tables on a poolside patio, offers traditional breakfast fare and an array of sandwiches, salads, entrées, and desserts at lunch; evenings it is transformed into **Papa Geppetto's** featuring California-style pizzas with gourmet toppings. Swinging doors lead to the 19th-century western-motif **White Horse Saloon,** which specializes in aged Black Angus prime rib dinners; a country-western trio entertains while you dine. **Papillon,** a plush pool bar in a white canvas tent overlooking a lake, is bordered by flower boxes. And **On the Rocks,** nestled in a rock cave surrounded by waterfalls, offers specialty drinks, snack fare, and ice-cream concoctions. In the lobby "rain forest," set amid cascading waterfalls, is **Trellises,** where a jazz ensemble entertains evenings. The **Rock Hyatt Club,** adjoining the video-game arcade, offers movies, music, and games for teens 13 to 17. The simpatico **Black Swan,** overlooking the golf course, serves contemporary American fare at dinner. Adjoining it is **Fairways,** a more casual venue with a working fireplace, open for all meals. And the **Pool Snack Bar** serves the pool by the villas.

Services 24-hour room service, babysitting, concierge (sells tickets to WDW parks and other nearby attractions), gratis transportation around property via shuttle buses and restored Victorian trolleys, hourly shuttle between the hotel and all WDW parks (round-trip fare is $4 a day), Mears airport shuttle.

Facilities Half-acre lagoonlike swimming pool spanned by a rope bridge and flowing through rock grottoes (with 12 waterfalls and two steep water slides), three secluded whirlpools, white-sand beach, 12 tennis courts (eight clay, four hard-surface, six lit for night play), award-winning 45-hole/par-72 Jack Nicklaus–designed golf course, nine-hole pitch-and-putt golf course, golf and tennis instruction/pro shops, equestrian center (lessons, trail rides), bicycle rental, boat rental (sailboats, sailboards, paddleboats, Sun Kat, canoes), 4.7-mile jogging path, 45-acre Audubon nature walk through pristine marshland with elevated boardwalks and descriptive signage, racquetball/volleyball/shuffleboard courts, croquet, children's playground, car-rental desk, full-service unisex beauty salon, full business center, state-of-the-art health club (offering sauna, steam, massage, and aerobics classes), shops (jewelry, gifts/sundries, pool accessories), helicopter landing pad, large high-tech video-game arcade, counselor-supervised child-care center/Camp Hyatt activity center, teen activities program.

EXPENSIVE

CYPRESS POINTE RESORT, 8651 Treasure Cay Lane, off Apopka-Vineland Rd. (FL 535), Lake Buena Vista, FL 32830. Tel. 407/238-2300, or toll free 800/749-8651. Fax 407/238-2886. 104 2- and 3-bedroom suites. A/C TV TEL

$ Rates: $175 two-bedroom suite for up to six people; $225 three-bedroom suite for up to nine people. Inquire about packages. AE, CB, DC, DISC, MC, V. **Parking:** Free self-parking.

This luxurious top-level vacation-ownership resort property is entered via a plant-filled lobby, with cages of tropical birds and an aquarium of colorful fish behind the registration desk. Very spacious accommodations (three-bedroom suites are 1,490 square feet) are housed in dormer-windowed stucco buildings painted in pleasing pastels with white trim—a very Caribbean look. They're simply gorgeous, with plushly furnished living rooms (equipped with large-screen remote-control cable TVs, VCRs, and CD/cassette players), large dining areas, additional dining set-ups on screened patios, fully equipped kitchens, whirlpools big enough for two in master bedrooms, and baths for each bedroom. Amenities abound—washers/dryers, irons and ironing boards, TVs/phones/AM/FM alarm-clock radios in living room and two bedrooms, and ceiling fans in all rooms (including the patio). Cypress Pointe is just minutes from Disney's main gate and adjacent to the Disney Village Marketplace.

Dining/Entertainment: Breakfast and light lunches are available poolside from a cabana bar, and beer and pizza are options during free movies shown nightly in an upstairs recreation room. Numerous restaurants are close by, many of which deliver food to the premises; you'll find a menu roster in your room.

Services: Guest services desk (sells tickets to WDW parks and other nearby attractions, most of them discounted), airport shuttle, babysitting. Round-trip fare to WDW parks is $6.

Facilities: Vast swimming pool with waterfall and "erupting volcano" whirlpool, sand volleyball court, basketball/shuffleboard courts, tennis court, children's playground and ball crawl, well-equipped health club, game room (billiards, darts, football), organized resort activities (movie nights, pool games, etc.), 24-hour convenience store (gift/sundries/movie rentals), small video-game arcade.

MARRIOTT'S ORLANDO WORLD CENTER, 8701 World Center Dr., on FL 536 between I-4 and FL 535, Orlando, FL 32821. Tel. 407/239-4200, or toll free 800/621-0638. Fax 407/238-8777. 1,503 rms, 85 suites. A/C MINIBAR TV TEL

$ Rates: $149–$189 for up to five people in a room (range reflects season). Pool-view room $10 additional per night. 14-day advance-purchase rates are $124–$154, subject to availability. $265–$2,400 suite. Inquire about packages and rates including full buffet breakfast. AE, CB, DC, DISC, ER, JCB, MC, Optima, V. **Parking:** Free self-parking, valet parking $8 per night.

This sprawling 230-acre resort, just two miles from WDW parks, is one of Florida's top venues for meetings and conventions. And the excellent service and array of facilities that make it so popular with corporate executives also make it a great choice for tourists. A grand palm-lined driveway, flanked by rolling golf greens, leads to the main building—a massive 27-story tower fronted by flower beds and fountains. In its 12-story atrium lobby, tropical plants and palms flourish in sunlight streaming through a lofty skylight, museum-quality 16th- and 17th-century chinoiseries and fine paintings set an elegant tone, and the sound of splashing fountains blends with soft piano music.

The tower houses spacious guest rooms cheerfully decorated in pastel hues with bamboo and rattan furnishings. All have desks, sofa beds, large closets (in which you'll find an iron and ironing board), and patios or balconies. Amenities include AM/FM alarm-clock radios, safes, remote-control cable TVs (with HBO, extensive pay-movie options, and video account review/message retrieval), and hairdryers in the bathrooms. Step outside the tower and you'll find magnificently landscaped grounds, punctuated by rock gardens, charming floral displays, shaded groves of pines and magnolias, fountains, and cascading waterfalls; black and white swans and ducks inhabit over a dozen lakes and lagoons spanned by graceful arched bridges.

Dining/Entertainment: With its rich mahogany and cherry paneling and 18th-century furnishings, the luxurious **Tuscany's** is Marriott's premier restaurant. It serves Italian haute-cuisine dinners featuring entrées such as lobster-filled ravioli and carved rack of lamb with white beans and roasted eggplant sauce. The **Mikado Japanese Steak House** is a serene setting for classic teppanyaki dinners overlooking rock gardens, reflecting pools, and a palm-fringed pond. The **Garden Terrace,** for family dining, is rather elegant with comfortable leather-upholstered furnishings amid lush tropical plantings and beautiful sienna lacquer paneling and trellising. It's open for breakfast, lunch, dinner, and buffet Sunday brunch. **JW's Steakhouse** is one of my favorite places in town for sun-dappled breakfasts and lunches on a screened balcony that yields breathtaking views of the lagoon and golf greens; or for cozy dinners in the rustic pine interior, **Champion's,** a simpatico sports-themed bar, airs athletic events on 16 TV monitors and one large-screen TV; other amusements here include blackjack, pool tables, video games, air hockey, and, some nights, music for dancing. The **Pagoda Lounge,** offering nightly piano-bar entertainment off the lobby, centers on an imposing Chinese black-lacquer pagoda under a sloped skylight. You can relax over cocktails in plush armchairs and sofas amid tropical blooms or on a lovely outdoor veranda overlooking the pool. **Palm's** serves drinks and light fare, including pizza, poolside. In high season it is augmented by the **Shrimp Shack,** vending peel-and-eat shrimp, and the hexagonal open-air **Pavilion** overlooking a pool and waterfalls and serving frozen drinks and snacks. **Stachio's,** adjoining the video-game arcade, serves light fare throughout the day.

Services 24-hour room service, babysitting, concierge from 7am to 11pm, shoeshine, nightly bed turndown on request, newspaper delivered to your room weekdays, Mears transportation/sightseeing desk (sells tickets to all nearby attractions, including WDW parks; also provides transport, by reservation, to WDW, other attractions, and airport), one-hour film developing. Round-trip fare between hotel and WDW parks is $4.50 per day, free for children under 12.

Facilities Three swimming pools (including a vast indoor pool, a larger-than-Olympic free-form pool with water slides and waterfalls, and a smaller pool with a volleyball net), four whirlpools, large children's wading pool, eight night-lit hard-surface tennis courts, 18-hole/par-71 Joe Lee–designed championship golf course, golf and tennis pro shops/instruction, 18-hole miniature golf course, two-mile jogging path, two volleyball courts, car-rental desk, full-service unisex beauty salon, very extensive business center, state-of-the-art health club (offering sauna, massage therapy, and aerobics classes), coin-op washers/dryers, shops (unique gifts/sundries, upscale resort wear, photo shop, toys, Disneyana), video-game arcade, Lollipop Lounge (a counselor-supervised child-care/activities center). Inquire as well about organized children's activities—games, movies, nature walks, and more.

RESIDENCE INN BY MARRIOTT, 8800 Meadow Creek Dr., just off FL 535, between Hwy. 536 and I-4, Orlando, FL 32821. Tel. 407/239-7700, or toll free 800/331-3131. Fax 407/239-7605. 688 suites. A/C TV TEL

$ Rates (including full breakfast): $150–$199 one-bedroom suite accommodating up to four people, $180–$249 two-bedroom suite accommodating up to six people. Range reflects season. Inquire about packages. AE, CB, DC, DISC, ER, JCB, MC, V. **Parking:** Free self-parking.

This delightful all-suite property, a converted luxury apartment complex, occupies 50 magnificently landscaped acres, with neatly manicured lawns, duck-filled ponds, fountains, and flower beds shaded by tall palms, pine trees, live oaks, and magnolias. Guests enjoy a serene environment that offers the seclusion of a private community (you have to drive through a security gate to enter) and can avail themselves of the extensive facilities at the adjoining Marriott Orlando World Center (see details above) with room-charge privileges. A lighted walkway connects the two properties via a gorgeous golf course.

Accommodations, housed in 86 two-story cream stucco buildings with Spanish-style terra-cotta roofs, are tastefully decorated in muted blue or green color schemes with soft peach and aqua accents. All offer fully equipped eat-in kitchens (some with washing machines and dryers), private balconies or patios, very ample closet space, and large, comfortable living rooms with sleeper sofas. Amenities include remote-control cable TVs (with HBO, Spectravision movie options, and VCRs; movie tapes can be rented), AM/FM alarm-clock radios, two phones (kitchen and bedroom), ceiling fans, and safes. Two-bedroom units have two baths.

Dining/Entertainment Breakfast—including your choice of entrées such as pancakes and French toast, breads, fresh fruits, fruit juices, and tea or coffee—is available in the gatehouse each morning. Many guests enjoy this meal al fresco on a covered open-air veranda overlooking the pool; others just take it to Disney World and eat it while waiting in line for the parks to open. A Pizza Hut is on the premises. Local restaurants also deliver food (there are menus in each room), and, of course, there are quite a few restaurants at the Marriott.

Services Guest services desk (sells tickets—most of them discounted—and provides transport to all nearby theme parks and attractions; round-trip to Disney parks costs $4.50), babysitting, complimentary daily newspaper, free shuttle transport around the property, same-day film developing, gratis food-shopping service, Mears airport shuttle.

Facilities Three large swimming pools (one with a rock waterfall), two beautiful secluded whirlpools, sports court (basketball, badminton, volleyball, paddle tennis, shuffleboard), one night-lit hard-surface tennis court, children's playground, coin-op washers/dryers, shops (large selection of deli/grocery items, gifts/sundries, toys, resort wear), two small video-game arcades. A recreation department organizes numerous free children's activities—arts and crafts, puppet making, video-game Olympics, outdoor sports, movies, and much more. These are on a daily basis in peak seasons, less frequently at other times. Do note all the additional facilities available to guests here at Marriott's Orlando World Center (see listing above).

SUMMERFIELD SUITES LAKE BUENA VISTA, 8751 Suiteside Dr., off Apopka-Vineland Rd. (FL 535), Lake Buena Vista, FL 32836. Tel. 407/238-0777, or toll free 800/833-4353. Fax 407/238-0778. 150 suites. A/C TV TEL

$ Rates (including extensive continental breakfast): $159–$199 one-bedroom suite for up to four people; $179–$249 two-bedroom suite for up to eight people. Range reflects season. Inquire about packages. AE, CB, DC, DISC, MC, V. **Parking:** Free self-parking.

This brand-new all-suite property, just minutes from Disney's main gate and adjacent to the Disney Village Marketplace, is an excellent choice for families. Immaculate accommodations in three-story terra-cotta–roofed stucco buildings surround a palm-fringed brick courtyard with fountains, big pots of flowering plants, umbrella tables, and gazebos. Spacious residential-style suites are attractively decorated in peach and teal with bleached oak furnishings. They contain fully equipped eat-in kitchens, comfortable living rooms with convertible sofas, big walk-in closets, and large dressing areas. Two-bedroom units have two baths, and all bedrooms have doors (insuring privacy). Amenities include irons and ironing boards, phones in each bedroom and the kitchen (with two lines, computer hookup, and voice-mail messaging), remote-control cable TVs in each bedroom and the living room (with free HBO, attraction-information stations, and pay-movie options), VCRs (a wide selection of movies can be rented), and AM/FM alarm-clock radios in each bedroom.

Dining/Entertainment: Guests enjoy an extensive continental buffet breakfast—fresh-baked muffins, fruit, hard-boiled eggs, toast, applesauce, assorted cereals, juice, and coffee or tea—in the pleasant dining room or at umbrella tables in the courtyard. An on-premises deli (which sells liquor as well as light fare) has a service window on the courtyard to serve swimmers and sunbathers. Local restaurants deliver food to the premises; you'll find a menu roster in your room.

Services: Room service (pizza delivery only), guest services desk (sells tickets to WDW parks and other nearby attractions, many of them discounted), shuttle available to airport and nearby attractions, free newspaper delivered to your room daily, complimentary grocery shopping, babysitting. Most important: There's free scheduled transport to and from the Disney parks throughout the day, representing a big savings for families.

Facilities: Large swimming pool, whirlpool, children's wading pool, car-rental desk, full business services, exercise room, coin-op washers/dryers, convenience shop, small video-game arcade.

VISTANA RESORT, 8800 Vistana Center Dr., off FL 535, between I-4 and FL 536, Lake Buena Vista, FL 32830. Tel. 407/239-3100, or toll free 800/877-8787. Fax 407/239-3062. 800 2-bedroom villas. A/C TV TEL

$ Rates: $175–$275 for up to six to eight people, range depending on season. Inquire about packages and weekly rates. AE, CB, DC, DISC, MC, Optima, V. **Parking:** Free self-parking.

This deluxe time-share property offers stunning two-bedroom, two-bath villas and extensive resort facilities on 119 beautifully landscaped acres encompassing shimmering lakes (home to ducks and black swans) and cascading waterfalls. Accommodations—ranging from sprawling ranch-style units to duplex town houses with cathedral pine ceilings—are individually furnished and decorated, though most utilize beachy resort pastels, bleached woods, wicker, and bamboo. All offer full living rooms (with convertible sofas and remote-control cable TVs equipped with VCRs), full dining areas (often there's a second dining set-up on the patio), two bedrooms (each with a TV, phone, and alarm-clock radio), fully equipped kitchens (the maid does your dishes), washers and dryers, and patios or balconies (some screened, many overlooking scenic waterways). Some master bedroom baths have whirlpool tubs, and there are ceiling fans in many rooms.

Dining/Entertainment   The gardenlike **Flamingo Cafe Restaurant & Lounge**—with seating at canvas umbrella tables and windows overlooking a weeping willow–shaded pond—specializes in barbecued chicken and ribs, steak, seafood, and pasta entrées. It's open for buffet breakfasts and à la carte lunches and dinners. Kids love the Flamingo's create-your-own-sundae bar. **Zimmie's,** a casual dining room with ceiling fans overhead and tables amid pine planters of philodendrons, serves hot and cold sandwiches, burgers, salads, and frozen drinks at lunch and dinner. And the **Oasis Poolside Cabana** offers drinks and light fare poolside.

Services   Limited room service (pizza and hot wings available from 11am to 10pm), babysitting, overnight photo processing, grocery shopping (you can have your room prestocked with food on request). Two guest services desks provide conciergelike assistance, also sell tickets (many of them discounted), and arrange transportation to/from Disney parks and all other nearby attractions. Round-trip fare to/from Disney parks costs $6.

Facilities   Five swimming pools (one of them an immense free-form affair with a rock waterfall, water volleyball, and water slide), five children's wading pools, seven outdoor whirlpools (some secluded), 13 tennis courts (nine clay, four hard-surface, two lit for night play), tennis pro shop/instruction, 18-hole/par-38 miniature golf course, basketball/sand volleyball/shuffleboard courts, bicycle rental, raft rental, children's playgrounds, full health club and recreation center (including sauna, steam, tanning salon, massage), game library, outdoor barbecue grills, 1½-mile/12-station jogging path, general store (includes extensive grocery selection, liquor, Disneyana, sundries, movie-rental library), three video-game arcades. A comprehensive daily activities schedule for adults and children includes nature walks, casino nights, Ping-Pong tournaments, arts and crafts, barbecues, karaoke, and more.

MODERATE

DOUBLETREE CLUB HOTEL, 8688 Palm Pkwy., between FL 535 and I-4, Lake Buena Vista, FL 32830. Tel. 407/239-8500, or toll free 800/228-2846. Fax 407/239-8591. 164 rms, 3 suites. A/C TV TEL

$ Rates: $59–$99 single or double, depending on season; $115–$175 suite. Extra person $10. Children under 18 free. AE, CB, DC, ER, Optima, MC, V. **Parking:** Free self-parking.

Located on a pleasant tree-lined parkway and overlooking a lake out back, the Doubletree Club has a lot to offer. Guests are greeted with fresh-baked chocolate-chip cookies at check-in, and the lobby contains a comfortably furnished 5,000-square-foot library and lounge stocked with books and current magazines. With its intimate lamp-lit seating areas and large-screen TV, it's like having your own living room—one where you can order drinks. Part of the room is a play area for children, with its own TV, toys, games, and children's magazines. Pristine guest rooms are attractively decorated in seafoam green and dusty rose with bleached wood furnishings and pretty prints on the walls. Many have convertible sofas. Amenities include remote-control cable TVs with Spectravision movie options and AM/FM alarm-clock radios. The Crossroads Shopping Center and Walt Disney World Village put dozens of shops, services (banks, post office, pharmacy), and restaurants in easy walking distance. And to compete with "official" hotels, the Doubletree offers free shuttle transport to and from Disney parks.

Dining/Entertainment   Part of the lobby lounge serves as a restaurant and bar offering daily buffet breakfasts, cocktails, and light, low-priced à la carte dinners—burgers, sandwiches, salads, pizza, and a few hot entrées—all under $7.

Services   Room service from 5pm to 10pm, complimentary shuttle to/from Disney parks, guest services desk (sells tickets, many of them discounted, and arranges transport to all nearby attractions), babysitting, complimentary daily newspaper.

Facilities   Nice-sized swimming pool and whirlpool, coin-op washers/dryers, children's playroom, exercise room, small video-game arcade.

HOLIDAY INN SUNSPREE RESORT LAKE BUENA VISTA, 13351 FL 535, between FL 536 and I-4, Lake Buena Vista, FL 32821. Tel. 407/239-4500, or toll free 800/FON-MAXX. Fax 407/239-7713. 507 rms. A/C TV TEL

$ Rates: $89–$129 for up to four people in a room, depending on the season. Inquire about packages. AE, CB, DC, DISC, JCB, MC, V. **Parking:** Free self-parking.

About a mile from Disney parks, this Holiday Inn caters to children in a big way. Kids "check-in" at their own pint-size desk and receive a free fun bag containing a video-game token coupon, a lollipop, and a small gift. And they're personally welcomed by animated raccoon mascots (Max and Maxine). Camp Holiday activities—magic shows, clowns, bingo, movies, sing-alongs, video games, arts and crafts, storytelling, and much more—are free of charge for kids 2 to 12. And parents can arrange (by reservation) for Max to come tuck a child into bed. Accommodations—in a six-story peach stucco building—are decorated in aqua, peach, and teal, with bleached oak furnishings, tropically themed paintings, and shell-motif lamps. All rooms have kitchenettes with refrigerators, micro-wave ovens, and coffee/tea makers. Amenities include remote-control cable TVs with local attraction-information channels, VCRs (tapes can be rented), AM/FM alarm-clock radios, hairdryers, and safes. Local calls are free. Open-air hallways add to the resort ambience.

Dining/Entertainment **Maxine's,** a pretty peach-walled dining room, is the setting for buffet and à la carte breakfasts and dinners, the latter featuring steak and seafood. **Max's Funtime Parlor,** serving gratis hot and cold hors d'oeuvres during happy hour, offers nightly bingo (with prizes) and karaoke; it also airs sporting events on a large-screen TV. **Pinky's Diner,** a skylit dining room with bamboo furnishings under canvas umbrellas, serves light fare (soup and salad bar, omelets, sandwiches, barbecued chicken and ribs); it's open from 6am (for breakfast fare) to midnight. Kids 12 and under eat all meals free, either in a hotel restaurant with parents or in Kid's Kottage—a cheerful facility where movies and cartoons are shown on a large-screen TV and dinner includes a make-your-own-sundae bar. The Barefoot Bar and Grill serves snack fare (pizzas, nachos, burgers) and frozen drinks poolside.

Services Room service from 7am to 2pm and 5pm to midnight, babysitting, guest services desk (sells tickets to all nearby attractions, including Walt Disney World parks), free scheduled transport to the Magic Kingdom/Epcot/Disney-MGM Studios (there's a charge for transport to other nearby attractions), telephone grocery shopping, Mears airport shuttle.

Facilities Large free-form swimming pool with lovely palm-fringed sun deck, two whirlpools, children's wading pool, poolside Ping-Pong and billiards, innovative children's playground, fitness center, coin-op washers/dryers, shops (extensive groceries/liquor, gifts/sundries, Disneyana), car-rental desk, video-game arcade, Camp Holiday (a counselor-supervised child-care/activity center for ages 2 to 12, open from 8am to midnight; parents can rent beepers to keep in touch with kids).

INEXPENSIVE

COMFORT INN, 8442 Palm Pkwy., between FL 535 and I-4, Lake Buena Vista, FL 32830. Tel. 407/239-7300, or toll free 800/999-7300. Fax 407/239-7740. 640 rms. A/C TV TEL

$ Rates: $39–$69 for up to four people. Range reflects season. Inquire about packages. AE, CB, DC, DISC, MC, V. **Parking:** Free self-parking.

This is an ideally located, large, and attractively landscaped property with two small manmade lakes amid expanses of manicured lawn and lush greenery. It offers great value for your hotel dollar, including free transport to/from Disney parks. Immaculate rooms, tastefully decorated in shades of mauve or rust, are housed in five-story stucco buildings. In-room amenities include cable TVs and complimentary safes. The Boardwalk Buffet, a sunny restaurant with windows all around, offers reasonably priced buffet meals at breakfast and dinner; kids under 12 eat free. The Comfort Zone, a bar/lounge, adjoins. And complimentary tea and coffee are served in the lobby every afternoon. The guest services desk sells tickets (most of them discounted) and provides transport to all nearby theme parks, dinner shows, and the airport. On-premises facilities include two nice-sized swimming pools, coin-op washers/dryers, a snack-vending machine area, a gift shop, and video-game arcade. Pets are permitted.

3. ACCOMMODATIONS ON U.S. 192/KISSIMMEE AREA

This very American stretch of highway dotted with fast-food eateries isn't what you'd call scenic, but it does contain many inexpensive hotels within one to eight miles of WDW parks.

MODERATE

HOLIDAY INN MAINGATE EAST, 5678 Irlo Bronson Memorial Hwy. (U.S. 192), between I-4 and Poinciana Blvd., Kissimmee, FL 34746. Tel. 407/396-4488, or toll free 800/FON-KIDS. Fax 407/396-8915. 670 rms. A/C TV TEL

$ Rates: $75–$105 for up to four people in a room, depending on the season. Inquire about packages. AE, CB, DC, DISC, JCB, MC, V. **Parking:** Free self-parking.

Just three miles from the entrance to the Magic Kingdom, Holiday Inn Maingate East, occupying 23 attractively landscaped acres, offers identical facilities to the Holiday Inn Sunspree Resort Lake Buena Vista described above—including its own Camp Holiday and all the kid-pleaser features (here the welcoming mascots are Holiday and Holly Hound). There's even a small merry-go-round in the lobby. Accommodations, in two-story motel-style buildings enclosing courtyard swimming pools, are decorated in muted blue and peach. Once again, facilities and in-room amenities are identical to those at the Lake Buena Vista property. Pets are permitted at this location.

Dining/Entertainment The **Vineyard Cafe,** decorated in grape purple and green, seats diners at canvas umbrella tables. Buffet and à la carte breakfasts and dinners are served, the latter featuring steak and seafood items. The **Court Street Bar** adjoins. **The People's Choice,** a food court, has six eateries—a pizza and pasta outlet, a deli, a soup and salad bar, and a bakery among them. **Tropical Treasures Pool Bar,** with seating on a wooden deck, serves up burgers, grilled sandwiches, and frozen tropical drinks.

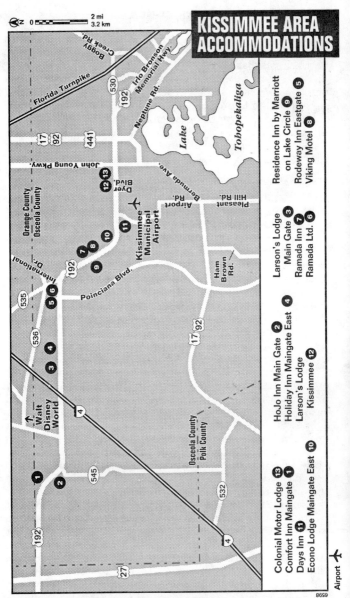

KISSIMMEE AREA ACCOMMODATIONS

0 2 mi / 3.2 km

Boggy Creek Rd.
Florida Turnpike
Irlo Bronson Memorial Hwy.
530
192
Neptune Rd.
17 92
441
John Young Pkwy.
Orange County / Osceola County
Dyer Blvd.
12 13
Bermuda Ave.
Lake Tohopekaliga
Airport Rd.
Pleasant Hill Rd.
International Dr.
535
536
192
Poinciana Blvd.
11
10
7 8
9
5 6
Kissimmee Municipal Airport
Ham Brown Rd.
4
3
Walt Disney World
4
Osceola County / Polk County
545
532
17 92
1
2
192
27
4
Airport

Colonial Motor Lodge 13
Comfort Inn Maingate 1
Days Inn 11
Econo Lodge Maingate East 10

HoJo Inn Main Gate 2
Holiday Inn Maingate East 4
Larson's Lodge Kissimmee 12

Larson's Lodge Main Gate 3
Ramada Inn 7
Ramada Ltd. 6

Residence Inn by Marriott on Lake Circle 9
Rodeway Inn Eastgate 5
Viking Motel 8

8659

Kids 12 and under eat all meals free, either in a hotel restaurant with parents or in the **Gingerbread House**—a cheerful facility where movies and cartoons are shown on a large-screen TV and dinner includes a make-your-own-sundae bar.

Services   Room service from 7am to 2pm and 5:30 to 10pm, babysitting, guest services desk (sells tickets to all nearby attractions, including Walt Disney World parks), free scheduled transport to the

Magic Kingdom/Epcot/Disney-MGM Studios (there's a charge for transport to other nearby attractions), telephone grocery shopping, Mears airport shuttle.

Facilities Two Olympic-size swimming pools, two whirlpools, children's wading pool, children's playground, two night-lit hard-surface tennis courts, sand volleyball, basketball court, coin-op washers/dryers, shops (groceries, liquor, gifts/sundries, Disneyana), car-rental desk, two video-game arcades, Camp Holiday (a counselor-supervised child-care/activity center for ages 3 to 12, open from 8am to midnight; parents can rent beepers to keep in touch with kids).

RESIDENCE INN BY MARRIOTT ON LAKE CECILE, 4786 **W. Irlo Bronson Memorial Hwy., between FL 535 and Siesta Lago Dr., Kissimmee, FL 34746. Tel. 407/396-2056,** or toll free 800/468-3027. Fax 407/396-2909. 159 suites. A/C TV TEL

$ Rates (including extended continental breakfast): $109–$115 studio accommodating up to four people; $115–$119 studio double (up to four people); $149–$169 bi-level penthouse (up to six people). Range reflects season. Inquire about packages. AE, CB, DC, DISC, ER, JCB, MC, Optima, V. **Parking:** Free self-parking.

★ This all-suite property has peacocks roaming its attractively landscaped grounds on the banks of beautiful 223-acre Lake Cecile. Like all Residence Inns, its accommodations are in two-story residential-looking cream stucco buildings fronted by neatly manicured lawns. Suites, tastefully decorated in gray and mauve, have fully equipped eat-in kitchens (the maid does your dishes) and comfortable living room areas with sleeper sofas. All but studio doubles have wood-burning fireplaces (logs are supplied), and cathedral-ceilinged penthouses have full baths upstairs and down. Many suites offer balconies overlooking the lake. Amenities include remote-control cable TVs (VCRs are available on request, and movie tapes can be rented), AM/FM alarm-clock radios, and in-room safes.

Dining/Entertainment The lovely gatehouse **lounge** off the lobby, with a lofty peaked ceiling and big, comfy sofas facing a working fireplace, is the setting for an extended continental breakfast each morning (muffins, danish, doughnuts, juices, cereals, fresh fruits, tea and coffee). And an al fresco **bar** serves light fare (hot dogs, pizza, sandwiches) and frosty drinks poolside on a canopied wooden deck with umbrella tables (drinks here are half price during happy hour). Local restaurants deliver food (there are menus in each room).

Services Guest services desk (sells tickets—most of them discounted—and provides transport to all nearby theme parks and attractions), complimentary daily newspaper, gratis food-shopping service, Mears airport shuttle. Round-trip fare to WDW parks is $7.

Facilities Small swimming pool, whirlpool, sports court (basketball, volleyball, badminton, paddle tennis), children's playground, coin-op washers/dryers, 24-hour food shop, picnic tables, barbecue grills. Lake activities include fishing, jet skiing, bumper rides, and waterskiing, and you can rent paddleboats, canoes, and sailboats.

INEXPENSIVE

COMFORT INN MAINGATE, 7571 W. Irlo Bronson Memorial Hwy. (U.S. 192), between Reedy Creek Blvd. and Sherbeth Rd., Kissimmee, FL 34747. Tel. 407/396-7500, or toll free 800/221-2222. Fax 407/396-7497. 281 rms. A/C TV TEL

$ Rates: $38–$74 for one or two people, depending on the season. Garden rooms $6–$10 additional. Extra person $8. Children 18 and under stay free. AE, CB, DC, DISC, ER, JCB, MC, V. **Parking:** Free self-parking.

Just one mile from Disney parks, this Comfort Inn houses clean, spiffy-looking standard motel accommodations in two-story peach stucco buildings. More upscale are garden rooms facing a lawn with a gazebo; decorated in teal, seafoam green, and peach, they're equipped with small refrigerators, coffee makers, and hairdryers. The Royal Palms Restaurant on the premises serves low-priced buffets and à la carte meals. A comfortable bar/lounge adjoins. And right next door are a 7-Eleven and an International House of Pancakes. The guest services desk sells tickets (most of them discounted) and provides transport to all nearby attractions and the airport; round-trip fare to WDW parks is $7. Facilities include a medium-sized swimming pool, children's playground, coin-op washers/dryers, and a small video-game arcade.

ECONO LODGE MAINGATE EAST, 4311 W. Irlo Bronson Memorial Hwy. (U.S. 192), between Hoagland Blvd. and FL 535, Kissimmee, FL 34746. Tel. 407/396-7100, or toll free 800/ENJOY-FL. Fax 407/239-2636. 173 rms. A/C TV TEL

$ Rates: $29–$79 for up to four people in a room, depending on the season. AE, CB, DC, DISC, JCB, MC, V. **Parking:** Free self-parking.

At this attractively landscaped Econo Lodge, accommodations are set well back from the highway in rustic two- and three-story buildings with cedar balconies and roofing. Well-maintained standard motel rooms are equipped with cable TVs and safes; small refrigerators can be rented. Snacks and soft drinks are sold in the lobby, and the pool bar serves light fare, including full breakfasts and lunches at umbrella tables under towering live oaks. The guest services desk sells tickets (most of them discounted) and provides transport to all nearby attractions and the airport; round-trip to WDW parks is $12. On-premises facilities include a large swimming pool, children's pool, volleyball, shuffleboard, horseshoes, coin-op washers/dryers, picnic tables, barbecue grills, and a small video-game arcade. This is one of six area hotels under the same ownership, all of which can be booked via the above toll-free number.

HOJO INN MAIN GATE, 6051 W. Irlo Bronson Memorial Hwy. (U.S. 192), just east of I-4, Kissimmee, FL 34747. Tel. 407/396-1748, or toll free 800/288-4678. Fax 407/649-8642. 358 rms, 9 family suites. A/C TV TEL

$ Rates: $60–$76 for up to four people, depending on the season. Children under 19 stay free. Add $10 for an efficiency unit with a kitchenette. $90–$106 family suite. Inquire about packages. AE, CB, DC, DISC, JCB, MC, V. **Parking:** Free self-parking.

This Howard Johnson's property just two miles from the Magic Kingdom offers attractive accommodations housed in pristine white stucco two- and three-story buildings. Completely renovated in 1992, they're nicely decorated with quilted lavender bedspreads, royal blue carpeting, and beach-themed paintings on the walls. In-room amenities include cable TVs with VCRs (movies can be rented in the lobby) and safes. Efficiency units have fully equipped kitchenettes with small refrigerators, two-burner stoves, and sinks. And family suites have both full kitchens and living rooms with convertible sofas.

Facilities here include a medium-sized swimming pool, whirlpool, kiddie pool, children's playground, coin-op washers/dryers, small 24-hour video-game arcade, car-rental desk, and pool table. A huge store next door sells resort wear, gifts and sundries, and Disneyana. Also adjoining the property: a large water park called Watermania and a particularly nice plant-filled International House of Pancakes open from 7am to 11pm (where kids under 12 with an adult eat for 99¢). On premises, a pool bar serves light fare and drinks, and coffee and tea are served gratis in the very pleasant lobby throughout the day. Guest services sells tickets to all Disney parks and nearby attractions (some of them discounted) and offers transportation to/from them and the airport. Transport to Disney parks is $7 per person round-trip.

LARSON'S LODGE KISSIMMEE, 2009 W. Vine St. (U.S. 192), at Thacker Ave., Kissimmee, FL 34741. Tel. 407/846-2713, or toll free 800/624-5905. Fax 407/846-8695. 200 rms. A/C TV TEL

$ Rates: $39–$79 for up to four people, depending on the season. Add $10 for an efficiency unit with a kitchenette. AE, CB, DC, DISC, MC, V. **Parking:** Free self-parking.

This friendly family-run property just eight miles from Walt Disney World has been operated by the Larsons since 1976. Standard motel units—decorated in teal and tan or teal and peach—have a vaguely southwestern look. They're equipped with remote-control cable TVs and in-room safes. More upscale are cheerful efficiency units that have living room areas and fully equipped kitchenettes with sinks, two-burner stoves, toasters, small refrigerators, microwave ovens, and coffee makers.

The guest services desk sells tickets to all nearby theme parks, including WDW (many of them discounted), and a shuttle bus plies the route between the property and all WDW parks at scheduled times throughout the day (round-trip fare is $10). Transport is also available to other nearby attractions and the airport. On-premises facilities and amenities include a large V-shaped swimming pool, a smaller free-form pool, a kiddie pool, a whirlpool, an innovative children's playground, a night-lit hard-surface tennis court, a gift/sundries shop, coin-op washers/dryers, and a nice-sized video-game arcade. Guests get free tickets to Watermania, the water park at the below-mentioned Larson's Lodge Main Gate. Pets are permitted. A shopping center is close by, and the Black Angus restaurant, serving all meals (dinner features steak and seafood), is on the premises; there's nightly entertainment in its adjoining western-motif lounge.

LARSON'S LODGE MAIN GATE, 6075 W. Irlo Bronson Memorial Hwy. (U.S. 192), just east of I-4, Kissimmee, FL 34747. Tel. 407/396-6100, or toll free 800/327-9074. Fax 407/396-6965. 128 rms. A/C TV TEL

$ Rates: $39–$79 single or double, depending on the season. Extra person $8. Children under 18 stay free. Add $15 for an efficiency unit with a kitchenette. AE, CB, DC, DISC, MC, V. **Parking:** Free self-parking.

With its large, on-premises water park (Watermania), children's playground, and poolside picnic tables and barbecue grills, Larson's Lodge is a good choice for families. It has a cheerful on-site Shoney's restaurant (open from 6am to midnight). Accommodations are standard motel units attractively decorated in peach and seafoam green with bleached oak furnishings. They're equipped with remote-control cable TVs (VCRs and movie tapes can be rented), coffee makers, and in-room safes. Efficiency units have fully equipped kitchenettes with sinks, two-burner stoves, small refrigerators, and microwave ovens. A supermarket is just a few minutes away by car.

The guest services desk sells tickets to all nearby theme parks, including WDW (many of them discounted), and a shuttle bus plies the route between the property and all WDW parks at scheduled times throughout the day (round-trip fare is $8). Transport is also available to other nearby attractions and the airport. On-premises facilities include a large swimming pool and whirlpool, shops (gifts/sundries, liquor, resort wear, Disneyana, jewelry, 24-hour photo developing), coin-op washers/dryers, a small video-game arcade, and a pool table. Guests enjoy gratis use of the tennis court at the above-mentioned Larson's Lodge Kissimmee and get free tickets to Watermania. Pets are permitted.

RODEWAY INN EASTGATE, 5245 W. Irlo Bronson Memorial Hwy. (U.S. 192), between Poinciana and Polynesian Isle blvds., Kissimmee, FL 34746. Tel. 407/396-7700, or toll free 800/423-3864. Fax 407/396-0293. 200 rms. A/C TV TEL

$ Rates: $31–$55 for up to four people. Range reflects view and season. Rates may be higher during major events. AE, CB, DC, DISC, ER, JCB, MC, V. **Parking:** Free self-parking.

The Rodeway's U-shaped configuration of two-story pink stucco buildings form an attractively landscaped courtyard around a large swimming pool. There are picnic tables and a children's play area on the lawn. Rooms are nicely decorated in teal, aqua, and mauve, with oak furnishings and grasspaper-look/bamboo-motif wall coverings.

The on-site Terrace Restaurant serves buffet breakfasts, and the comfy Half Time Lounge, where sporting events are aired on a seven-by-seven-foot screen, has a pool table and dart boards. Other facilities include a small video-game arcade off the lobby, coin-op washers/dryers, and a shop selling gifts, sundries, and Disneyana. Guest services sells tickets to all Disney parks and nearby attractions (many of them discounted) and offers transportation to/from them and the airport. Transport to Disney parks is $7.50 per person round-trip.

BUDGET

COLONIAL MOTOR LODGE, 1815 W. Vine St. (U.S. 192), between Bermuda and Thacker aves., Kissimmee, FL 34741. Tel. 407/847-6121, or toll free 800/325-4348. Fax 407/847-0728. 83 rms, 40 apts. A/C TV TEL

$ Rates (including continental breakfast): $24–$42 for up to four people, $44.95–$89.95 for up to six people in a two-bedroom apt. Range reflects season. AE, CB, DC, DISC, MC, V. **Parking:** Free self-parking.

This well-run motor lodge is entered via a white colonial-style building with peach columns and shutters and a Federalist eagle over the door. The pleasantly furnished lobby is the setting for a gratis continental breakfast each morning. Snack and fruit juices are sold in vending machines. Standard motel rooms decorated in rust and tan with whitewashed pine-paneled walls offer remote-control cable TVs with HBO and alarm clocks. Two-bedroom apartments, in two-story white buildings fronted by small gardens, represent a good choice for families. In addition to two full bedrooms, they have living rooms and fully equipped eat-in kitchens.

Facilities include two Junior Olympic-size outdoor pools and a kiddie pool. Adjacent to the Colonial are an International House of Pancakes and a shopping center with a dry cleaner and Laundromat. The Black Angus, a steak and seafood restaurant, is across the street. And a supermarket, 7-Eleven, Hardy's, and Kentucky Fried Chicken are a block away. Guest services sells tickets to all Disney parks and nearby attractions (some of them discounted) and offers transportation to/from them and the airport. Round-trip transport to Disney parks is $11 per person.

DAYS INN, 4104 and 4125 W. Irlo Bronson Memorial Hwy. (U.S. 192), at Hoagland Blvd. N., Kissimmee, FL 34741. Tel. 407/846-4714, or toll free 800/647-0100 or 800/DAYS-INN. Fax 407/932-2699. 194 rms, 32 efficiency units. A/C TV TEL

$ Rates (including continental breakfast): $29–$59 for up to four people, depending on season; $37–$63 efficiency unit; $55–$75 Jacuzzi room (for one or two people). Rates may be higher during major events. AE, CB, DC, DISC, ER, MC, V. **Parking:** Free self-parking.

These two Days Inn properties on either side of U.S. 192 share facilities, which include coin-op washers and dryers, a gift shop, two swimming pools, and a small video-game arcade. Several restaurants (which deliver food), a large shopping mall with a 12-theater movie house, and a supermarket are in close walking distance. Rooms at both locations are clean and attractive standard motel units. Best bet are efficiency units with fully equipped kitchenettes (two-burner stoves, sinks, small refrigerators) at 4104. On the other hand, at 4125 you can ask for a room with a large Jacuzzi. All accommodations offer remote-control cable TVs (with free HBO and pay-movie options) and in-room safes, and both locations serve a gratis continental breakfast (juice, coffee, tea, doughnuts) in their lobbies each morning. Guest services at 4104 sells tickets (many of them discounted) and arranges transport to all nearby attractions, including WDW parks. Round-trip fare to WDW parks $7. Airport transfers can also be arranged.

RAMADA INN, 4559 W. Irlo Bronson Memorial Hwy. (U.S. 192), between Siesta Lago Dr. and Bass Rd./Old Vineland Rd., Kissimmee, FL 34746. Tel. 407/396-1212, or toll free 800/446-5669. Fax 407/396-7926. 114 rms. A/C TV TEL

$ Rates: $23.95–$40.95 for up to four people, depending on season; $6 per night additional for efficiency unit. AE, DC, DISC, MC, V. **Parking:** Free self-parking.

This Ramada offers standard motel rooms decorated in blues and greens with mauve and white wall coverings. They're equipped with cable TVs (with free HBO), AM/FM alarm-clock radios, and safes; refrigerators are available on request for $6 a night. Efficiency units offer two-burner stoves, extra sinks, and small refrigerators (no eating or cooking utensils are provided). Facilities include coin-op washers/dryers, a swimming pool, children's playground, and picnic tables. The 1950s-style Hollywood Diner—which has an adjoining bar/lounge—serves American fare at all meals; one child under 12 per paying adult eats free. Shuttle service to WDW parks is available for $9 per person, round-trip. Pets are accepted.

RAMADA LTD., 5055 W. Irlo Bronson Memorial Hwy. (U.S. 192), between Poinciana Blvd. and FL 535, Kissimmee, FL 34746. Tel. 407/396-2212, or toll free 800/446-5669. Fax 407/396-0253. 107 rms. A/C TV TEL

$ Rates (including continental breakfast): $27.95–$45 for up to four people, depending on season. AE, DC, DISC, MC, V. **Parking:** Free self-parking.

Less than four miles from Walt Disney World parks, this Ramada houses its rooms in a three-story mauve and pale gray stucco building. Accommodations are standard motel rooms with oak furnishings, forest green carpeting, mint green walls, and splashy floral-print bedspreads. They're equipped with cable TVs (with free HBO movies), AM/FM alarm-clock radios, and safes; refrigerators are available on request for $6 a night. Facilities include a swimming pool and coin-op washers/dryers. Continental breakfast is served in the lobby each morning. Shuttle service to WDW parks is available for $7 per person, round-trip. Pets are accepted.

VIKING MOTEL, 4539 W. Irlo Bronson Memorial Hwy. (U.S. 192), between FL 535 and Hoagland Blvd. N., Kissimmee, FL 34746. Tel. 407/396-8860. Fax 407/396-2088. 49 rms. A/C TV TEL

$ Rates: $25–$60 single or double, depending on season. Extra person $5. Add $10 for kitchenette units. AE, DISC, MC, V.
Parking: Free self-parking.

Kids love this family-owned property housed in a fantasy castle, with towers topped by little Viking ships. Owners Bert and Christine Langenstroer are from Germany, and they've prettified their motel's Alpine-style balconies with neat flower boxes. Immaculate rooms have forest green carpeting and peach stucco walls hung with old-fashioned lithograph portraits in oval frames and kitschy landscape paintings. All are equipped with cable TVs (with free HBO), safes, and Magic Fingers bed massagers, and some have refrigerators. A few units offer kitchenettes with two-burner stoves, small refrigerators, sinks, microwave ovens, toasters, and coffee makers; these units also have cozy breakfast nooks. On-premises facilities include coin-op washers/dryers, a shuffleboard court, a Viking-themed playground and sandbox, and a small free-form swimming pool with outdoor tables under thatched umbrellas and barbecue grills on the sun deck. A Waffle House restaurant and a miniature golf course are next door. The guest services desk sells tickets, many of them discounted, to nearby attractions, though it does not carry WDW park tickets. Transportation is, however, available to WDW parks (round-trip fare is $8 per person), other area attractions, and the airport. The Viking is six miles from the Magic Kingdom.

4. ACCOMMODATIONS ON INTERNATIONAL DRIVE

Properties listed here are 7 to 10 miles north of WDW parks and close to Universal Studios and Sea World.

EXPENSIVE

PEABODY ORLANDO, 9801 International Dr., between Beeline Expy. and Sand Lake Rd. (across from the Civic Center), Orlando, FL 32819. Tel. 407/352-4000, or toll free 800/PEABODY. Fax 407/351-0073. 835 rms, 57 suites. A/C MINIBAR TV TEL

$ Rates: $190–$230 for up to three people in a room; $250

Peabody Club; $395–$1,300 suite. Children under 18 free. Seniors 50 and over get a $1 discount per year of age. Rates are slightly reduced May–Sept 15. Inquire about packages as well as holiday and summer discounts. AE, CB, DC, DISC, ER, JCB, MC, V. **Parking:** Free self-parking, valet parking $6 per night.

This deluxe 27-story resort hotel—its porte-cochère facade fronted by splashing fountains, waterfalls, and lush tropical plantings—has some especially famous avian residents. Every morning at 11am, five fluffy ducks proudly parade along a red carpet to the beat of John Philip Sousa's *King Cotton* march, their journey culminating at a marble fountain in the lobby. They frolic there throughout the day, until the duckmaster directs them back to their "Royal Duck Palace" at 5pm. But ducks are just a fillip here. The Peabody, in the grand hotel tradition, pampers guests with sumptuous surroundings and attentive service. Its skylit atrium lobby and other public areas are enhanced by stunning displays of live orchids, towering palms, bamboo, ficus, and magnolia trees. Luxurious rooms, decorated in muted teal, peach, mauve, and cream, have bamboo and bleached wood furnishings and walls hung with quality artworks. Amenities include two phones (bedroom and bath) with two lines and modem capacity, remote-control cable TVs with Spectravision and laser-disc movie set-ups (more than 500 movies are available from a video library), AM/FM alarm-clock radios, and, in the bath, cosmetic lights, fine European toiletries, a hairdryer, and a small TV. The concierge-level Peabody Club, with rooms on the top three floors, offers individualized concierge service and a beautiful lounge. Perks include continental breakfast, afternoon hot and cold hors d'oeuvres, and evening desserts and coffee; gratis entrance to the Athletic Club; free valet parking; and rubber ducks in the tub. The Peabody is about 15 minutes by car from WDW parks and very close to Sea World and Universal Studios.

Dining/Entertainment **Dux,** the Peabody's elegant signature restaurant, features Florida regional cuisine dinners in a plush candlelit and crystal-chandeliered setting; it does not, however, serve duck. **Capriccio,** for sophisticated northern Italian fare, is open for dinner and champagne Sunday brunches. Its adjoining lounge features cappuccino and espresso, Italian hors d'oeuvres, and drinks in an intimate setting. The **B-Line Diner,** a 24-hour art deco eatery in the nouvelle diner-chic tradition, dishes up American specialties such as turkey hash and barbecued beef sandwiches prepared with culinary institute panache. From the **B-Line Express** window, a 24-hour counter operation fronted by a tempting array of cakes and pastries, you can order take-out fare from the restaurant's menu. (See details on all three of the above in Chapter 6.) The **Peabody Pool Bar** serves cold, frothy specialty drinks and snacks. A singer and trio perform jazz, blues, and show tunes in the atrium **Lobby Bar** nightly from 7pm to 1am. The lobby is also the setting for weekday afternoon teas with petit fours, pastries, scones with Devonshire cream, and finger sandwiches. The adjoining **Mallards Lounge,** its walls hung with framed paintings of every kind of duck in the world, is a cozy gathering place; sports events are aired on the TV over the bar. And al fresco jazz concerts take place on the fourth-floor recreation level spring and fall.

Services   24-hour room service, babysitting, 24-hour concierge, shoeshine, nightly bed turndown on request, gratis newspaper delivered to your room daily, "Double Ducker" shuttle bus making round-trip runs between the hotel and all WDW parks throughout the day (unlimited daily round-trips cost $5), Mears transportation/ sightseeing desk (sells tickets to all nearby attractions, including WDW parks and dinner shows; also provides transport, by reservation, to attractions and airport).

Facilities   Double-Olympic-length swimming pool, indoor and outdoor whirlpools, large children's wading pool with waterfall fountain, four hard-surface night-lit tennis courts, golf privileges at four nearby courses, seven-mile jogging path, car-rental desk, Delta Air Lines desk, full-service unisex beauty salon, full business center, state-of-the-art health club (offering tanning, sauna, steam, massage therapy, Nautilus, and aerobics classes), shops (unique gifts/sundries, upscale mèn's/women's apparel, athletic sportswear, resort wear, poolside sundries), small video-game arcade, the Children's Hotel (a counselor-supervised child-care/activities center). Hot-air balloon rides, deep-sea fishing, scuba lessons, and other amusements/ excursions can be arranged.

MODERATE

COURTYARD BY MARRIOTT, 8600 Austrian Court, off International Dr. between Sand Lake Rd. and Beeline Expy. (Hwy. 528), Orlando, FL 32819. Tel. 407/351-2244, or toll free 800/321-2211. Fax 407/351-1933. 140 rms, 11 suites. A/C TV TEL

$ Rates: $89 single, $99 double (for up to four people); suite $105 single, $115 double (for up to four people). Extra person $10. AE, CB, DC, DISC, MC, V. **Parking:** Free self-parking.

Located in a secluded complex of hotels and restaurants off International Drive, the Courtyard occupies a tan stucco four-story building with a green tile roof. It's fronted by lush tropical plantings, and most rooms overlook a lovingly landscaped central courtyard with a gazebo that is ideal for picnics. Courtyard is a moderately priced link in the Marriott chain, with lower prices achieved via limited services (for instance, there's no bellman, though you can get a luggage cart). But don't envision a Spartan, no-frills atmosphere. This is a delightful property, with a pleasant, plant-filled lobby and accommodations that are both tasteful and immaculate. Decorated in soft blue-gray and mauve with nice-sized dressing areas, the rooms are furnished in mahogany pieces and equipped with remote-control cable TVs (with HBO, Spectravision movie, and visitor-information channels), AM/ FM alarm-clock radios, and boiling-water dispensers for making tea or coffee (both available free at the front desk). King-bedded rooms have sleeper couches. And spacious suites have full sofa-bedded living rooms with extra phones and TVs plus small refrigerators. Accommodations facing the courtyard have patios.

Dining/Entertainment   A plant-filled lobby **restaurant** with bleached oak beams and columns serves full and continental buffet breakfasts daily. The adjoining plushly furnished **lounge,** which has a working fireplace and a TV, serves overstuffed subs and frozen tropical drinks from 4 to 10pm Monday through Friday. In addition, several local eateries deliver food (there are menus in each room).

Services   The guest services desk sells tickets (most of them discounted) and provides transport to all nearby theme parks and attractions and the airport. Round-trip fare to WDW parks costs $10.

Facilities   Swimming pool, whirlpool, exercise room, small video-game arcade, coin-op washers/dryers.

HERITAGE INN ORLANDO, 9861 International Dr., between Beeline Expy. and Sand Lake Rd., Orlando, FL 32819. Tel. 407/352-0008, or toll free 800/447-1890. Fax 407/352-5449. 150 rms. A/C TV TEL

$ Rates: $59–$159 single or double, depending on view and season. Extra person $10. Up to two children under 18 free. Inquire about packages. AE, CB, DC, DISC, ER, MC, V. **Parking:** Free self-parking.

Ⓢ   Centered on a white-trimmed pale-peach octagonal building crowned by a windowed cupola, the Heritage Inn evokes 19th-century Florida—the leisurely era of riverboat travel and gracious plantations. Ceiling fans whirr slowly over verandas and balconies furnished with wicker rocking chairs, and a charmingly landscaped courtyard with neat lawns and flower beds encompasses a large free-form swimming pool backed by verdant woodlands and a wide canal. The balustraded Victorian lobby, flanked by graceful staircases and housing an elegant dining room, is handsomely furnished in period pieces. Overhead, you'll view the beautiful cupola—painted peach and Wedgwood green—from within. Charming guest rooms are housed in two-story peach buildings on either side of the octagon. Furnished in handsome maple or mahogany pieces, they have dark teal carpeting and ecru walls adorned with floral friezes and 19th-century folk art. French doors open onto patios, balconies, or courtyards, and baths have art nouveau lighting fixtures. In-room amenities include cable TVs with free HBO and Spectravision movie options, phones with modem jacks, wood-bladed chandelier ceiling fans, safes, and small refrigerators. Larger deluxe rooms offer sleeper sofas, microwave ovens, and hairdryers.

Dining/Entertainment   The above-mentioned **Plantation Dining Room,** with white wainscoted walls and pretty floral-print period wallpaper, seats diners at oak tables under a massive Victorian globe chandelier. Open for all meals—including a Sunday champagne brunch, at which a pianist entertains—it offers a moderately priced American menu. The Victorian-look **Front Porch Lounge,** with oak parquet floors, a pressed-tin ceiling, and lace-curtained French doors, is popular with locals. It features happy hour buffets weekdays from 5:30 to 7pm.

Services   Room service from 7 to 10:30am and 5 to 10pm, guest services desk (sells tickets, many of them discounted, and arranges transport to all nearby attractions, including WDW parks), babysitting, Mears airport shuttle. Round-trip fare to WDW parks costs $8.

Facilities   Large swimming pool.

ORLANDO MARRIOTT, 8001 International Dr., at Sand Lake Rd., Orlando, FL 32819. Tel. 407/351-2420, or toll free 800/421-8001. Fax 407/351-5016. 1,060 rms, 16 suites. A/C TV TEL

$ Rates: $79–$120 single or double, depending on view and season; $110–$300 suite. Extra person $10. Children under 18 stay free. Inquire about packages. AE, DC, DISC, MC, V. **Parking:** Free self-parking.

This verdant 48-acre resort contrasts neatly manicured lawns and flower beds with dense stands of palm, fern gullies, lush tropical foliage, sprightly fountained pools, and serene lagoons. Accommodations, housed in pale pink stucco bi-level villas, are attractively decorated in resort mode, with light wood and bamboo/rattan furnishings, pretty floral-print bedspreads in pastel hues, and beach-themed paintings on the walls. Half have balconies or patios, and about a fifth offer full kitchens. In-room amenities include remote-control color TVs with free HBO and pay-movie stations, AM/FM alarm-clock radios, safes, and desk and bedside phones. Many are also equipped with hairdryers, electric shoeshine machines, and irons/ironing boards.

Dining/Entertainment   The candlelit **Grove Steakhouse**—a southwestern setting with steer horns mounted on the walls and seating areas divided by cactus gardens—is open for dinner nightly. The menu highlights steaks, prime rib, and lobster. The **Chelsea Cafe,** a handsome oak-paneled restaurant with turn-of-the-century-style lighting fixtures suspended from a pressed-tin ceiling, serves à la carte American fare throughout the day along with buffet breakfasts and dinners. A 24-hour **Pizza Hut** and the adjacent **Marmalade Tree,** both offering seating on a shaded brick patio overlooking the tennis courts, serve pizza, light fare, and Häagen-Dazs ice cream. The **Crocodilly** and **Whoppadilly Bars** proffer frozen tropical drinks to sunbathers at the East and West Pools, respectively. The **Lobby Bar** is a cozy setting for continental breakfast, specialty wines, and cocktails. And at **Illusions,** a DJ plays Top 40 tunes. If you don't feel like dancing, there's a blackjack table (you can't win money, it's just for fun), a pool table, and an electric dart board. Monday-night football is aired on a large-screen TV, and complimentary hors d'oeuvres are served daily from 5 to 7pm.

Services   Room service from 6am to 11pm (pizza 24 hours), babysitting, guest services desk (sells tickets, many of them discounted, and arranges transportation to/from Disney parks and all other nearby attractions), 24-hour gratis tram service around the property, Mears airport shuttle. Round-trip fare to WDW parks costs $8.

Facilities Three swimming pools (one quite large), two children's wading pools, whirlpool, four hard-surface night-lit tennis courts, sand volleyball court, children's playground, exercise room, 1.4-mile jogging trail, coin-op washers/dryers, car rental, unisex hair salon, shops (Disneyana, resort wear, gifts, groceries, sundries, pool accessories, liquor), two video-game arcades.

RESIDENCE INN BY MARRIOTT, 7975 Canada Ave., just off Sand Lake Rd. a block east of International Dr., Orlando, FL 32819. Tel. 407/345-0117, or toll free 800/ 227-3978. Fax 407/352-2689. 176 suites. A/C TV TEL

$ Rates (including extended continental breakfast): $94 studio accommodating up to four people, $105 studio double (up to four people); $144 bi-level penthouse (up to six people). Inquire about packages. AE, MC, V. **Parking:** Free self-parking.

Marriott's Residence Inns are designed to offer home-away-from-home comfort. Accommodations, in two-story residential-looking brick and stucco buildings with weathered pine trim, are surrounded by neatly manicured lawns, shrubbery, and beds of geraniums. Staying here is like having your own luxurious Orlando apartment, with a private entrance and a large, fully equipped eat-in kitchen (the maid does your dishes). Suites are handsomely decorated in forest green and mauve (or teal and mauve), with pretty floral-print bedspreads in complementary hues and oak furnishings. All have comfortable living room areas with convertible sofas, coffee tables, and armchairs; all but studio doubles have wood-burning fireplaces; and penthouses have full baths upstairs and down. Amenities include remote-control cable TVs with free HBO and pay-movie options, AM/FM radios, alarm clocks, and in-room safes. Pets are allowed.

Dining/Entertainment The comfortably furnished **gatehouse,** off the lobby, is the setting for an extended continental breakfast (muffins, juices, cereals, fresh fruits, breads, tea and coffee) daily and complimentary beer, wine, soft drinks, and hot and cold hors d'oeuvres (cocktail franks, nachos, popcorn) Monday to Thursday from 5 to 7pm. This cozy lounge is equipped with a 27-inch TV and stereo. Guests can also enjoy breakfast and snacks outdoors at umbrella tables by the pool. Local restaurants deliver food (there are menus in each room).

Services Guest services desk (sells tickets—most of them discounted—and provides transport to all nearby theme parks and attractions), complimentary daily newspaper, gratis food-shopping service, Mears airport shuttle. Round-trip fare to WDW parks costs $7.

Facilities Swimming pool, whirlpool, basketball court, sand volleyball court, gratis use of Bally health club nearby, coin-op washers/dryers, food shop, picnic tables, barbecue grills.

SUMMERFIELD SUITES, 8480 International Dr., between Beeline Expy. and Sand Lake Rd. (near the Civic Center), Orlando, FL 32819. Tel. 407/352-2400, or toll free 800/833-4353. Fax 407/352-4631. 146 suites. A/C TV TEL

$ Rates (including extended continental breakfast): $139–$159 one-bedroom suite (for up to four people), $159–$199 two-bedroom suite (for up to six people). Range reflects room size and season. Inquire about packages. AE, CB, DC, DISC, MC, V. **Parking:** Free self-parking.

This delightful five-story cream stucco hotel is built around a nicely landscaped central courtyard. Open-air balconies adorned with potted plants serve as hallways, creating a welcoming resort ambience. Spacious, neat-as-a-pin residential-style suites, very attractively decorated in peach and teal with bleached oak furnishings, contain fully equipped eat-in kitchens (the maid does your dishes), comfortable living rooms, big walk-in closets, and large dressing areas. Two-bedroom units have two baths. All bedrooms have doors (insuring privacy), and you'll find a large desk in the master bedrooms. Amenities include irons and ironing boards, phones (with two lines, computer hookup, and voice-mail messaging) in each bedroom and the kitchen, remote-control satellite TVs (with free HBO, attraction-information station, and pay-movie options) in each bedroom and the living room (the latter with a VCR; rent your choice of 200 movies downstairs), and AM/FM alarm-clock radios in each bedroom. A large shopping center is across the street, WDW parks are about 15 minutes away by car, Sea World and Universal Studios are very close, and numerous restaurants are in the area. This is a great choice for families.

Dining/Entertainment An extensive continental buffet breakfast—fresh-baked muffins, fruit, hard-boiled eggs, toast, applesauce, assorted cereals, juice, and coffee or tea—is served in a charming peach-walled **dining room** hung with delightful watercolors of tropical fish. The cozy **lobby bar** is a popular gathering place evenings. A **cabana bar** proffers drinks and snacks poolside. And local restaurants (you'll find a menu roster in your room) deliver food to the premises.

Services Babysitting, concierge/tour desk (sells tickets to WDW parks and other nearby attractions), newspapers delivered to your room daily, transport between the hotel and all WDW parks (round-trip fare is $7), shuttle available to airport and nearby attractions, complimentary grocery shopping.

Facilities Nice-sized swimming pool with fountain and bi-level sun deck, whirlpool, children's wading pool, car-rental desk, full business services, exercise room, coin-op washers/dryers, 24-hour shop (gifts/sundries/groceries/Disneyana/video-movie rental), small video-game arcade.

INEXPENSIVE

FAIRFIELD INN BY MARRIOTT, 8342 Jamaican Court, off

International Dr. between Sand Lake Rd. and Beeline Expy. (Hwy. 528), Orlando, FL 32819. Tel. 407/363-1944, or toll free 800/228-2800. Fax 407/363-1944. 135 rms. A/C TV TEL

$ Rates (including continental breakfast): $29–$74 for up to four people. Range reflects season. Extra person $7. AE, CB, DC, DISC, ER, MC, V. **Parking:** Free self-parking.

Jamaican Court, in a secluded area off International Drive, is a neatly landscaped complex of hotels and restaurants, including this handsome three-story tan stucco property with blue roofing and doors. It has spiffy-looking rooms decorated in rust, tan, and Federalist blue with oak furnishings. In-room amenities include remote-control cable TVs with free HBO and attractions-information channels, AM/FM radios, alarm clocks, and phones equipped with 25-foot cords and modem jacks. Guests enjoy a few thoughtful extras here: 100-watt bulbs in the lamps, candies on your pillow at check-in, complimentary daily newspapers, and free local calls. A continental breakfast of bagels, rolls, doughnuts, juices, fresh fruit, tea, and coffee is served in the lobby each morning. In addition, there are many freestanding and hotel restaurants right in Jamaican Court, and several local eateries deliver food (there are menus in each room).

The guest services desk sells tickets (most of them discounted) and provides transport to all nearby theme parks and attractions and the airport; round-trip to Disney parks costs $10. There's a small swimming pool on the premises, and the lobby has a microwave oven for guests' use.

ORLANDO DINING

Since most Orlando visitors spend the majority of their time in the Walt Disney World area, I've focused on the best dining choices throughout that vast enchanted empire. Also listed are some worthwhile restaurants beyond the realm. Parents will be pleased to note that just about every place in town offers a low-priced children's menu and usually provides some kind of kid's activity (mazes, coloring, paper dolls) as well. *Note:* Since the clientele at even the fanciest Epcot World Showcase restaurants are coming directly from the parks, you don't have to dress up for dinner. See also listings for dinner shows in Chapter 9.

Listings are divided by the following price categories: very expensive (dinner, typically, is more than $40 per person for a full meal, including a glass of wine, tip, and tax), expensive ($30 to $40), moderate ($20 to $30), inexpensive ($15 to $20), and budget ($15 and under). Keep in mind that the above categories refer to dinner prices, and some very expensive restaurants offer affordable lunches. Also, I'm going by the assumption that you're not stinting when you order. Some restaurants, for instance, have entrées ranging from $12 to $20. In most cases, you can dine for less if you order carefully. My favorite restaurants are marked with a star, those offering particularly good value for the money with a dollar sign.

1. IN WALT DISNEY WORLD

The following listings encompass restaurants at the Magic Kingdom, Epcot, Disney-MGM Studios, and Walt Disney World Village.

AT EPCOT

An ethnic meal at one of the World Showcase pavilions is part of the Epcot experience. If you want to have lunch or dinner at a World Showcase or Future World restaurant, make reservations at Earth Center as soon as you enter the park in the morning. That will insure optimum choice of dining time and cuisine. Guests at WDW-owned and official hotels can make reservations by phone up to three days in advance (ask CRO for details when you reserve, or call the guest services or concierge desk at your hotel). And during slower seasons, you can very often just walk up to an Epcot restaurant and make a reservation on the spot. *Note:* In addition to the below-listed there are plenty of walk-in eateries throughout the park that don't require reservations; check your **Epcot Guidebook** for details. All the establishments listed below offer lunch and dinner daily (hours vary with park hours), serve alcoholic beverages, and take American Express, MasterCard, and Visa.

WORLD SHOWCASE

These restaurants are arranged geographically, beginning at the Canada pavilion and proceeding counterclockwise around the World Showcase Lagoon.

Canada Located in the Victorian Hotel du Canada, with its French Gothic facade and steeply pitched copper roofs, **Le Cellier** has a castlelike ambience with dark oak wainscoting, seating in tapestried chairs under vaulted stone arches, and amber light emanating from black wrought-iron sconces. It's a self-service buffeteria, for which no reservations are required. Regional dishes include Cheddar cheese soup, poached fresh salmon, a pork- and potato-filled pie called tourtière, chicken and meatball stew, maple syrup pie, and Canadian beers. Appetizers cost $2.50 to $5.20; entrées $6.75 to $8.75 at lunch, $8.95 to $15.25 at dinner.

United Kingdom The plank-floored **Rose & Crown,** entered via a cozy pub with a pungent aroma of ale, evokes Victorian England with dark oak wainscoting, stained-glass, and English and Scottish folk music. It additionally offers outdoor seating at umbrella tables overlooking the lagoon. Servers in period costume enhance the village-inn ambience. The menu features traditional items like fish-and-chips, steak-and-kidney pie, and sherry trifle. Dinner might begin with an appetizer of Scotch egg (a hard-boiled egg encased in sausage meat, fried, and served cold with mustard sauce). Continue with an entrée of prime rib with Yorkshire pudding, conclude with raspberry fool (whipped cream and crushed raspberries atop a shortbread cookie), and wash it all down with a pint of Irish lager beer, Bass ale, or Guinness stout. Appetizers are $3.95 to $7.20; lunch entrées $8.75 to $10.75, dinner entrées $9.95 to $19.95. Traditional afternoon tea, with scones, pastries, and finger sandwiches, is served daily at 4pm; cost is $9.95.

France Chefs de France is under the auspices of a world-famous culinary triumvirate—Paul Bocuse, Roger Vergé, and Gaston LeNôtre. Its art nouveau/fin-de-siècle interior, under a coffered cherrywood ceiling, is agleam with mirrors and brass candelabra chandeliers. Etched-glass and brass dividers create intimate dining areas, tables are elegantly appointed, and—a cute Disney touch—your butter is molded into the shape of a chef. To start off, I recommend the seafood cream soup with crab dumplings (as featured by Vergé at Moulin de Mougins). Entrée selections at dinner include a superb broiled salmon in sorrel cream sauce à la façon de

Bocuse (it's served with ratatouille and new potatoes) and Vergé's sautéed beef tenderloin with raisins and brandy sauce. And classic French desserts range from Le Nôtre's soufflé Grand-Marnier to a pêche Melba crêpe filled with peaches and vanilla ice cream and topped with raspberry sauce. The distinguished chefs also composed the restaurant's wine list, any item of which can be purchased at Au Palais du Vin, a wine shop in the pavilion. Appetizers cost $3.75 to $7.50 at lunch, $3.50 to $8.50 at dinner; entrées $8.95 to $14.50 at lunch, $14.25 to $21.75 at dinner.

The ✪ **Bistro de Paris,** upstairs from Chefs de France and serving dinner only, offers similar fare in a more serene country-French setting. Also under the auspices of Bocuse, Vergé, and LeNôtre, it's rather elegant, with seating in burgundy tufted-leather banquettes, French windows adorned with swagged draperies, candlelit white-linened tables, and art nouveau lighting fixtures. Highlights here include Bocuse's duck foie gras salad appetizer with fresh greens and artichoke hearts, and Vergé's classic bouillabaisse served with garlic sauce and croutons. Another notable entrée: Bocuse's roast red snapper wrapped in thin-sliced potato crust and served on a bed of sautéed spinach with red wine lobster sauce. Stay with Bocuse for dessert; his crème brûlée is unbeatable. Appetizers cost $7.25 to $13.95, entrées $19.75 to $24.95.

Lighter fare is available throughout the day at **Au Petit Café,** a sidewalk bistro adjacent to Chefs de France on an awninged terrace overlooking the lagoon. It's a great venue for watching IllumiNations. Traditional café fare is featured—ham and cheese croissants, quiche Lorraine, salade niçoise, and a few heartier entrées such as coq au vin and brochette of prawns with rice and basil butter. No reservations are required. Entrées range from $7.25 to $14.50.

Morocco The palatial ✪ **Restaurant Marrakesh**—with its hand-set mosaic tilework, latticed teak shutters, and intricate cut-brass chandeliers suspended from a ceiling painted with elaborate Moorish motifs—represents 12 centuries of Arabic design. Exquisitely carved faux-ivory archways frame the central dining area, where belly dancers perform to *oud, kanoun,* and *darbuka* music. The Moroccan *diffa* (traditional feast) that lets you sample a variety of dishes is recommended. At dinner it includes a hearty saffron-seasoned harira soup flavored with onions, tomatoes, lentils, and lamb; beef *brewats* (minced beef seasoned with coriander, ginger, cinnamon, and saffron, rolled in thin pastry layers, and fried); roast lamb served with almond- and raisin-studded rice; braised tagine of chicken with green olives and preserved lemon; couscous with seasonal vegetables; Moroccan pastries; and mint tea. Combination appetizer plates are another way to experience culinary diversity. French and Moroccan wines are available to complement your meal. Appetizers cost $3.50 to $5.95; entrées $9.95 to $12.95 at lunch, $12.95 to $17.95 at dinner; Moroccan diffa is $27.95 for two at lunch, $49.95 for two at dinner.

Japan The **Mitsukoshi Restaurant** centers on a teppanyaki steakhouse where diners sit at grill tables and white-

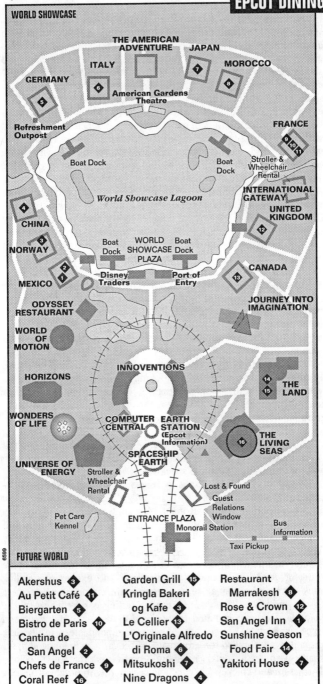

EPCOT DINING

N

WORLD SHOWCASE

GERMANY 5

ITALY 6

THE AMERICAN ADVENTURE

JAPAN 7

MOROCCO 8

American Gardens Theatre

Refreshment Outpost

FRANCE 9 10 11

Boat Dock

Boat Dock

Stroller & Wheelchair Rental

World Showcase Lagoon

INTERNATIONAL GATEWAY

UNITED KINGDOM 12

CHINA 4

Boat Dock

WORLD SHOWCASE PLAZA

Boat Dock

NORWAY 3

MEXICO 2 1

Disney Traders

Port of Entry

CANADA 13

JOURNEY INTO IMAGINATION

ODYSSEY RESTAURANT

WORLD OF MOTION

HORIZONS

INNOVENTIONS

THE LAND 14 15

WONDERS OF LIFE

COMPUTER CENTRAL

EARTH STATION (Epcot Information)

THE LIVING SEAS 16

UNIVERSE OF ENERGY

SPACESHIP EARTH

Stroller & Wheelchair Rental

Lost & Found

Guest Relations Window

Pet Care Kennel

ENTRANCE PLAZA

Monorail Station

Bus Information

Taxi Pickup

FUTURE WORLD

6599

Akershus 3	Garden Grill 15	Restaurant
Au Petit Café 11	Kringla Bakeri	Marrakesh 8
Biergarten 5	og Kafe 3	Rose & Crown 12
Bistro de Paris 10	Le Cellier 13	San Angel Inn 1
Cantina de	L'Originale Alfredo	Sunshine Season
San Angel 2	di Roma 6	Food Fair 14
Chefs de France 9	Mitsukoshi 7	Yakitori House 7
Coral Reef 16	Nine Dragons 4	

hatted chefs perform samurailike culinary moves—rapidly dicing, slicing, stir-frying, and propelling cooked food onto your plate with amazing dexterity. Kids especially love watching the chef wield his cleaver and utensils. Intimate dining areas are created by lacquered shoji screens, and walls are embellished with murals and paintings of cranes, willows, irises, sea motifs, and bamboo groves. Since you share a table with strangers, teppanyaki makes for a convivial dining experience. An elaborate dinner for two (of which an abbreviated version is available at lunch) includes a shrimp appetizer, green salad with ginger dressing, soup (ask for the *miroshiru*—soybean soup with tofu and mushrooms), grilled fresh vegetables with udon noodles, succulent morsels of grilled beef tenderloin and lobster, steamed rice, choice of dessert (perhaps chestnut cake), and green tea. And even à la carte entrées include plenty of extras. Kirin beer, plum wine, and sake are among your beverage options, along with specialty drinks (some of them nonalcoholic for kids) such as a *tachibana* (light rum, orange curaçao, and mandarin orange juice). Appetizers cost $4.75 to $5.95; entrées $8.95 to $14.95 at lunch, $14.25 to $24.50 at dinner; complete dinner described above costs $38 for two at lunch, $58 for two at dinner.

Adjoining the teppanyaki rooms is a U-shaped **tempura counter** where you can eat shrimp, scallops, chicken, and fresh vegetables that have been lightly battered and deep-fried. Some sushi and sashimi items are served here as well. Entrées cost $9.25 to $11.50 at lunch, $14.25 to $20.50 at dinner. No reservations required for counter seating.

Another gem in this complex is a peaceful plant-filled **cocktail lounge** with large windows overlooking the lagoon and torii gate—a very pleasant setting for appetizers (perhaps shrimp tempura or sashimi) and warm sake. Japanese music plays softly in the background. Menu items are $4.50 to $7.95, and no reservations are required.

And housed in a replica of the 16th-century Katsura Imperial Villa in Kyoto is **Yakitori House,** a cafeteria serving teriyaki, yakitori, and other Japanese snack fare.

Italy   ✪ **L'Originale Alfredo di Roma Ristorante**—patterned after Alfredo De Lelio's celebrated establishment in Rome—evokes a seaside Roman palazzo with crystal candelabra chandeliers suspended from a high coffered ceiling and beautiful *trompe l'oeil* frescoes of 16th-century patrician villas inspired by Veronese. In the entrance foyer, three arched windows look into an exhibition kitchen where pasta dough is kneaded and noodles are hung up to dry. Charming Italian waiters and exuberant strolling musicians—who play accordion, guitar, and tambourine—create a festive ambience. If you want a quieter setting, ask for a seat on the veranda. De Lelio invented fettuccine Alfredo—and it remains an excellent entrée choice here. Also recommendable are ziti in a piquant vodka-spiked tomato cream sauce, garlicky linguine al pesto made with fresh Italian basil and tossed with pignoli nuts and Parmesan, and chicken alla parmigiana served with potato croquette and an array of fresh vegetables. Noteworthy antipasto selections include sage-stuffed baked mushrooms, stuffed clams, and deep-fried zucchini. An extensive array of Italian wines is available. And there's a sublime tiramisu for dessert. On your way in or out, note the entrance room walls; they're covered with photographs of celebrity diners in Rome—everyone from Douglas Fairbanks and Mary Pickford (who discovered Alfredo's on their honeymoon and told *tout* Hollywood) to Dwight and Mamie Eisenhower. Appetizers cost $3.50 to $6.95; entrées $9.75 to $14.95 at lunch, $12.25 to $24.75 at dinner.

Germany Lit by streetlamps (to suggest nighttime), **The Biergarten** simulates a Bavarian village courtyard at Oktoberfest with autumnal trees, a working water wheel, and geranium-filled flower boxes adorning Tudor-style houses. The setting was inspired by the town of Rothenburg. Waiters are in lederhosen, waitresses in peasant dresses, and entertainment is provided by oom-pah bands, singers, dancers, and a strolling accordionist. Musical shows, which take place five to seven times a day (depending on the season) incorporate performances on instruments such as a 15-foot Alpine horn and cowbells. Guests are encouraged to dance as the band strikes up polkas and waltzes and to sing along with yodelers and folksingers. Beck's beer (served in 33-ounce steins) and carafes of Liebfraumilch accompany traditional Bavarian fare—appetizers of goulash soup, potato pancakes, and herring with apple salad; entrée platters of sauerbraten with dumplings and red cabbage or knockwurst and weisswurst with wine kraut and boiled potatoes; and apple strudel or Black Forest cake for dessert. Appetizers cost $3.25 to $7.50; entrées $8.95 to $11.50 at lunch, $10.95 to $20.50 at dinner.

China One of the most attractive of the World Showcase restaurants, ✪ **Nine Dragons,** with windows overlooking the lagoon, has intricately carved rosewood paneling and furnishings, lacquer screens embellished with cherry blossoms, and a beautiful dragon-motif ceiling. Begin with a selection of dim sum (appetizers) such as honey-glazed spareribs, delicious shrimp toast, pan-fried dumplings (pot stickers) stuffed with pork and vegetables, and ginger-nuanced steamed dumplings stuffed with pork, shrimp, and water chestnuts. Entrées highlight dishes from four regions of China—Mandarin duck shredded with green and red peppers and served with pancakes; from Shanghai a saucy stir-fried boneless chicken with onions, carrots, and green peas; Cantonese tender sliced sirloin and broccoli stir-fried in oyster sauce; and Szechuan deep-fried shrimp ambrosia in a Mao Tai liqueur-spiked fruit sauce. You can order Chinese or California wines with your meal, but I especially love fresh melon juice, either non-alcoholic or mixed with rum or vodka. And for dessert there's red-bean ice cream with fried banana or Chinese pastries. Appetizers cost $4.25 to $6.50; entrées $8.95 to $17.95 at lunch, $9.95 to $22.50 at dinner. A multicourse sampler lunch (soup, spring roll, entrée, pastries, and tea) is $10.95; $38.95 buys an elaborate meal for two at dinner.

Norway **Akershus** re-creates a 14th-century castle fortress that stands in Oslo's harbor. Its pristine white stone interior, with

FROMMER'S SMART TRAVELER: RESTAURANTS

1. Eat your main meal at lunch, when prices are lower and you can enjoy haute-cuisine entrées for a fraction of what they'd cost at dinner.
2. Some accommodations listed in this book include breakfast in rates or have rooms with fully equipped kitchens; for families, these can represent substantial savings.
3. Dining at Walt Disney World can get expensive. Save money by bringing a picnic lunch (purchase fixings at the local supermarket). You won't have to traipse back to your car to get it; there are coin-op lockers in all the Disney parks.
4. The least expensive restaurants in the Walt Disney World area are along U.S. 192 in Kissimmee—a stretch of highway where every fast-food chain in America is represented. Head over there for cheap eats.

glossy oak floors, lofty pine and cherrywood-beamed ceilings, and leaded-glass windows, features intimate dining niches divided by Gothic stone archways. Soft lighting emanates from gas lamps (on crisply white-linened tables), wrought-iron and brass candelabra chandeliers, and flickering sconces. The meal is an immense smörgåsbord of traditional *småvarmt* (hot) and *koldtbord* (cold) dishes— smoked pork with honey mustard, strips of venison in cream sauce, gravlax in mustard sauce, smoked mackerel, poached salmon, fish mousse in herb dressing, Norwegian tomato herring, an array of Norwegian breads and cheeses, smoked turkey, stuffed pork loin, potato salad, red cabbage, boiled red potatoes, eggs Nordique, and much more. Norwegian beer and aquavit complement a list of French and California wines. For dessert order a "veiled maiden"—an applesauce and whipped cream concoction. Norwegian hosts and hostesses can answer all your questions. Lunch buffet costs $11.50 for adults, children 4 to 12 pay $4.75, 3 and under free. Dinner buffet costs $17.25 for adults, $7.50 for children 4 to 12, 3 and under free. Desserts and beverages are à la carte. A la carte children's entrées are $3.99.

Another facility in this pavilion, the **Kringla Bakeri og Kafe,** offers covered outdoor seating and inexpensive light fare—open-faced sandwiches like smoked salmon stuffed with hard-boiled egg, cheese and fruit platters, waffles sprinkled with powdered sugar, and fresh-baked Norwegian pastries. No reservations are required.

Mexico   The ✪ **San Angel Inn** evokes a hacienda courtyard under a starlit sky in the shadow of a crumbling Yucatán pyramid and dense jungle foliage. It is nighttime: Tables are candlelit (even at lunch), and lighting is very low. The Popocatepetl volcano erupts in the distance, spewing molten lava, and you can hear the sounds of faraway birds. Thunder, lightning, and swiftly moving clouds add a dramatic note, but the overall ambience is soothing. The fare is authentic and prepared from scratch. Order an appetizer of *queso fundido* (melted cheese with Mexican pork sausage, served with homemade corn or flour tortillas). At dinner, filet of blackened mahi-mahi in spicy chili sauce, served with Mexican rice and vegetables, is a house specialty. Also very good are *mole poblano* (chicken simmered with more than 20 spices and a hint of chocolate), and *filete ranchero* (grilled tenderloin of beef served over corn tortillas with sauce ranchero, poblano pepper strips, Monterey jack cheese, onions, and refried beans). Dinner entrées are served with soup or salad and Mexican rice. Order a side dish of guacamole. Combination platters are available at both meals. There's chocolate Kahlúa mousse pie for dessert, and drink options include Dos Equis beer and margaritas. Appetizers cost $5.75 to $8.50 (they're large enough to share); entrées $8.95 to $14.95 at lunch, $12.50 to $22.50 at dinner.

Cantina de San Angel, a cafeteria with outdoor seating at umbrella tables overlooking the lagoon, offers inexpensive tacos, burritos, enchiladas, and combination plates, along with frozen margaritas.

FUTURE WORLD

As at World Showcase above, Future World restaurants are arranged geographically, beginning at the Living Seas pavilion and proceeding counterclockwise.

Living Seas Pavilion Dine "under the sea" at the enchanting **Coral Reef,** where tables ring a 5.6-million-gallon aquarium inhabited by more than 4,000 denizens of the deep. Tiered seating—much of it in semicircular booths—ensures everyone a good view, and diners are given "fish-identifier" sheets with labeled pictures so they can put names to the species swimming by. The strains of Debussy's *La Mer* and Handel's *Water Music* playing softly in the background enhance the Piscean vibes. And the menu features (what else?) fresh fish and seafood. A satisfying appetizer is the seas' sampler—a platter of mesquite-grilled jumbo shrimp, baked oysters Rockefeller topped with spinach and cream sauce, and garlicky baked clams with an herb- and white wine–seasoned breadcrumb topping. Smoked fish is a specialty. Try hickory-smoked grouper served on braised napa cabbage with bacon and tomato-basil sauce or smoked shrimp and assorted seafood tossed with fettuccine, spinach, and shiitake mushrooms. Non-seafood eaters can dine on beef tenderloin or broiled chicken, and low-priced hot dogs with french fries are an option for kids. Desserts range from fresh strawberries in Grand Marnier served in a white chocolate conch shell to a white chocolate mousse topped with dark chocolate Mickey Mouse ears. Coral Reef features premium wines by the glass and also offers a nightly entrée matched with a selected label. Appetizers cost $4.25 to $9.75; entrées $11.50 to $19.25 at lunch, mostly $19.75 to $23.50 at dinner.

The Land The revolving **Garden Grill,** on the upper level of this pavilion, seats diners in comfortable upholstered semicircular booths. As you dine, you'll travel past desert, prairie, farmland, and rain forest environments. A planter of seedlings on each table further promotes The Land's ecology-awareness theme, and many menu selections feature produce grown in its on-premises greenhouses. Your meal here might begin with an appetizer of spicy chicken wings with celery stalks and tangy blue cheese dressing. Entrées range from a platter of barbecued smoked pork with steak fries to spicy Cajun jambalaya (rice tossed with andouille sausage, chicken, and shrimp). For dessert, there's a fruit crisp à la mode. Wine and beer are available. Appetizers cost $2.75 to $5.50, entrées $7.95 to $15.50.

The Land also houses a lower-level food court called the **Sunshine Season Food Fair,** where vendors proffer an array of low-priced items—barbecued chicken and beef, homemade soups and fresh salads, immense cinnamon rolls, fresh fruit and cheeses, pastas, baked potatoes stuffed with Cheddar cheese and broccoli, sandwiches, oven-fresh cakes and pastries, ice cream, and more. Colorful umbrella tables under a skylit dome ring a splashing fountain.

IN THE MAGIC KINGDOM

There are three major restaurants in the Magic Kingdom offering full-service dining—the Liberty Tree Tavern, King Stefan's Banquet Hall, and Tony's Town Square. Reservations for these—and the Diamond Horseshoe Jamboree—must be made at the restaurant's door the day you wish to dine (do it immediately on entering the park in the morning). Guests at WDW-owned and official hotels can make reservations by phone up to three days in advance (ask CRO for details when you reserve, or call the guest services or concierge desk at your hotel). All the establishments listed below take American Express, MasterCard, and Visa, and no Magic Kingdom restaurants serve alcoholic beverages. In addition to the restaurants I've listed, you'll find dozens of fast-food eateries throughout the park. Consult your *Magic Kingdom Guidebook* for details.

Main Street Inspired by the Disney movie *Lady and the Tramp*, **Tony's Town Square Restaurant** is Victorian plush, with rich cherrywood beams and paneling, stained-glass, cut-glass mirrors, and globe lighting fixtures. Walls are hung with original cels from the movie. There's additional seating in a sunny plant-filled solarium. This is the only full-service restaurant serving breakfast in the Magic Kingdom (no reservations required for that meal only), and it opens early; you can eat here while waiting for the other lands to open. Breakfast items include frittatas served with buttermilk biscuits, Lady and the Tramp–shaped waffles, and French toast tossed in cinnamon sugar and served with warm maple or fruit syrup. The rest of the day, the menu is Italian, featuring appetizers such as a

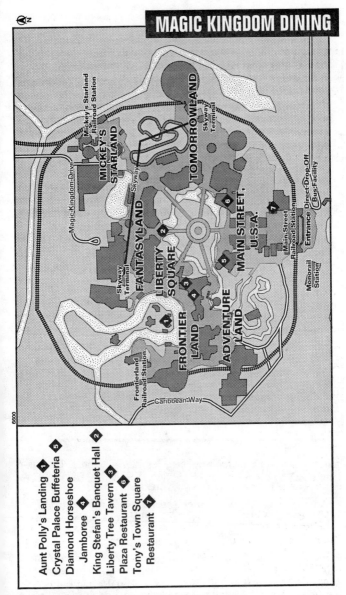

Aunt Polly's Landing 1
Crystal Palace Buffeteria 5
Diamond Horseshoe
Jamboree 4
King Stefan's Banquet Hall 2
Liberty Tree Tavern 3
Plaza Restaurant 6
Tony's Town Square
Restaurant 7

five-cheese pizza and fried calamari with marinara sauce. The lunch menu lists a variety of pastas, calzones, meatball and sausage subs, and salads. At dinner your options range from garlicky sautéed shrimp and seasonal vegetables over linguine in a light cream sauce to a 12-ounce sirloin steak/sautéed lobster combination, also served with linguine in cream sauce. Desserts include spumoni, gelatos, and

FROMMER'S COOL FOR KIDS: RESTAURANTS

In a town where the major attractions are amusement parks, just about every restaurant is child-oriented. Do see the listings for meals hosted by Disney characters on p. 139. Some additional suggestions include:

Cape May Cafe Clambake Buffet   *(see p. 131)* This old-fashioned nightly clambake at Disney's Beach Club Resort is fun for the whole family.

Chef Mickey's   *(see pp. 122 and 140)* Great food pleases mom and dad, and kids love the nightly appearances by Mickey Mouse. If you want to linger over dinner, the kids can retreat to a lounge where cartoons are shown.

Mickey's Tropical Luau   *(see p. 140)* Not just a meal but a Polynesian floor show featuring Minnie, Mickey, Pluto, and Goofy along with a cast of South Sea Islanders. At Disney's Polynesian Resort. Character breakfasts here, too.

Hoop-Dee-Doo Musical Revue   *(see p. 215)* I've never met anyone who didn't have a great time at this whoopin' and hollerin' country music dinner show in Fort Wilderness Pioneer Hall.

Sci-Fi Dine-In Theater Restaurant   *(see p. 119)* A drive-in movie theater where you sit in actual convertible cars and the waitstaff is on roller skates. At Disney-MGM Studios.

Italian pastries. Open for breakfast, lunch, and dinner. Breakfast items cost $2.75 to $7.75; appetizers $4.50 to $7.95; entrées $6.95 to $14.50 at lunch, $15.50 to $21.95 at dinner.

Another appealing Main Street–area eatery is the **Crystal Palace Buffeteria** housed in a replica of a glass edifice constructed for the Great London Exhibition of 1851 in Hyde Park. An exquisite Victorian structure, topped by glass domes, it has a pristine white wood interior with a lime-green ceiling. Multipaned windows and a stained-glass frieze enhance the crystalline motif, and baskets of flowers suspended from the rafters and a central octagonal planter add garden-conservatory ambience. Additional seating is offered on a covered veranda cooled by ceiling fans. All in all, it's a rather elaborate setting for a cafeteria. Breakfast—served from a half-hour before park opening—offers items ranging from bacon and eggs with roasted potatoes to sausage biscuits with gravy. Lunch fare includes salads and sandwiches (from poor boys to grilled turkey), along with hot entrées—also offered at dinner—such as spit-roasted chicken seasoned with fresh rosemary and thyme, served with fresh vegetables and mashed potatoes. And for dessert there's fresh-baked apple pie, carrot cake, or cheesecake. Open for breakfast, lunch, and dinner. Breakfast items cost $2.50 to $5.50; entrées $7.50 to $10.50 at lunch, $7.95 to $15.50 at dinner.

Near the end of Main Street is the pretty **Plaza Restaurant,** with an art nouveau interior—café-curtained windows, etched mirrors, and shell-motif lighting fixtures. It serves burgers and sandwiches (tuna and Swiss on whole wheat, a Reuben or pastrami on rye, hot roast beef double-deckers) which you can wash down with a vanilla, chocolate, or strawberry shake, or skip the shake and leave room for a hot-fudge sundae topped with whipped cream and a maraschino cherry. There's waiter service, but you don't need reservations. Open from lunch to park closing. Sundaes are $3.75 to $5.75 (for an elaborate create-your-own concoction); sandwiches, burgers, and salads, $6.95 to $9.95.

Frontierland Highly recommended is the **Diamond Horseshoe Jamboree,** combining a light meal with a 40-minute western-themed musical revue (details in Chapter 7).

I also like **Aunt Polly's Landing** on Tom Sawyer's Island, reached via a short raft trip across the Rivers of America. With its outdoor tables on a porch overlooking the water, it provides a tranquil respite from park hyperactivity. Inexpensive light fare includes sandwiches—peanut butter and jelly, fried chicken, ham and cheese—and soft drinks. And you can relax over refreshing lemonade while the kids explore the island's dark caves and abandoned mines. It's open for lunch only.

Liberty Square The **Liberty Tree Tavern** replicates an 18th-century pub, with beamed cherrywood ceilings, peg-plank oak floors, displays of pewterware in oak hutches, and a vast brick fireplace hung with copper pots. Diners sit at sturdy candlelit tables, waitstaff is in period garb, background music is appropriate to the period, and paintings on redwood illustrate historic scenes of colonial America. Even the windows have panes of hand-pressed glass, a detail typical of Disney thoroughness. Entrées range from New England pot roast braised in burgundy and served with mashed potatoes and vegetables to a traditional roast turkey dinner with all the trimmings. Precede these with a bowl of creamy New England clam chowder. Meals are accompanied by baskets of three-grain bread and apple butter. At lunch there are sandwiches such as prime rib smothered with onions and brown gravy, served with fried potatoes. And all-American desserts include a Mickey Mouse–shaped strawberry shortcake, apple pie topped with cinnamon ice cream, and red velvet cake. Little Patriots get a special menu with games, puzzles, and a cutout portrait, suitable for hanging, perhaps of "Thomouse" Jefferson. Open for lunch and dinner. Appetizers cost $4.75 to $6.95; entrées are $10.50 to $15.25 at lunch (sandwiches $7.50 to $10.25), $12.95 to $18.50 at dinner.

Fantasyland Housed in Cinderella Castle, the focal point of the park, **King Stefan's Banquet Hall** has a Gothic interior with leaded-glass windows and heraldic banners suspended from a vaulted ceiling. Suits of armor and shields are on display, and servers in 13th-century garb address guests as "Milord" and "Milady." Sturdy oak tables are candlelit. The only anachronistic note: Background music is from Disney movies. The menu features hearty cuts of beef such as prime rib and grilled sirloin served with fresh sautéed vegetables and soup (or salad at dinner). And while you're piling on cholesterol, might as well opt for the fried cheese appetizer— Havarti, smoked Gouda, and mozzarella served with marinara sauce. Less caloric entrées include pasta tossed with mixed seafood and fresh vegetables and a vegetarian plate, and at lunch there are salad entrées. The crown-shaped kid's menu lists burgers, hot dogs, chicken tenders, and macaroni and cheese. And dessert choices include a hot fudge sundae, berry and apple cobbler topped with cinnamon ice cream, and a southern classic—red velvet cake. *Note:* Cinderella often greets guests in the downstairs entrance hall where the Disney family crest (three lions) is displayed over a fireplace. Open for lunch and dinner. Appetizers $3.25 to $6.95; entrées $8.95 to $15.95 at lunch, $20.25 to $24.95 at dinner.

AT DISNEY-MGM STUDIOS

There are over a dozen eateries in this Hollywood-themed park with movie-lot monikers like the Studio Commissary and Starring Rolls Bakery. The two below-listed are my favorites. Both require reservations, which should be made at the Hollywood Junction Red Car Station on Sunset Boulevard or at the restaurants themselves when you enter the park in the morning. Guests at WDW-owned and official hotels can make reservations by phone up to three days in advance (ask CRO for details when you reserve, or call the guest services or concierge desk at your hotel). Both serve lunch and dinner, have full bars, and take American Express, MasterCard, and Visa.

The **Hollywood Brown Derby,** modeled after the famed L.A. celebrity haunt where Louella Parsons and Hedda Hopper held court, evokes its West Coast counterpart with interior palm trees, roomy semicircular leather booths, derby-shaded sconces, and mahogany-paneled walls hung with hundreds of caricatures of major stars who patronized the restaurant—everyone from Bette Davis to Sammy Davis. Brown Derby legend abounds: It was at this Hollywood shrine that Clark Gable proposed to Carole Lombard, Wallace Beery poured ketchup over his sponge cake, and Lucille Ball and Jack Haley chucked dinner rolls at each other across the tables! A pianist entertains while you dine. The Derby's signature dish is the Cobb salad, invented by owner Bob Cobb in the 1930s—almost a puree of finely chopped greens mixed with avocado, Roquefort cheese, bacon, and tomatoes. It's a good appetizer choice, as are the pan-fried Maryland crabcakes (to which a hint of cayenne adds piquancy) served with spicy marinara sauce. Dinner entrées come with a choice of soup or salad (select the oyster Brie, available à la carte at lunch—an ambrosial champagne-flavored soup garnished with a slice of lemon). Go on to an entrée of baked grouper meunière served atop pasta in a light lemony white wine cream sauce. Grapefruit cake with vanilla icing is the Derby's signature dessert. There's a full bar, and after-dinner drinks are a specialty. Appetizers cost $5.25 to $7.75 at lunch, $5.75 to $8.75 at dinner; entrées, $9.75 to $15.95 at lunch, $15.25 to $25.75 at dinner.

The **Sci-Fi Dine-In Theater Restaurant** replicates an archetypical 1950s Los Angeles drive-in movie emporium. Diners are ensconced in flashy chrome-trimmed convertible cars (complete with fins and whitewalls) under a twinkling starlit sky with the Hollywood hills as a backdrop. Friendly carhops bring your food order and complimentary popcorn. While you eat, you can watch the movie screen, where a mix of zany newsreels (e.g., *News of the Future*) is interspersed with cartoons, horror movie clips (*Frankenstein Meets the Space Monster*), and coming attractions. Menu items have names like Terror of the Tides (deep-fried shrimp, served with fries and coleslaw), 20,000 Leafs Under the Sea (a seafood salad in citrus vinaigrette dressing), and Monster Mash (oven-roasted turkey with all the trimmings). And though the restaurant basically appeals to kids (whose menu items are all under $5), beverages include wine and beer (there's a full bar) as well as milkshakes. Finish up with The Cheesecake that Ate New York. Your bill is presented as a speeding ticket. Entrées cost $6.25 to $12.50 at lunch, $7.50 to $17.95 at dinner.

WALT DISNEY WORLD VILLAGE/PLEASURE ISLAND

Located about 2½ miles from Epcot off Buena Vista Drive, Walt Disney World Village is a very pleasant complex of cedar-shingled shops and restaurants overlooking a scenic lagoon. Pleasure Island, a nighttime entertainment center, adjoins. *Note:* You don't have to pay the entrance fee to Pleasure Island to dine at the Fireworks Factory or Portobello Yacht Club.

VERY EXPENSIVE

THE EMPRESS ROOM, aboard the *Empress Lilly* in Walt Disney World Village. Tel. 828-3900.
Cuisine: FRENCH. **Reservations:** Required (*note:* You can reserve up to 30 days in advance). **Parking:** Free self-parking and validated valet parking.
$ Prices: Appetizers $9–$15; main courses $26–$34. AE, MC, V.
Open: Dinner seatings daily 6:30–9:30pm.

The *Empress Lilly* (named for Walt Disney's wife) is a plush replica of a 19th-century Mississippi riverboat permanently moored on the shores of Lake Buena Vista. It houses several restaurants and lounges, among them this ornate dining room with gold satin-damask wall coverings and a crystal candelabra chandelier suspended from an intricately carved domed plaster ceiling. Gilded etched-glass dividers create intimate dining alcoves where patrons are royally ensconced in apricot velvet Louis XV–style chairs at white-linened tables, each adorned with a rose in a silver vase. Jackets are required for men.

The exquisitely presented fare (almost, but not quite, too beautiful to eat) is every bit as *haute* as its setting. Two hors d'oeuvres are especially wonderful: Sautéed oysters and jumbo lump crabmeat on a bed of fennel are glazed with champagne sauce and garnished with julienned vegetables. And escargots en croûte, deriving its garlicky flavor from Boursin cheese, is served on yellow tomato butter sauce marbleized with puréed watercress. A warm salad of boneless duck and quail eggs over greens, garnished with morsels of black truffle and prosciutto bacon and drizzled with balsamic vinaigrette, is also delightful. Ditto a Pernod-spiked creamy shellfish soup, replete with oysters, mussels, shrimp, and scallops. Entrées—served in silver cloches—include roast breast of duck with mandarin honey-vinegar sauce served over a bed of tri-grain rice with crisp sautéed watercress and garnishes as thrilling as gifts—a morsel of honeycomb, fresh duck liver, and Peking kumquats. Sorbets served in frosted-glass flowers refresh your palate between courses. Dessert—perhaps a soufflé Grand Marnier topped with crème anglaise (if you want a soufflé, order it at the beginning of the meal)—is followed by complimentary chocolates infused with rum and amaretto and rolled in crushed pistachios. And coffee is accompanied by a silver tray laden with cinnamon sticks, rock and anisette sugar, shaved chocolate, and unsweetened whipped cream. Needless to say, an extensive wine list complements the menu.

EXPENSIVE

FISHERMAN'S DECK, aboard the *Empress Lilly* in Walt Disney World Village. Tel. 828-3900.
   Cuisine: SEAFOOD. **Reservations:** Required (*note:* you can reserve up to 30 days in advance). **Parking:** Free self-parking, valet parking $4.
$ **Prices:** Appetizers $4.95–$8.50; main courses $5.75–$9.95 at lunch, $17.25–$23 at dinner. AE, MC, V.
   Open: Lunch daily 11:30am–2pm; dinner daily 5:30–10pm.
This very appealing restaurant aboard Disney's triple-decker white paddlewheeler is decorated in 18th-century style. Semicircular in shape, its seating—in plush tufted-velvet Louis XVI–style chairs—faces a curved window wall overlooking Lake Buena Vista. White-linened tables are lit by shaded pewter candle lamps at dinner, and said windows are elegantly framed by Federalist blue velvet draperies with gold fringe. Early arrivals at dinner enjoy gorgeous sunsets.

Tempting appetizers include baked sea scallops served in the shell with buttery garlic-breadcrumb topping and fresh oysters baked with shiitake mushrooms and pesto sauce topped with a gratinée of

Monterey Jack cheese. An entrée of hot and spicy sautéed Mississippi catfish is served with green rice (mixed with finely chopped parsley and scallions) and Cajun mushroom sauce. Also accompanied by green rice is shrimp Imperial—baked crabmeat-stuffed shrimp with lobster cream sauce and fresh seasonal vegetables. Finish up with angel-food cake under a scoop of vanilla-bean ice cream and hot butter pecan-raisin sauce. Children's entrées are under $4. The lunch menu lists sandwiches and salads in addition to entrées such as seafood crêpes and speckled trout teriyaki.

MODERATE

FIREWORKS FACTORY, 1630 Lake Buena Vista Dr., Pleasure Island. Tel. 934-8989.

Cuisine: AMERICAN REGIONAL. **Reservations:** Recommended. **Parking:** Free self-parking, valet parking $4.

$ Prices: Appetizers $4.95–$6.95; main courses $5.95–$8.95 at lunch, $9.95–$23.95 at dinner. AE, MC, V.

Open: Daily 11:30am–11:30pm (dinner served from 4pm); light fare and drinks served to 2am.

According to Disney legend, Captain Merriweather Adam Pleasure, the mythological 19th-century ship merchant and adventurer who developed Pleasure Island, manufactured fireworks as a hobby and staged dazzling spectaculars every July 4th. Pleasure was lost at sea in 1839, but his former corrugated-tin warehouse survives in the form of this "explosively" exuberant casual restaurant. The Factory has big red pipes overhead and exposed-brick walls hung with neon signs and vintage advertisements for fireworks. Dozens of unopened boxes of beer are strewn around the floor, and missile fireworks are prominently displayed. In the bar area, sporting events are aired on TV monitors. Tables are covered with bright-plaid plastic cloths.

Lunch or dinner, you might start off with a "3 and 3 combo" of spicy chicken wings tossed in Louisiana hot sauce, fried catfish, and applewood-smoked shrimp served with barbecue sauce, blue cheese, and house dressing. Follow that up with a Macon County barbecue platter—mesquite-smoked pork, sliced brisket, and shredded chicken, served with corn on the cob and a baked potato (fries at lunch). Dinner entrées include grilled herbed and citrus-soaked chicken served with New Orleans dirty rice and vegetables, roast duck in loganberry sauce with wild rice and vegetables, and steamed Dungeness crab with drawn butter, served with sweet corn and a baked potato. For dessert: a giant tollhouse cookie served warm in a cast-iron skillet topped with vanilla ice cream and hot fudge. In addition to "dynamite" cocktails (try a 21 Rum Salute) and wines, the Fireworks Factory offers more than 45 varieties of domestic and imported beer, ale, and stout, including several microbrewery selections.

PORTOBELLO YACHT CLUB, 1650 Lake Buena Vista Dr., Pleasure Island. Tel. 934-8888.

Cuisine: NORTHERN ITALIAN. **Reservations:** Not accepted (arrive early to avoid a wait). **Parking:** Free self-parking, valet parking $4.

$ Prices: Appetizers $5.95–$10.95; main courses $6.95–$9.95 at lunch, $12.95–$22.95 at dinner; pizzas $6.95–$7.95. AE, MC, V.

Open: Daily 11:30am–midnight (dinner served from 4pm).

Occupying a gabled Bermuda-style house, the Yacht Club is nautically themed, its interior, though casual, evoking a luxury cruise ship. Inside, robin's-egg-blue walls are plastered with photographs of racing yachts, navigational charts, and yachting flags, and shelves are lined with racing trophies. From the lively mahogany-paneled bar, you can watch oak-fired pizzas being prepared in an exhibition kitchen. And, weather permitting, you can dine al fresco, on an awninged patio overlooking Lake Buena Vista.

Those oak-fired pizzas have crisply thin crusts and toppings such as *quattro formaggi* (mozzarella, Romano, Gorgonzola, and provolone with sun-dried tomatoes). And lunch or dinner, you might follow an antipasto of steamed clams and mussels served with garlic croutons in buttery white wine sauce with an entrée of charcoal-grilled half chicken marinated in olive oil, garlic, and fresh rosemary, served with roasted garlic mashed potatoes (grilled polenta at lunch) and seasonal vegetables. Or choose a pasta dish such as bucatini with plum tomatoes, Italian bacon, garlic, and fresh basil. Entrées are served with sourdough bread and roasted spreadable garlic cloves. There's an extensive award-winning list of Italian and California wines (many of them hard-to-find vintages), supplemented by a selection of grappas, single-malt scotches, and cognacs. A dessert of *crema bruccioto* (white-chocolate custard with a caramelized sugar glaze) served with fresh berries is recommended.

INEXPENSIVE

CHEF MICKEY'S, Walt Disney World Village. Tel. 828-3900.

Cuisine: AMERICAN. **Reservations:** Recommended (only 20% of tables are allotted via reservations, with the rest reserved for walk-ins, but you can reserve up to 30 days in advance; walk-ins should arrive early to avoid a wait). **Parking:** Free self-parking (use lot A).

$ Prices: Breakfast fare $1.95–$6.25; appetizers $3.95–$6.95; main courses $5.75–$10.25 at lunch, mostly $9.75–$15 at dinner. AE, MC, V.

Open: Breakfast daily 9–11am; lunch daily 11:30am–2pm; dinner daily 5–10pm.

Rustically attractive, Chef Mickey's plant-filled interior has ficus trees growing towards a skylight and exposed-brick walls hung with signed photographs of Disney characters. About half of the seats overlook Buena Vista Lagoon. One dining area is ski lodgey with redwood-paneled walls and a beamed pine cathedral

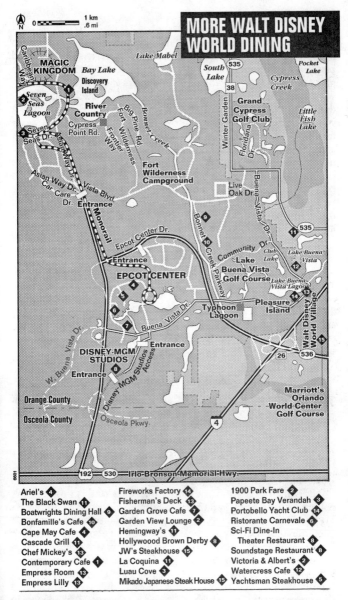

MORE WALT DISNEY WORLD DINING

Ariel's ④	Fireworks Factory ⑭	1900 Park Fare ②
The Black Swan ⑪	Fisherman's Deck ⑬	Papeete Bay Verandah ③
Boatwrights Dining Hall ⑨	Garden Grove Cafe ⑦	Portobello Yacht Club ⑭
Bonfamille's Cafe ⑩	Garden View Lounge ②	Ristorante Carnevale ⑥
Cape May Cafe ④	Hemingway's ⑪	Sci-Fi Dine-In
Cascade Grill ⑪	Hollywood Brown Derby ⑧	Theater Restaurant ⑧
Chef Mickey's ⑬	JW's Steakhouse ⑮	Soundstage Restaurant ⑧
Contemporary Cafe ①	La Coquina ⑪	Victoria & Albert's ②
Empress Room ⑬	Luau Cove ③	Watercress Cafe ⑫
Empress Lilly ⑬	Mikado Japanese Steak House ⑮	Yachtsman Steakhouse ⑤

ceiling, another offers a view of white-hatted chefs at work in an exhibition kitchen. And should you have to wait for a table, you can do so in a lounge where kids can watch cartoons on a large-screen TV, while adults view sporting events at the bar. Mickey turns out some pretty terrific food here (a cookbook of his recipes is available), and, at dinner, he table-hops, greeting patrons and signing autographs.

An appetizer of light and fluffy crabcakes Boca—to which nuances of Tabasco, cayenne, mustard, and Worcestershire sauce add zest—is served up in a black ceramic frying pan. This is also a good place to try conch chowder. Lunch choices include burgers, sandwiches, and salads, as well as entrées of beef or chicken fajitas. At dinner there's cheesy crisp-baked salmon lasagne served on a spinach–pine nut cream sauce. Or you might opt for a hearty rack of fork-tender barbecued ribs marinated in hot honey-mustard sauce and served with grilled corn (served in the husk), a big slab of homemade cornbread, and fabulous homemade coleslaw. Leave room for dessert—peach cobbler topped with vanilla-bean ice cream or a very good key lime pie. Mom and Dad can linger over coffee while the kids watch more cartoons in the lounge. The breakfast menu features traditional items—muffins and bagels, waffles, omelets, eggs Benedict, corned beef hash, and so on.

2. LAKE BUENA VISTA AREA

This section is largely comprised of notable restaurants at Disney resorts and other area accommodations. Since most of these are gorgeous properties, they're fun to visit. Before or after your meal, take a stroll around the grounds and public areas.

VERY EXPENSIVE

THE BLACK SWAN, Grand Cypress Resort, 1 N. Jacaranda, off FL 535. Tel. 239-1999.
   Cuisine: AMERICAN REGIONAL. **Reservations:** Recommended. **Parking:** Free self-parking, validated valet parking.
$ Prices: Appetizers $7.25–$10.50; main courses $20.95–$29.95. AE, CB, DC, DISC, ER, JCB, MC, V.
   Open: Dinner daily 6–10pm.

Overlooking the magnificent emerald fairways of this posh resort's golf course, the Black Swan has a lodgelike, split-level interior with a big working fireplace (don't worry if it's hot outside, there's air conditioning) and a cross-beamed knotty-pine cathedral ceiling. Large, pine-framed windows overlook the ninth hole, and that verdant view is echoed by lovely floral arrangements and planters of greenery. Golfers make up the majority of the clientele. It's not unusual here to see someone rise up excitedly from a table and demonstrate how he eagled the 17th and birdied the 18th hole to win a match. Barring that, dinner entertainment consists of a pianist at a white baby grand.

   Hearty portions are presented on large white Villeroy & Boch platters—veritable canvases for the chef's aesthetically exquisite arrangements. For instance, a red and white ravioli appetizer (one side of the ravioli pocket is egg pasta, the other tomato pasta) stuffed with lump crabmeat and Boursin cheese, is served atop asparagus cream sauce to which thin asparagus spears add an elegant design element while chopped red and yellow peppers add tang and color. And a consommé of lobster with black truffles is beautifully garnished with lobster caviar and decorative gold leaf. Fresh buffalo mozzarella layered with five baby field greens, thinly sliced onions, and plum tomatoes drizzled with pesto vinaigrette makes an excellent salad course. The menu changes seasonally. On my last visit I selected an entrée of sautéed jumbo prawns served with a bouquetière of six fresh steamed vegetables and key lime pasta in a citrusy cilantro-flavored vinaigrette garnished with diced avocado and tomato. A friend's roast rack of lamb (thick, juicy slices grilled in a coating of honey mustard and crushed pecans) was also noteworthy. Whatever you eat, save room for the Swan's superb desserts such as a warm, crisp apple tart on caramel sauce topped with honey-vanilla ice cream and whipped cream. There's an extensive wine list, and dessert libations (cognacs, ports, etc.) are featured. *Note:* Park your car at the main entrance to the adjacent Hyatt Regency Grand Cypress, 1 Grand Cypress Blvd., off FL 535; a complimentary van will take you from there to the restaurant.

VICTORIA & ALBERT'S, Disney's Grand Floridian Beach Resort, 4401 Floridian Way. Tel. 824-2383.

Cuisine: AMERICAN REGIONAL WITH INTERNATIONAL IN-FLUENCES. **Reservations:** Required. **Parking:** Free self-parking, validated valet parking.

$ Prices: Prix-fixe meal $80 per person, $25 additional for Royal Wine Pairing. AE, MC, V.

Open: Two dinner seatings daily, 6–6:45pm and 9–9:45pm.

It's not often one describes a dining experience as flawless, but at Victoria & Albert's, the World's most elite restaurant (Walt Disney World, that is), I experienced nothing less than idyllic perfection. The intimate dining room is plushly furnished and girded by a circular colonnade. Brocaded walls are hung with gilt-framed ink drawings, and an exquisite floral arrangement—above which a chinoiserie chandelier is suspended from a beautifully painted dome—serves as an aesthetic centerpoint. Diners sit in leather-upholstered Louis XIII–style chairs at tables lit by silver-shaded Victorian lamps and exquisitely appointed with Royal Doulton china, Sambonet silver from Italy, and Schott-Zweisel crystal from Germany. A maid and butler provide deft and gracious service, and a harpist playing softly while you dine enhances the celestial ambience.

Dinner, a seven-course affair, is described in a personalized menu sealed with a gold wax insignia. The fare changes nightly. On a recent visit, I began with an hors d'oeuvre of Florida lobster tail with aïoli on mitzuma lettuce. It was supplanted by a more formal appetizer—vermouth-poached jumbo sea scallops served in a crisp rice-noodle basket on shallot-chive sauce with garnishes of flying fish caviar and Chinese tat soi leaves. A shot of peppered vodka added piquancy to a velvety plum tomato bisque sprinkled with smoked bacon and lightly topped with pesto cream sauce. For an entrée I selected a fan of pinkly juicy sautéed Peking duck breast with wild rice and crabapple chutney. A salad of esoteric greens in an orange sherry vinaigrette cleared the palate for the next course—English Stilton served with pine-nut bread, port wine, and a pear poached in burgundy, cognac, and cinnamon sugar. The conclusion: a sumptuous hazelnut and Frangelico soufflé, followed by coffee and chocolate truffles. This is a highly nuanced cuisine to be slowly savored. There is, of course, an extensive *recherché* wine list. I suggest you opt for the Royal Wine Pairing, which provides an appropriate wine with each course and lets you sample a variety of selections from the restaurant's distinguished cellars. Jackets are required for men, and smoking is not permitted.

EXPENSIVE

ARIEL'S, Disney's Beach Club Resort, 1800 Epcot Resorts Blvd. Tel. 934-3357.
   Cuisine: SEAFOOD. **Reservations:** Recommended. **Parking:** Free self- and valet parking.
$ Prices: Appetizers $4.25–$8.95; main courses mostly $17.95–$24. AE, MC, V.
   Open: Dinner daily 6–10pm.

Named for the *Little Mermaid* character, this exquisite restaurant overlooking Stormalong Bay is awash in seafoam green, peach, and coral. White-linened tables, lit by shaded lamps, are elegantly appointed with fish and seashell–motif china; a prismed 2,000-gallon coral-reef tank is filled with tropical fish; walls are hung with oil paintings of scenes from the movie; and whimsical fish mobiles and glass bubbles dangle from a vaulted ceiling. You'll feel like you're dining in an underwater kingdom.

Appetizers (which supplement a complimentary smoked clam dip) include scrumptious New England silver dollar crabcakes served with a spicy tartar sauce. And a Cajun-style shellfish gumbo is replete with chunks of shrimp, lobster, and smoky andouille sausage. For your entrée, a traditional Spanish paella—an array of fresh lobster, scallops, mussels, calamari, and shrimp inside a ring of saffroned rice—is highly recommended. Also excellent: Maine lobster sautéed with shiitake mushrooms, lemon, and garlic and served atop a nest of tricolor angelhair pasta with two sauces—a buttery lobster sauce (sauce américaine) and herbed cream sauce. A few non-seafood options are offered as well, among them USDA choice New York strip steak grilled over a hickory and oak fire and oven-roasted boneless game hen stuffed with wild rice and lentils served with a light pesto sauce. Desserts include a rich Chambord raspberry chocolate cake, and an extensive award-winning wine list indicates which selections best complement your entrée. A children's menu lists items like chicken nuggets and spaghetti with meat sauce in the $4 to $6 range.

HEMINGWAY'S, Hyatt Regency Grand Cypress, 1 Grand Cypress Blvd., off FL 535. Tel. 239-1234.
   Cuisine: FLORIDA SEAFOOD. **Reservations:** Recommended. **Parking:** Free self- and validated valet parking.

$ Prices: Appetizers $6.25–$7.50 at lunch, $6.50–$8.75 at dinner; main courses $7.25–$16.75 at lunch, $17.75–$23.50 at dinner. AE, CB, DC, DISC, ER, JCB, MC, V.

Open: Lunch Tues–Sat 11:30am–2:30pm; dinner daily 6:30–10pm.

Fronted by a waterfall that cascades into stone-bedded streams, Hemingway's evokes Key West and honors its most famous denizen. Waiters are dressed as beachboys and walls are hung with sepia photographs of Papa in Key West and his fishing and hunting trophies. A warren of intimate dining areas under a high weathered-pine ceiling have oak-framed glass doors, making for an outdoorsy feeling. The restaurant is decorated in muted greens, with comfortable upholstered bamboo and rattan furnishings. Elegantly appointed tables are adorned with orchids and lit by gleaming brass hurricane lamps; fans whirr lazily overhead; and glossy oak floors are strewn with Persian rugs. Weather permitting, you can sit on a screened wooden deck near the waterfall. Or, if you have a party of six to eight people, reserve a private open-air dining room. It's lovely.

Ask not for whom the bell tolls but rather for an appetizer of deep-fried baby squid and grilled eggplant in garlicky herb-seasoned tomato coulis. Or begin with skewers of grilled chicken breast served with artichokes, julienned tomatoes, and an aïoli cilantro sauce. Among the entrées, golden brown beer-battered coconut shrimp is served with roast potatoes, a colorful array of al dente vegetables (zucchini, carrots, corn, and red and green peppers sautéed with onions, garlic, and herbs), and orange marmalade–horseradish sauce. And crabcakes (made with jumbo lump crabmeat) are deliciously light, moist, and fluffy, perkily nuanced with Tabasco. Ask for Cajun tartar sauce with them. For dessert key lime pie appropriately reaches its apogee here, though the apple strudel—studded with raisins and walnuts and topped with vanilla cream sauce and Häagen-Dazs—is equally ambrosial. Order both and share. The lunch menu offers some marvelous seafood sandwiches and salads. In the adjoining Hurricane Lounge—a most congenial setting with a beautiful oak bar—specialties include a variety of island rums and the Papa Doble, a potent tropical rum and fruit libation invented by Hemingway himself (legend has it he once drank 16 of them at one sitting!).

JW's STEAKHOUSE, Marriott's Orlando World Center, 8701 World Center Dr. Tel. 238-8829.

Cuisine: STEAK/SEAFOOD. **Reservations:** Recommended.

Parking: Free self-parking and validated valet parking.

$ Prices: Breakfast fare $1.95–$9.95. Appetizers $3.95–$6.95 at lunch, $8.75–$9.95 at dinner; main courses $6.95–$10.95 at lunch, mostly $17.25–$28 at dinner. AE, CB, DC, DISC, ER, JCB, MC, Optima, V.

I always think golf-course restaurants have a uniquely simpatico ambience, and this one is especially alluring. Its woodsy, plant-filled interior, under a 30-foot cathedral pine ceiling, has grass-green carpeting and teak-shuttered windows. But the view here is too gorgeous to be glimpsed through windows. Weather permitting, sit outside on the screened and awninged balcony overlooking a duck-filled lagoon spanned by graceful arched bridges and verdant golf greens framed by pines, palms, and magnolias. Seating is in comfortable upholstered garden furnishings, and cooling fans whirr slowly overhead.

JW's is an especially lovely venue for al fresco breakfasts, whether you opt for a fresh-baked bran muffin and coffee or a heartier morning meal—perhaps an 8-ounce grilled New York strip steak with eggs and home-fries. Lunch choices include sandwiches, chili, and salads (I like the baby shrimp and rotini pasta tossed with cucumbers, green peppers, and mandarin oranges and served in Armenian lavash bread). And a typical dinner here might consist of an appetizer of traditional baked onion soup au gratin, followed by a juicy steak, lamb chops, or grilled Pacific Northwest salmon filet. Entrées include stuffed baked potato, Caesar salad, and warm sourdough bread. Portions are immense, but save room for dessert—a screaming double-double (chunks of macadamia-nut brownie topped with vanilla Häagen-Dazs, chocolate and raspberry syrup, and whipped cream). There's a full bar and an extensive wine list.

MIKADO JAPANESE STEAK HOUSE, Marriott's Orlando World Center, 8701 World Center Dr., off FL 536. Tel. 238-8664.

Cuisine: JAPANESE TEPPANYAKI. **Reservations:** Recommended. **Parking:** Free self-parking and validated valet parking.

$ Prices: Appetizers $4.50–$6.95; main courses $12.95–$28.95. **Open:** Dinner daily 6–10pm.

This gorgeous 230-acre resort houses a beautiful teppanyaki restaurant traditionally constructed by Japanese craftsmen. Its serene interior, with intimate seating areas created by shoji screens, has glossy parquet floors, a sloped beamed ceiling, beautifully paneled skylit pagoda areas, and windows overlooking rock gardens, reflecting pools, and a palm-fringed pond. Japanese music helps set the tone. Plan to arrive early and enjoy a preprandial cocktail at sunset on the wooden deck overlooking the swimming pool.

Meals here are teppanyaki style—which means you're seated with other patrons at a grill-topped table. A highly trained chef wheels a cart full of raw food to the table and with samurailike dexterity trims, chops, sautés, and flips it onto your waiting plate. It's a dazzling display, and the chefs are not only nimble-fingered but entertaining. Appetizer selections include softshell crab, smoked salmon and cucumber sushi, and assorted tempura vegetables and shrimp. Entrées offer various combinations of steak (New York sirloin or filet mignon), shrimp, scallops, lobster, chicken, and fresh fish. They include a complimentary hors d'oeuvre of grilled shrimp or scallops, soup (select the tastier miso), a salad with sesame or ginger dressing, steamed rice (yummy fried rice is available for an additional $1.95), vegetables (onions, zucchini, and mushrooms stir-fried with sesame and spices), and green tea. A decanter of warm sake is recommended. And green tea or ginger ice cream makes a refreshing dessert. Low-priced meals are available for children.

YACHTSMAN STEAKHOUSE, Disney's Yacht Club Resort, 1700 Epcot Resorts Blvd. Tel. 934-3415.

Cuisine: STEAK. **Reservations:** Recommended. **Parking:** Free self- and valet parking.

$ Prices: Appetizers $6.95–$10.95; main courses $16.95–$25.50. AE, MC, V.

Open: Dinner daily 6–10pm.

The Yacht Club, a gorgeous resort inspired by New England's grand turn-of-the-century summer mansions, houses a fittingly elegant signature restaurant. Lacquered knotty-pine beams, paneling, and plank flooring create a warm woody feel that is enhanced by burgundy leather-upholstered oak chairs. And shaded lamps cast a soft glow on beautifully appointed tables. USDA grain-fed beef—hand selected to ensure top marbling for natural juices and tenderness—is aged, cured, cut, and ground on the premises. You can see these prime cuts on display in a glass-enclosed beef-aging room, and an exhibition kitchen provides a tantalizing glimpse of sizzling steaks, chops, and seafood being grilled over oak and hickory.

You might begin your meal here with an appetizer of smoked salmon with Grand Marnier caper dressing or garlicky escargots marinated in dry vermouth and served en croûte with rich burgundy sauce. A salad course (perhaps a classic Caesar tossed tableside) is recommended. Beef entrées—such as succulent filet mignon (available in 6- or 10-ounce servings), slow-roasted prime rib of beef au jus, an 18-ounce Kansas City strip steak served on the bone (it's a cattle drive tradition), or a filet mignon and crabmeat-stuffed lobster combination—are served with baked potato, a board of fresh-baked bread, and a choice of béarnaise or bordelaise sauces. Other dishes run the gamut from lamb chops with apple mint butter and rosemary gin sauce to crisp-grilled chicken in apricot brandy sauce, both accompanied by savory rice. Side dishes, such as a skillet of fresh mushrooms sautéed in cognac and creamed spinach, are noteworthy. And if you have room for dessert, selections include a chocolate mousse cake spiked with Jack Daniels and, for the truly intrepid, a brownie fudge sundae. An extensive wine list is available, and a children's menu offers full meals for $3.75 to $6.50.

MODERATE

PEBBLES, 12551 FL 535 in the Crossroads Shopping Center, in Lake Buena Vista. Tel. 827-1111.

Cuisine: CALIFORNIA-STYLE AMERICAN. **Reservations:** Not accepted. **Parking:** Free self-parking.

$ Prices: Appetizers mostly $3.95–$5.95; sandwiches and salads

$4.95–$8.50; main courses $9.95–$19.95. AE, CB, DC, DISC, MC, V.

Open: Daily 11am–1am.

Plant-filled and oak-paneled, Pebbles is one of Orlando's most popular restaurants. The multilevel dining room centers on a sunken bar under a cross-beamed skylight ceiling, and though it's a large space, white wooden shutters and windowed enclosures create a warren of intimate dining areas. Lush tropical greenery, fountains, statues of water birds, and canvas tenting contribute to the garden-party ambience. During the day, sunshine streams in through numerous windows; at night flickering hurricane lamps provide romantic lighting. Weather permitting, you can dine at umbrella tables on an outdoor deck overlooking Lake Buena Vista. During busy seasons a guitar soloist entertains at dinner; otherwise, the background music is light jazz.

The same menu is offered throughout the day, enhanced by lunch and dinner specials. Start off with a "lite bite" of creamy baked chèvre served atop chunky tomato sauce with hot garlic bread. Pebbles offers the option of a casual meal—perhaps a Cheddar burger on toasted brioche, honey-roasted spareribs, or a Caesar salad tossed with grilled chicken. Or you can select a more serious entrée such as tender leg of smoked duck that has been rubbed with fennel, glazed with triple sec, and slow roasted to sear in flavorful juices. It's served atop a bed of angelhair pasta tossed with Asian peppers and spices. Also excellent is rack of lamb baked in a coating of chèvre, Dijon mustard, and rosemary-flavored breadcrumbs and served with roasted potatoes and an array of vegetables baked with asiago dill cheese. Dessert of choice: the gold brick sundae—a scoop of vanilla ice cream encased in a candylike chocolate/almond shell and served atop caramel sauce with fresh strawberries. There's a full bar, and many premium wines are offered by the glass.

INEXPENSIVE

BOATWRIGHT'S DINING HALL, Disney's Dixie Landings Resort, 1251 Dixie Dr., off Bonnet Creek Pkwy. Tel. 934-5000.

Cuisine: CAJUN. **Reservations:** Recommended at dinner. **Parking:** Free self-parking.

$ Prices: Breakfast items $3.50–$6.95; appetizers $3.95–$7.95; main courses $9.25–$14.95; sandwiches $6.25. AE, MC, V.

Open: Breakfast daily 7–11:30am; dinner daily 5–10pm.

Boatwright's is themed to look like an 1800s boat-building factory, complete with the wooden hull of a Louisiana lugger (fishing boat) suspended from its lofty beamed ceiling. An untypically pretty factory, it has oak plank floors, peach stucco walls hung with antique boat-building tools, and two large working brick fireplaces. Wooden toolboxes on the bare oak tables contain a salt shaker that doubles as a level, a wood-clamp sugar dispenser, a pepper-grinder-cum-ruler, a jar of unmatched utensils, shop rags (to be used as napkins), and a little metal pail of crayons for the kids.

Cajun breakfasts offer intriguing possibilities. French toast here is made with sourdough-sweet potato baguette tossed in rich egg custard, deep-fried, and coated with cinnamon sugar. Another option: a pan of sautéed crawfish, mushrooms, green onions, and tomatoes in mustard cream sauce (served with home-style potatoes topped with two basted eggs, meat sauce, and an oven-fresh buttermilk biscuit). At dinner, appetizer selections include deep-fried bacon-wrapped oysters and scallops and roasted baby back ribs with stone-ground honey-mustard sauce, served on a mound of onion straws. Among your entrée choices are rich bouillabaisse redolent of oaken cognac and a blackened seafood dish (shrimp, scallops, and bayou catfish served over brown-buttered pasta in creamy garlic sauce), both served with salad and oven-fresh pumpernickel and sweet-potato bread. For dessert: homemade fruit cobblers topped with vanilla ice cream and smothered in whipped cream.

BONFAMILLE'S CAFE, Disney's Port Orleans Resort, 2201 Orleans Dr., off Bonnet Creek Pkwy. Tel. 934-5000.

   Cuisine: CREOLE. **Reservations:** Recommended at dinner.
   Parking: Free self-parking.
$ Prices: Breakfast items $3.50–$6.95; appetizers $4.95–$7.95; main courses mostly $8.25–$11.25; salads and po'boy sandwiches $3.95–$6.95. AE, MC, V.
   Open: Breakfast daily 7–11:30am; dinner daily 5–10pm.

Named for a character in *The Aristocats,* the charming Bonfamille's is patterned after a fountained French Quarter courtyard. Exposed-brick walls are hung with paintings of New Orleans, lighting emanates from fan/globe fixtures, big baskets of flowering plants are suspended from beams overhead, and Dixieland jazz plays softly in the background. During breakfast it's light and sunny, and evenings, candle lamps provide soft lighting.

Louisiana-style breakfasts range from fresh hot beignets and café au lait to a skillet of crawfish and andouille sausage in zesty Créole sauce and melted sharp Cheddar. The latter is served with home-style fried potatoes topped with basted eggs and a hot buttermilk biscuit. Pancakes stuffed with blueberries and drenched in pecan honey butter are another possibility. A typical dinner here: an appetizer of chilled shrimp and crawfish served with rémoulade sauce, followed by a spicy kebab of grilled seafood and vegetables on a bed of pecan rice, and a dessert of Bourbon Street pudding topped with strawberry and caramel bourbon sauces. After dinner, head over to the hotel's Scat Cats Lounge where family entertainment—sing-alongs and live music with lots of audience participation—is featured Thursday to Monday evenings through midnight.

CAPE MAY CAFE, Disney's Beach Club Resort, 1800 Epcot Resorts Blvd. Tel. 934-3415.

Cuisine: CLAMBAKE BUFFET. **Reservations:** Not accepted. **Parking:** Free self- and valet parking.

$ Prices: Adults $16.95, ages 6–11 $8.95, under 6 free. Lobster is additional. AE, MC, V.

Open: Dinner daily 5:30–9:30pm.

A hearty 19th-century-style New England clambake is featured nightly at this charming peach and seafoam-green restaurant, where sand sculptures, paintings of turn-of-the-century beach scenes, croquet mallets, and furled striped beach umbrellas evoke an upscale seaside resort. Diners sit in oversized chairs at birchwood tables. Large towel napkins are provided. Aromatic stews and chowders, steamed clams and mussels, corn on the cob, chicken, lobster, and redskin potatoes are cooked up in a crackling rockweed steamer pit that serves as the restaurant's centerpiece. And these traditional clambake offerings are supplemented by dozens of salads (pasta, seafood, fruit, vegetables), hot entrées (barbecued baby back ribs, smoked sausage, fried chicken, pasta dishes), and a wide array of oven-fresh breads and desserts. There's a full bar.

3. INTERNATIONAL DRIVE AREA

Some of the best area restaurants are along International Drive within about 10 minutes of Walt Disney World parks by car.

EXPENSIVE

DUX, Peabody Orlando Hotel, 9801 International Dr. Tel. 345-4550.

Cuisine: AMERICAN REGIONAL. **Reservations:** Recommended. **Parking:** Free self-parking, validated valet parking.

$ Prices: Appetizers $5.50–$5.95 at lunch, $7.50–$13.25 at dinner; main courses $8.75–$12.50 at lunch, $22–$28.50 at dinner. AE, CB, DC, DISC, ER, JCB, MC, Optima, V.

Open: Dinner Mon–Sat 6–11pm.

Named for the hotel's signature ducks that parade ceremoniously into the lobby each morning to Sousa's *King Cotton* march, this is one of central Florida's most highly acclaimed restaurants. And since the Peabody is the headquarters hotel for nearby Universal Studios, you're likely to see a celebrity or two among the diners. The deluxe Dux is decorated in shimmery hues of rust and gold, soft lighting emanates from amber-shaded sconces, and textured gold walls are hung with ornately framed mirrors and watercolors representing 72 ducks! Diners are comfortably ensconced in upholstered bamboo chairs and cushioned banquettes at candlelit, white-linened tables set with flowers and beautiful ceramic show plates. A lavish dessert display table with a floral centerpiece serves as a visual focus.

Chef Mike McSweeney serves only free-range birds and veal, imports truffles from France and caviar from Russia, and pays local farmers to grow baby vegetables and other produce to his specifications. His menu changes seasonally. At a recent dinner, appetizer selections included a fabulous pastry of sherried lobster meat with sautéed leeks and wild mushrooms wrapped in a phyllo-dough pocket, garnished with lobster slices and caviar, and finished with a buttery basil-white wine coulis. Another stunning choice was grilled Maine sea scallops topped with foie gras and tangy compote (rhubarb, mixed with chopped figs, peppers, and yellow tomatoes) in blackberry/port wine sauce. Also worthy of mention was a velvety Pernod-laced lobster bisque garnished with crème fraîche, lobster caviar, and finely shredded roasted beets. An entrée of mesquite-grilled Gulf Coast snapper was served with applewood-roasted corn salsa, slices of grilled balsamic-marinated Chinese eggplant, and puréed Washington cherries in a red Zinfandel sauce. Another of baked Atlantic salmon came wrapped in a crispy grated-potato crust on a platter arrayed with haricots verts, ragoût of pearl onions, roasted garlic, wild mushrooms, and an edible flower garnish. Dessert was a sublime trilogy of crèmes brûlées—one topped with fresh raspberries and sprigs of mint, a second flavored with coffee beans, and a third with candied ginger. An extensive, award-winning wine list is available.

MODERATE

CAPRICCIO, Peabody Orlando Hotel, 9801 International Dr. Tel. 352-4000.
Cuisine: NORTHERN ITALIAN. **Reservations:** Recommended. **Parking:** Free self-parking, validated valet parking.
$ Prices: Appetizers $4.75–$7.50; main courses $10.50–$22.50 (with most pizza and pasta dishes priced below $12); Sun champagne brunch buffet $24.95 for adults, $12.95 for children 4–12, under 4 free. AE, CB, DC, DISC, ER, JCB, MC, Optima, V.
Open: Dinner Tues–Sun 6–10pm; brunch Sun 11am–2:30pm.

Capriccio's striking Italian *moderne* interior features a gleaming black-and-white-checkerboard marble-tile floor and black Italian marble tables elegantly appointed with Tuscan-look Villeroy & Boch show plates. Brass-trimmed cut-glass dividers frame intimate dining areas, banquettes are flanked by massive Corinthian columns, and large potted ferns add a note of palm court elegance. An exhibition kitchen occupying an entire wall showcases chefs tending mesquite-burning pizza ovens and grills, and a dessert display table is graced by a lavish floral centerpiece.

Talented young chef Mark Mattern's seasonal menus bring verve, imagination, and international scope to traditional northern Italian cooking. On a recent visit I enjoyed appetizers of eggplant Napoleon (mesquite-grilled, balsamic-marinated eggplant layered with goat cheese, sun-dried and Roman tomatoes, and fresh basil on a tangy tomato sauce) and fried calamari served with three *aïolis* (aïoli is a garlicky Basque mayonnaise) flavored, respectively, with sun-dried tomato, basil, and saffron. His superb salads—such as warm quail tossed with seasonal greens, autumn pears, and Gorgonzola cheese in a raspberry vinaigrette—also make an excellent beginning. I adored a pasta dish of *bucatini* (a long, fat, hollow pasta) tossed with chunks of mesquite-grilled chicken and mushrooms in a slightly garlicky herbed white wine/pesto sauce finished with tomato concasse. Listed under pizzas was a haute-cuisine *calzone* (a doughy pocket stuffed with sun-dried tomatoes, ricotta, mozzarella, provolone, sautéed spinach, and fresh pesto, served with fresh marinara sauce). And an entrée of mesquite-grilled mild Italian fennel sausage with caramelized onions, roasted red bell peppers, and fried polenta in a buttery balsamic sauce was divine. The kitchen turns out fabulous oven-fresh breads such as herbed focaccia and *bruschetta* (mesquite-grilled sourdough rubbed with pesto and roasted garlic and topped with mozzarella, pecorino cheese, and Roman tomatoes) accompanied by extra virgin olive oil that has been marinated in rosemary, thyme, and garlic. Dip and exult. But do save room for Capriccio's exquisite desserts, which include the definitive *zuppa inglese* (sponge cake layered with fresh berries, kiwi, and Grand Marnier–spiked whipped cream on raspberry-marbelized crème anglaise with garnishes of chocolate shavings and sprigs of fresh mint). An extensive, award-winning wine list—over 450 labels—is available. Consult your server (they're all very knowledgeable here) for suggestions to complement your meal. *Note:* Capriccio's champagne Sunday brunch is described in "Champagne Sunday Brunch," in "Specialty Dining," below.

MING COURT, 9188 International Dr., between Sand Lake Rd. and Beeline Expy., just across from the Peabody Orlando Hotel. Tel. 351-9988.
   Cuisine: CHINESE REGIONAL. **Reservations:** Recommended. **Parking:** Free self-parking.
$ Prices: Appetizers $4.50–$7.95; dim sum items mostly $1.95–$2.50; main courses $4.50–$7.95 at lunch, mostly $12.50–$18.95 at dinner. AE, CB, DC, DISC, JCB, MC, V.
   Open: Lunch daily 11am–2:30pm; dinner daily 4:30pm–midnight.

I was thrilled to find an Orlando restaurant whose culinary offerings are on a par with the finest Chinese haute cuisine of New York and California. Ming Court is fronted by a serpentine "cloud wall" crowned by engraved sea-green Chinese tiles (it's a celestial symbol; you dine above the clouds here, like the gods). Its candlelit interior is stunningly decorated in soft earth tones (subtle hues of rust, ochre, and tan) with unfinished oak wainscoting. Glass-walled terrace rooms overlook lotus ponds filled with colorful koi, a plant-filled area under a lofty skylight ceiling evokes a starlit Ming dynasty courtyard, and an interior green-roofed gazebo that seats 8 to 10 people is perfect for small private parties. Beautiful Chinese paintings and pottery are on display, and between 7 and 10pm nightly a musician plays classical Chinese music on a *zheng* (a long zither).

The menu offers specialties from diverse regions of China—all of them uniquely spiced and sauced and prepared with the finest ingredients (including fresh Florida fish and seafood). Begin by ordering a variety of appetizers such as wok-charred Mandarin pot stickers, crispy wontons stuffed with vegetables and cream cheese, and wok-smoked shiitake mushrooms topped with sautéed scallions. Entrées will open up new culinary vistas to even the most sophisticated diners. Lightly battered deep-fried chicken breast is served with a delicate lemon-tangerine sauce. Szechuan charcoal-grilled filet mignon, marinated in olive oil and crushed herbs, is topped with a toasted onion/garlic/chili sauce and served with stir-fried julienne vegetables. Lamb chops, topped with finely chopped cantaloupe, arrive atop broad rice noodles in coconut cream/Madras curry sauce studded with pine nuts. And crispy stir-fried jumbo Szechuan shrimp is enhanced by a light fresh tomato sauce nuanced with sake, ginger, chili oil, scallion, garlic, and cilantro. At lunch you can order dim sum items in addition to regular menu offerings. An extensive wine list includes everything from Pouilly-Fuissé to Chinese rice wines, plum wines, and sake. And as a concession to Western palates, Ming Court features sumptuous desserts such as a moist cake layered with mandarin oranges, key lime, and fresh whipped cream in orange-vanilla sauce.

SIAM ORCHID, 7575 Republic Dr., between Sand Lake Rd. and Carrier Dr. Tel. 351-0821.
    Cuisine: THAI. **Reservations:** Recommended. **Parking:** Free self-parking.
$ **Prices:** Appetizers $3.55–$5; main courses $10.25–$18.95. AE, DC, DISC, MC, V.
    Open: Dinner daily 5–11pm.

Patterned after a palace in northern Thailand, Siam Orchid centers on a platform used to display wood carvings of angels and musicians representing figures from the *Ramayana,* an ancient Hindu epic poem. The split-level dining room, with lofty knotty-pine cathedral ceilings on either side, seats diners in cushioned booths and banquettes and bamboo chairs at white-linened tables, some of them overlooking a lake. For intimate dining request a *khun toke*—a private carved teak enclosure that is the Thai answer to Japanese tatami rooms. Walls are hung with Thai art, and Thai music further enhances the ethnic ambience. On your way out, browse in the adjoining shop stocked with lacquerware and wood carvings from Thailand.

Owners Tim and Krissnee Martsching grow many necessary ingredients—fresh chiles, mint, cilantro, lemongrass, and wild lime—in their own garden, and their fare is authentic and delicious. Begin with *tom kha gai* (a savory chicken and mushroom soup flavored with lemon juice, lemongrass, wild ginger, and coconut milk). Continue with shared appetizers such as *satay* (skewered pork or chicken, marinated in coconut cream and mild curry, grilled, and served with hot peanut sauce) or *tod man* (crispy fried chicken patties flavored with lemongrass, basil, and wild lime leaf). Both are served with cucumber salad in a sweet vinaigrette. Not to be missed (share an order) is *pad Thai* (soft rice noodles tossed with ground pork, fresh minced garlic, shrimp, crab claws, crabmeat, crushed peanuts, and bean sprouts in a tangy-sweet sauce). Curries are another specialty. Try the royal Thai replete with chunks of chicken, potato, and onion in a yellow curry sauce or *panang* (tender beef or chicken cooked in red curry sauce with mushrooms, basil leaves, and eggplant). There's a full bar, and beverage choices include sake, plum wine, and Thai beers along with French, German, and American wines. Homemade coconut ice cream topped with crushed peanuts makes a refreshing dessert.

INEXPENSIVE

B-LINE DINER, Peabody Orlando Hotel, 9801 International Dr. Tel. 345-4460.
    Cuisine: AMERICAN. **Reservations:** Not accepted. **Parking:** Free self-parking, validated valet parking.
$ **Prices:** Appetizers $5.50–$8.25; main courses $3.25–$8.25 at breakfast, $6.75–$9.50 at lunch, $7.25–$17.25 at dinner. AE, CB, DC, DISC, ER, JCB, MC, Optima, V.
    Open: Daily 24 hours.

This popular local eatery is of the nouvelle art deco diner genre, which is to say it's an idealized version of America's ubiquitous roadside establishments. A high-gloss peach and gray interior, with black-and-white tile floor, gleams with chrome edging that adorns everything from a cove ceiling to peach Formica tables. Seating is in comfortable leatherette booths or Breuer chairs, windows are shaded by venetian blinds, and a jukebox is stocked with oldies tunes. You can also sit on stools along the sleek black marble-topped counter facing an open kitchen. It's lined with glass-domed cake trays, here filled with duck-shaped cookies. Gorgeous flower arrangements add further upscale panache. Just your average greasy spoon (not!).

    The menu, in the shape of a Wurlitzer jukebox, offers sophisticated versions of diner food such as turkey meatloaf served with smashed potatoes, fresh vegetables, and cranberry relish; spicy Jamaican jerk chicken wings; a ham and cheese sandwich (on baguette); and sautéed pork médaillons with Thai sauce and papaya salsa. Other items—such as grilled tuna with vegetable couscous and red pepper coulis, classic French onion soup, and a felafel sandwich on pita bread—bear no relation to traditional diner fare. Portions are hearty. You may notice a glass display case of scrumptious fresh-baked desserts when you come in—everything from banana cream pie to white chocolate/Grand Marnier mousse cake. If you can guess how many ducks are behind a glass wall by the dessert display, you'll win a free piece of cake or pie. The dessert area adjoins **B-Line Express,** a 24-hour take-out counter. There's a full bar. And kids get their own low-priced menu, a duck-themed coloring/activities book, and crayons.

ENZO'S, 7600 Dr. Phillips Blvd., in the Marketplace Shopping Center, off Sand Lake Rd. just west of I-4. Tel. 351-1187.

Cuisine: ITALIAN. **Reservations:** Not accepted. **Parking:** Free self-parking.

$ Prices: Appetizers $3.95–$5.95 at lunch, $4.50–$6.50 at dinner; panini (sandwiches) $4.75–$5.95; main courses $4.50–$6.95 at lunch, $8.50–$12.75 at dinner. AE, CB, DC, DISC, MC, V.

Open: Mon–Thurs 11:30am–10pm, Fri–Sat 11:30am–11pm, Sun 4:30–10pm.

Upon entering this charming little restaurant-cum-Italian charcuterie, you'll walk past display cases filled with olives, antipasti, deli meats, pâtés, and cheeses and shelves stocked with homemade pastas, virgin olive oils, jars of sun-dried tomatoes, and other fancy foodstuffs. And if that's not enough to whet your appetite, you'll also glimpse chefs tending a pizza oven in an exhibition kitchen. The dining area is cheerful and inviting, with glossy pine-plank floors, peach walls hung with fine art prints, and tables covered with red-and-white-striped oilcloth. There's also counter seating; Enzo's is a casual kind of place. Café-curtained windows and large plants in terra-cotta pots enhance the simpatico atmosphere, as do Italian music (most of it operatic arias) and exuberant Italian waiters.

Pretty much the same menu is available throughout the day, offering a variety of dining experiences. Families troop in for pizzas—either the traditional American kind or Napoli pies with more sophisticated toppings (perhaps crushed tomatoes, mozzarella, and shiitake mushrooms) and crisp, delicate crusts. Until 4:30pm, you can also opt for *panini* (sandwiches on crusty Italian bread) with fillings such as Italian sausage, grilled onions, and peppers; they're served with potato salad. A more serious dinner might begin with an appetizer of paper-thin slices of Norwegian salmon and onion served with extra virgin olive oil, capers, lemon, and red peppers. Homemade pastas include *bucatini* (thick, hollow pasta) tossed with mushrooms, fresh-grated Parmesan, prosciutto, bacon, and peas in a robust sauce. And Enzo's most fabulous entrée is *pollo alla cecco* (roasted breast of free-range chicken with rosemary potatoes roasted with the skins and a ratatouillelike mixture of crushed tomatoes, diced zucchini and eggplant, onions, and peppers in herbed olive oil). Beer and wine are available. For dessert try *zuccotto* (Italian sponge cake soaked in Grand Marnier, layered with fresh fruit and crème anglaise, and topped with chocolate shavings). In busy seasons, arrive off-hours to avoid a wait.

4. CASSELBERRY/ORLANDO

Generally, people visiting this area don't drive 40 minutes to downtown Orlando or Casselberry to eat. Buckets, however, is close to major sightseeing attractions in Orlando. Rolando, in Casselberry, is for those of you who want to experience authentic Cuban cuisine while you're in Florida.

For further Orlando eateries, check out the Church Street Station listing in Chapter 9.

INEXPENSIVE

BUCKETS, 1825 N. Mills Ave., just across the street from Loch Haven Park museums. Tel. 894-5197.
   Cuisine: AMERICAN. **Reservations:** Recommended (required Friday/Saturday nights).
$ Prices: Appetizers $4.95–$6.95; main courses $4.95–$10.95 at lunch, $8.95–$17.95 at dinner. Sun brunch $14.95. AE, DC, DISC, MC, V.
   Open: Breakfast Mon–Fri 7am–10am, Sat–Sun 7am–11pm; lunch/brunch daily 11am–4pm; dinner Sun–Thurs 4–10pm, Fri–Sat 4–11pm; late-night menu Sun–Thurs till midnight, Fri–Sat till 1am.

This is a great choice when you're visiting Orlando sights such as Leu Gardens and Loch Haven Park museums. Its attractive interior has white stucco walls hung with photographs of a wine cellar, a teak ceiling, and big teak-framed windows overlooking Lake Rowena. There's additional lake-view seating on an open-air deck under a canvas awning. At dinner, there's live entertainment—light jazz or acoustical guitar.

Lunch items include salads (such as pasta and veggies or chicken Caesar topped with asiago cheese and almonds), sandwiches (such as smoked turkey breast with mozzarella cheese and tomato salsa), and hot entrées ranging from blackened catch of the day to stir-fried chicken with fresh vegetables and yellow rice tossed with walnuts. At dinner you might follow up an appetizer of baked seafood-stuffed mushrooms or fried calamari with baked tortellini in homemade marinara sauce, shrimp scampi served over pasta, jumbo lump crabcakes, barbecued ribs, or grilled filet mignon. Sunday brunch is a $14.95 prix-fixe meal including an appetizer, entrée, and unlimited champagne or mimosas. There's a full bar and an extensive wine list.

ROLANDO'S, 870 E. FL 436 (Semoran Blvd.), between Red Bug Rd. and U.S. 17-92, in Casselberry. Tel. 767-9677.
   Cuisine: CUBAN. **Reservations:** Not accepted. **Parking:** Free self-parking. **Directions:** Take I-4 east to the East-West Expy., head east, and make a left on FL 436.

$ Prices: Appetizers 85¢–$1.75; main courses $3.75–$4.75 at lunch, mostly $5.75–$11.50 at dinner. AE, DISC, MC, V.
Open: Tues–Thurs 11am–9:15pm, Fri–Sat 11am–10:15pm, Sun 1–8:15pm.

About 40 minutes from Walt Disney World, this inexpensive mom-and-pop eatery—run by Rolando and Maria Vieitez with daughters Mirtha and Maritza—serves up huge portions of totally authentic Cuban fare. Its two dining rooms are pleasant but plain, with Formica tables, stucco walls hung with photographs of Cuba, and pots of philodendrons suspended from the ceiling. Soft lighting adds a bit of ambience.

I recommend ordering up a bunch of appetizers to share: deep-fried ripe plantains, *papas rellenas*—breaded deep-fried balls of mashed potato stuffed with spicy *picadillos* (garlicky ground beef cooked with onions, olives, raisins, and green peppers in a tomato sauce)—flavorful Cuban tamales topped with picadillos, and slightly sweet batter-fried corn fritters that are light as air. An entrée of roast chicken is brushed with crushed garlic, white wine vinegar, cumin, and oregano and briefly deep-fried just before serving. And tender shredded beef is simmered in a richly seasoned tomato-based sauce with potatoes, olives, peas, pimentos, onions, green peppers, and sweet red peppers. Entrées are served with fresh-baked hot Cuban bread and butter, house salad, rice, and plantains or *yuca* (a chewy root plant). Take the plantains. You might additionally consider an order of black bean soup. For dessert try the *dulce de tres leche* (a meringue-topped yellow cake mixed with condensed milk, evaporated milk, and cream). At lunch a hearty sandwich of hot Cuban bread stuffed with slices of ham, roast pork, Swiss cheese, and pickles is served with black bean soup. Beer and wine are available.

5. SPECIALTY DINING

MEALS WITH DISNEY CHARACTERS

Especially for the 10-and-under set, it's a thrill to dine in a restaurant where costumed Disney characters show up to greet the customers, sign autographs, pose in family photos, and interact with little kids. And for adults, it's lots of fun to watch the kids going nuts over Mickey or Donald. The following restaurants throughout the Walt Disney World complex offer character breakfasts and dinners. All accept American Express, MasterCard, and Visa.

The delightful New England–themed **Cape May Cafe,** at Disney's Beach Club Resort, 1800 Epcot Resorts Blvd. (tel. 934-3415), serves lavish buffet character breakfasts daily from 7:30 to 11am. Food tables are laden with quiches, waffles, hot and cold cereals, egg dishes, roast beef hash, bread pudding, fruit fritters, cheese blintzes, bacon and cheese crêpes, biscuits with sausage gravy, fresh-baked pastries and muffins, and many other goodies. Admiral

Goofy and his crew—Chip 'n' Dale and Pluto—(characters may vary) are hosts. Adults pay $12.95, children 3 to 11 pay $7.95, under 3 free. Reservations are not accepted; arrive early to avoid a wait.

At the very attractive **Chef Mickey's** in Walt Disney World Village (tel. 828-3900), Mickey is on hand to greet dinner patrons each night from 5 to 10pm. Reservations are suggested; however, only 20% of tables are alloted via reservations, with the rest reserved for walk-ins. On the other hand, you can reserve up to 30 days in advance. Walk-ins should arrive early to avoid a wait. This is an especially appealing choice, since there's first-rate food for adults, and the menu also offers burgers, chicken bits, and other kid pleasers in the $3.25 to $3.75 range. See full listing above.

The **Contemporary Cafe,** at Disney's Contemporary Resort, 4600 N. World Dr. (tel. 824-1000), replicates an indoor formal garden with faux topiary, trelliswork, planter dividers, and tables under bright yellow canvas umbrellas. It is the setting for buffet character breakfasts from 8 to 11am daily. On hand to meet, greet, and mingle with guests are Goofy, Pluto, Chip 'n' Dale, Tigger, and Prince John (from *Robin Hood*). The prix-fixe buffet ($12.95 for adults, $7.95 for children 3 to 11, under 3 free) features a wide array of breakfast foods—eggs, potatoes, French toast, pancakes, bacon and sausage, apple cobbler, bread pudding, and much more. Reservations are not accepted; arrive early to avoid a wait.

Five opulently Victorian dining rooms aboard the *Empress Lilly* (tel. 828-3900)—a plushly furnished triple-decker paddlewheeler docked on Lake Buena Vista in Walt Disney World Village—are used for morning character breakfasts. There are two seatings daily at 8:30am and 10am (arrive at least 20 minutes ahead of time). A prix-fixe menu ($10.95 for adults, $7.95 for children 3 to 9, under 3 free), features sausage and eggs and a Mickey-shaped waffle. Donald, Mickey, Minnie, and Pluto are on hand to greet the guests, and Disney movie music and friendly waiters enhance the party atmosphere. The restaurant is amenable to menu substitutions for fussy kids, and adults who want a lighter meal can also ask for a fruit and yogurt plate. Reservations are essential, and can be made anytime in advance; do so as soon as you decide the dates of your trip.

The plant-filled **Garden Grove Cafe,** at the Walt Disney World Swan, 1200 Epcot Resorts Blvd. (tel. 934-3000), is an airy three-story domed greenhouse with festive striped canvas awnings, colorful wooden birds perched overhead, and a central terra-cotta fountain. It is the setting for character breakfasts Wednesday and Saturday from 8 to 11am and dinners Thursday from 6 to 10pm. Breakfast offers a choice of à la carte or buffet meals (the latter is $11.95 for adults, $6.95 for children 4 to 12, 3 and under free). Dinner is à la carte, featuring steak and seafood. Character meals here are hosted by Goofy, Pluto, Pooh, and Tigger. Reservations suggested.

Luau Cove, at Disney's Polynesian Resort, 1600 Seven Seas Dr. (tel. W-DISNEY), is the setting for an island-themed character show called **Mickey's Tropical Luau** daily at 4:30pm. It's an abbreviated version of the Polynesian Luau Dinner Show described in Chapter 9,

"Orlando Nights," featuring Polynesian dancers along with Mickey, Minnie, Pluto, and Goofy. Your prix-fixe meal ($28 for adults, $21.50 for ages 12 to 20, $12.50 for ages 3 to 11, under 3 free) includes tropical fruit salad, a trio of entrées (seafood stir-fry, barbecued ribs, and teriyaki chicken), rice, coconut-almond bread with mandarin-orange butter, and a Disney character ice-cream bar. Guests are presented with shell leis on entering. Reserve far in advance.

The Polynesian also hosts **Minnie's Menehune Character Breakfast** buffets (tel. 824-1391) daily from 7:30 to 10:30am in the French Polynesian–themed **Papeete Bay Verandah**. A wide selection of hot and cold breakfast foods is featured—omelets, French toast, biscuits, cereals, fresh-baked pastries, fresh fruits and more. Adults pay $12.95, children 3 to 11 pay $7.95, under 3 free. Minnie, Goofy, and Chip 'n' Dale appear. Reservations are essential.

Disney's exquisitely elegant Grand Floridian Beach Resort, 4001 Grand Floridian Way (tel. 824-2383), hosts character meals in its festive exposition-themed restaurant, **1900 Park Fare.** The room is decorated with old-fashioned carved wooden merry-go-round animals, colorful flags and banners, antique toys, and circus-themed paintings. Big Bertha—a French band organ that plays pipes, drums, bells, cymbals, castenets, and xylophone—provides music. Mary Poppins, Winnie the Pooh, Goofy, Pluto, Chip 'n' Dale, and Minnie Mouse appear at elaborate buffet breakfasts served daily between 7:30am and noon. An assortment of fresh fruits, breakfast meats, egg dishes, home fries, pancakes, French toast, waffles, fresh-baked pastries and muffins, bagels and cream cheese, hot and cold cereals, cheese blintzes, and fruit cobblers, are featured. Adults pay $14.95, children 3 to 11 pay $9.75, under 3 free.

Mickey and Minnie appear at nightly buffets (featuring prime rib, stuffed pork loin, fresh fish, and more) from 5 to 9pm. Adults pay $17.95, children 3 to 11 pay $9.75, under 3 free. Reservations are essential for both meals.

The lively Venetian festival–themed **Ristorante Carnevale,** at the Walt Disney World Dolphin, 1500 Epcot Resorts Blvd. (tel. 934-4025), is colorfully decorated with masks, balloons, curlicues of ribbon, and Pierrot hats. Floor-to-ceiling windows overlook Crescent Lake. All of this combines to create a simpatico setting for Sunday character brunches served from 8:30am to 12:30pm hosted by Chip 'n' Dale, Goofy, and Pluto. A bountiful buffet runs the gamut from Italian dishes (frittatas, rigatoni primavera, chicken marsala) to traditional brunch fare (waffles, omelets, chocolate-chip pancakes). Adults pay $15.95, children ages 3 to 12 pay $7.95, under 3 free. Reservations suggested.

One of the most popular WDW character breakfasts takes place at the **Soundstage Restaurant** at Disney-MGM Studios, adjacent to the Magic of Disney Animation (tel. 824-4321). Characters from the movie *Aladdin*—the genie, Jafar, and Aladdin or Jasmin—plus Mickey in Moroccan garb, visit tables and sign autographs in this exotic Middle Eastern–motif restaurant adorned with shelves of brass coffee urns and murals of onion-domed mosques. A vast buffet—fresh and dried fruits, breakfast meats, eggs, pastries, muffins and bagels, cereals, waffles, and blintzes—evokes an Arab marketplace, and there's a magic lamp on every table. It takes place daily from 8:30 to 10:30am. Cost is $12.95 for adults, $7.95 for kids 3 to 11, free for kids under 3. Reservations are essential.

The plant-filled **Watercress Café,** at the Buena Vista Palace, 1900 Buena Vista Dr. (tel. 827-2727), has paintings of parrots and flamingos adorning peach stucco walls and large windows overlooking Lake Buena Vista. It's the setting for Sunday morning character breakfasts (8 to 10:30am) featuring Minnie, Goofy, and Pluto. You can order à la carte or buffet meals. The buffet costs $9.75 for adults, $4.95 for kids 4 to 12, under 4 free. Reservations are not accepted; arrive early to avoid a wait.

AFTERNOON TEA

It's worth having afternoon high tea in the **Garden View Lounge** at Disney's Grand Floridian Beach Resort, 4401 Floridian Way (tel. 824-3000), not only because it's a lovely and leisurely custom, but because it provides an opportunity to see this palatial accommodation. Served daily from 3 to 6pm it offers a choice of complete teas such as the Buckingham Palace Tea ($15), which includes your choice of scones with Devonshire cream and preserves, crumpets, tea sandwiches (filled with watercress, tomato, and cucumber and egg), and pastries. Other choices include nut breads, English trifle, and strawberries and cream, and liqueurs and ports are available. The setting is divine. The plushly furnished lounge, decorated in tints of peach and celadon, offers comfortable seating amid potted palms. A wall of Palladian windows overlooks formal gardens. Tea is served at exquisitely appointed marble tables set with English china, and a pianist entertains.

The **Peabody Orlando Hotel,** 9801 International Dr. (tel. 352-4000), hosts a delightful afternoon tea in its gorgeous skylit atrium lobby with seating amid lofty palm trees overlooking a waterfall and fountain. And frolicking in that fountain while you sip your Earl Grey and nibble on scones are the Peabody's five resident ducks. A full tea, priced at $6.50 and served weekdays from 3 to 4:30pm, includes a goodly selection of fine and herbal teas; thin-sliced tea sandwiches filled with smoked salmon, cucumber and watercress, and chicken salad; a scone with Devonshire cream and strawberry preserves; and a fresh-baked pastry.

JAPANESE BREAKFAST

Tired of the same old bacon and eggs? The **Cascade Grill** at the Hyatt Regency Grand Cypress, 1 Grand Cypress Blvd. (tel. 239-1234), offers a traditional Japanese breakfast of miso soup, grilled salmon, steamed rice, seaweed, fresh fruit, and green tea presented on a special tray. Price is $15.25. American breakfasts here are great, too. The menu features items like crabcakes Benedict and Spanish frittatas. And the gardenlike setting is gorgeous. Down a grand spiral staircase, the restaurant centers on an exquisite mermaid-motif fountain sculpture backed by a waterfall, and windows all around overlook Lake Windsong and verdant landscaping. The grill opens at 6:30am.

CHAMPAGNE SUNDAY BRUNCH

Sip unlimited champagne, peruse the papers, and hang out for a couple of hours eating and schmoozing at **Capriccio,** the attractive northern Italian restaurant at the Peabody Orlando Hotel, 9801 International Dr. (tel. 352-4000). It features a lavish champagne brunch buffet from 11am to 2:30pm. Items vary a bit week to week. On my last visit the spread included Italian cold cuts, a variety of tempting salads (couscous, asparagus and ham, pasta, seafood, and more), fruits, cheeses, vegetables, smoked seafood, smoked salmon, seafood terrines, pâtés, peel-and-eat shrimp, a carving station (for steamship of beef with horseradish sauce and leg of lamb with apple mint jelly), waffles, fruit crêpes, Italian sausage, egg dishes (including eggs Benedict, frittatas, and omelets), pasta dishes such as angelhair with pesto and rigatoni marinara, hot entrées such as pan-seared chicken breast with Parmesan polenta and jumbo sea scallops with citrus butter sauce, pizzas (by the slice), a wide array of fresh-baked breakfast breads (muffins, coffee cake, croissants, sticky buns, danish), assorted desserts including tiramisu, zuppa inglese, key lime pie, peanut butter pie, and chestnut cake, and coffee or tea. If you bring the kids (and I always feel long, leisurely meals are more enjoyable without them), they can adjourn to the video-game arcade while you linger. Price is $24.95 for adults, $12.95 for children 4 to 12, under 4 free.

Another exquisite Sunday brunch venue is **La Coquina,** at the Hyatt Regency Grand Cypress, 1 Grand Cypress Blvd. (tel. 239-1234). In this beautiful dining room, with windows all around overlooking the swans and flamingos on Lake Windsong, diners repose at elegantly appointed, flower-bedecked, white-linened tables. Buffet items—alluringly arrayed on French market carts—include pâtés and terrines, smoked fish, raw bar offerings, a vast selection of cheeses, cold soups (perhaps creamy burgundy apple), cold cuts, bagels and cream cheese, wooden baskets filled with fresh-baked breads and pastries (also muffins and croissants), beautiful salads (pasta, seafood, duck, chicken), dried and fresh fruits, Belgian waffles and pancakes, many desserts, coffee or tea, and a large selection of entrées such as poached eggs in Mornay sauce, seafood croquettes with ancho chili sauce, escargots encased in phyllo pastry, chicken Cordon Bleu, eggs Benedict, and pork tenderloin with spicy papaya relish. The buffet is served from 10:30am to 2:30pm, and the price ($38 for adults, $15.95 for children under 12) includes unlimited champagne. Reservations are suggested.

CHAPTER 7

WHAT TO SEE & DO IN THE WALT DISNEY WORLD AREA

We all know what the big attraction is here—the one that put Orlando on the map. With the exception of conventioneers (and I'm sure many of them sneak off to the parks as well), most people who come to Orlando have come to meet the Mouse.

SUGGESTED ITINERARIES

You won't see all the attractions at any of the parks in a single day. Read through the upcoming descriptions, decide which are musts for you, and try to get to them. My favorite rides and attractions are starred.

A DAY IN THE MAGIC KINGDOM

Get to the park well before opening time, tickets in hand. When the gates open, head for the kiosk just outside Disneyana Collectibles, and make a reservation for a lunchtime show at the Diamond Horseshoe Jamboree. Then hightail it to Frontierland and ride Splash Mountain before long lines form. When you come off, it will still be early enough to beat the lines at another major attraction. Double back to Adventureland and do Pirates of the Caribbean. Then relax and take it slow. Complete whatever else interests you in Adventureland, and enjoy Frontierland attractions until it's time for your lunch show. After lunch, continue visiting Frontierland attractions as desired or proceed to the Hall of Presidents and the Haunted Mansion in Liberty Square. By 2:30pm (earlier in peak seasons), you should snag a seat on the curb in Liberty Square along the parade route. After the parade, continue around the park taking in Fantasyland and Tomorrowland attractions. If SpectroMagic is on during your stay, don't miss it.

If you have little kids (8 and under) in your party, after making the above-mentioned lunch reservations for Diamond Horseshoe Jamboree, take the WDW Railroad from Main Street to Mickey's Starland to see the show. Work your way through Fantasyland until lunch. After lunch visit the Country Bear Jamboree in Frontierland and proceed to Adventureland for the Jungle Cruise, Swiss Family Treehouse, and Tropical Serenade. Once again, stop in good time to get parade seats (in Frontierland). Little kids need to sit right up front to see everything. That's a long enough day for most little kids, and your best plan is to go back to your hotel for a nap or swim. If, however, you wish to continue, return to Frontierland and/or Fantasyland for the rides you didn't complete earlier.

TWO DAYS AT EPCOT

Day 1: As above, arrive early, tickets in hand. Make your first stop at Earth Station to make lunch reservations at the San Angel Inn Restaurant in Mexico for about 1pm. If you like, also make dinner reservations at the World Showcase restaurant of your choice (*note:* Disney hotel guests can make these in advance). Then head for the lagoon, and take the launch to Germany. While cruising the lagoon, check your show schedule, and decide which shows to incorporate into your day. Don't stop in Germany. First take in Italy and American Adventure (check show times for the latter) before working your way back counterclockwise around the Germany, China, and Norway pavilions. You should arrive in Mexico just in time for a leisurely lunch, after which you can visit its attractions. If you've dawdled, you'll have to skip something to make your reservation. After lunch, continue on the same side of the park, visiting World of Motion, Horizons, Wonders of Life, the Universe of Energy, and the east wing of Innoventions in Future World. Frankly, unless crowds are very light, you can't see everything in all of the above-mentioned showcase pavilions and themed areas in one day. So rather than do it all, hit the highlights you don't want to miss. If you have only one day at Epcot, plan dinner in the park, and stay for IllumiNations (usually at 9pm, but check your schedule). Otherwise, leave the park, have dinner elsewhere (see Chapters 6 and 9 for suggestions), and catch IllumiNations your second night.

Day 2: First stop: Earth Station to make dinner reservations for the World Showcase restaurant of your choice. Check your show schedule, and make your reservation early enough to allow time to find a seat on the lagoon at least a half hour before IllumiNations begins. Then take the launch across the lagoon to Morocco, walk to Japan, and after seeing its attractions (don't miss the show here), continue clockwise to Morocco, France, the United Kingdom, and Canada. Stop for a light early lunch at a casual restaurant—perhaps Au Petit Café in France or Le Cellier in Canada (no reservations required at either). After lunch visit Journey Into Imagination, The Land, the Living Seas, Spaceship Earth, and the west wing of Innoventions, have dinner, and watch IllumiNations.

IN THE WORDS OF WALT DISNEY

"Family fun is as necessary to modern living as a kitchen refrigerator."

"Part of the Disney success is our ability to create a believable world of dreams that appeals to all age groups."

A DAY AT DISNEY-MGM STUDIOS THEME PARK

Since show times change seasonally, you may have to revise this itinerary a bit when you visit. Upon entering the park, stop at the Hollywood Brown Derby (details in Chapter 6), and make reservations for a 1pm lunch. Then make a beeline for the new Twilight Zone of Terror, as it will no doubt have the longest lines as the day progresses. Afterwards, head over to the Magic of Disney Animation, followed by the Voyage of the Little Mermaid, the Backstage Studio Tour, and, if time allows, Inside the Magic, prior to lunch. After lunch do the Great Movie Ride, Superstar Television, the Monster Sound Show, Indiana Jones Epic Stunt Spectacular, Jim Henson's Muppet Vision 3-D movie (not to be missed), and Star Tours, ending up at Beauty and the Beast in the Backlot Theater. You may have to make some adjustments to program in the Aladdin's Royal Caravan parade (preferably in the afternoon); check your show schedule for times. In peak seasons stay on for fireworks.

IF YOU HAVE EXTRA DAYS

If you're staying longer than the four days accounted for above, you'll probably want to spend at least one of them in the Magic Kingdom and/or Epcot seeing whatever you've missed. If you have an additional day, spend it at Universal Studios, which is chockablock with thrilling high-tech rides and attractions. Still more time? By now you need rest and refreshment. You'll find it at Typhoon Lagoon, a fabulous water theme park. Spend the morning splashing about there, and in the afternoon tour Discovery Island.

---

1. WALT DISNEY WORLD

Walt Disney World, attracting more than 13 million annual visitors, is one of the world's most popular travel destinations. And why not? It provides a welcome retreat from personal and global problems to a star-spangled all-American fantasyland where wonderment, human progress, and old-fashioned family fun are the major themes. And these themes are presented in a dazzling format of spectacular parades and fireworks displays, 3-D and 360-degree movies, and adventure-filled journeys through time and space. Though it's not inexpensive, you'll seldom hear people complain about not getting their money's worth. Disney delivers!

The **Magic Kingdom** opened in 1971. Later additions include Epcot, where guests take exhilarating voyages around the world and into the future; **Disney-MGM Studios,** centered on "Hollywood Boulevard" and providing a thrilling behind-the-scenes look at motion-picture and TV studios; **Pleasure Island,** an ongoing street festival in a six-acre complex of nightclubs and shops, featuring live concerts nightly; **Walt Disney World Village,** a charming lakeside enclave of shops and restaurants; **Typhoon Lagoon,** a 56-acre water park where you can catch the world's largest manmade waves or plummet down steep water flumes; **River Country,** another fabulous water park; and **Discovery Island,** an utterly delightful nature preserve and aviary.

COMING SOON **Blizzard Beach,** a new water park with the zany theme of "a ski resort in the tropics," is set to open in mid-1995.

TIPS FOR PLANNING YOUR VISIT How you plan your time at Walt Disney World will depend on a number of factors, including the ages of children in your party, what you've seen on previous visits, your specific interests, and whether you're traveling at a peak time or off-season (when lines are shorter and you can cram more in). Planning, however, is essential. Unless you're staying for considerably more than a week, you can't possibly experience all the rides, shows, and attractions here—not to mention the vast array of recreational facilities. And you'll only wear yourself to a frazzle trying. It's far better to follow a relaxed itinerary, including leisurely meals and recreational activities, than to make a demanding job out of trying to see everything. *Note:* Many of these suggestions are also applicable at non-Disney theme parks.

Information Before leaving home, call or write the **Walt Disney World Co.,** Box 10,000, Lake Buena Vista, FL 32830-1000 (tel. 407/824-4321) for a copy of the very informative *Walt Disney World Vacation Guide*—an invaluable planning aid. When you call, also ask about special events that will be on during your stay (see also "When to Go," in Chapter 2 of this book). Once you've arrived in town, **guest services** and **concierge desks** in all area hotels— especially Disney properties and official hotels—have up-to-the-minute information about happenings in the parks. Stop by to ask questions and pick up literature, including a schedule of park hours and special events. If you have questions your hotel can't answer, call **824-4321.** There are also **information locations** in each park— at City Hall in the Magic Kingdom, Earth Station at Epcot, and the Guest Services Building in Disney-MGM Studios.

Create an Itinerary for Each Day Read the above-mentioned *Walt Disney World Vacation Guide* and the detailed descriptions in this book of every nook and cranny of the Disney parks, and plan your visit to include all shows and attractions that pique your interest and excitement. It's a good idea to make a daily itinerary, putting these in some kind of sensible geographical sequence, so you're not zigzagging all over the place. Familiarize yourself in advance with the layout of each park. I repeat this advice—do schedule in sit-down shows, recreational activities (a boat ride or swim late in the afternoon can be wonderfully refreshing), and at least some unhurried meals. My suggested itineraries are above.

Buy Tickets in Advance You can purchase four- or five-day passes (see details below) at the Orlando airport, at many hotels, or by contacting the **Central Reservations Office** (tel. 407/824-8000) prior to your trip (allow 21 days for processing your request). In the latter case there's a $2 postage and handling charge. Of course, you can always purchase tickets at any of the parks, but why stand on an avoidable line? *Note:* One-day tickets can be purchased only at park entrances.

Arrive Early Unless you're an incorrigible night person, always arrive at the parks a good 30 to 45 minutes before opening time, thus avoiding a traffic jam entering the park and a long line at the gate. Early arrival also lets you experience one or two major attractions before big lines form. In high season parking lots sometimes fill up and you may even have to wait to get in.

In the Parks Upon entering any of the three major Disney parks, you'll be given an **entertainment schedule** and a comprehensive **park guidebook** that contains a map of the park and lists all attractions, shops, shows, and restaurants. If by some fluke you haven't obtained these, they are available at the above-mentioned information locations in each park. If, as suggested above, you've formulated an itinerary prior to arrival, you already know the major shows (check show schedules for additional ideas) you want to see during the day and what arrangements you need to make. If you haven't done this, use your early arrival time, while waiting for the park to open, to figure out which shows to attend, and, where necessary, make reservations for them as soon as the gates swing open. Some restaurant reservations also need to be made first thing in the morning. Make as many lunch, dinner, and show reservations in advance as possible (see Chapters 6 and 9 for details).

Lost Children All parks have a place for separated adults and children to meet up. Find out where it is when you come into the park (it's in your park guidebook), and tell your kids to ask a park attendant to take them there if you get separated. Children under 7 should have name tags.

Sunshine Prepare for a day exposed to the Florida sun. Bring sunscreen, and consider a visored hat.

Pets Don't leave your pet in a parked car, even with a window cracked. The interior of a car becomes incredibly hot baking in the Florida sun. A dead pet will not enhance your trip. Pets are not permitted in the parks, but there are four kennels in the WDW complex. Those at the Transportation and Ticket Center in the

FROMMER'S FAVORITE ORLANDO EXPERIENCES

Splash Mountain   This new Magic Kingdom attraction combines gorgeous scenery with Disney magic and a theme park thrill—a five-story splashdown! Don't chicken out. It's great.

The Daily Parade and SpectroMagic   The daily 3pm parade at the Magic Kingdom is enchanting. And SpectroMagic, which takes place after dark and adds high-tech dazzle to Disney's genius for spectacle, is simply awe-inspiring.

The Making of Me   Martin Short teaches the facts of life in this delightful and very charming 15-minute film at Epcot's Wonders of Life pavilion.

Cranium Command   Another Wonders of Life feature, this hilarious multimedia attraction is one of Epcot's best. It stars a handful of "Saturday Night Live" actors and other comedians.

Wonders of China   This 360-degree Circle-Vision™ film at Epcot's China pavilion explores 6,000 years of Chinese history and ranges the country's landscape in stunning cinematography.

Jim Henson's Muppet Vision 3D   High-tech 3-D Muppets, with lots of special-effects wizardry. A delight. At Disney-MGM Studios.

Aladdin's Royal Caravan   Disney-MGM Studios' exotic version of the Magic Kingdom parade, complete with scimitar dancers, fire-eaters, and snake charmers.

Universal Studios   Steven Spielberg is the park's creative consultant! How can you go wrong? Not-to-be-missed attractions here: Back to the Future, Jaws, Kongfrontation, and Earthquake: The Big One.

Cypress Gardens   Two hundred acres of gorgeous botanical gardens punctuated by lakes and lagoons, waterfalls, and sculpture.

Harry P. Leu Gardens   A delightful 56-acre botanical garden in Orlando on the shores of Lake Rowena.

Magic Kingdom and near the entrance to Fort Wilderness board animals overnight. Day accommodations are offered at kennels just outside the Entrance Plaza at Epcot and at the entrance to Disney MGM-Studios.

? DID YOU KNOW . . . ?

- It's not a small world after all! Covering 43 square miles, Walt Disney World is about the size of San Francisco.
- In a recent year, guests at Universal Studios consumed 1,101,245 burgers —the equivalent of 22 King Kongs—and 131 miles of hot dogs
- The manatees at Sea World each eat about 10% of their body weight daily. Their daily diet consists of about 100 pounds of romaine lettuce along with assorted fruits and vegetables, especially apples.
- The pesticide DDT was developed solely in Orlando by a group of government entomologists who were exploring its military uses. Though later abandoned as dangerously toxic, DDT was widely used during World War II.
- The famous Florida sinkhole, appearing in Winter Park in May of 1981, consumed several Porsche cars, part of a city street, a home, and a large corner of a public swimming pool. It became a central Florida tourist attraction, with vendors lining up nearby to hawk T-shirts and sinkhole-related merchandise.

Dining Try to eat lunch before noon or after 2pm. That way you can hit popular rides when most people are eating (and lines are a bit shorter), and eat when restaurants are less crowded.

Shopping All of the Disney parks have dozens of shops filled with kid-pleasing items. To avoid a lot of whining and pleading, agree in advance on the amount a child can spend on souvenirs. Leave shopping for the last activity of the day, so that you don't have to lug your purchases around.

Best Days to Visit The busiest days at the Magic Kingdom and Epcot are Monday to Wednesday, at Disney-MGM Studios Wednesday to Friday. Surprisingly, weekends are the least busy at all parks. In peak seasons, especially, arrange your visits accordingly.

Pace Yourself In high season, especially, when the parks are open late, take a break in the afternoon. Go back to your hotel for a nap or swim, and return in the early evening when it's cooler and lines are shorter. There's something magical about the parks at night.

Leaving the Parks If you leave any of the parks and plan to return later in the day, be sure to get your hand stamped on exiting.

Parking Parking—free to guests at WDW resorts—otherwise costs $5 per day no matter how many parks you visit. Be sure to note down your parking location before leaving your car. There is a spot for this information on your parking ticket. Also remember to lock your car and roll up the windows. There are special handicapped lots at each park (call 824-4321 for details). Don't worry about parking far from the entrance gates; trams constantly ply the route.

Remember to Have Fun A theme park provides a unique opportunity to spend some quality time with the kids, but your attitude can make or break the experience. For instance, it's more fun to chat, play games, and tell stories on long lines than to grouse about them. Parents set the tone. So get your priorities in order, and go with the flow.

The Easy Way Staying at Disney properties simplifies many of the above tasks and procedures. See the full list of perks for Disney and "official" hotel guests in Chapter 5.

OPERATING HOURS Hours of operation vary somewhat throughout the year. The Magic Kingdom and Disney-MGM Studios are generally open 9am to 7pm, with extended hours—sometimes as late as midnight—during major holidays and the summer months. Epcot hours are generally 9am to 9pm, once again with extended holiday hours. Typhoon Lagoon is open from 10am to 5pm most of the year (with extended hours during some holidays), 9am to 8pm in summer. River Country and Discovery Island are open from 10am to 5pm most of the year (with extended hours during some holidays), 10am to 7pm in summer. *Note:* Epcot and MGM sometimes open a half hour or more before posted time. Keep in mind, too, that Disney hotel guests enjoy early admission to the Magic Kingdom on designated days for a full lineless hour.

TICKETS There are several ticket options. Most people get the best value from four- and five-day passes. All passes offer unlimited use of the WDW transportation system. Prices quoted below include sales tax.

The **Four-Day Value Pass** provides admission for: one day at the Magic Kingdom, one day at Epcot, one day at Disney-MGM Studios, and one day at your choice of any of those three parks; you can use it on any four days following purchase. Cost is $132 for ages 10 and over, $103.50 for children 3 to 9, under 3 free. (*Note:* guests at Disney resorts can purchase a **Four-Day Super Pass** that allows them any combination of visits to the three major parks for the same price.)

The **Five-Day Around the World Pass** provides admission for: one day at the Magic Kingdom, one day at Epcot, one day at Disney-MGM Studios, and two days at your choice of one park each of the two additional days, including Typhoon Lagoon, River Country, Discovery Island, and Pleasure Island for a period of seven days beginning the first date stamped. It costs $179.60 for ages 10 and over, $142.60 for children 3 to 9, under 3 free. (*Note:* guests at Disney resorts can purchase a **Five-Day Super Duper Pass** that allows them any combination of visits to all Disney parks for the same price.)

A **one-day, one-park ticket for the Magic Kingdom, Epcot, or Disney-MGM Studios** is $36.95 for ages 10 and over, $29.55 for children 3 to 9, under 3 free.

A **one-day ticket to Typhoon Lagoon** is $22.79 for adults, $17.49 for children ages 3 to 9, under 3 free.

A **one-day ticket to River Country** is $14.84 for adults, $11.66 for children ages 3 to 9, under 3 free.

A **one-day ticket to Discovery Island** is $10.07 for adults, $5.57 for children ages 3 to 9, under 3 free.

A **combined one-day ticket for River Country and Dis-**

📖 DID YOU KNOW . . . ?

- The movie portion of Universal Studio's Back to the Future attraction took two years to make and was the most expensive film per minute ever made.
- Mickey Mouse has more than 80 different outfits, ranging from a scuba suit to a tuxedo. Minnie has only 50.
- There are enough Mickey Mouse ear hats sold each year to cover the head of every man, woman, and child in Pittsburgh.
- In a typical week in Orlando, 396 new jobs are created, 1,117 new residents move in, 243 marriages and 325 births are recorded, retail sales total $188 million, and more than 230,000 visitors arrive in town.
- You could fit New York's Empire State Building into the Vehicle Assembly Building at the Kennedy Space Center 3¾ times.
- Shamu, the killer whale at Sea World, eats more than 65,000 pounds of fish a year.
- Every day an average of 100 pairs of sunglasses are turned into the Lost and Found at the Magic Kingdom.

covery Island is $17.76 for adults, $12.99 for children ages 3 to 9, under 3 free.

If you are staying at any Walt Disney World resort or official hotel you are also eligible for a money-saving **Be Our Guest Pass** priced according to length of stay. It also offers special parks.

If you plan on visiting Walt Disney World more than one time during the year, inquire about a money-saving **annual pass.**

THE MAGIC KINGDOM

Centered around Cinderella Castle—its medieval spires Walt Disney World's most recognizable symbol after Mickey Mouse—the Magic Kingdom occupies about 100 acres, with 45 major attractions and numerous restaurants and shops in seven themed sections or "lands." From the parking lot, you have to take a short monorail or ferry ride to the Magic Kingdom entrance. During peak attendance times, arrive at the Magic Kingdom no later than an hour prior to opening time to avoid long lines at these conveyances. Sections of the parking lot are named for Disney characters (Goofy, Pluto, Minnie, and so on), and aisles are numbered. Upon entering the park, consult your *Magic Kingdom Guidebook* map to get your bearings. It details every shop, restaurant, and attraction in every land. Also consult your **entertainment schedule** to see what's on for the day. There are parades, musical extravaganzas featuring Disney characters, fireworks, band concerts, barbershop quartets, Disney character appearances, and more. If you have questions, all park employees are very knowledgeable, and City Hall, on your left as you enter, is both an information center, and, along with Mickey's Starland (details below) a likely place to meet up with costumed characters. There's a stroller rental shop just after the turnstiles to your right, and the Kodak Camera Center, near Town Square, supplies all conceivable photo-

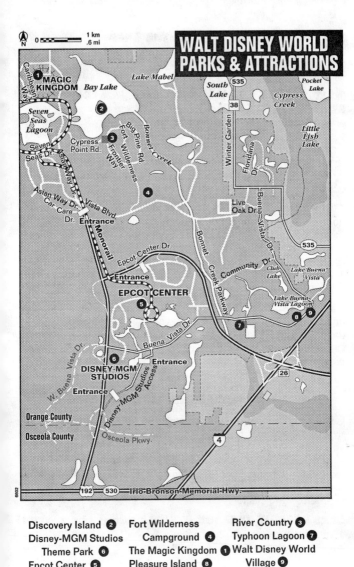

WALT DISNEY WORLD PARKS & ATTRACTIONS

Discovery Island ❷
Disney-MGM Studios Theme Park ❻
Epcot Center ❺
Fort Wilderness Campground ❹
The Magic Kingdom ❶
Pleasure Island ❽
River Country ❸
Typhoon Lagoon ❼
Walt Disney World Village ❾

---

graphic needs, including camera and camcorder rentals and two-hour film developing.

MAIN STREET U.S.A.

Designed to replicate an archetypical turn-of-the-century American street—albeit one that culminates in a 13th-century castle—this is the gateway to the Kingdom. Don't dawdle on Main Street when you enter the park; leave it for the end of the day when you're heading back to your hotel.

WALT DISNEY WORLD RAILROAD & OTHER MAIN STREET VEHICLES You can board an authentic 1928 steam-powered railroad here for a 15-minute journey clockwise around the perimeter of the park. There are stations in Frontierland, Mickey's Starland, and Tomorrowland. There are also horse-drawn trolleys, horseless carriages, jitneys, omnibuses, and fire engines plying the short route along Main Street from Town Square to Cinderella Castle.

MAIN STREET CINEMA A mannequin is in charge of the ticket booth here, so you can sneak right in without paying. Just kidding—there's no charge for admission. Main Street Cinema is an air-conditioned hexagonal theater where vintage black-and-white Disney cartoons (including the 1928 *Steamboat Willie* in which Mickey and Minnie debuted) are aired continually on six screens. Viewers have to watch these standing; there are no seats.

PENNY ARCADE At this old-fashioned penny arcade, even the prices evoke nostalgia. Its 1¢ hand-cranked Cail-o-scopes (one of them featuring Charlie Chaplin), test-your-grip machines, old pinball games, kiss-o-meter, Gypsy fortune-teller, and shooting gallery evoke pleasant childhood memories to those of a certain age and are a novelty to the Nintendo generation.

ADVENTURELAND

Cross a bridge to your left, and stroll into an exotic jungle of lush tropical foliage, thatch-roofed huts, and carved totems. Amid dense vines and stands of palm and bamboo, drums are beating, and swashbuckling adventures are taking place. *Note:* If you're heading toward Adventureland or Frontierland first thing in the morning, wait for the gates to open at the bridge in front of the Crystal Palace, to your left as you enter.

SWISS FAMILY TREEHOUSE This attraction is based on the 1960 Disney movie version of Johann Wyss's *Swiss Family Robinson,* about a shipwrecked family of five who created an ingenious

---

IN THE WORDS OF WALT DISNEY

"Sheer animated fantasy is still my first and deepest production impulse. The fable is the best storytelling device ever conceived. . . . And, of course, animal characters have always been the personnel of fable—animals through which the foibles as well as the virtues of humans can best and most hilariously be reflected."

"Never get bored or cynical. Yesterday is a thing of the past."

dwelling for themselves in the branches of a sprawling banyan tree. Using materials and furnishings salvaged from their downed ship, the Robinsons created bedrooms, a kitchen, a library, and a living room. Visitors traverse a rope-suspended bridge and ascend the 50-foot tree for a close-up look into these rooms. Do note the Rube Goldberg rope-and-bucket device with bamboo chutes that dips water from a stream and carries it to treetop chambers. The "tree" itself, designed by Disney "Imagineers," has 330,000 polyethylene "leaves" sprouting from a 90-foot span of branches; although it isn't real, it is draped with actual Spanish moss.

JUNGLE CRUISE What a cruise! In the course of about 10 minutes, your boat sails through an African veldt in the Congo, an Amazon rain forest, the Mekony River in Southeast Asia, and along the Nile. Lavish scenery, with ropes of hanging vines, cascading waterfalls, and lush tropical and subtropical foliage (most of it real), includes dozens of Audio-Animatronic™ birds and animals— elephants, zebras, lions, giraffes, crocodiles, tigers, even fluttering butterflies. On the shore you'll pass a *Raiders*-like Cambodian temple cave fronted by a Buddha and guarded by snakes; a rhino and jackal chasing terrified African beaters up a tree; and a jungle camp taken over by apes. But the adventures aren't all on shore. Passengers are menaced by everything from water-spouting elephants to fierce warriors who attack with spears. The guide keeps up an amusing patter.

★ **PIRATES OF THE CARIBBEAN** This is Disney magic at its best. You'll proceed through a long grottolike passageway to board a boat into a pitch-black cave. Therein, elaborate scenery and hundreds of Audio-Animatronic™ figures (including lifelike dogs, cats, chickens, and donkeys—even drunken pigs) depict a rambunctious pirate raid on a Caribbean town. To a background of cheerful "yo-ho-yo-ho" music, the sound of rushing waterfalls, squawking sea gulls, and screams of terror, passengers pass through the line of fire in a raging pirate battle and view tableaux of fierce-looking pirates chasing maidens, swigging rum, looting, and plundering. This might be scary for kids under 5.

TROPICAL SERENADE In a large hexagonal Polynesian-style dwelling, with a thatched roof, bamboo beams, and tapa-bark murals, 250 tropical birds, chanting totem poles, and singing flowers whistle, tweet, and warble songs such as "Let's All Sing Like the Birdies Sing." The audience is encouraged to sing along. In the background you can hear the sound of a gurgling stream. The show is hosted by four feathered friends named José, Michael, Pierre, and Fritz, all with appropriate national accents—who perch atop an "enchanted" fountain. Highlights include a thunderstorm in the dark (the gods are angry!), a light show over the fountain, and, of course, the famous "in the tiki, tiki, tiki, tiki, tiki room" song. Like it or not, you'll find yourself singing it all day. An amusing preshow, in which

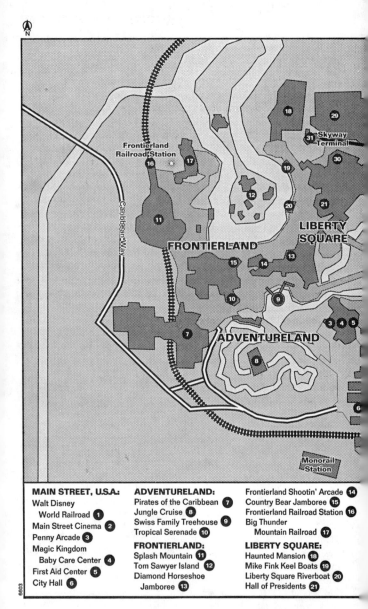

MAIN STREET, U.S.A:

Walt Disney
World Railroad **1**
Main Street Cinema **2**
Penny Arcade **3**
Magic Kingdom
Baby Care Center **4**
First Aid Center **5**
City Hall **6**

ADVENTURELAND:

Pirates of the Caribbean **7**
Jungle Cruise **8**
Swiss Family Treehouse **9**
Tropical Serenade **10**

FRONTIERLAND:

Splash Mountain **11**
Tom Sawyer Island **12**
Diamond Horseshoe
Jamboree **13**

Frontierland Shootin' Arcade **14**
Country Bear Jamboree **15**
Frontierland Railroad Station **16**
Big Thunder
Mountain Railroad **17**

LIBERTY SQUARE:

Haunted Mansion **18**
Mike Fink Keel Boats **19**
Liberty Square Riverboat **20**
Hall of Presidents **21**

two wisecracking parrots relate their jungle adventures, takes place out front while you wait. This is a must for young children.

FRONTIERLAND

From Adventureland, step into the wild and woolly past of the American frontier, where Disney employees are clad in denim

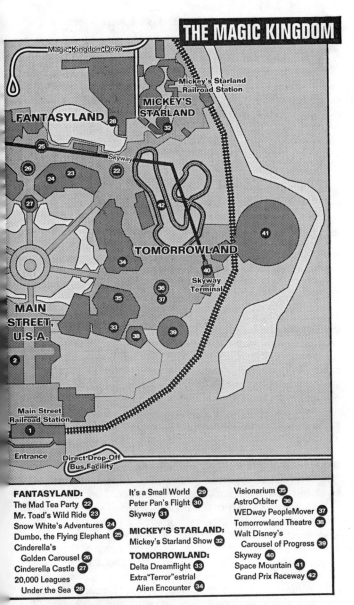

THE MAGIC KINGDOM

FANTASYLAND:
The Mad Tea Party **22**
Mr. Toad's Wild Ride **23**
Snow White's Adventures **24**
Dumbo, the Flying Elephant **25**
Cinderella's
  Golden Carousel **26**
Cinderella Castle **27**
20,000 Leagues
  Under the Sea **28**

It's a Small World **29**
Peter Pan's Flight **30**
Skyway **31**

MICKEY'S STARLAND:
Mickey's Starland Show **32**

TOMORROWLAND:
Delta Dreamflight **33**
Extra"Terror"estrial
  Alien Encounter **34**

Visionarium **35**
AstroOrbiter **36**
WEDway PeopleMover **37**
Tomorrowland Theatre **38**
Walt Disney's
  Carousel of Progress **39**
Skyway **40**
Space Mountain **41**
Grand Prix Raceway **42**

and calico, sidewalks are wooden, rough-and-tumble architecture runs to log cabins and rustic saloons, and the landscape is southwestern scrubby with mesquite, saguaro cactus, yucca, and prickly pear. Across the river is Tom Sawyer Island, reachable via log rafts.

SPLASH MOUNTAIN Themed after Walt Disney's 1946 film,

Song of the South, Splash Mountain takes you on an enchanting journey in a hollowed-out log craft along the canals of a flooded mountain, past 26 brilliantly colored tableaux of backwoods swamps, bayous, spooky caves, and waterfalls. Riders are caught up in the bumbling schemes of Brer Fox and Brer Bear as they pursue the ever-wily Brer Rabbit, who, against the advice of Mr. Bluebird, has left his briar-patch home in search of adventure and the "laughing place." The music from the film forms a delightful audio backdrop. Your log craft twists, turns, and splashes—sometimes plummeting in total darkness—all leading up to a thrilling five-story, 45-degree angle splashdown from mountaintop to briar-filled pond at 40 miles per hour! And that's not the end. The ride continues, and finally it's a Zip-A-Dee-Doo-Dah kind of day.

BIG THUNDER MOUNTAIN RAILROAD This mining-disaster-themed roller coaster—its thrills deriving from hairpin turns and descents in the dark rather than sudden steep drops—is situated in a 200-foot-high redstone mountain with 2,780 feet of track winding through windswept canyons and bat-filled caves. You enter the ride via the ramshackle headquarters of the Big Thunder Mining Company and board a runaway train that careens through the ribs of a dinosaur, under a thundering waterfall, past spewing geysers and bubbling mudpots, and over a bottomless volcanic pool. Riders are threatened by flash floods, earthquakes, rickety bridges, and avalanches. Audio-Animatronic™ characters (such as the longjohn-clad fellow navigating the floodwaters in a bathtub) and animals (goats, chickens, donkeys, possums), enhance the scenic backdrop, and several hundred-thousand dollars worth of authentic antique mining equipment, amassed from many auctions, adds verisimilitude. Keep your eyes open for interesting detail.

DIAMOND HORSESHOE JAMBOREE This 40-minute show provides an opportunity to sit down in air-conditioned comfort and enjoy a rousing western revue. The "theater" is a re-creation of a turn-of-the-century saloon. Owner/bartender Sam plays the washboard, tells silly jokes, and shoots at the audience (with a water gun). Lily (a Mae West type) and her troupe of dance-hall girls do a cancan (Sam, in drag, joins in). And the cowboys perform feats of fast fiddling and foot-stomping acrobatic dances. There's a vague story line behind the action, which includes lots of good-natured audience participation. There are five shows daily; plan on going around lunchtime so you can eat during the show. The menu features deli or peanut butter and jelly sandwiches served with chips, and there are brownies for dessert. Make reservations when you enter the park just outside Disneyana Collectibles on the east side of Main Street in Town Square. Seating is reserved, so you can arrive shortly before show time.

COUNTRY BEAR JAMBOREE Call me corny. I've always

loved the Country Bear Jamboree, a 15-minute show featuring a troupe of fiddlin', banjo strummin', harmonica playin' Audio-Animatronic™ bears belting out rollicking country tunes and crooning plaintive love songs. The chubby Trixie, decked out in a satiny skirt, laments lost love, as she sings "Tears Will Be the Chaser for Your Wine." Teddi Barra descends from the ceiling in a swing to perform "Heart We Did All That We Could." Other star performers include a country-western group called the Five Bear Rugs, Liver Lips McGrowl, and the seven-foot-tall master of ceremonies, Henry. In the rousing show finale the entire cast joins in a foot-stompin' singalong. Wisecracking commentary comes from a mounted buffalo, moose, and deer on the wall. A special holiday show plays throughout the Christmas season each year.

TOM SAWYER ISLAND Board Huck Finn's raft for a one-minute float across the river to the densely forested Tom Sawyer Island, where kids can explore the narrow passages of Injun Joe's cave (complete with scary sound effects like whistling wind), a walk-through windmill, a serpentine abandoned mine, or Fort Sam Clemens, where an Audio-Animatronic™ drunk is snoring off a bender. Maintaining one's balance while crossing rickety swing and barrel bridges is also fun. Narrow winding dirt paths lined with oaks, pines, and sycamores create an authentic backwoods island feel. It's easy to get briefly lost and stumble upon some unexpected adventure. You might combine this attraction with lunch at Aunt Polly's restaurant, which serves light fare (fried chicken, sandwiches, and the like) and has outdoor tables on a porch overlooking the river. Adults can rest weary feet over coffee, while the kids explore the island.

FRONTIERLAND SHOOTIN' ARCADE Combining state-of-the-art electronics with a traditional shooting-gallery format, this vast arcade presents an array of 97 targets (slow-moving ore cars, buzzards, gravediggers) in a three-dimensional 1850s gold-mining town scenario. Fog creeps across the graveyard, and the setting changes as a calm starlit night turns stormy with flashes of lightning and claps of thunder. Coyotes howl, bridges creak, and skeletal arms reach out from the grave. If you hit a tombstone, it might spin around and mysteriously change its epitaph. To keep the western ambience authentic, newfangled electronic firing mechanisms loaded with infrared bullets are concealed in genuine Hawkins 54-caliber buffalo rifles. When you hit a target, elaborate sound and motion gags are set off. Fifty cents buys you 25 shots.

LIBERTY SQUARE

Serving as a transitional area between Frontierland and Fantasyland, Liberty Square evokes 18th-century America with Federal and Georgian architecture, Colonial Williamsburg–type shops, and neat flower beds bordering manicured lawns. Thirteen lanterns, symbolizing the colonies, are suspended from the Liberty Tree, an immense live oak. You might encounter a fife and drum corps marching along Liberty Square's cobblestone streets. The Liberty Tree Tavern here (details in Chapter 6) is my favorite Magic Kingdom restaurant.

THE HALL OF PRESIDENTS In this red-brick colonial hall, a giant bell suspended in its tower, all American presidents—from George Washington to Bill Clinton (whose actual voice was recorded for this attraction)—are represented by Audio-Animatronic™ figures who act out important events in the nation's history, from the signing of the Declaration of Independence through the space age. The show begins with a film, projected on a 180-degree, 70mm screen, about the importance of the Constitution. The curtain then rises on the 42 assembled American leaders, and, as each is spotlighted, he nods or waves with presidential dignity, Lincoln then rises and speaks, occasionally even referring to his notes. In a stunning example of Disney thoroughness, painstaking research was done in creating the figures and scenery, with each president's costume reflecting not only period fashion but period fabrics and tailoring techniques! The presidential figures look amazingly real. Poet and author Maya Angelou narrates. In the entrance hall you can see many of the historically themed paintings that were created for the above-mentioned film.

THE HAUNTED MANSION What better way to exhibit Disney special-effects wizardry than a haunted mansion? Macabre attendants harry groups of visitors past a graveyard, turning them over to a ghost host who encloses them in a windowless, doorless portrait gallery (are those eyes following you around?), lit by gargoyle torchiers, where the floor seems to be descending. Its ambience enhanced by inky darkness, spooky music, eerie howling, and mysterious screams and rappings, this mansion is replete with bizarre scenes and objects: a ghostly banquet and ball, a graveyard band, a suit of armor that comes alive, cobweb-covered chandeliers, luminous spiders, a talking head in a crystal ball, weird flying objects, and much more. At the end of the ride, a ghost joins you in your car. The experience is more amusing than terrifying, so you can take small children inside.

BOAT RIDES A steam-powered sternwheeler called the *Richard F. Irvine* and two Mike Fink Keel Boats (the *Bertha Mae* and the *Gullywhumper*) depart from Liberty Square for scenic cruises along the Rivers of America. The passing landscape evokes the wild west. Both ply the identical route and make a restful interlude for foot-weary parkgoers.

FANTASYLAND

The attractions in this happy "land"—themed after Disney film classics such as *Snow White, Peter Pan,* and *Alice in Wonderland*—are especially popular with young visitors. And a new stage show based on the Disney film *The Lion King* will open here soon. If your kids are 8 or under, you might want to make it your first stop in the Magic Kingdom. *Note:* Two rides here—Snow White's Adventures and Mr. Toad's Wild Ride—are a bit scary. If your under-5 frightens easily, skip them.

MAD TEA PARTY   This is a traditional amusement park ride à la Disney with an *Alice in Wonderland* theme. Riders sit in oversized pastel-hued teacups on saucers that career around a circular platform, tilt, and spin. In the center of the platform is a big teapot, out from which pops a mouse. Believe it or not, this can be a pretty wild ride—or a tame one. It depends on how much you spin, a factor under your control via a wheel in the cup.

MR. TOAD'S WILD RIDE   This ride is based on the 1949 Disney film, *The Adventures of Ichabod and Mr. Toad,* which was itself based on one of my favorite children's classics, the divine *Wind in the Willows.* A gang of weasels has tricked Mr. J. Thaddeus Toad into trading the deed to his beloved ancestral mansion, Toad Hall, for a stolen car. In colorful cars named for characters (Weasel, Toady, Moley), riders navigate a series of dark rooms, hurtling into solid objects—a fireplace, a bookcase, a haystack—and through barn doors into a coop of squawking chickens. They're menaced by falling suits of armor, snorting bulls, and an oncoming locomotive in a pitch-black tunnel, and are sent to jail (for car theft), to hell (complete with pitchfork-wielding demons), and through a fiery volcano. The ride's interior space is illuminated by invisible ultraviolet light, which makes whites and neons in the scenery glow.

20,000 LEAGUES UNDER THE SEA   Based on the Jules Verne classic, this submarine voyage travels beneath the waters of Fantasyland's lagoon. Via portholes, passengers look out at ersatz undersea vegetation and creatures—talking fish, giant clams, sea horses, mermaids, and sea serpents among them. And in addition to observing engaging sights—including the classical remains of the lost continent of Atlantis—they experience an underwater volcano, a squid attack, and a storm at sea. Authenticity is enhanced by appropriate sound effects and official-sounding commentary from the control room.

IN THE WORDS OF WALT DISNEY

"Fantasy, if it's really convincing, can't become dated, for the simple reason that it represents a flight into a dimension that lies beyond the reach of time . . . nothing corrodes or gets run down . . . And nobody gets any older."

"We have never lost our faith in family entertainment—stories that make people laugh, stories about warm and human things, stories about historic characters and events, and stories about animals."

SNOW WHITE'S ADVENTURES You might not remember that *Snow White,* originally a Grimms fairy tale, was a little scary, and this boat ride in the dark concentrates on some of its more sinister elements—the evil queen, the cackling witch proffering a poisoned apple to Snow White, skeletons in cages, and a crocodile lurching at riders. Even the trees are menacing.

CINDERELLA CASTLE At the end of Main Street, in the center of the park, you'll come to a fairyland castle, 180 feet high and housing a restaurant (King Stefan's Banquet Hall) and shops. Mosaic murals inside depict the Cinderella story, and Disney family coats of arms are displayed over a fireplace. Cinderella herself, dressed for the ball, often makes appearances in the lobby area.

CINDERELLA'S GOLDEN CAROUSEL It's a beauty, built by Italian wood-carvers in the Victorian tradition in 1917 and refurbished by Disney artists who added 18 hand-painted scenes from the Cinderella story on the wooden canopy above the horses. The carousel organ plays Disney classics such as "When You Wish upon a Star."

DUMBO, THE FLYING ELEPHANT This is a very tame kiddie ride in which the cars—large-eared baby elephants (Dumbos)—go around and around in a circle gently rising and dipping. But it's very exciting for wee ones.

IT'S A SMALL WORLD You know the song—and if you don't you will. It plays continually as you sail "around the world" through vast rooms designed to represent different countries. They're inhabited by appropriately costumed Audio-Animatronic™ dolls and animals—all singing "It's a small world after all . . ." in tiny doll-like voices. This cast of thousands includes Chinese acrobats, Russian kazatski dancers, Indian snake charmers in front of the Taj Mahal, French cancan dancers, Irish leprechauns, singing geese and windmills in Holland, Arabs on magic carpets, mountain goats in the Swiss Alps, African drummers and lunging hyenas in the jungle, a Venetian gondolier, and Australian koala bears. Cute. Very cute.

PETER PAN'S FLIGHT Riding in airborne versions of Captain Hook's ship, passengers careen through dark passages while experiencing the story of *Peter Pan.* The adventure begins in the Darlings's nursery, and includes a flight over nighttime London to Never-Never Land, where riders encounter mermaids, Indians, a ticking crocodile, the lost boys, Princess Tiger Lilly, Tinkerbell, Hook, Smee, and the rest—all to the movie music "You Can Fly, You Can Fly, You Can Fly." It's fun.

SKYWAY Its entrance close to Peter Pan's Flight, the Skyway is an aerial tramway to Tomorrowland that makes continuous trips throughout the day.

MICKEY'S STARLAND

This small land adjacent to Fantasyland, with a topiary maze of Disney characters and a block of Duckburg architecture, is accessible from Main Street via the Walt Disney World Railroad. It includes a Walk of Fame à la Hollywood, with Disney character "voiceprints" activated when you step on a star; a hands-on fire station; storefronts that come alive at the push of a button; Grandma Duck's Farm (a petting zoo); funhouse mirrors; a treehouse; and an interactive video area. And Mickey's house is here, too, complete with living room TV tuned to the Disney channel, a shopping list of six kinds of cheese tacked to the refrigerator, and his familiar outfits hanging on a clothesline in the yard. Pluto's doghouse is out front.

The main attraction is **Mickey's Starland Show,** which is presented on a stage behind his house. While waiting to enter the theater, you can watch Disney cartoon videos on monitors in the preshow room. The show—a lively musical—features the Goof Troop, Chip 'n' Dale, a perky hostess named CJ, and a vocal computer-control system called Dude. The story line: The show is about to start, but Mickey is missing! While CJ frantically searches for him, Goofy and his son, Max, get accidentally locked in the house. But it all works out in the end. The cheerful cartoon-inspired scenery, audience participation, and dramatic special effects are all designed to appeal to young viewers. After the show there's an opportunity to meet Mickey backstage in his dressing room.

TOMORROWLAND

This futuristic land focuses on space travel and exploration, but much like the Contemporary Hotel (built to complement it), its early 1970s architecture and vision of the future have become as retro-looking today as an old *Star Trek* episode. Don't think the folks at Disney haven't noticed. At this writing, they're revamping the exhibit to reflect the future as a galactic, science fiction–inspired community inhabited by humans, aliens, and robots.

Its major new attraction, **Extra"terror"estrial Alien Encounter,** will feature an interplanetary "teletransporter" capable of beaming living beings between planets light years apart. But as this revolutionary device is being marketed to earthlings by representatives from another planet, the demonstration goes awry, resulting in a shocking close encounter with a fearsome extraterrestial! Scheduled opening is in 1996.

As we go to press, two other new attractions are in the works and may be open by the time you're reading this. In **Visionairium**—a fourth-dimension adventure that will combine Circle-Vision™, Audio-Animatronic™ figures, and high-tech special effects—guests will time-travel back to centuries past and forward to those yet to come. And **AstroOrbiter** will spin guests around in rockets amid whirling planets.

WALT DISNEY'S CAROUSEL OF PROGRESS Originally seen at New York's 1964–65 World's Fair, this 22-minute show was recently revamped to reflect later technological advances. Shown in a revolving theater, it features an Audio-Animatronic™ family (including grandparents, a freeloading cousin, and a dog) in humorous tableaux demonstrating a century of development in electric gadgetry, contraptions, and modern electronics. The action begins on Valentine's Day in a turn-of-the-century home, where telephones, Victrolas, indoor running water, and gaslight are the marvels of the age; train travel and horseless trolleys are coming into vogue; and there's even talk of "flying contraptions." We travel through time, tracking advances and their detriments (e.g., car travel leads to the commuter rat race), culminating circa the year 2000 on Christmas Eve. Gifts include virtual-reality headgear and a voice-activation system. Unfortunately, grandma yells out her virtual-reality game score of 975, which the voice-activating oven takes for a command; it blows up, nuking the holiday turkey. A pre-show featuring Walt Disney traces the history of this production.

DELTA DREAMFLIGHT The history and wonder of aviation—from barnstorming to space shuttles—is captured in this whimsical fly-through adventure presented by the official airline of Walt Disney World. High-tech special effects and 70mm live-action film footage add dramatic 3-D-style verisimilitude. Guests travel from a futuristic airport up a hillside to witness a flying circus, parachutists, stunt flyers, wing walkers, crop dusters, and aerial acrobats. The action moves on to the ocean-hopping age of commercial flight, as passengers are transported to a Japanese tea garden, Mt. Fuji, and Paris at sunset. Finally, your vehicle is pulled into a giant jet engine and sent into hypersonic flight through psychedelic tunnels of light for a journey to outer space at a simulated speed of 300 m.p.h.

STARJETS This is a tame, typical amusement park ride. The "jets" are on arms attached to a "missile" and they move up and down while traveling in a circle. It will eventually be replaced by the above-mentioned AstroOrbiter.

WEDWAY PEOPLEMOVER A futuristic means of transportation, the PeopleMover has no engine. It works by electromagnets, emits no pollution, and uses little power (don't ask me to explain it; I didn't do so well in physics). Narrated by a computer guide named Horack I, it offers an overhead look at Tomorrowland, including a pretty good preview of Space Mountain. If you're only in the Magic Kingdom for one day, this can be skipped.

SKYWAY Its Tomorrowland entrance just west of Space Mountain, this aerial tramway to Fantasyland makes continuous round-trips throughout the day.

⭐ **SPACE MOUNTAIN** In a precursor to the concept of preshows, Space Mountain entertains visitors on its long, long lines with space-age music, exhibits, and meteorites, shooting stars, and space debris whizzing about overhead. These "illusioneering" effects, enhanced by appropriate audio, continue during the ride itself, which is something like a cosmic roller coaster in the inky starlit blackness of outer space. Your rocket climbs high into the universe, before racing—at what feels like breakneck speed—through a serpentine complex of aerial galaxies, making thrilling hairpin turns and rapid plunges. The exit from Space Mountain is a moving sidewalk, past scenes of Audio-Animatronic™ figures who demonstrate the future uses of electronic media in displays such as Astrodate 2250—farm communications on a once-barren planet. *Note:* Though the line may seem long, take heart; Space Mountain accommodates 3,000 people an hour.

GRAND PRIX RACEWAY This is a great thrill for kids—including pre-drivers-license teens—who get to put the pedal to the metal, steer, and *vroom* down a speedway in an actual gas-powered sports car. Maximum speed on the four-minute drive around the track is about 7 m.p.h., and kids have to be at least 4 feet, 4 inches tall to drive alone.

PARADES, FIREWORKS & MORE

You'll get an *Entertainment Show Schedule* when you enter the park, which lists all kinds of special goings-on for the day. These include concerts (everything from steel drums to barbershop quartets), encounters with Disney characters, holiday events, and the three major happenings listed below.

⭐ **THE 3 O'CLOCK PARADE** You haven't really seen a parade until you've seen one at Walt Disney World. The spectacular daily parade kicks off at 3pm year-round on Main Street and meanders through Liberty Square and Frontierland. The route is outlined on your *Entertainment Show Schedule*. The only problem: In slow seasons you have to snag a seat along the curb a good half hour before it begins—even earlier during peak travel times. That's a long time to sit on a hard curb. Consider packing inflatable pillows. But the parade is worth a little discomfort. Disney characters from Mickey Mouse to Roger Rabbit are represented by 40-foot Macy's-style balloon figures. There are elaborate floats, stunning costumes, dazzling special effects, and a captivating cavalcade of acrobats, court jesters, stilt-walkers, dancers, Mardi Gras bands, storybook characters (Snow White, Cinderella, Sleeping Beauty), and a Royal Guard of rhinos, elephants, and hippos. Great music, too.

SPECTROMAGIC Along a darkened parade route (the same one as above), 72,000 watts of dazzling high-tech lighting effects (including holography) create a glowing array of pixies and peacocks, sea horses and winged horses, flower gardens and fountains. Roger Rabbit is the eccentric conductor of an orchestra producing a rainbow of musical notes that waft magically into the night air. There are dancing ostriches from *Fantasia,* whirling electric butterflies, flowers that evoke Tiffany glass, bejeweled coaches, luminescent ElectroMen atop spinning whirlyballs, and, of course, Mickey, surrounded by a sparkling confetti of light. And the music and choreography are on par with the technology. It's like nothing you've ever seen before. Once again, very early arrival is essential to get a seat on the curb. SpectroMagic takes place nightly in summer, on selected nights during Christmas and Easter vacation times, and during other special celebrations. Consult your *Entertainment Show Schedule* for details.

FIREWORKS Like SpectroMagic, Fantasy in the Sky Fireworks, immediately preceded by Tinker Bell's magical flight from Cinderella Castle, take place nightly in summer, on selected nights during Christmas and Easter vacation times, and during other special celebrations. Consult your *Entertainment Show Schedule* for details. Suggested viewing areas are Liberty Square, Frontierland, and Mickey's Starland.

EPCOT

In 1982, Walt Disney World opened its second major attractions park, the world's fair–like Epcot (Experimental Prototype Community of Tomorrow). Its aims are described in a dedication plaque: "May Epcot entertain, inform and inspire. And, above all . . . instill a new sense of belief and pride in man's ability to shape a world that offers hope to people everywhere." Ever growing and changing, Epcot today occupies 260 acres so stunningly landscaped as to be worth visiting for botanical beauty alone. Do stop and smell the roses. There are two major sections, Future World and World Showcase.

Epcot is huge, and walking around it can be exhausting (some people say its acronym stands for "Every Person Comes Out Tired"). Don't try to do it all in one day. And conserve your energy by taking launches across the lagoon from the edge of Future World to Germany or Morocco. There are also double-decker buses circling the World Showcase Promenade and making stops at Norway, Italy, France, and Canada. Unlike the Magic Kingdom, Epcot's parking lot is right at the gate. Sections of the parking lot are named for Epcot themes (Harvest, Energy, etc.), and aisles are numbered. Stop by **Earth Station** (Epcot's information center) when you come in to pick up an **Epcot Guidebook** and **entertainment schedule,** and, if you so desire, make reservations for lunch or dinner. Many

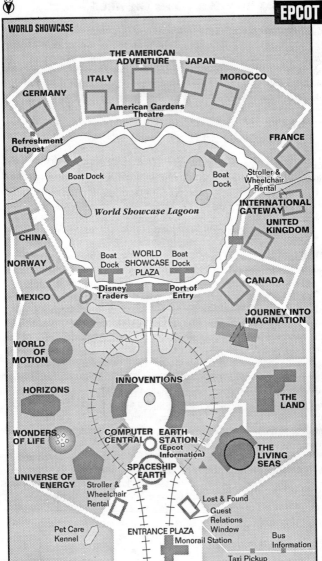

WORLD SHOWCASE

N

THE AMERICAN ADVENTURE

JAPAN

ITALY

MOROCCO

GERMANY

American Gardens Theatre

FRANCE

Refreshment Outpost

Boat Dock

Boat Dock

Stroller & Wheelchair Rental

World Showcase Lagoon

INTERNATIONAL GATEWAY

UNITED KINGDOM

CHINA

NORWAY

Boat Dock

WORLD SHOWCASE PLAZA

Boat Dock

CANADA

MEXICO

Disney Traders

Port of Entry

JOURNEY INTO IMAGINATION

WORLD OF MOTION

THE LAND

INNOVENTIONS

HORIZONS

THE LIVING SEAS

WONDERS OF LIFE

COMPUTER CENTRAL

EARTH STATION (Epcot Information)

SPACESHIP EARTH

UNIVERSE OF ENERGY

Stroller & Wheelchair Rental

Lost & Found

Guest Relations Window

Pet Care Kennel

ENTRANCE PLAZA

Monorail Station

Bus Information

FUTURE WORLD

Taxi Pickup

6604

Epcot restaurants are described in Chapter 6. Then check out your show schedule and incorporate shows you want to see into your itinerary. Strollers can be rented to your left at the Future World entrance plaza and in World Showcase at the International Gateway between the United Kingdom and France.

Since most people begin the day by touring Future World, the best way to beat the crowds is to head directly to World Showcase. Arrive early, tickets in hand. Take a launch across to either side of the lagoon, and work your way down to the right or left, taking in World Showcase and Future World attractions on one side of the park. By the time you reach Future World in the afternoon, traffic there will be lighter. The second day, follow the same method and cover the other side of the park.

FUTURE WORLD

The northern section of Epcot (where you enter the park) comprises Future World, centered on a giant geosphere known as Spaceship Earth. Future World's 10 themed areas, sponsored by major American corporations, focus on discovery, scientific achievements, and tomorrow's technologies in areas running the gamut from energy to undersea exploration.

SPACESHIP EARTH Spaceship Earth, housed in a massive silvery "geosphere" 180 feet high and 165 feet in diameter, is Epcot's most cogent symbol. Inside, a show presented by AT&T, created by sci-fi writer Ray Bradbury, and narrated by Walter Cronkite, takes visitors on a 15-minute journey through the history of communications beginning 40,000 years ago. We board time-machine vehicles and are drawn into a whirling space-warp vortex to the distant past. An Audio-Animatronic™ Cro-Magnon shaman recounts the story of a hunt while others record it on cave walls. The link between communications and survival is established. We advance thousands of years to ancient Egypt, where hieroglyphics adorn the walls of columns and temples and writing is recorded on papyrus scrolls, becoming portable. With typical Disney thoroughness, the hieroglyphics are authentic, and words being recorded by a scribe are taken from an actual letter sent by a pharoah to one of his agents. By the 9th century B.C., the Phoenicians have developed a 22-letter alphabet, simplifying communications; sailor-merchants, they spread their invention throughout the known world. As our time machine moves ahead, the Greeks have added vowels to the alphabet and refined its use as a tool to express new inner needs—speculative thought, art, and philosophy; the theater is born. Roman roads expand the network of communications, and the vast Islamic empire furthers the dispersion of manuscripts that enhance knowledge of science, astronomy, and art. In the Middle Ages, we see Benedictine monks painstakingly reproducing classical and religious wisdom by hand, prior to the revolutionary development of the Gutenberg press in 1456. Man's increasing ability to disseminate ideas becomes a catalyst for the Renaissance, which, in turn, spawns the Age of Invention. Technologies develop at a rapid pace, enlarging our communications spectrum via steam power, electricity, the telegraph, telephone, radio, movies, and TV. It is but a short step to the age of computers and electronic communications; centuries of information can now reach us in an instant. We are catapulted into outer space to see spaceship earth from a new perspective, returning via a kaleido-scopic passageway in a dazzling special-effects finale that places the audience amid interactive global networks. High-tech special effects, animated sets, and laser beams create an exciting experience in this "global neighborhood," and new shows demonstrate emerging technologies such as voice recognition, video telepathy, and the much-touted information highway.

As you leave Spaceship Earth, you'll enter Earth Station, an electronic information center with guest-relations booths and touch-sensitive video monitors (where you can make reservations for Epcot restaurants). Staff here can answer all questions.

THE LIVING SEAS This United Technologies–sponsored pavil-ion contains the world's sixth "ocean," a 5.6 million-gallon saltwater aquarium (including a complete coral reef), inhabited by more than 4,000 sea creatures—sharks, barracudas, parrot fish, rays, and dolphins among them. Rockwork at the entrance simulates a natural coastline, with waves cascading into tidal pools. While waiting on line, visitors pass exhibits tracing the history of undersea exploration, including a glass diving barrel used by Alexan-der the Great in 332 B.C. and Sir Edmund Halley's first diving bell (1697). A 2½-minute multimedia preshow highlighting today's under-sea technology (sophisticated robotics and computers) is followed by a seven-minute film demonstrating the formation of the earth and seas as a means to support life.

After the films, visitors enter hydrolators for a rapid descent to the sunlit ocean floor. Upon arrival, they board Seacabs that wind around a 400-foot-long tunnel to enjoy stunning close-up views (through acrylic windows) of ocean denizens in a natural coral-reef habitat. The ride concludes in the Seabase Concourse, which is the visitors center of Seabase Alpha, a prototype ocean-research facility of the future. Here exhibits include a 22½-foot scuba tube used by Seabase Alpha scientists to enter and leave the waters. And seven information-al modules contain numerous exhibits focusing on ocean ecosystems, harvestable resources grown in controlled undersea environments, marine mammals (dolphins, sea lions, manatees), earth systems (the relationship between the planet's seas and its landmasses), the study of oceanography from space, undersea exploration (featuring an Audio-Animatronic™ deep-sea submersible robot), and life in a coral-reef community. Many of these exhibits are hands-on. You can expand your knowledge of oceanography via interactive computers or step into a diver's JIM Suit and use controls to complete diving tasks.

THE LAND Sponsored by Nestlé, this largest of the Future World pavilions highlights man's relation to food and nature in a variety of intriguing attractions.

A 13-minute excursion in a canopied boat,   ✪ **Living with the Land** takes us through three ecological environments, each popu-lated by Audio-Animatronic™ denizens. In the rain forest—with its dense foliage and tangle of vines, tree ferns, cascading waterfalls, and serene lagoon—we meet up with chattering birds and insects, whooping howler monkeys, and crocodiles. Its humidity is replaced by the dry, oppressive heat of an African desert, where we experience a sandstorm. It subsides as we approach a fog-filled tunnel en route to America's midwestern windswept plains—scene of a thunder and lightning storm that precipitates a grass fire, rousing a swarm of locusts. We sail on, into pastoral American autumn scenery, where a film in a barn theater examines 100 years of American farming from early plows to modern machinery. And from here on, new farming methods and experiments—such as hydroponics, aeroponics, aquaculture, desert farming, even plants growing in simulated Martian and lunar soil!—are showcased in real gardens. The food grown here is utilized in Walt Disney World restaurants. If you'd like a more serious overview, take a 45-minute **guided walking tour** of the growing areas. They're given every half hour between 9:30am and 4:30pm. You have to sign up at the Broccoli & Co. shop near the entrance to Food Rocks, and the boat tour is a recommended prerequisite. I found it fascinating.

Under construction as we go to press, ✪ **Circle of Life**—a 15-minute, 70mm motion picture based on the Disney feature, *The Lion King*—will utilize a combination of live and animated characters. It will star Simba, Timon, and Pumbaa in a cautionary environmental tale. Timon and Pumbaa are building a monument to the good life called Hakuna Matata Village, but their project, as Simba points out, is damaging the savannah for other animals. Simba relates a story about how other creatures (humans) once nearly destroyed their beautiful planet, and how they finally learned from their mistakes and cleaned up the land, air, and water.

Food Rocks, another new show under development at this writing, features Audio-Animatronic™ rock performers transformed into culinary favorites—Pita Gabriel, Chubby Cheddar, and the Peach Boys, among others—to deliver an entertaining message about nutrition.

JOURNEY INTO IMAGINATION In this wondrous pavilion, presented by Kodak and housed in glass pyramids, even the fountains are magical, with arching streams of water that leap into the air like glass rods.

A major new attraction, ✪ **Honey I Shrunk the Audience,** a 3-D movie based on the Disney hit film *Honey I Shrunk the Kids* (and its sequel, *Honey I Blew Up the Kid*), will open shortly after we go to press. Its 3-D thrills will be enhanced by moving seats and other special effects. Many of the cast members from the two films will appear. The action begins at an awards ceremony at the Imagination Institute where Dr. Szalinski is being honored with the "Inventor of the Year" award. But while demonstrating his latest inventions, he inadvertently shrinks the entire audience. While waiting to get in, you'll enjoy a charmingly narrated slide montage of Kodak moments. It's a real tearjerker.

Journey Into Imagination Ride: Visitors board moving cars for a 14-minute ride, hosted by a red-bearded adventurer named Dreamfinder and his sidekick, Figment—a mischievous baby dragon with a childlike ability to dream. After a simulated flight across the nighttime sky, we enter the "Imaginarium," where a dream-catching machine is vacuuming up "sparks of imagination, ideas, and natural elements" into a giant storage bag. We then ride past whimsical tableaux in which Audio-Animatronic™ characters explore the creative worlds of the fine arts, literature, the performing arts (complete with laser-light dancers), science (Dreamfinder's lab is filled with magical gadgetry), and image technology (aka movies). The ride culminates at:

Image Works, housing dozens of hands-on electronic devices and interactive computers. Here you can activate different musical instruments by stepping on hexagons of colored light (remember Tom Hanks in *Big*?), participate in a TV drama, paint on a magic palette, draw patterns with laser beams, operate a giant kaleidoscope, wend your way through the Rainbow Corridor of a sensor maze, and conduct an electronic philharmonic orchestra.

INNOVENTIONS The pair of crescent-shaped buildings to your right and left just beyond Spaceship Earth (formerly called CommuniCore East and CommuniCore West) contain numerous exhibits that are being revamped at this writing. Both buildings will soon house a major new and constantly evolving exhibit called Innoventions that will showcase cutting-edge and future products for home, work, and play. Guests will preview the latest developments in interactive TV, hand-held personal digital assistants, micro-discs, electronic games and toys, high-definition TV, voice-activated appliances, computerized home management, automobile navigation equipment, telephone technologies, group video games, and more. With new systems such as CD-ROM and interactive CDs, visitors will be able to "tour" the Egyptian pyramids and choose preferred viewing angles. Leading manufacturers will sponsor many of the exhibit areas (there will be 15 major displays). There will also be live stage demonstrations and interactive hands-on displays.

The two-story **Epcot Discovery Center,** which will be located on the right side of Innoventions, will include an information resource area where guests can get answers to all their questions about Epcot attractions in particular and Walt Disney World in general. For instance, if after visiting The Land, you would like to learn more about hydroponics, they can print out an information sheet on it. The Discovery Center will also house a shop called **Field Trips** featuring educational products and software.

IN THE WORDS OF WALT DISNEY

"In my view, wholesome pleasure, sport, and recreation are as vital to this nation as productive work and should have a large share in the national budget."

WORLD OF MOTION Everything you always wanted to know about transportation—past, present, and future—is explored in this General Motors–sponsored, vast wheel-shaped, gleaming stainless-steel pavilion.

Its highlight is the **World of Motion Show,** a whimsical 15-minute ride-through attraction—utilizing animated scenery, 70mm film, and a cast of 140 Audio-Animatronic™ characters—that documents civilization's eternal quest for movement. It begins with sore-footed cavemen, early attempts at riding animals (test-driving a zebra), and the invention of the wheel. Leonardo is shown experimenting with ideas for flight, the era of railroads is represented by a train being held up by masked desperadoes, and an astonished horse looks on as a man cranks up a car. Just about every mode of transport is covered—from paddlewheelers to ocean liners, from wagon trains to barnstorming planes. We proceed—always to a cheerful background score called "It's Fun to Be Free"—to the widening travel opportunities presented by auto and air travel. And, this being Walt Disney World, the ride climaxes with a dizzying journey through computer-graphics space for a look at the future—spaceship transportation.

Transcenter, the other major attraction here, offers a behind-the-scenes look at General Motors' advanced engineering and manufacturing facilities, its prototype vehicles of the future, and its concerns in creating nonpolluting engines and fuel economy. Here you can test your knowledge of automotive signals, learn how robotics are used in automobile manufacturing (via a humorous show starring a wisecracking toucan and an assembly-line robot named Tiger), find out about the use of computer diagramming in car design, and, of course, sit down in the prototype models and examine the controls.

HORIZONS The theme of this pavilion is the future, which presents an unending series of new horizons. In the line area, designed as a futuristic transportation center, a public address system pages passengers bound for exotic destinations. We board sideways-facing gondolas for a 15-minute journey into the next millennium. The first tableau honors visionaries of past centuries (like Jules Verne) and looks at outdated visions of the future and classic sci-fi movies. We ascend to an area where an IMAX film projected on two 80-foot-high screens presents a kaleidoscope of brilliant micro and macro images—growing crystals, colonies in space, solar power, a space shuttle launching, DNA molecules, and a computer chip. We then travel to 21st-century cityscapes, desert farms, floating cities under the ocean's surface, and outer space colonies populated by Audio-Animatronic™ denizens who use holographic telephones, magnetic levitation trains, and voice-controlled robotic field hands. For the return to earth from a space colony, riders have a choice of three futuristic transportation systems—a personal spacecraft, desert Hovercraft, or mini-submarine.

WONDERS OF LIFE Housed in a vast geodesic dome fronted by a 75-foot replica of a DNA molecule, this pavilion, presented by Metropolitan Life, offers some of Future World's most engaging shows and attractions.

Starring zany comedian Martin Short, ✪ **The Making of Me** is the sweetest introduction imaginable to the facts of life. In a captivating 15-minute film combining live action with animation, Short travels back in time to witness his parents as children, their meeting at a college dance, their wedding, and their decision to have a baby. Along with him, we view his development inside his mother's womb (via spectacular in-utero photography) and witness his birth. If you've not yet told your kids about sex, you couldn't find a better springboard to that important conversation.

In ✪ **Body Wars,** audience members join ex-fighter pilot Jack Braddock on a medical rescue mission inside the immune system of a human body. Our objective: to save Dr. Cynthia Lair, a miniaturized immunologist who has been accidentally swept into the bloodstream (while studying the body's response to a splinter) and come under attack from white blood cells! After passing through dermatopic purification stations and undergoing miniaturization (to the size of a single cell), visitors board moving theaters for this motion-simulator ride that utilizes special computer-graphics and 70mm motion-picture footage to evoke a wild journey through gale-force winds (in the lungs) and pounding heart chambers. Leonard Nimoy directed.

In ✪ **Cranium Command,** a totally delightful multidimensional theater attraction, Buzzy, an Audio-Animatronic™ brain-pilot-in-training, is charged with the seemingly impossible mission of controlling the brain of Bobby, a typical 12-year-old boy. A five-minute animated film introduces the story line and characters. Cranium Command is a training center for brain pilots, in which Buzzy has to prove his ability at the helm. The boy's left brain (logic) is played by Charles Grodin, his right brain (emotion/creativity) by Jon Lovitz, his out-of-control adrenal gland by Bob Goldthwait, his "pumped-up" heart by Kevin Nealon and Dana Carvey (as Hans and Franz of "Saturday Night Live"), and his oft-upset stomach by George Wendt (Norm from "Cheers"). The audience is seated inside Bobby's head as Buzzy guides him through a day of typical preadolescent traumas—running for the school bus, meeting a girl, fighting bullies, and a run-in with the school principal.

Finally, there's **Fitness Fairgrounds,** a large area filled with fitness-related shows, exhibits, and participatory activities. These include an eight-minute multimedia presentation called Goofy About Health (stressed-out Goofy has the *Unhealthy Livin' Blues* until he reforms and extols the joys of healthy living), the Anacomical Players (a live improvisational theater troupe who perform 15-minute health-related comic skits), and Coach's Corner (your tennis, golf, or baseball swing is videotaped and replayed in slow-motion, with specific video tips for improvement provided by Chris Evert, Nancy Lopez, and Gary Carter, respectively). You can also do a light workout on a video-enhanced exercise bike here, receive a personalized computer-generated evaluation of your health habits, play sensory games, and take a video voyage to investigate the effects of drugs, tobacco, and alcohol on your heart. There's much, much more. You could easily spend hours here.

UNIVERSE OF ENERGY   Sponsored by Exxon, this pavilion— its roof glistening with solar panels—aims to better our understanding of America's energy problems and potential solutions via a 35-minute ride-through attraction with visitors seated in solar-powered "traveling theater" cars (hard to explain, you'll see what I mean).

The experience begins with an introductory kinetic multi-image preshow tracing our use of energy from primitive to modern times. On a massive screen in Theatre I, an animated motion picture depicts the earth's molten beginnings, its cooling process, and the first stirrings of life—microscopic ocean plants. As they die, their organic matter accumulates on the ocean floor, are compressed into shale, and begin a slow transformation (over eons) into oil and gas. Meanwhile, life is evolving in the primeval forest, and a similar process ensues as dying leaves form a spongy mass of peat that sinks deep under the mud and sand to emerge after many millennia as coal.

We move from Theatre I to travel back 275 million years into an eerie storm-wracked landscape of the Mesozoic era—a time of violent geological activity. Here, we're menaced by giant Audio-Animatronic™ dragonflies, pterodactyls, dinosaurs, earthquakes, and streams of molten lava before entering a steam-filled tunnel and traveling through the bowels of a volcano to emerge back in the 20th century in Theatre II. In this new setting, which looks like a NASA mission control room, a 70mm film, projected on a massive 210-foot wraparound screen, depicts the challenges of the world's increasing energy demands and the emerging technologies that will help meet them. The film takes us from the Alaska pipeline to desert oil drums in the Middle East, to ocean oil tankers, and outer space, where satellites help us locate new gas and oil deposits.

Our moving seats now return to Theatre I where swirling special effects herald a film about how energy impacts our lives in areas such as mobility, communications, agriculture, health, education, and recreation. It ends on a dramatically upbeat note complete with a light show and musical crescendo—a vision of an energy-abundant future.

WORLD SHOWCASE

Surrounding a 40-acre lagoon at the park's southern end is World Showcase—a permanent community of 11 miniaturized nations, all with authentically indigenous landmark architecture, landscaping, background music, restaurants, and shops. The cultural facets of each nation are explored in art exhibits, dance performances, and innovative rides, films, and attractions. And all of the employees in each pavilion are natives of the country represented.

CANADA Our brothers to the north are represented by diverse architecture ranging from a mansard-roofed replica of Ottawa's 19th-century French-style Château Laurier (here called the Hôtel du Canada) to a British-influenced rustic stone building modeled after a famous landmark near Niagara Falls. An Indian village—complete with rough-hewn log trading post and 30-foot replicas of Ojibwa totem poles—signifies the culture of the northwest, while the Canadian wilderness is reflected by a steep mountain (a Canadian Rocky), a waterfall cascading into a whitewater stream, and a "forest" of evergreens, stately cedars, maples, and birch trees. Don't miss the stunning floral displays of azaleas, roses, zinnias, chrysanthemums, petunias, and patches of wildflowers inspired by the Butchart Gardens in Victoria, B.C. The pavilion's highlight attraction is *O Canada!*—a dazzling 360-degree Circle-Vision™ film that reveals Canada's scenic splendor from sophisticated Montréal to the thundering flight of thousands of snow geese departing an autumn stopover near the St. Lawrence River. Other scenes (there are more than 50) depict a chuckwagon race in the Calgary stampede, the pine-covered mountains of Banff National Park, a fishing village off the Newfoundland coast, herds of reindeer on Tuktoyaktuk Peninsula in the Northwest Territory, and an aerial view of the majestic snow-covered Rockies. The film is 18 minutes in length. Canada pavilion shops carry sandstone and soapstone carvings, fringed leather vests, snowshoes, lumberjack shirts, duck decoys, fur-lined parkas, moccasins, toy tomahawks and teepees, a vast array of Eskimo stuffed animals and Native American dolls, turquoise jewelry, and, of course, maple syrup.

UNITED KINGDOM Centered on Brittania Square—a formal London-style park, complete with copper-roofed gazebo bandstand and a statue of the Bard—the U.K. pavilion evokes Merry Olde England. Four centuries of architecture are represented along quaint cobblestoned streets; troubadours and minstrels entertain in front of a traditional British pub; and a formal garden with low box hedges in geometric patterns, flagstone paths, and a stone fountain replicates the landscaping of 16th- and 17th-century palaces. High Street and Tudor Lane shops display a broad sampling of British merchandise— toy soldiers, Paddington bears, hobbyhorses, personalized coats of arms, tobaccos and pipes, Scottish clothing (cashmere and Shetland sweaters, golf wear, tams, knits, and tartans), shortbreads, Royal Doulton china, and Waterford crystal. A tea shop occupies a replica of Anne Hathaway's thatch-roofed 16th-century cottage in Stratford-upon-Avon, while other emporia represent the Georgian, Victorian, Queen Anne, and Tudor periods. Background music ranges from "Greensleeves" to the Beatles.

FRANCE Focusing on La Belle Epoque (1870–1910)—a flourishing

⭐ period for French art, literature, and architecture—this pavilion is entered via a replica of the beautiful cast-iron Pont des Arts footbridge over the "Seine." It leads to a park with pleached sycamores, Bradford pear trees, flowering crape myrtles, and sculpted parterre flower gardens that was inspired by Seurat's painting *A Sunday Afternoon on the Island of La Grande Jatte*. A one-tenth replica of the Eiffel Tower constructed from Gustave Eiffel's original blueprints looms above *les grands boulevards*, and period buildings feature copper mansard roofs and casement windows. The highlight attraction is *Impressions de France*. Shown in a palatial (mercifully sit-down) theater à la Fontainebleau, this 18-minute film is a breathtakingly scenic journey through diverse French landscapes projected on a vast 200-degree-view wraparound screen. Enhanced by music of French composers, it takes us from charming farm and fishing villages to the sophistication of Paris and the Côte d'Azur. We soar over the steep cliffs of Etretat in Normandy and the French Alps near Mont Blanc, attend a traditional Brittany wedding, visit Versailles, and see vineyards at harvest time. Emporia in the covered shopping arcade, with art nouveau Métro facades at either end, have interiors ranging from a turn-of-the-century bibliothèque to a French château. Merchandise includes French art prints, cookbooks, cookware, fashions, wines, pâtés, bonbons, berets, Madeline and Babar books and dolls, and perfumes. Another marketplace/tourism center revives the defunct Les Halles, where Parisians used to sip onion soup in the wee hours. The heavenly aroma of a *boulangerie* penetrates the atmosphere, and mimes, jugglers, and strolling chanteurs entertain.

MOROCCO This exotic pavilion—its architecture embellished with intricate geometrically patterned tilework, minarets, hand-painted wood ceilings, and brass lighting fixtures—is heralded by a replica of the Koutoubia Minaret, the prayer tower of a 12th-century mosque in Marrakesh. The Medina (old city), entered via a replica of an arched gateway in Fez, leads to Fez House (a traditional Moroccan home) and the narrow winding streets of the *souk*, a bustling marketplace where all manner of authentic hand-crafted merchandise is on display. Here you can peruse or purchase pottery, brassware, sheepskin bags, baskets, hand-knotted Berber carpets, colorful Rabat carpets, prayer rugs, and wall hangings. There are weaving demonstrations in the *souk* throughout the day. The Medina's rectangular courtyard centers on a replica of the ornately tiled Najjarine Fountain in Fez, the setting for musical entertainment. The pavilion's Royal Gallery contains an ever-changing exhibit of Moroccan art, and the Center of Tourism offers a continuous three-screen slide show. Along the pavilion's banks, an ancient-looking water wheel lifts water from the lagoon to nourish a formal garden. Morocco's landscaping also includes citrus and olive trees, date palms, and banana plants.

JAPAN Heralded by a flaming red *torii* (gate of honor) on the banks of the lagoon and the graceful blue-roofed Goju No To pagoda (its five stories representing earth, water, fire, wind, and sky), this pavilion focuses on Japan's ancient culture. The pagoda, topped by a bronze spire with gold wind chimes and a water flame, was inspired by a shrine built at Nara in 700 A.D. In a traditional Japanese garden, cedars, yew trees, bamboo, "cloud-pruned" evergreens, willows, and flowering shrubs frame a contemplative setting of pebbled footpaths, rustic bridges, waterfalls, exquisite rock landscaping, and a pond of golden koi. The Yakitori House is based on the renowned 16th-century Katsura Imperial Villa in Kyoto, designed as a royal summer residence and considered by many to be the crowning achievement of Japanese architecture. Exhibits ranging from 18th-century Bunraki puppets to samurai armor take place in the moated White Heron Castle, a replica of the Shirasagi-Jo, a 17th-century fortress overlooking the city of Himeji. And the Mitsukoshi Department Store (Japan's answer to Macy's) is housed in a replica of the Shishinden (Hall of Ceremonies) of the Gosho Imperial Palace built in Kyoto in 794 A.D. It sells lacquer screens, kimonos, kites, fans, collectible dolls in traditional costumes, origami books, tea sets, samurai swords, Japanese Disneyana, incense burners, bonsai plants, pottery, even modern electronics. In the courtyard, artisans demonstrate the ancient arts of *anesaiku* (shaping brown rice candy into dragons, unicorns, and dolphins), *ikebana* (flower arranging), *sumi-e* (calligraphy), and *origami* (paper folding). Be sure to include a show of traditional Japanese music and dance at this pavilion in your schedule. It's one of the best in the World Showcase.

THE AMERICAN ADVENTURE Housed in a vast Georgian-style structure, *The American Adventure* is a 29-minute dramatization of U.S. history utilizing a 72-foot rear-projection screen, rousing music, and a large cast of lifelike Audio-Animatronic™ figures, including narrators Mark Twain and Ben Franklin. The "adventure" begins with the voyage of the *Mayflower* and encompasses major historic events. We view Jefferson writing the Declaration of Independence, the expansion of the frontier, Mathew Brady photographing a family about to be divided by the Civil War, the stock market crash of 1929, Pearl Harbor, and the *Eagle* heading toward the moon. John Muir and Teddy Roosevelt discuss the need for national parks, Susan B. Anthony speaks out on women's rights, Frederick Douglass on slavery, Chief Joseph on the situation of Native Americans. Twelve life-size statues flanking the stage symbolically represent aspects of the American spirit such as Independence, Knowledge, Compassion, and Pioneering. While waiting for the show to begin, you'll be entertained by the wonderful Voices of Liberty Singers performing American folk songs in the Main Hall. Note the quotes from famous Americans on the walls here. Formally symmetrical gardens shaded by live oaks, sycamores, elms, and holly complement the pavilion's 18th-century architecture; ivy suspended from lampposts is shaped into Liberty Bells; and a rose garden includes varieties named for American presidents. A shop called Heritage Manor Gifts sells American food products, Coca-

Cola memorabilia, patchwork baby quilts, Confederate and Davy Crockett hats, books on American history, historically costumed dolls, classic political campaign buttons, and vintage newspapers with banner headlines like "Nixon Resigns!" An artisan in the shop makes jewelry out of coins.

ITALY   One of the prettiest World Showcase pavilions, Italy lures visitors over an arched stone footbridge to a replica of Venice's intricately ornamented pink and white Doge's Palace (built between the 9th and 16th centuries). Other architectural highlights include the 83-foot Campanile (bell tower) of St. Mark's Square topped by a gold-leafed angel, Venetian bridges, Corinthian columns, and a central piazza enclosing a version of Bernini's Neptune Fountain with a delightful statue of the sea god flanked by water-spewing dolphins. A garden wall suggests a backdrop of provincial countryside, and Mediterranean citrus, olive trees, cypress, and pine frame a formal garden. Gondolas are moored on the lagoon. Shops—some of them in the Arcata d'Artigiani, a Tuscan-style open-air market—sell baskets, leather, Benetton clothing, Perugina chocolates, biscotti, cameo and filigree jewelry, Murano and Venetian glass, alabaster figurines, and inlaid wooden music boxes. A troupe of street actors perform a contemporary version of 16th-century commedia dell'arte in the piazza.

GERMANY   Enclosed by towered castle walls, this festive pavilion is centered on a cobblestoned *Platz* with pots of colorful flowers girding a fountain statue of St. George and the Dragon. An adjacent clock tower is embellished with whimsical glockenspiel figures that herald each hour with quaint melodies. The pavilion's outdoor Biergarten—where it's Oktoberfest all year long—was inspired by medieval Rothenberg. And 16th-century building facades replicate a merchant's hall in the Black Forest (embellished with statues of three Hapsburg emperors) and the town hall in Frankfurt's Römerberg Square. Shops here carry Hummel figurines, crystal, glassware, cookware, cuckoo clocks, cowbells, music boxes, pewterware, German wines and specialty foods, toys (German Disneyana, teddy bears, dolls, and puppets), Christmas ornaments, art reproductions, and books. An artisan demonstrates the molding and painting of Hummel figures, another paints exquisitely detailed scenes on eggs. Background music runs the gamut from oom-pah bands to Mozart symphonies.

CHINA   Bounded by a serpentine wall that snakes around its outer perimeter, the China pavilion is entered via a vast triple-arched ceremonial gate inspired by the Temple of Heaven in Beijing, a summer retreat for Chinese emperors. Passing through the gate, you'll see a half-size replica of this ornately embellished red and gold circular temple, built in 1420 during the Ming dynasty. Gardens simulate those in Suzhou, with miniature waterfalls, fragrant lotus ponds, groves of bamboo, stately pines, scrub oaks, corkscrew willows, and weeping mulberry trees. The highlight attraction here is *Wonders of China,* a 20-minute, 360-degree Circle-Vision™ film that explores 6,000 years of dynastic and Communist rule and the breathtaking diversity of the Chinese landscape. Narrated by 8th-century Tang dynasty poet Li Bai, it includes scenes of the Great Wall (begun 24 centuries ago!), a performance by the Beijing Opera, a Manchurian ice-sculpture festival, the Forbidden City in Beijing with 9,000 rooms in six palaces, Yangtze River gorges, rice terraces of Hunan Province, the Gobi Desert, and tropical rain forests of Hainan Island. Adjacent to the theater, an art gallery fronted by a hanging lotus gate and atrium courtyard houses changing exhibits of Chinese art. A bustling marketplace festooned with colorful streamers and banners offers an array of merchandise including silk robes, lacquer and carved-jade furniture, jade figures, cloisonné vases, paper umbrellas, silk rugs and embroideries, stuffed pandas, kites, dolls, fans, pottery, wind chimes, and Chinese clothing. Note the towering stone elephant nearby: Legend has it that if you throw a stone on its back and it remains there, luck will follow you the rest of your days. Artisans here paint wooden ducks and demonstrate calligraphy.

NORWAY   Centered on a picturesque cobblestone courtyard, this pavilion evokes ancient Norway. A *stavekirke* (stave church), styled after the 13th-century Gol Church of Hallingdal, its eaves embellished with wooden dragon heads, houses changing exhibits. A replica of Oslo's 14th-century Akershus Castle, next to a cascading woodland waterfall, is the setting for the pavilion's featured restaurant. Other buildings simulate the red-roofed cottages of Bergen and the timber-sided farm buildings of the Nordic woodlands. There's a two-part attraction here. **Maelstrom,** a boat ride in a dragon-headed Viking vessel, traverses Norway's fjords and mythical forests to the music of *Peer Gynt*—an exciting journey during which you'll be menaced by polar bears prowling the shore and trolls who cast a spell on the boat and propel it backward into raging rapids. The watercraft crashes through a narrow gorge and spins into the North Sea where a violent storm, complete with crashing waves and lightning, is in progress. But the storm abates, and passengers disembark safely in a 10th-century Viking village to view the 70mm film *Norway,* which documents a thousand years of history. Featured images include *Oseberg bat* (a 1,000-year-old Viking ship), a fiery nighttime view of an oil rig silhouetted against 45-foot waves of the tumultuous North Sea, a small fishing village, festive national holiday celebrations in Oslo, and soaring jumps at the Holmenkollen ski resort. Shops feature hand-knit wool hats and sweaters, toys (Legos—there's a table where kids can play with them while you shop—troll dolls, children's books, Viking swords), pewterware, and jewelry made from Norwegian gemstones.

MEXICO   You'll hear the music of marimba and mariachi bands as you approach the festive showcase of Mexico, fronted by a towering

Mayan pyramid modeled on the Aztec temple of Quetzalcoatl (God of Life) dating to the 3rd century A.D. It is adorned with fierce serpent heads, symbols of fertility and renewal, and surrounded by dense Yucatán jungle landscaping (fan palms, bamboo, banana trees, jacarandas, and trumpet trees). Upon entering the pavilion, you'll find yourself in a museum of pre-Columbian artifacts. Down a ramp is a small lagoon, the setting for **El Rio del Tiempo** (River of Time), where visitors board boats for eight-minute cruises through Mexico's past and present. Passengers get a close-up look at the above-mentioned pyramid and the erupting Popocatepetl volcano. Dance performances focusing on the cultures of Mayan, Toltec, Aztec, and colonial Mexico are presented in film segments and by an Audio-Animatronic™ cast of folk-costumed Dondi look-alikes in vignettes ranging from a Day of the Dead skeleton band atop an archway to children breaking a piñata. Additional film footage focuses on Mexican tourist spots. The show culminates in a Mexico City fiesta with exploding fiber-optics fireworks. Shops in and around the Plaza de Los Amigos (a "moonlit" Mexican *mercado* with a tiered fountain and streetlamps) display an array of leather wallets and handbags, baskets, sombreros, big paper flowers, piñatas, pottery, embroidered dresses and blouses, maracas, papier-mâché birds, worry dolls, turquoise jewelry, carved onyx animals, cut-tin candle lamps, weavings, and blown-glass objects (an artisan gives demonstrations). La Casa de Vacaciones, sponsored by the Mexican Tourist Office, provides travel information.

ILLUMINATIONS & SHOWS

IllumiNations, a 16½-minute spectacular using high-tech lighting effects, darting laser beams, fireworks, strobes, and rainbow-lit dancing fountains, takes place nightly. A backdrop of classical music by international composers (representing World Showcase nations) enhances the drama. Each nation is highlighted in turn. Colorful kites fly over Japan, the giant Rockies loom over Canada, a gingerbread house rises in Germany, and so on. Find a seat around the lagoon about a half hour before show time.

Live shows, especially those in World Showcase, make up an important part of the Epcot experience. Among others, these might include lion dancers in China, oom-pah bands playing lively polkas in Germany, Caledonian bagpipers in Canada, jesters and stilt-dancing puppeteers in the United Kingdom, and Moroccan belly dancers. Two especially good shows are the Voices of Liberty singers at The American Adventure Pavilion and the traditional music and dance displays in Japan. Check your show schedule when you come in, and plan your day to include some of them.

✪ The new **Splashtacular,** a 20-minute futuristic musical extravaganza centering on Epcot's vast CommuniCore fountain, features a cast of lavishly costumed dancers (in notably vibrant colors like bright yellow, kelly green, and shocking pink), stilt-walkers, space aliens, and Disney characters. Mickey (decked out à la *Fantasia* in silver conductor's tuxedo and tails) is the star. Dazzling special effects include hundreds of laser-like jets of water crashing 150 feet skyward in a stunning aquatic dance. In a story line pitting good against evil, a wicked alien sorceress conjures up an intergalactic nemesis called TerrosaurX (he has 30 metal-spike teeth and drools!). Towering 45 feet above the stage, and heralded by a sinister army of silver guards on stilts, he menaces hapless earthlings. Upon his arrival, the dancers' costumes lose all their color, and the fountains cease to flow. But Mickey—with his magic conducting wand—triumphs over the fearsome monster, and the show ends in a brilliant technicolor finale complete with rainbows, hundreds of bubbles, dancing butterflies, and fireworks. A soaring symphonic score and rousing song and dance numbers add drama and verve to the proceedings. Check your show schedule for presentation times.

In **The Magical World of Barbie,** presented at the outdoor America Gardens Theater (just across from The American Adventure Pavilion in World Showcase), Barbie, Ken, Skipper, Stacy, and the rest of their ever-exuberant doll family and friends come to life in a perky 30-minute around-the-world stage show. Amid lively music and dance numbers (everything from Prokofiev to 1960s beach songs), Barbie and pals travel to the Australian outback with "Wombat Dundee" to see kangaroos and koalas and splash the audience in a surfing scene, attend "Guy de Croissant's" Paris fashion show (a disaster until Barbie saves the day by accessorizing his designs), and show up at a Russian ballet theater and in the African jungle— always, of course, in appropriate outfits from their vast wardrobes. There's a grand finale with doves and streamers released over the audience. Barbie's 40-foot glittering fuschia stretch limo is parked in front of the theater. By the way, I picked up this bit of trivia from Mattel™ reps at the première show: Barbie's full name is Barbara Millicent Roberts, and her birthday is March 9, 1959.

DISNEY-MGM STUDIOS THEME PARK

In 1989, Walt Disney World premiered its third "magical kingdom," Disney-MGM Studios, offering exciting movie- and TV-themed shows and behind-the-scenes "reel-life" adventures. Heralded by the 130-foot-high Mouseketeer-hatted "Earffel Tower," its main streets include Hollywood and Sunset boulevards, with art deco movie sets evocative of Hollywood's glamorous golden age. There's also a New York Street lined with Gotham landmarks (the Empire State, Flatiron, and Chrysler buildings) and typical New York characters including wisecracking workmen, peddlers hawking knockoff watches, and cops. More importantly, this is a working movie and TV studio, where shows are in production even as you tour the premises.

Arrive at the park early, tickets in hand. Unlike the Magic Kingdom and Epcot, Disney-MGM's 110 acres of attractions can pretty much be seen in one day. The parking lot is right at the gate. If you don't get a **Disney-MGM Studios Guidebook** and/or **entertainment schedule** when you enter the park, you can pick them up at Guest Services. First thing to do is check show times and work out an entertainment schedule based on highlight attractions and geographical proximity. Then, if you so desire, make restaurant reservations for lunch or dinner (my favorite restaurants here are described in Chapter 6). Strollers can be rented at Oscar's Super Service inside the main entrance. Major attractions include:

THE TWILIGHT ZONE TOWER OF TERROR In a thrilling journey to another dimension, you'll enter the once-grand but now deserted (and haunted) Hollywood Tower hotel, and wend your way through the dimly lit lobby and library (a walk made more interesting by deceptive optical-illusion effects) to the boiler room. Here, you'll board the ride vehicle (a giant elevator) and ascend past mysterious hotel hallways, beckoned by ghostly guests enroute. The climax: The creaking hotel "elevator" malfunctions in descent, sending passengers on a terrifying 13-story free-fall plunge into The Twilight Zone! Rod Serling narrates.

THE MAGIC OF DISNEY ANIMATION You'll see Disney characters come alive at the stroke of a brush or pencil as you tour actual glass-walled animation studios and watch artists at work. Walter Cronkite and Robin Williams (guess who plays straight man?) explain what's going on via video monitors, and they also star in a very funny eight-minute Peter Pan–themed film about the basics of animation. It's painstaking work: To produce an 80-minute film, the animation team must complete more than 120,000 individual cels (drawings/paintings on clear celluloid sheets) of characters and scenery! Original cels from famous Disney movies, and some of the many Oscars won by Disney artists, are on display here. The tour also includes very entertaining video talks by animators and a grand finale of magical moments from Disney classics such as *Pinocchio, Snow White, Bambi,* and *Cinderella.* This very popular attraction should be visited first thing in the morning; long lines form later in the day.

BACKSTAGE STUDIO TOUR This 25-minute tram tour takes you behind the scenes for a close-up look at the vehicles, props, costumes, sets, and special effects used in your favorite movies and TV shows. You'll see costumers at work in the wardrobe department (Disney has the world's largest costume collection—more than two million garments), house facades of "The Golden Girls" and "Empty Nest" on Residential Street, and carpenters building sets in the scenic shop. All very interesting until the tram ventures into Catastrophe Canyon where an earthquake in the heart of desert oil country causes canyon walls to rumble and riders are threatened by a raging oil fire, massive explosions, torrents of rain, and flash floods! Then you're taken behind the scenes to see how filmmakers use special effects to

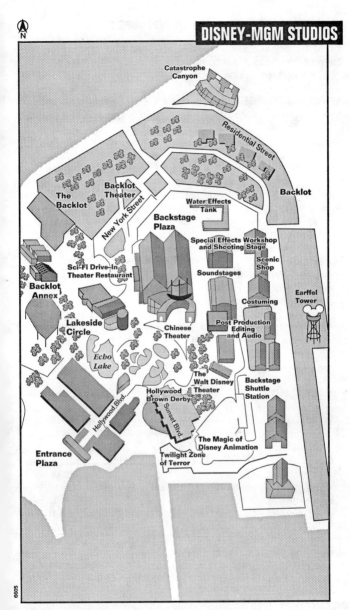

Catastrophe
Canyon

Residential Street

The
Backlot

Backlot
Theater

New York Street

Backlot

Water Effects
Tank

Backstage
Plaza

Special Effects Workshop
and Shooting Stage

Sci-Fi Drive-In
Theater Restaurant

Soundstages

Scenic
Shop

Backlot
Annex

Lakeside
Circle

Chinese
Theater

Costuming

Post Production
Editing
and Audio

Earffel
Tower

Echo
Lake

The Walt Disney
Theater

Backstage
Shuttle
Station

Hollywood
Brown Derby

Hollywood Blvd.

Sunset Blvd.

Entrance
Plaza

Twilight Zone
of Terror

The Magic of
Disney Animation

6605

create such disasters. Almost as interesting as the ride is the preshow.
While waiting on line, you can watch entertaining videos hosted by
Tom Selleck and Carol Burnett of well-known actors and directors
on overhead monitors: Penny Marshall talking about the piano scene
in *Big*, Leonard Nimoy on the challenge of directing babies in *Three
Men and a Baby*, Richard Dreyfuss sharing how he landed the role
in *Jaws* that launched his movie career, Mel Brooks on why he was

"forced" to become a director/producer, and many more. After the tram tour, visit Studio Showcase, a changing walk-through display of sets and props from popular movies.

INSIDE THE MAGIC   Movie and TV special effects and production facets are the focus of this behind-the-scenes walking tour of studio facilities. You'll see how a naval battle—complete with burning ships, torpedos, and undersea explosions—is created, then view the results on videotape. Two young volunteers from the audience help demonstrate how miniaturization was achieved in *Honey, I Shrunk the Kids.* You'll visit three studio soundstages, including the home of Ed McMahon's "Star Search" (on some tours you'll get to see movies or TV shows being filmed from a soundproof catwalk); view a short comedy called *The Lottery* starring Bette Midler and learn how its special effects were achieved; check out a video postproduction area to see a scene from *Star Wars* before and after editing (C-3PO, R2-D2, and George Lucas explain how it's done on video monitors); and move on to audio postproduction where Mel Gibson and Pee Wee Herman shed light on the process of mixing dialogue, music, and sound effects to create a sound track. The tour ends in a sit-down theater with a screening of coming Disney attractions hosted by Mickeys Eisner and Mouse. A very entertaining video preshow features Goldie Hawn and Rick Moranis. To find the entrance to this attraction follow the big pink footsteps of Roger Rabbit.

VOYAGE OF THE LITTLE MERMAID   Hazy light, creating an underwater effect in a reef-walled theater, helps set the mood for this charming musical spectacular based on the Disney feature film. The show combines live and Audio-Animatronic™ performers with more than 100 puppets, movie clips, and innovative special effects—bubbles, mist, cascading water, lightning, laser beams, stage smoke, and fireworks. Sebastian sings the movie's Academy Award–winning song, "Under the Sea"; the ethereal Ariel shares her dream of becoming human in a live performance of "Part of Your World"; and the evil, tentacled Ursula, 12 feet tall and 10 feet wide, belts out "Poor Unfortunate Soul," in which she tempts Ariel to part with her most precious possession, her voice. It all has a happy ending, as most of the young audience knows it will; they've seen the movie. The preshow takes place in a room cluttered with nautical artifacts.

THEATER OF THE STARS   This 1,500-seat amphitheater is currently presenting a 25-minute live Broadway-style production of ***Beauty and the Beast*** based on the Disney movie version. Musical highlights from the show range from the rousing "Be Our Guest" opening number to the poignant title song featured in a romantic waltz-scene finale complete with the release of white doves. A highlight is "The Mob Song" scene in a dark forest, in which villagers led by Gaston (the beast's rival for Belle) and armed with axes, hoes, and pitchforks set out on a rampage to "kill the beast," setting up the emotional climax: Belle speaks the three magic words that heal the beast's heart and transform him into a handsome prince. Sets and costumes are lavish, production numbers spectacular. Consider going to the last show; it makes for a feel-good (and sit-down) ending to your day. Arrive early to get a good seat. One feminist comment: When is someone going to do a version of this tale in which the beast is a woman and a man loves her for her inner qualities? *Note: Beauty and the Beast* has been enjoying a long run here; a new show, based on a more recent Disney hit, may be in progress by the time you visit.

JIM HENSON'S MUPPET VISION 3D This utterly delightful film starring Kermit and Miss Piggy combines Jim Henson's puppets with Disney Audio-Animatronics™ and special-effects wizardry, 70mm film, and cutting-edge 3-D technology. Wow! The coming-at-you action includes flying Muppets, cream pies, cannonballs, high winds, fiber-optics fireworks, bubble showers, even an actual spray of water. Kermit is the host, Miss Piggy sings "Dream a Little Dream of Me," Statler and Waldorf critique the action (which includes numerous mishaps and disasters) from a mezzanine balcony, and Nicki Napoleon and his Emperor Penguins (a full Muppet orchestra) provide music from the pit. Kids in the first row get to interact with the characters. In the preshow area, guests view a hilarious Muppet video on overhead monitors and see movie props belonging to Muppet superstars. Note the cute fountain out front.

STAR TOURS A wild galactic journey based on the *Star Wars* trilogy (George Lucas collaborated on its conception), this action-packed adventure uses dramatic film footage and flight-simulator technology to transform the theater into a vehicle careening through space. We enter a preshow area—where R2-D2 and C-3PO are running an intergalactic travel agency—and board 40-passenger "spacecraft" for a voyage to the Moon of Endor. En route, we encounter robots, aliens, and droids, among them our inexperienced pilot, RX-24. No sooner has he extricated our spaceship from an asteroidlike tunnel of frozen ice fragments than he's drawn into combat with a massive Imperial Star Destroyer. The ship lurches out of control, and passengers experience sudden drops, violent crashes, and oncoming laser blasts. The harrowing ride ends safely, and we exit into a "droid and baggage claim" area that leads to a *Star Wars* merchandise shop.

THE GREAT MOVIE RIDE Audio-Animatronic™ replicas of movie stars enact some of the most famous scenes in filmdom on this thrilling ride through movie history. You'll relive magic moments from the 1930s through the present—Bergman and Bogart's classic airport farewell in *Casablanca,* Rhett carrying Scarlett up the stairs of Tara for a night of passion, Brando bellowing "Stellllaaaa," Sigourney Weaver fending off slimy *Alien* foes, Gene Kelly singin' in the rain, Johnny Weissmuller's trademark Tarzan yell and vine swing across the jungle, 60 dancers performing a Busby Berkeley number atop a revolving tiered cake, and many more. Action is enhanced by dramatic special effects as you experience everything from the highjacking of your ride vehicle by an outlaw to thieves blowing up a safe and setting the bank on fire in a western town. "Fasten your seat belts. It's going to be a bumpy night." The setting for this attraction is a full-scale reproduction of Hollywood's famous Mann's Chinese Theatre, complete with hand, foot, and paw prints (Mickey and Kermit) of the stars out front.

MONSTER SOUND SHOW Four "Foley artists" (Foley is the Hollywood sound-effects system named for its creator, Jack Foley) are chosen from the audience to create sound effects for a two-minute comic Gothic thriller starring Chevy Chase and Martin Short. Sound effects include thunder, rain, creaking doors, falling chandeliers, footsteps, ringing bells, and explosions. We see the film three times, first with professional sound, then without sound as volunteers frantically try to create an appropriate track, and finally with the sound effects they've provided. Errors in timing and volume make it all quite funny, as a knock at the door or crashing glass comes just a few seconds too late. The show features some of the 20,000-plus ingenious gadgets created by sound master Jimmy Macdonald during his 45 years with Disney Studios. David Letterman narrates a terrific video preshow, including one of his famous "top-ten" lists, in this case "most entertaining sounds" (number 10: "A sweaty fat guy getting up out of a vinyl beanbag chair"). In a postshow area called Soundworks, guests can attempt to reproduce flying saucer sounds from the film *Forbidden Planet,* dub the voice of Roger Rabbit, and create the gallop of the Headless Horseman in *Legend of Sleepy Hollow.*

SUPERSTAR TELEVISION This 30-minute show takes guests through a broadcast day that spans television history. During the preshow, "casting directors" choose a few dozen volunteers from the audience to reenact 15 famous television scenes (arrive early and station yourself near the stage if you want to snag a role). The broadcast day begins with a 1955 black-and-white "Today" show featuring Dave Garroway (the date is July 18, the day Disneyland opened) and continues with a classic "I Love Lucy" episode (the candy factory), a scene from "General Hospital," the Ed Sullivan show, "Bonanza," "Gilligan's Island," Walter Cronkite doing the news (Neil Armstrong's moon landing), a Three Stooges sequence (a volunteer gets a pie in the face), "Cheers," "The Golden Girls," "Home Improvement," "Howard Cosell's Sportsbreak" (the interviewee is a young volunteer who has ostensibly just hit a home run at Shea Stadium), the "Tonight" show, and "Late Night With David Letterman." There's even a Sony commercial. Real footage is mixed with live action, and though occasionally a star is born, it's more often fun watching amateur actors freeze up, flub lines, and otherwise deviate from the script.

INDIANA JONES EPIC STUNT SPECTACULAR Visitors get a glimpse into the world of movie stunts in this dramatic 30-minute show that re-creates major scenes from the *Raiders of the Lost Ark* series. It takes place in a vast 2,000-seat amphitheater. The show opens on an elaborate Mayan temple backdrop. Indiana Jones crashes dramatically onto the set in a free fall, and, as he searches with a torch for the golden idol, he encounters booby traps, fire and steam, and spears popping up from the ground, before being chased by a vast rolling boulder. The set is then dismantled to reveal a colorful Cairo marketplace where a swordfight ensues and the action includes jumps from high places, virtuoso bullwhip maneuvers, lots of gunfire, and a truck bursting into flame. An explosive finale takes place in a desert scenario. The action is enhanced by movie theme music and entertaining narrative, and throughout, guests get to see how elaborate stunts are pulled off. Volunteers are chosen to participate as extras during the preshow.

PARADES, SHOWS, FIREWORKS & MORE

Aladdin's Royal Caravan, a dazzling Disney parade based on the movie, takes place once or twice daily (check your entertainment schedule for route and times). Its exotic cast includes a 26-foot genie on a bejeweled float, brass bands, amazing acrobats, scimitar dancers, golden camels, a giant out-of-control ape, a rope climber, a fire-eater, a snake charmer, magicians, a harem, and the grand entrance of Prince Ali and Princess Jasmine on Abu (transformed from a monkey into an elephant), followed by Aladdin's old nemesis, the villainous Jafar, now reduced to pushing the honey bucket behind them. Don't miss it. Find a curbside seat (or grab a bench near the Monster Sound Show) along the parade route a half hour before it begins.

The Sorcery in the Sky fireworks show is presented nightly during summer and peak seasons. Check your entertainment schedule to see if it's on.

The **Star Today** program features frequent appearances by major stars such as Betty White, Howie Mandel, Sally Struthers,

---

IN THE WORDS OF WALT DISNEY

"A family picture is one the kids can take their parents to see and not be embarrassed."

"I don't like downbeat pictures, and I cannot believe that the average family does either . . . when I go to the theater, I don't want to come out depressed."

Alice Ghostley, and Marlee Matlin. They appear at attractions, record their handprints in front of the Chinese Theater, and appear at question-and-answer sessions with park guests. Check your entertainment schedule to see if it's on.

Teenage Mutant Ninja Turtles emerge from the sewers to demonstrate their radical moves, sing, order pizza, and sign autographs in a "totally awesome" show on New York Street several times each day.

The ***Honey I Shrunk the Kids* Movie Set,** an 11,000-square-foot playground based on the film, is located near New York Street. Everything in it is larger than life. A thicket of grass is 30 feet tall, mushroom caps are three stories high, and a friendly "ant" makes a suitable seat. Play areas—enhanced by sounds such as the buzzing of giant crickets and bees—include a massive cream cookie, a 52-foot garden hose (with leaks), cereal loops nine feet in diameter (cushioned for jumping), a waterfall cascading from a leaf to a dell of fern sprouts (the sprouts form a musical stairway, activated when guests step from sprout to sprout), tree stump slides, a root maze with a flower petal slide, a "film strip" slide in a giant Kodak film can, and a huge spider web with 11 levels to climb.

Centering on a gleaming 14½-foot bronze Emmy, the **Academy of Television Arts & Sciences Hall of Fame Plaza,** adjacent to SuperStar Television, honors TV legends. Bronze statues of television luminaries Carol Burnett, Sid Caesar, Bill Cosby, Mary Tyler Moore, Red Skelton, Danny Thomas, and Milton Berle are displayed, along with one of Walt Disney. Additional statues will be added each year. ATAS holds its annual Hall of Fame induction ceremonies at the Disney-MGM Studios.

TYPHOON LAGOON

Ahoy swimmers, floaters, run-aground boaters!
A furious storm once roared 'cross the sea
Catching ships in its path, helpless to flee . . .
Instead of a certain and watery doom
The winds swept them here to TYPHOON LAGOON

Such is the Disney legend relating to Typhoon Lagoon, which you'll see posted on consecutive signs as you enter the park. Located off Lake Buena Vista Drive halfway between Walt Disney World Village and Disney-MGM Studios, this is the ultimate in water theme parks. Its fantasy setting is a palm-fringed tropical island village of ramshackle, tin-roofed structures, strewn with cargo, surfboards, and other marine wreckage left by the "great typhoon." A storm-stranded fishing boat dangles precariously atop the 95-foot-high Mt. Mayday, the steep setting for several major park attractions. Every half hour the boat's smokestack erupts, shooting a 50-foot geyser of water into the air. Colorful tropical birds enhance the island ambience. In summer, arrive no later than 9am to avoid long lines.

The park is often filled to capacity by 10am and closed to later arrivals. Beach towels and lockers can be obtained for a minimal fee, and all beach accessories can be purchased at Singapore Sal's. Light fare is available at two eateries—Leaning Palms and Typhoon Tillie's Galley and Grog, a beach bar called Let's Go Slurpin' sells beer and soft drinks, and there are also picnic tables (consider bringing picnic fare; you can keep it in your locker until lunchtime). Guests are not permitted to bring their own flotation devices into the park. A full day's worth of water attractions and activities includes:

TYPHOON LAGOON   This large and lovely lagoon, the size of two football fields and surrounded by white sandy beach (complete with volleyball set-up), is the park's main swimming area. The chlorinated water's turquoise hue evokes the Caribbean. Large waves for surfing and bobbing crash against the shore every 90 seconds. A foghorn sounds to warn you when a wave is coming. Young children can wade in the lagoon's more peaceful tidal pools—Blustery Bay or Whitecap Cove.

CASTAWAY CREEK   Hop onto a raft or inner tube and meander along this 2,100-foot lazy river. Circling the lagoon, Castaway Creek tumbles through a misty rain forest, past caves and secluded grottoes. It has a themed area called Water Works where jets of water spew from shipwrecked boats and a Rube Goldberg assemblage of broken bamboo pipes and buckets spray and dump water on passersby. There are exits along the route where you can leave the creek; if you do the whole thing, it takes about a half hour. Tubes are complimentary.

WATER SLIDES   Humunga Kowabunga consists of two 214-foot Mt. Mayday water slides that drop you down the mountain before rushing into a cave and out again at 30 m.p.h. Three longer (about 300 feet each), but less steep slides—Jib Jammer, Rudder Buster, and Stern Burner—take you on a serpentine route through waterfalls and bat caves, past nautical wreckage at about 20 m.p.h. before depositing you in a bubbling catch pool; each offers slightly different views and thrills. There's seating for nonparticipatory parents whose kids have commissioned them to "watch me."

WHITEWATER RIDES   Mt. Mayday is the setting for three whitewater rafting adventures—Keelhaul Falls, Mayday Falls, and Gangplank Falls—all of them offering steep drops, coursing through caves, and passing lush scenery. Keelhaul Falls has the most winding spiral route, Mayday Falls the steepest drops and fastest water, while the slightly tamer Gangplank Falls uses large tubes so the whole family can ride together.

SHARK REEF   Guests are given free snorkel equipment (and instruction) for a 15-minute swim through this 362,000-gallon simulated coral-reef tank populated by about 4,000 rainbow parrot-fish, queen angelfish, yellowtail damselfish, rock beauties, blue tang, puddingwife fish, and other colorful denizens of the deep. Underwater scenery includes shipwrecked boats, and there's a rock waterfall at one end. If you don't want to get in the water, you can observe the fish via portholes in a walk-through area. Shark Reef is housed in a sunken upside-down tanker.

KETCHAKIDDIE CREEK   Many of the above-mentioned attractions require guests to be at least four feet tall. This section of the park is a kiddie area exclusively for those *under* four feet. An innovative water playground, it has bubbling fountains to frolic in, mini–water slides, a pint-sized whitewater tubing adventure, spouting whales and squirting seals, rubbery crocodiles to climb on, grottoes to explore, and waterfalls to loll under.

RIVER COUNTRY

One of the many recreational facilities at the Fort Wilderness Resort campground, this mini–water park is themed after Tom Sawyer's swimming hole. Kids can scramble over manmade boulders that double as diving platforms for a 330,000-gallon clearwater pool. Two 16-foot water slides also provide access to the pool. Attractions on the adjacent Bay Lake, which is equipped with ropes and ships' booms for climbing, include a pair of flumes—one 260 feet long, the other 100 feet—that corkscrew through Whoop-N-Holler Hollow; White Water Rapids, which carries inner-tubers along a winding 230-foot creek with a series of chutes and pools; and the Ol' Wading Pool, a smaller version of the swimming hole designed for young children. There are pool and beachside areas for sunning and picnicking, plus a 350-yard boardwalk nature trail through a cypress swamp. Beach towels and lockers can be obtained for a minimal fee. Light fare is available at Pop's Place. To get here without a car take a launch from the dock near the entrance to the Magic Kingdom or a bus from its Transportation and Ticket Center.

DISCOVERY ISLAND

This lushly tropical 11½-acre zoological sanctuary—just a short boat ride away from the Magic Kingdom entrance, the Contemporary Resort, or Fort Wilderness Resort—provides a tranquil counterpoint to Disney World dazzle. Plan to spend a leisurely afternoon strolling its scenic mile-long nature trail, which, shaded by a canopy of trees, winds past gurgling streams, groves of palm and bamboo, ponds and lagoons filled with ducks and trumpeter swans, a bay that is a breeding ground for brown pelicans, and colonies of rose-hued flamingos. Peacocks roam free, and aviaries house close to 100 species of colorful exotic birds, including macaws, cockatoos, roseate spoonbills, scarlet ibis, kookaburras, bald eagles, toucans, parrots, partridges, king vultures, East African crowned cranes, and white-crested hornbills. Discovery Island denizens also include Patagonian cavies (they're a kind of guinea pig), alligators and caimans, Galápagos tortoises, small primates, and muntjac miniature deer from Southeast Asia. Two different bird shows and a reptile show are scheduled several times throughout the day; they take place outdoors with seating on log benches. Guests can also look through a viewing area to see the nursery complex of the island's animal hospital, where baby birds and mammals are often hand-raised.

2. UNIVERSAL STUDIOS

✪ Universal Studios Florida, 1000 Universal Studios Plaza (tel. 363-8000), is a working motion-picture and television-production studio that invites the public in for a glimpse behind the scenes. As you stroll along "Hollywood Boulevard" and "Rodeo Drive," you'll pass more than 40 full-scale sets and large props from famous movies (from the hedges used in *Edward Scissorhands* to New York's Central Park). On hand to greet visitors are Hanna-Barbera characters (Yogi Bear, Scooby Doo, Fred Flintstone, and others). While waiting on line, you'll be entertained by excellent preshows. Work out a show schedule when you arrive.

MAJOR ATTRACTIONS After 75 years of moviemaking, Universal knows how to create a supercolossal theme park experience. Steven Spielberg is the park's creative consultant, and thrilling rides and attractions utilize cutting-edge technology—such as OMNIMAX™ 70mm film projected on seven-story screens—to create unprecedented special effects. Top attractions include:

E.T. Adventure This is the movie sequel Spielberg said he'd never make. Visitors are given a passport to E.T.'s planet, which needs his healing powers to rejuvenate it. You'll soar with E.T. on a mission to save his ailing planet, through the forest and into space, aboard a star-bound bicycle—all to the accompaniment of that familiar movie theme music.

Back to the Future The year is 2015. The incompetent but evil Biff has penetrated Doc Brown's Laboratory of Future Technology, imprisoned Doc, and taken off in the DeLorean. On a mission to save the time machine from Biff, visitors blast through the space-time continuum, plummeting into volcanic tunnels ablaze with molten lava, colliding with Ice Age glaciers, thundering through caves and canyons, and are briefly swallowed by a dinosaur, in a spectacular multisensory adventure. Actors Christopher Lloyd (Doc) and Tom Wilson (Biff) appear on video.

Kongfrontation It's the last thing the Big Apple needed. King Kong is back! As you stand in line—in a replica of a grungy, graffiti-scarred New York subway station—CBS newsman Roland Smith reports on Kong's terrifying rampage. Everyone must evacuate to Roosevelt Island. So it's all aboard the Roosevelt Island tram. Cars collide and hydrants explode below, police helicopters hover overhead putting us directly in the line of fire, the tram malfunctions, and, of course, we encounter Kong, 32 feet tall, 13,000 pounds, with over 100 facial expressions. He emits banana breath in our faces, and menaces passengers, dangling the tram over the East River. A great thrill—or just another day in New York.

Earthquake, The Big One You board a BART train in San Francisco for a peaceful subway ride, but just as you pull into the Embarcadero station there's an earthquake—the big one—8.3 on the Richter scale! As you sit helplessly trapped, vast slabs of concrete collapse around you, a propane truck bursts into flames, a runaway train comes hurtling at you, and the station floods (60,000 gallons of water cascade down the steps). Your feet will get wet. Earthquake is preceded by several interesting preshows narrated by Charlton Heston, during which the audience is briefed for roles as extras and taken behind the scenes to see how special effects were achieved.

Ghostbusters There are so many ghosts these days, Ghostbusters just has to sell franchises. Lewis Tully delivers a zany high-pressure sales pitch to the audience, and volunteers come up on stage and get slimed. Tully demonstrates flushing ghosts into the Ectoplasmic Container Chamber and discusses starter kits in three price ranges. But the ghosts, of course, break loose from Gozer's Temple, and demons lunge at the audience.

Jaws You're in the charming New England town of Amity. Did you really think it was safe to go back into the water? Guests are assured the waters are shark-free, but as your boat heads out to the open seas, an ominous dorsal fin appears on the horizon. What follows is a series of terrifying face-to-glistening-jaw attacks from a three-ton, 32-foot-long great white shark who tries to sink its teeth into passengers. Just as you begin to feel safe in the confines of a deserted boat house, "Jaws" breaks through the walls sending oars, lobster traps, and buoys hurtling through the air. And there's more trouble ahead. The boat is surrounded by a 30-foot wall of flame from burning fuel. I won't tell you how it ends, but here's a hint: The pungent stench of charred shark flesh comes into it.

Nickelodeon Studios Tour Kids get a bang out of touring the studios of their own cable network, the premises of which are fronted by a slime geyser. Along the tour route guests get a look at the soundstages where shows such as "Clarissa Explains It All" are produced; view concept pilots for Nick shows; visit the kitchen where Gak and Green Slime are produced (you can touch and taste, if you like); play games typical of Nickelodeon shows; and try out new Sega video games. There's lots of audience participation, and a volunteer will get slimed.

Wild, Wild, Wild West Show Stunt people demonstrate falls from balconies, gun and whip fights, dynamite explosions, and other oater staples.

The Beetlejuice Graveyard Revue Dracula, Wolfman, the Phantom of the Opera, Frankenstein and his bride, and Beetlejuice put on a funky—and very funny—rock music show with pyrotechnic special effects and MTV-style choreography.

The FUNtastic World of Hanna-Barbera This motion-simulator ride takes guests careening through the universe in a spaceship piloted by Yogi Bear to rescue Elroy Jetson. Prior to this wild ride, you'll learn about how cartoons are created. After it, in an interactive area, you can experiment with animation sound effects—boing! plop! splash!

ADDITIONAL ATTRACTIONS   Other attractions here include:

A **Rocky and Bullwinkle** character show with those scheming no-goodnik spies, Boris and Natasha.

The **Gory, Gruesome, & Grotesque Horror Make-up Show,** all about makeup and special effects in movies such as the transformation scenes from *An American Werewolf in London, The Fly,* and *The Exorcist.* The lobby of the theater houses a collection of movie props, costumes, and behind-the-scenes videos from the movie *Jurassic Park,* most notably the 26-foot-long ailing triceratops.

Lucy: A Tribute, honoring America's queen of comedy, consists of a vast collection of Lucy-Desi memorabilia, home movies, costumes, props, awards, fan letters, a scale model of the "I Love Lucy" soundstage, and a Lucy computer trivia game.

Fievel's Playland, based on the Spielberg movie, is a very innovative western-themed playground with giant props and sets (in which kids experience being mouse-size), including a 200-foot-long water ride, a 30-foot spider web to climb, and a Gulliver-sized harmonica that makes music as kids glide down the keys.

At **Murder She Wrote,** you're on the set with Angela Lansbury trying to solve a crime involving a rare black pearl. Via computer, the audience gets to make postproduction executive decisions—choose the murder weapon, the murderer, and Jessica's dinner companion. Robert Wagner narrates the preshow.

At **Alfred Hitchcock's 3-D Theatre** a volunteer is chosen from the audience to play Norman Bates. The attraction is a tribute to the "master of suspense" who directed 53 films, eight of them for Universal. The late Tony Perkins narrates a reenactment of the famous shower scene from *Psycho,* and *The Birds,* as if it weren't scary enough, becomes an in-your-face 3-D movie.

Lassie, Benji, Mr. Ed (descendants of, actually), and other animal superstars perform their famous pet tricks in the **Animal Actors Show.**

During **Screen Test Home Video Adventure,** a director, crew, and team of "cinemagicians" put visitors on the screen in an exciting video production.

And **Dynamite Nights Stunt Spectacular,** a nightly show, combines death-defying stunts with a breathtaking display of fireworks.

In the works at this writing is a new attraction based on Steven Spielberg's movie *The Flintstones.* Visitors will be able to tour Bedrock and interact with Fred, Wilma, Barney, Betty, and Dino.

Over 25 shops in the park sell everything from Lucy collectibles to Bates Motel towels, and restaurants run the gamut from Mel's Drive-In (of *American Graffiti* fame), to the Hard Rock Cafe, to Schwab's.

ADMISSION   A one-day ticket costs $35 for ages 10 and over, $28 for children 3 to 9. A two-day ticket is $55 for ages 10 and over, $44 for children 3 to 9. An annual pass (admission for a full year) is $87.50 for ages 10 and over, $70 for children 3 to 9. Ages 2 and under free. Parking costs $5 per vehicle, $6 for RVs and trailers.

OPEN Universal Studios is open 365 days a year. Hours are basically 9am to 7pm, extended during summer and holidays. Call before you go.

DIRECTIONS Take I-4 east, making a left on Sand Lake Road, then a right onto Turkey Lake Road, and follow the signs.

---

3. SEA WORLD

This popular 175-acre marine-life park, at 7007 Sea World Dr. (tel. 351-3600), explores the mysteries of the deep in a format that combines entertainment with wildlife-conservation awareness. Its beautifully landscaped grounds, centering on a 17-acre lagoon, include flamingo and pelican ponds (more than 1,500 birds, primarily waterfowl, make their home in the park), and a lush tropical rain forest. Sea World's involvement in marine-life research, education, animal rescue and release programs, and preserving and breeding endangered species is impressive. Shamu, a killer whale, is the star of the park. Do work out a show schedule upon entering the premises.

MAJOR ATTRACTIONS There are 10 major shows and attractions:

Mission: Bermuda Triangle Combining a high-definition underwater adventure film with state-of-the-art flight-simulator technology, this attraction takes visitors aboard a scientific research submarine. Your "mission": to explore the 444,000-square-mile expanse of the Atlantic Ocean known as the Bermuda Triangle, in which thousands of people and hundreds of ships and planes have vanished without a trace. Computer-controlled movements authentically replicate a real deep-sea expedition. Your "cabin" pitches, lunges, and sways with the waves as you plunge into the ocean to study the magnetic anomalies of this enigmatic area. Hugh Downs narrates a preshow video and briefs mission participants. It's all very rational and scientific . . . until an underwater earthquake threatens the expedition!

Terrors of the Deep This exhibit houses 220 specimens of venomous and otherwise scary sea creatures in a tropical reef habitat. Immense acrylic tunnels provide close encounters with slithery eels and three dozen sharks. Barracudas, lionfish, and poisonous pufferfish are also on display. A theatrical presentation focusing on sharks puts across the message that pollution and uncontrolled commercial fishing make humankind the ultimate "terror of the deep."

Manatees: The Last Generation? For centuries sea-going cultures have been fascinated by the gentle manatee, which some believe is the basis for mermaid myths (though you'd have to be at sea a long, long time for a manatee to suggest a woman). Today the Florida manatee is in danger of extinction, with as few as 2,000 remaining. Underwater viewing stations, innovative cinema techniques, and interactive displays combine to create an exciting format for teaching visitors about the manatee and its fragile ecosystem. In a winding tropical 3½-acre lagoonlike setting, visitors view the world from a manatee's perspective, perceiving what the creatures hear, see, and feel. Also on display here are hundreds of other native fish as well as alligators, turtles, and shorebirds, and there's a nursing pool for manatee mothers and their babies.

Sea World Theatre: Window to the Sea A multimedia presentation—which begins with a ballet of dancing waters shimmering in a rainbow of colored lights—takes visitors behind the scenes at Sea World and explores a variety of marine subjects. These include an ocean dive in search of the rare six-gilled shark, a killer whale giving birth, babies born at Sea World (dolphins, sea horses, penguins, walruses), dolphin anatomy, and underwater geology.

Shamu: New Visions Sea World trainers develop close relationships with killer whales, and in this partly covered open-air stadium, they direct performances that are extensions of natural cetacean behaviors—twirling, waving tails and fins, rotating while swimming, and splashing the audience (sit pretty far back if you don't want to get soaked). Trainers also ride the whales. An informative video, narrated by James Earl Jones and projected on a vast 16- by 20-foot monitor, adds an underwater perspective to the show. The stadium includes a research and breeding area where you might see killer whale calves. The evening show here, called *Shamu: Night Magic,* utilizes rock music and special lighting effects; I suggest attending it instead of the daytime show. It's a fun way to wind up your day at Sea World.

The Whale and Dolphin Discovery Show At Discovery Cove—a big partially covered open-air stadium—whales and Atlantic bottlenose dolphins perform flips and high jumps, swim at rapid speeds, twirl, swim on their backs, and give rides to trainers, all to the accompaniment of calypso music. Once again, these are extensions of natural behaviors that showcase the abilities of these creatures. A child volunteer gets to work as an apprentice trainer. While you're being seated, a guitarist leads a sing-along. Those sitting up front get wet.

The Gold Rush Ski Show This wacky waterski exhibition features a cantankerous prospector and a talented team of cowboy waterskiers performing long-distance jumps, water ballet (performed by the miners' mail-order brides), flips, and backward and barefoot skiing. Their antics are accompanied by rollicking hoedown music and dance.

Penguin Encounter This display of hundreds of penguins and alcids (including adorable babies) native to the Antarctic and Arctic regions also serves as a living laboratory for protecting and preserving polar life. On a moving walkway, you'll view six different penguin species congregating on rocks, nesting, and swimming underwater. If you want to observe their antics for a longer period, there is a viewing area for that purpose. The attraction is augmented by video displays about penguins and an additional area for puffins and murres—flying Arctic cousins of penguins.

Hotel Clyde and Seamore   Two sea lions, along with a cast of otters and walruses, appear in this fishy *Fawlty Towers* comedy with a conservation theme.

Shamu's Happy Harbor   This innovative three-acre play area provides facilities for kids to climb a four-story net tower with a 35-foot crow's nest lookout, fire water cannons, play steel drums, swing on tires, operate remote-controlled vehicles, navigate a water maze, do a ball crawl, and propel themselves upward on an air bounce. One section is especially for children under 42 inches tall.

ADDITIONAL ATTRACTIONS   The park's other attractions include:

Pacific Point Preserve is a 2½-acre naturalistic setting with beaches and ocean waves that duplicates the rocky northern Pacific coast. It is home to California sea lions and harbor and fur seals.

A **Tropical Reef** aquarium, fronted by a tide pool of touchables—sea anemones, starfish, sea cucumbers, and sea urchins. Inside, the 160,000-gallon manmade coral reef is home to 1,000 brightly hued tropical fish—including blue surgeon fish, sargeant majors, porkfish, French angelfish, guitarfish, and conch—displayed in 17 vignettes of undersea life.

Stingray Lagoon, where visitors enjoy hands-on encounters with harmless southern diamond and cownose rays. You can buy them treats and feed them as well; their diet consists of clams, shrimp, smelt, and squid.

A **Dolphin Community Pool,** where guests can feed and touch Atlantic bottlenose dolphins.

Ocean-themed **musical spectaculars** that take place in the park's Nautilus Theatre.

A **Hawaiian dance troupe** that entertains with island songs and dances in an outdoor facility at Hawaiian Village; if you care to join in, grass skirts and leis are available.

You can ascend 400 feet to the top of the **Sea World Sky Tower** for a revolving 360-degree panorama of the park and beyond (there's an extra charge of $3 per person for this activity).

And at the 5½-acre **Anheuser-Busch Hospitality Center**—set amid tropical lagoons, waterfalls, and lush landscaping—you can view turn-of-the-century brewery equipment and a restored beer wagon, try free samples of Anheuser-Busch beers (there are soft drinks for kids) and snacks, and stroll through the stables to watch the famous Budweiser Clydesdale horses being groomed. There's indoor and terrace seating overlooking a lake. Anheuser-Busch is the owner of Sea World.

The **Aloha! Polynesian Luau Dinner and Show**—a musical revue featuring South Seas food, song, and fire dancing—takes place nightly at 6:30pm. Park admission is not required. Cost is $29.63 for adults, $20.09 for children 8 to 12, $10.55 for children 3 to 7, under 3 free. Reservations are required (tel. 407/363-2559, or toll free 800/227-8048).

There are, of course, numerous restaurants, snack bars, and food kiosks throughout the park, offering everything from chicken and biscuits to mesquite-grilled ribs. My favorites are the Bimini Bay Café—a very pleasant full-service restaurant featuring seafood and basic American fare—and Mango Joe's, specializing in fajitas and offering al fresco seating at umbrella tables overlooking the lagoon. Dozens of shops carry marine-related gifts, toys, clothing, diving gear, and souvenirs, as well as wilderness/conservation-oriented items.

Visitors can take a 90-minute behind-the-scenes **tour** of the park's breeding, research, and training facilities and/or attend a **45-minute presentation** about Sea World's animal behavior and training techniques. Cost for either tour is $5.95 for ages 10 and over, $4.95 for children 3 to 9, 2 and under free.

ADMISSION A one-day ticket costs $32.95 for ages 10 and over, $28.95 for children 3 to 9. A two-day ticket is $37.95 for ages 10 and over, $33.95 for children 3 to 9. A one-year pass is $59.95 for ages 10 and over, $49.95 for children 3 to 9. Ages 2 and under free. There are discounts for seniors, military, AAA members, and the handicapped. Discounted admissions in conjunction with Cypress Gardens (see Chapter 10) and Busch Gardens in Tampa are also available; call for details or inquire at the gate. Parking costs $5 per vehicle, $7 for RVs and trailers.

OPEN The park is open 365 days a year, 9am to 7pm, later during summer and holidays when there are also laser/fireworks spectaculars and additional shows at night.

DIRECTIONS Take I-4 to the Beeline Expressway (Hwy. 528) and follow the signs.

4. ADDITIONAL AREA ATTRACTIONS

KISSIMMEE

Kissimmee sights are close to the Walt Disney World area—about a 10- to 15-minute drive.

FLYING TIGERS WARBIRD AIR MUSEUM, 231 N. Hoagland Blvd., off U.S. 192 between Armstrong Blvd. and Yates Rd. Tel. 933-1942.

Flying Tigers is actually a World War II aircraft restoration facility where vintage planes are rebuilt and test-flown. Seventy-five percent of the displays—which run the gamut from 1920s antiques to 1970s fighter jets—are permanent, the rest are in shop on a temporary basis. On free guided tours, which depart every 30 minutes throughout the day, you'll visit the rebuilding facility where planes in various stages of assemblage are being restored. Exhibits include a U.S. Navy pilot trainer, many World War II bombers (including the B-17 "Flying Fortress" bomber that flew 140 missions), Navy helicopters, Vietnam torpedo bombers, cargo planes, and a rare World War II Paisacki Hup 1, as well as actual bombs, military jeeps and command cars from World War II and the Korean War, models of Russian planes, models of U.S. war planes from the beginnings of flight through Desert Storm, and much, much more. Visitors can sit in the cockpit of a jet fighter simulator, or—for a more realistic Red Baron fantasy experience—arrange to go up in a 1935 three-seat open biplane (call ahead for information on the latter, as well as other flight and piloting opportunities, some for families). An on-premises shop sells everything from airplane model kits and air force patches to grenades (not live ones). There are picnic tables on the grounds.

Admission: $6 adults, $5 seniors over 60 and children under 12.
Open: Daily 9:30am–5:30pm.

GATORLAND, 14501 South Orange Blossom Trail (U.S. 441), between Osceola Pkwy. and Hunter's Creek Blvd. Tel. 855-5496, or toll free 800/393-JAWS

Founded in 1949 with a handful of alligators living in huts and pens, Gatorworld today features 5,000 alligators and crocodiles on a 55-acre spread. Breeding pens, nurseries, and rearing ponds are situated throughout the park, which also displays monkeys, snakes, deer, goats, birds, sheep, Florida lake turtles, a Galapagos tortoise, and a bear. A petting zoo is on the premises. A 2,000-foot boardwalk winds through a cypress swamp and a 10-acre breeding marsh with an observation tower. Or you can take the free Gatorland Express Train around the park. There are three shows scheduled throughout the day—gator wrestling, gator jumping, and an informative snake show. Facilities include an open-air restaurant (where you can sample smoked gator ribs and nuggets), a shop (Gatorland also functions as a alligator-breeding farm for meat and hides; you'll find a wide array of alligator leather products here, not to mention canned gator chowder), and a picnic area.

Admission: $11.61 for adults, $8.43 for children 3–11, under 3 free. Parking is free.
Open: Daily 8am–dusk.

GREEN MEADOWS FARM, 1368 Poinciana Blvd., off U.S. 192 between Polynesian Blvd. and S.R. 535. Tel. 846-0770.

 If your children are 8 or younger, a visit to this delightful 40-acre farm—home to over 200 animals—will give you better value for your money than any major theme park. On guided two-hour farm tours, visitors view, learn about, and in some cases feed or pet, sheep, goats, exotic chickens, turkeys, ducks, pigs, donkeys, ostriches, peacocks, and bison. Kids especially love to see the baby animals, and for parents, it's really fun to watch the kids in this setting. Everyone also gets a turn to milk a cow, and a hayride and pony ride are included in the entrance fee. Call before you go to find out about special events such as shows, pumpkin harvesting, and barn dances. There's a large shaded picnic area, so pack your lunch and make a day of it.

Admission: $12 adults, children under 3 free.

Open: Daily 9:30am–4pm. **Closed:** Thanksgiving and Christmas.

SPLENDID CHINA, Formosa Gardens Blvd. off W. Irlo Bronson Memorial Hwy. (U.S. 192), between Entry Point Blvd./Sherbeth Rd. and Black Lake Rd. Tel. 396-7111.

This 76-acre outdoor attraction features more than 60 miniaturized replicas of China's most noted manmade and natural wonders, spanning 5,000 years of history and culture. Visitors enter via a bustling commercial street in the "water city" of Suzhou (the Venice of the East) circa AD 1300 to view a short orientation film about China. Park highlights include: a half-mile-long copy of the 4,200-mile Great Wall; the Forbidden City's 9,999-room Imperial Palace, built in 1420; Tibet's sacred Potala Palace, former mountain home of the Dalai Lama; carved Buddhist grottoes with statuary dating from AD 477 to AD 898; the massive Leshan Buddha, carved out of a mountainside between AD 713 and AD 803; the Stone Forest of Yunan, a natural formation of towering limestone peaks; and the Mongolian mausoleum of Genghis Khan. Live shows (acrobats, martial-arts demonstrations, storytelling, dance, puppetry, and more) take place throughout the day on stages around the park and in a 900-seat open-air amphitheater; check your entertainment schedule. Over a dozen shops sell Chinese merchandise. Food concessions, a gourmet restaurant, and a Chinese cafeteria are on the premises. Two-hour guided walking tours, departing several times a day, cost $5 per person (children under 12 free), and one-hour golf-cart tours ($45 per six-person cart) depart every half hour. There is also recorded commentary at each attraction.

Admission: $23.55 for adults, $13.90 for children 5–12, under 5 free. Parking is free.

Open: Daily from 9:30am–9:30pm.

WATER MANIA, 6073 W. Irlo Bronson Memorial Hwy. (U.S. 192), just east of I-4. Tel. 396-2626.

This conveniently located 36-acre water park offers a variety of aquatic thrill rides and attractions. You can boogie-board or body-surf in continuous wave pools, float lazily along an 850-foot river, enjoy a whitewater tubing adventure, and plummet down spiraling water slides and steep flumes. Or dare to ride the Abyss—an enclosed tube slide that corkscrews through 300 feet of darkness, exiting into a splash pool. There's a rain forest–themed water playground for children. A miniature golf course and wooded picnic area—with arcade games, a beach, and volleyball—adjoin.

Admission: $19.95 adults, $17.95 children 3–12, under 3 free. Parking is $2.

Open: Daily. Hours vary seasonally (call before you go). **Closed:** Nov 29–Dec 25.

A WORLD OF ORCHIDS, 2501 Old Lake Wilson Rd. (C.R. 545), off U.S. 192. Tel. 396-1887.

Lovers of horticulture will enjoy touring this 30,000-square-foot conservatory filled with tropical trees (including 64 varieties of palms and 21 of bamboo), ferns, lush tropical foliage, and, most notably, thousands of orchids—many of them rare—magnificently abloom at all times. Streams, waterfalls, koi ponds, and birds enhance this little enchanted garden. Free guided tours are given by resident horticulturalists at 11am and 3pm weekdays, 11am and 2 and 4pm on weekends. *Note:* If this is the kind of attraction you enjoy, be sure to also visit Harry P. Leu Gardens in Orlando (details below).

Admission: $8.95 adults, $6.95 ages 15–18, under 15 free.

Open: Daily 10am–6pm. **Closed:** New Year's Day, Memorial Day, July 4th, Thanksgiving, and Christmas.

INTERNATIONAL DRIVE

Like Kissimmee attractions, these are about a 10- to 15-minute drive from the Disney area.

RIPLEY'S BELIEVE IT OR NOT! MUSEUM, 8201 International Dr., 1½ blocks south of Sand Lake Rd. Tel. 363-4418.

It's always fun to peruse a Ripley collection of oddities, curiosities, and fascinating artifacts from faraway places. Among the hundreds of items and mannequins on display here are a 1,069-pound man, a two-headed kitten, a five-legged cow, a ¾-scale model of a 1907 Rolls-Royce made from a million matchsticks, a mosaic of the *Mona Lisa* created from 1,426 pieces of toast, torture devices from the Spanish Inquisition, a Tibetan flute made from human bones, an Ecuadorean shrunken head, a painting on a grain of rice, a "disappearing" nude bather (they do it with mirrors), Ubangi women with wooden plates in their lips, Burmese Padaung women who stretch their necks up to 15 inches long by wearing heavy brass rings around them, and the Lighthouse Man from China (a tour guide, he had a 7-inch candle inserted into his head). There are exhibits on Houdini and Florida sinkholes, and a film documents daredevil stunts at Niagara Falls. Guests are greeted by a hologram of Robert Ripley.

Admission: $8.95 adults, $5.95 children 4–11, under 4 free.

Open: Daily 10am–11pm.

WET 'N WILD, 6200 International Dr., at Republic Dr. Tel. 351-WILD or toll free 800/992-WILD.

When temperatures soar, head for this 25-acre water park and cool off by jumping waves, careening down steep flumes, and running rapids. Among the highlights: The Surge, the longest, fastest multipassenger tube ride anywhere in the United States, with 580 feet of exciting banked curves, Surf Lagoon, a vast pool with four-foot ocean waves; Bomb Bay (enter a bomblike casing 76 feet in the air for a speedy vertical flight straight down to a target pool); Black Hole (step into a spaceship and board a two-person raft for a 30-second, 500-foot, twisting, turning, space-themed reentry through total darkness propelled by a 1,000-gallon-a-minute blast of water!); Raging Rapids, a simulated whitewater tubing adventure with a waterfall plunge; and Lazy River, a leisurely float trip. There are additional flumes, a challenging children's water playground, a sunbathing area, and picnic area. Food concessions are located throughout the park, lockers and towels can be rented, and you can purchase beach accessories at the gift shop.

Admission: $20.95 adults, $17.95 children 3–9, under 3 free. Parking is free.

Open: 365 days a year. Hours vary seasonally (call before you go). **Directions:** Take I-4 east to Exit 30, and follow the signs.

ORLANDO

All of the below-listed Orlando attractions are in close proximity to one another, making for a pleasant day's excursion. Loch Haven Park is about 35 minutes by car from the Disney area. You can probably also incorporate Winter Park sights in the same day (see Chapter 10 for details).

HARRY P. LEU GARDENS, 1730 N. Forest Ave., between Nebraska St. and Corrine Dr. Tel. 246-2620.

This delightful 56-acre botanical garden on the shores of Lake Rowena offers a serene respite from theme park razzle-dazzle. Meandering paths lead through forests of giant camphors, moss-draped oaks, palms, cycads, and camellias (one of the world's largest collections, comprising some 2,000 plants in 50 species; they bloom October through March). Exquisite formal rose gardens (the largest in Florida, displaying 75 varieties) are enhanced by Italian fountains, a gazebo, and statuary. Other highlights include orchids, azaleas, desert plants, beds of colorful annuals and perennials, a flowering tree garden (mimosa, cherry, plum, and others), and a 50-foot floral clock. The gardens were created by Orlando businessman Harry P. Leu, who donated his 49-acre estate to the city in the 1960s. Free 20-minute tours of the Leu House, built in 1888 and restored to reflect the period between 1910 and 1930, take place on the hour and half hour. The house is a veritable decorative-arts museum filled with beautiful Victorian, Chippendale, and Empire pieces and other furnishings and objets d'art. It takes about two hours to see the house and gardens. Inquire about lectures and workshops, including some for children.

Admission: $3 for adults, $1 for children 6–16, under 6 free.

Open: Daily 9am–5pm. Leu House tours Tues–Sat 10am–3:30pm, Sun–Mon 1–3:30pm. **Closed:** Christmas. **Directions:** Take I-4 east to Exit 43 (Princeton Street), follow Princeton Street east, make a right on Mills Avenue and a left on Virginia Drive; look for the gardens on your left.

ORANGE COUNTY HISTORICAL MUSEUM, 812 E. Rollins St., between Orange and Mills aves., in Loch Haven Park. Tel. 897-6350.

Sharing a building with the Orlando Science Center (details below), this museum focuses on Florida history, beginning with prehistoric projectile points, a Timucuan canoe, and tooled animal bones from hunting cultures that existed here 12,000 years ago. Other exhibits include: displays of Seminole pottery and clothing; items from a pioneer kitchen; artifacts from an 1892 courthouse; a chronicle of the citrus industry and the role it played in the development of central Florida; and re-creations of a turn-of-the-century country store, a Victorian parlor, and the old *Orlando Sentinel* composing room. Also on the premises is Fire Station No. 3, a restored 1926 firehouse containing historic fire trucks, equipment, and memorabilia. The permanent collection is supplemented by changing exhibits of local, national, and international significance.

Admission: $2 for adults, $1.50 for seniors 55 and over, $1 for children 6–12, under 6 free.

Open: Mon–Sat 9am–5pm, Sun noon–5pm. **Closed:** Martin Luther King Day, Memorial Day, July 4th, Labor Day, Thanksgiving, Christmas, and New Year's Day. **Directions:** Take I-4 east to Exit 43 (Princeton Street) and follow the signs to Loch Haven Park.

ORLANDO MUSEUM OF ART, 2416 N. Mills Ave., in Loch Haven Park off Hwy. 17-92. Tel. 896-4231.

Founded in 1924, the Orlando Museum of Art displays its permanent collection of 19th- and 20th-century American art, pre-Columbian artifacts dating from 1200 BC to AD 1500, and African objects on a rotating basis. These holdings are augmented by long-term loans focusing on Mayan archaeology (recently discovered ceramics, sculptured stucco, and jade pieces from Belize) and arts of the African sub-Saharan region (cast bronze works, intricate beaded objects, and wood figures from the ancient kingdoms of Yoruba and Benin). Art Encounter is an interactive hands-on area for young children, where they might weave on a giant loom, piece together a pre-Columbian pot, or play African instruments. And recent temporary exhibits have ranged from Hudson River School landscapes to works of Andy Warhol. Inquire about guided tours, workshops for adults and children, gallery talks, and other activities. Museum shops (one especially geared to children) and a restaurant are on the premises.

Admission: $4 for adults, $2 for children 4–11, under 4 free. Parking is free.

Open: Tues–Sat 9am–5pm, Sun noon–5pm. Art Encounter hours are Tues–Fri and Sun noon–5pm, Sat 10am–5pm. **Closed:**

Mon, New Year's Day, Memorial Day, July 4th, Labor Day, Thanksgiving, and Christmas. **Directions:** Take I-4 east to Exit 43 (Princeton Street) and follow the signs to Loch Haven Park.

ORLANDO SCIENCE CENTER, 810 E. Rollins St., between Orange and Mills aves., in Loch Haven Park. Tel. 896-7151.

The Orlando Science Center specializes in hands-on interactive exhibits. In its Tunnel of Discovery you can pedal a bicycle to generate electricity, play with an echo tube, encase yourself in a giant soap bubble, create a tornado, or learn about anatomy from an immense soft-sculpture doll named Stuffee. NatureWorks focuses on the flora and fauna of four Florida habitats—cypress swamp, sand pine scrub, sinkhole lake, and pine flatwood. In WaterWorks, an area for pre-kindergarten through fourth grade, children can play with water-creature puppets, learn how water moves objects by building dams and canals, crawl under a glass-bottom turtle tank, touch starfish and sponges, and examine discovery drawers filled with fossils, plants, insects, and bones. In addition, you can examine pond life in a water lab, search for cardinals in a bird-watching area, find out what the weather is back home, take in a free planetarium show, or touch live frogs and turtles during daily reptile and amphibian demonstrations. About 50% of the museum is given over to changing exhibits on subjects ranging from dinosaurs to exotic insects. A café serves light fare at outdoor umbrella tables, and a large gift shop carries many interesting science projects for children. Inquire about workshops for children and nighttime planetarium shows and laser-show rock concerts.

Admission: $6.50 for adults, $5.50 for children 3–11, under 3 free.

Open: Mon–Thurs and Sat 9am–5pm, Fri 9am–9pm, Sun noon–5pm. **Closed:** Thanksgiving and Christmas. **Directions:** Take I-4 east to Exit 43 (Princeton Street) and follow the signs to Loch Haven Park.

5. SPORTS & RECREATION

SPECTATOR SPORTS
THE MAJOR ARENAS

As we go to press, construction is underway on the multimillion-dollar **Walt Disney World International Sports Center,** a 100-acre facility for amateur sports. It will include a 5,000-seat main-event stadium, as well as a 2,000-seat professional-level tennis arena, baseball diamonds, and much more. The center is scheduled to open in 1996.

The **Orlando Centroplex** administers six public sports and entertainment facilities in the downtown area. These include three major sporting arenas: the **Florida Citrus Bowl,** the **Orlando Arena,** and **Tinker Field.**

FLORIDA CITRUS BOWL, 1610 W. Church St., at Tampa St. Tel. 849-2020 for information, 839-3900 to charge tickets.

The Florida Citrus Bowl seats 70,000 people for major sporting events including the annual New Year's Day Citrus Bowl classic, college football games, NFL pre-season games, mud and monster truck racing, motocross, and World Cup soccer games.

Prices: Vary with events. Parking is $5.

Open: Year-round. **Directions:** Take I-4 east to the East-West Expy. and head west to Hwy. 441, make a left on Church St. and follow the signs.

ORLANDO ARENA, 600 W. Amelia St., between I-4 and Parramore Ave. Tel. 849-2020 for information, 839-3900 to charge tickets.

This 15,500-seat arena is the home of the NBA Orlando Magic basketball team during their October-through-April season, the NHL Tampa Bay Lightning hockey team (same season), and the Orlando Predators (arena football, May through August). The McDonald's American Cup Gymnastic Competition takes place here every March, and the National Championship Finals Rodeo every November. In the past the arena has also hosted key events such as the NCAA Basketball Championship Tournament, U.S. Figure Skating Championships, and the NBA All-Star Weekend. Call to find out what's on when you're in town.

Prices: Vary with events. Tickets to Orlando Magic games (about $17–$45) have to be acquired far in advance; they usually sell out by September before the season starts. Parking costs $4.

Open: Year-round. **Directions:** Take I-4 east to Amelia Ave., turn left at the traffic light at the bottom of the off-ramp, and follow signs. For up-to-the-minute parking information turn your car radio to 1620 AM.

TINKER FIELD, 287 S. Tampa Ave., between Colonial Dr. (Hwy. 50) and Gore St. Tel. 872-7593 for information and to charge tickets.

From April to September, the Orlando Cubs (the Chicago Cubs' Class AA Southern League affiliate) play at Tinker Field, which adjoins the Citrus Bowl. Various other baseball and softball events take place here throughout the year. Call for details.

Prices: Tickets to Cubs games $3–$5. Parking is $3.

Open: Year-round. **Directions:** Take I-4 east to the East-West Expy. and head west to Hwy. 441, make a left on Church St. and follow the signs.

GREYHOUND RACING

SANFORD-ORLANDO KENNEL CLUB, 301 Dog Track Rd., between FL 427 and U.S. 17/92, in Longwood. Tel. 831-1600.

This is a pleasant way to spend a day or evening, especially if you opt to watch the races over lunch or dinner in the glassed-in clubhouse restaurant. There are a variety of ways to bet on the greyhounds; if you've never done it before, pick up a free brochure that explains trifectas, quinelas, boxing, and wheeling and also shows you how to read your ticket. You can also buy tip sheets here recommending computer and expert picks. Each meet includes 14 races. You must be at least 18 years old to enter the track. The restaurant is moderately priced and has a full bar. Reservations are suggested.

Prices: Admission $1, plus $1 admission to the restaurant. Parking is free, preferred parking (closer to the entrance) $1, valet parking $2.

Open: Nov–early May. Nighttime races Mon–Sat at 7:30pm; matinees Mon, Wed, and Sat at 1pm. **Directions:** From the Walt Disney World area, take I-4 east, make a right at Exit 48 (FL 436), and a left at FL 427 (Longwood Ave.). It's about a 40-minute drive.

SEMINOLE GREYHOUND PARK, 2000 Seminola Blvd., just east of U.S. 17/92, in Casselberry. Tel. 699-4510.

Seminole offers a very similar set-up to the above. Its attractive third-floor restaurant, Osceola Terrace, has tiered seating with big picture windows overlooking the track and TV monitors enhancing the view at higher tables. Prices are moderate, and there's a full bar. Reservations are suggested. Each meet here includes 14 or 15 races. Children are welcome but must be at least 18 years old to enter the betting area.

Prices: Admission $1, seniors 55 and over free at matinees, $2 for clubhouse seating, $3 for restaurant seating. Children under 18 pay half price throughout. Parking is free, preferred parking (closer to the entrance) $1, valet parking $2.

Open: May–Oct. Nighttime races Mon–Sat at 7:30pm; matinees Mon, Wed, and Sat at 1pm. **Directions:** From the Walt Disney World area, take I-4 east, make a right at Exit 48 (FL 436), a left at U.S. 17/92, and right on Seminola Blvd., which dead-ends at the track. It's about a 40-minute drive.

JAI ALAI

ORLANDO JAI-ALAI, 6405 S. U.S. 17/92, at FL 436 in Fern Park. Tel. 339-6221.

The action-packed Basque sport of jai-alai (it's the world's fastest game) is vaguely similar to racquetball. It's played on a 180-foot court with three walls. The ball is hurled at speeds of up to 150 miles an hour from baskets strapped to the players' wrists, and the object of the game is to throw the ball with such force, spin, and/or placement that the opponent is unable to return it before it bounces twice. A score of seven points wins. There are two opposing singles or doubles teams on the court at all times. Your program offers extensive information about how the game is played and how to wager, and the public-address announcer elucidates what is happening on the court.

Best bet is to watch the action from the moderately priced, and very attractive, open-air Terrace Restaurant, with some tables as close as 20 feet from the court. There's a color TV monitor at every table. Fare is American/continental; there's a full bar; reservations are suggested. Children are admitted into the fronton with parents, but not allowed in the betting area. *Note:* The fronton also features inter-track wagering; you can place bets here on thoroughbred and harness races as well as Miami jai-alai.

Prices: Admission $1, reserved seats $2, restaurant seating $3, box seats $5–$6. Seniors 55 and over free at matinees. Parking is free, valet parking $1.50.

Open: Year-round Wed–Sun. Evening games at 7:30pm Wed–Sat, matinees at noon Thurs and Sat and 1pm Sun. **Directions:** From the Walt Disney World area, take I-4 east, make a right at Exit 47A (Maitland Exchange), a right at U.S. 17/92, and look for the fronton two miles along on your right. It's about a 40-minute drive.

RECREATION

Recreational facilities of every description abound in Walt Disney World and the surrounding area. These are especially accessible to guests at Disney-owned resorts, official hotels, and Fort Wilderness Resort and Campground, though many other large resort hotels also offer comprehensive facilities (see details in Chapter 5). The Disney facilities listed below are all open to the public, no matter where you're staying. For further information about WDW recreational facilities call 407/824-4321. Guests at Disney properties can inquire when making hotel reservations or at guest services/concierge desks.

BICYCLING Bike rentals (single and multispeed bikes for adults, tandems, and children's bikes) are available from the **Bike Barn** (tel. 824-2742) at Fort Wilderness Resort and Campground. Rates are $3 per hour, $8 per day ($1 additional for tandems); overnight rentals are $15 ($18 for tandems). Both Fort Wilderness and Disney's Village Resort offer good bike trails.

BOATING Walt Disney World, with its many manmade lakes and lagoons, owns the nation's largest fleet of pleasure boats. At the **Walt Disney World Village Marina** you can rent Water Sprites, canopy boats, Sun Kats, and 20-foot pontoon boats. For information call 828-2204. The **Bike Barn** at Fort Wilderness (tel. 824-2742) rents canoes ($4 per hour, $10 per day) and paddleboats ($5 per half hour, $8 per hour). See hotel facilities listings in Chapter 5 for additional boating options.

BOWLING The **Dowdy Pavilion World Bowling Center,** 7540 Canada Ave., between Sand Lake Road and Carrier Drive (tel. 352-BOWL), with 32 lanes, is a state-of-the-art operation. Bowlervision™ monitors over the lanes track your ball speed, and the center also offers variations on 10-pin bowling such as crapshoot, par bowling, and golf; an instruction sheet is provided. The center opens daily at 9am; closing times vary (call ahead). Closed Christmas Eve and Christmas Day. To get here from the Disney World area take International Drive north, turn right at Sand Lake Road and left on Canada Avenue. It's about a 10-minute drive.

FISHING Fishing excursions on Lake Buena Vista—mainly for largemouth bass—may be arranged from 2 to 14 days in advance by calling the **Walt Disney World Village Marina** (tel. 828-2204). Equipment can be rented. No license is required. The fee is $70 for one person for two hours, $90 for two people, $110 for three to six people, $25 for each additional hour; those rates include gear, guide, and refreshments. Similar excursions are offered on Bay Lake in Fort Wilderness (tel. 824-2757). If you'd like to take your catch home, Walt Disney World has an arrangement with a local taxidermist.

You can also rent fishing poles at the **Bike Barn** (tel. 824-2742) to fish in Fort Wilderness canals. No license is required.

FLYING **The Flying Tigers Warbird Air Museum** offers a variety of flight and piloting experiences including scenic seaplane flights over central Florida's lake region, a ride in a 1935 open-cockpit barnstormer, night flights to see theme-park fireworks and laser shows from the air, and hands-on dual-instruction adventures in an historic World War II fighter trainer. Call 933-1942 for details.

A slightly more offbeat experience is offered by an organization called **Fighter Pilots USA.** Ever dreamed of suiting up, jumping into a fighter plane, and engaging in high-speed one-on-one dogfighting? This is your chance to experience the excitement of aerial combat. Actual F-16 pilots are your instructors. To schedule a "mission" call 931-4333, or toll free 800/56-TOPGUN. No license is required. Cost is $750 per person.

GOLF Walt Disney World operates five championship 18-hole, par-72 golf courses and one nine-hole, par-36 walking course. All are open to the general public and offer pro shops, equipment rentals, and instruction. For tee times and information call 824-2270 up to seven days in advance (up to 30 days for Disney resort and official property guests). Call 407/W-DISNEY for information about golf packages.

HAYRIDES The hay wagon departs from Pioneer Hall at **Fort Wilderness** nightly at 7pm and 9:30pm for hour-long, old-fashioned hayrides with singing, jokes, and games. Cost is $5 for adults, $4 for children 3 to 11, under 3 free. Children under 12 must be accompanied by an adult. No reservations; it's first-come, first-served.

HORSEBACK RIDING Disney's Fort Wilderness Resort and Campground offers 50-minute scenic **trail rides** daily, with four to six rides per day. Cost is $16 per person. Children must be at least 9 years old. For information and reservations up to five days in advance, call 824-2832.

ICE SKATING **Rock on Ice! Skating Arena,** in the Dowdy Pavilion, 7500 Canada Ave., between Sand Lake Road and Carrier

Drive (tel. 352-9878), is a gorgeous Olympic-size indoor rink with high-tech lighting and sound systems. A DJ spins Top 40 tunes. There are ice-skating games with prizes throughout the day. Facilities include video games, a snack bar, and a complete skate shop offering a large selection of figure skating and hockey equipment. Rental skates are $1.50. Admission is $4.50 to $6, depending on the season. Hours vary seasonally; call ahead. To get here from the Disney World area take International Drive north, turn right at Sand Lake Road and left on Canada Avenue. It's about a 10-minute drive.

JOGGING   Many of the Disney resorts have scenic jogging trails. For instance, the **Yacht and Beach Club** resorts share a 2-mile trail, **Disney's Village Resort** has a 3.5-mile course with 32 exercise stations, the **Caribbean Beach Resort's** 1.4-mile promenade circles a lake, **Dixie Landings** has a 1.7-mile riverfront trail, and **Fort Wilderness's** tree-shaded 2.3-mile jogging path has exercise stations about every quarter mile. After your run, you can cool off in a hotel pool. Pick up a jogging trail map at any Disney property's guest services desk.

TENNIS   Twenty-two lighted tennis courts are located throughout the Disney properties. Most are free and available on a first-come, first-served basis. If you're willing to pay for court time, courts can be reserved at two Disney resorts: the Contemporary (up to two weeks in advance, fee is $10 per hour) and the Grand Floridian (up to a month ahead of time, fee is $12 per hour). The Contemporary offers a large pro shop, a ball machine, rebound walls, and equipment rentals. To reserve a court or lesson time with resident pros call 824-3578 at the Contemporary, 824-2433 at the Grand Floridian.

WATER PARKS/SWIMMING   See Walt Disney World listings for River Country and Typhoon Lagoon as well as parks listed in "Additional Area Attractions," above.

WATERSKIING   Waterski trips (including boats, drivers, equipment, and instruction) can be arranged at the **Fort Wilderness** marina (tel. 824-2621). Make reservations up to seven days in advance (no later than two days in advance). Cost is $75 per hour.

ORLANDO SHOPPING

You probably didn't come down here to shop, but I doubt you'll leave without a purchase or two. All Orlando area theme parks abound with emporia, in addition to which Walt Disney World has its own shopping complex.

1. SHOPPING IN WALT DISNEY WORLD

Just about every shop throughout the parks carries Disneyana—plush Mickey Mice, *Little Mermaid* T-shirts, etc. But you may be surprised at some of the other merchandise on display here. Among the many dozens of shops, the following are especially notable:

IN THE MAGIC KINGDOM

MAIN STREET AREA The vast **Disneyana Collectibles** carries limited-edition movie cels, antique Disney clocks and porcelain figures, collectible dolls, and items such as a 1947 Donald Duck cookie jar that is today worth $2,000! Why did you ever let Mom throw out your old toys?

The Emporium, in Town Square, houses the park's largest selection of Disneyana—everything from Mickey logo golf balls to Winnie the Pooh slippers. There's a wonderful collection of music boxes here. Note the Audio-Animatronics™ window displays.

The **Market House**—basically an old-fashioned candy store—also carries an interesting line of pipes and tobaccos. Disney-themed kitchenware, too, including Mickey and Minnie corn picks, cupcake papers, ice-cube molds, and cookie cutters.

Over at the **Harmony Barber Shop,** where nostalgic men's grooming items are sold (moustache wax, spice colognes, shaving mugs), a barbershop quartet performs on the hour, except at 3pm, throughout the day.

The **House of Magic** is the place to acquire double-headed nickels, folding quarters, squirting calculators, invisible ink, and other items with which to amaze and impress your friends.

At **Crystal Arts** you can watch craftspeople create intricate animals, cut-glass vases and bowls, and other glittering items.

And at the **Shadow Box,** silhouette artists create cut-out portraits of customers on black paper.

ADVENTURELAND Traders of Timbuktu carries carved wooden and soapstone animals, masks, and cowhide drums from Kenya, among other exotic wares.

Adventure (Raiders-look) clothing is available from **Elephant Tales.**

The **Zanzibar Shell Shop** is the place for shell mobiles and hangings.

Island Supply carries nature/ecology-themed books, toys, clothing, posters, and T-shirts.

The **House of Treasure** retails pirate merchandise—hats, Captain Hook T-shirts, ships in bottles, skull-and-crossbone keychains, and toy muskets and daggers.

And rather fun is **Lafitte's Portrait Deck,** where you can have a costumed photo taken in any of six elaborate Disney sets.

FRONTIERLAND Mosey into the **Frontier Trading Post** for western-look leather items, cowboy boots and hats, turquoise jewelry, western and Native American sculpture, and toy rifles.

Similar wares are found at **Prairie Outpost & Supply.**

LIBERTY SQUARE Olde World Antiques is an actual antiques emporium selling items ranging from an 18th-century pine hutch to 19th-century Staffordshire china.

The adjoining **Silversmith** carries Revere-style silver and pewter butter dishes, candlesticks, bowls, trays, and picture frames, along with valuable items such as a 46-piece set of Benjamin Franklin sterling silverware in a cherrywood chest ($3,500).

Over at **Heritage House** you can purchase parchment copies of famous American documents as well as actual historic framed letters (one signed by Andrew Johnson in 1864 was priced at $2,350). Old campaign buttons, Civil War hats, and presidential signatures are here, too.

FANTASYLAND It's always the holiday season at **Mickey's Christmas Carol**—supply central for Disney-motif ornaments, caroller dolls, Christmas stockings, and charming Christmas-themed music boxes.

The **King's Gallery,** inside Cinderella Castle, is cluttered with family crests, tapestries, suits of armor, and other medieval wares. An artisan demonstrates damascening—a form of metal engraving that originated in Damascus circa A.D. 600.

TOMORROWLAND Kids love browsing over **Space Port's** *Star Trek* and *Star Wars* merchandise and games, sonic blaster guns, robots, alien masks, and astronaut-costumed Mickeys. *Note:* Shops in Tomorrowland are subject to change as this area is undergoing a major revamp.

EPCOT

The most fascinating shops are found in **World Showcase** pavilions, which comprise an international bazaar selling everything from Berber rugs to Japanese kimonos. You'll find descriptions of merchandise available at each of these pavilions in World Showcase descriptions in Chapter 7.

DISNEY-MGM STUDIOS

There's some really interesting shopping here. **Sid Cahuenga's One-Of-A-Kind** sells autographed photos of the stars, original movie posters, and star-touched items. Obviously, the inventory of the latter is ever changing. On my last visit it included a bracelet that once belonged to Joan Rivers, Richard Dreyfuss's director's chair from *Lost in Yonkers*, Cher's black spiked wig, and an original letter written by Tyrone Power.

Over at **Cover Story** you can have your photograph put on the cover of your favorite magazine—anything from *Forbes* to *Psychology Today* to *Golf Digest*. Costumes are available.

Celebrity 5 & 10, modeled after a 1940s Woolworth's, has movie-related merchandise—*Gone With the Wind* memorabilia, MGM Studio T-shirts, movie posters, Elvis mugs, James Dean clocks, and more.

And major park attractions all have complementary merchandise outlets selling Indiana Jones adventure clothing, *Little Mermaid* stuffed characters and logo wear, *Star Wars* souvenirs, and so on.

DISNEY VILLAGE MARKETPLACE

Just 2½ miles from Epcot, this complex of restaurants and shops on the shores of Buena Vista Lagoon makes for a very pleasant browse. Designed to evoke a quaint seaside town, the Marketplace (tel. 828-3058) has about 20 weathered-wood and shingled shops offering a wide variety of giftware, Disneyana (the Mickey Character Shop here has the largest selection of Walt Disney merchandise in WDW), toys, resort wear (including many logo items), designer clothing for men and women, Christmas-year-round merchandise, jewelry, crystal, housewares, country/folk crafts, shells, surfboarding gear, wines and spirits, and sports shoes. Artisans demonstrate crafts such as glass-blowing, pottery-making, silhouette-cutting, and caricaturing at various locations throughout the complex, and many special events—ranging from boat shows to Easter-egg hunts—take place here. There's plenty of free parking. See Chapter 6 for restaurant suggestions here. You can also rent mini-speedboats, paddleboats, and FloteBotes at the marina here. The Marketplace is open daily from 9:30am to 10pm.

CROSSROADS OF LAKE BUENA VISTA

Also under Walt Disney World auspices, this retail center at Exit 27 off I-4 (tel. 827-7300) is anchored by a 24-hour Goodings supermarket with a full-service pharmacy. Other shops sell sportswear, children's clothing, electronics, books, cards, gifts, shoes, and Disney merchandise. Services include a post office, dry cleaner, eyeglass store, and bank. And, of course, there are several restaurants and fast-food outlets. It's just like a shopping center in the real world.

2. ORLANDO AREA MALLS

FACTORY OUTLETS

Belz Factory Outlet World, 5401 W. Oak Ridge Rd., at the north end of International Drive (tel. 354-0126 or 352-9600), is the largest of these, with 160 stores in two huge enclosed malls and three shopping annexes. It offers an immense range of merchandise at savings up to 75% off retail prices. There's even a carousel for the kids. Among its emporia: 18 shoestores (including Bass, Bally, and Capezio); 14 housewares shops (including Fieldcrest/Cannon, Corning, Oneida, and Mikasa); and more than 60 clothing shops for men, women, and children (including London Fog, Van Heusen, Jonathan Logan, Guess Jeans, Crazy Horse, Aileen, Danskin, Jordache, Gitano, Harvé Benard, Calvin Klein, and Anne Klein). You can also shop for books and records, electronics, sporting goods, health and beauty aids, jewelry, toys, gifts, accessories, lingerie, and hosiery here. Open Monday through Saturday from 10am to 9pm, Sunday from 10am to 6pm.

Close to the above is the **Quality Outlet Center,** on International Drive a block east of Kirkman Road (tel. 423-5885). It has about 20 outlets, including Arrow, American Tourister, a vast book warehouse, Corning-Revere (glassware and cookware), Florsheim shoes, Magnavox, Laura Ashley, Linens 'N Things, Mikasa, Royal Doulton, and Villeroy & Boch. Once again, big savings. Open Monday through Saturday from 9:30am to 9pm, Sunday from 11am to 6pm.

Manufacturer's Outlet Mall, U.S. 192, a mile east of FL 535 in Kissimmee (tel. 396-8900), houses about 25 stores, including Van Heusen, Nike, London Fog, Leggs/Hanes/Bali, Bass shoes, Fieldcrest/Cannon, Aileen, and Levis. Open Monday through Saturday from 10am to 9pm, Sunday from 11am to 5pm.

INTERNATIONAL DRIVE AREA MALLS

The Mercado, 8445 International Dr., just south of Sand Lake Road (tel. 345-9337)—a Mediterranean-style shopping center with brick and cobblestone streets, terra-cotta-roofed buildings, brightly colored awnings, and splashing fountains—is home to the Orlando/Orange County Visitor Information Center. During the day, animated bird shows amuse the kids; evenings, there's a one-man band (he plays rock, jazz, pop, and big band) in the central courtyard. More than 60 specialty shops here include Once Upon A Star (movie-motif gifts and clothing), Candlelite (handcrafted candles), American Cola Company (Coca-Cola and Anheuser-Busch memorabilia), House of Ireland (china, crystal, claddagh jewelry), Historic Families (find your family's coat of arms), Earth Matters (conservation/ecology-themed merchandise), Lady Bug (needlecrafts), The Magic Shop (novelties, tricks, and pranks), and The Looking Glass (blown glass). It makes good browsing, and there are over a dozen restaurants and bars on the premises as well as more prosaic shops selling clothing, toys, electronics, and jewelry. Open daily from 10am to 10pm, till 11pm late spring through the end of August.

The **Florida Mall**, 8001 Orange Blossom Trail, at Sand Lake Road (tel. 851-6255), is your basic massive shopping mall with more than 200 shops, restaurants, and services. Centered on a 500-room Sheraton Hotel, it is anchored by six department stores—Belk Lindsey, two Dillard's stores, J. C. Penney, Gayfers, and Sears. In addition there are more than 10 jewelry shops, about 50 clothing and accessory shops (including mall regulars such as Benetton, The Gap/Gap Kids, The Limited, and Victoria's Secret), over a dozen shoestores, bookstores, electronics stores, eateries, and much, much more. Open Monday through Saturday from 10am to 9:30pm, Sunday from 11am to 6pm.

ORLANDO NIGHTS

My hat's off to those of you who after a long day traipsing around amusement parks still have the energy to venture out at night in search of entertainment. You'll find plenty to do. And this being a kid's world, many evening shows are geared to families.

In addition to the below-listed suggestions check the "Calendar" section of Friday's *Orlando Sentinel* for up-to-the-minute details on local clubs, visiting performers, concerts, and events. It has hundreds of listings. A recent edition would have informed you of entertainment options including a dance performance by *Stars of the Bolshoi Ballet,* a production of *La Traviata* by the Orlando Opera Company, and concerts by Garth Brooks, Jethro Tull, Bette Midler, Art Garfunkel, Rod Stewart, George Benson, Travis Tritt, New Riders of the Purple Sage, Mickey Gilley, and Tears for Fears. That's all in one week!

Tickets to many performances are handled by Ticketmaster. Call 839-3900 to charge tickets.

1. MAJOR CONCERT HALLS & AUDITORIUMS

These three large entertainment facilities administered by the **Orlando Centroplex** host the majority of big-name performers playing the Orlando area.

BOB CARR PERFORMING ARTS CENTRE, 401 W. Livingston St., between I-4 and Parramore Ave. Tel. 849-2020 for information, 839-3900 to charge tickets.

This 2,500-seat theater is the home of the Orlando Opera Company and the Southern Ballet Theater, both of which perform during October-to-May seasons here. It also offers concerts and comedy shows (a recent year's performers included Patti LaBelle, B. B. King, Manhattan Transfer, David Sanborn, Stephen Curtis Chapman, George Carlin, Barry Manilow, Bruce Hornsby, and Crosby, Stills, and Nash). The Orlando Broadway Series here (September to May) features original-cast Broadway shows such as *Cats, Les Misérables, The Secret Garden, Crazy for You, Evita,* and the *Magic of David Copperfield.*

Prices: Concert prices vary with performers. Ballet tickets $12–$30, opera $19–$41, Broadway Series $20–$45.

Open: Year-round. **Directions:** Take I-4 east to Amelia Ave., turn left at the traffic light at the bottom of the off-ramp, and follow signs. For up-to-the-minute parking information, turn your car radio to 1620 AM. **Parking:** $4.

FLORIDA CITRUS BOWL, 1610 W. Church St. at Tampa St. Tel. 849-2020 for information, 839-3900 to charge tickets.

This 70,000-seat arena is the setting for major rock concerts starring headliners such as Paul McCartney, George Michael, Pink Floyd, Genesis, Guns n' Roses, Metallica, and the Rolling Stones.

Prices: Vary with performer.

Open: Year-round. **Directions:** Take I-4 east to the East-West Expy. and head west to Hwy. 441, make a left on Church St. and follow the signs. **Parking:** $5.

ORLANDO ARENA, 600 W. Amelia St., between I-4 and Parramore Ave. Tel. 849-2020 for information, 839-3900 to charge tickets.

This 15,000-seat arena offers an array of family-oriented entertainment, including Ringling Bros. Barnum & Bailey Circus every January, the Tour of World Figure-Skating Champions in April or May, *Walt Disney's World on Ice* in September, and *Sesame Street Live* in October. It also hosts about 30 varied music and comedy concerts a year featuring performers such as Elton John, Billy Joel, Neil Diamond, Bruce Springsteen, Bette Midler, the Grateful Dead, and Garth Brooks. Call to find out who's on when you're in town.

Prices: Vary with events.

Open: Year-round. **Directions:** Take I-4 east to Amelia Ave., turn left at the traffic light at the bottom of the off-ramp, and follow signs. For up-to-the-minute parking information turn your car radio to 1620 AM. **Parking:** $4.

2. WALT DISNEY WORLD DINNER SHOWS

Two distinctly different dinner shows are hosted by Walt Disney World. Other nighttime park options include SpectroMagic, fireworks, and IllumiNations (details in Chapter 7).

HOOP-DEE-DOO MUSICAL REVUE, Disney's Fort Wilderness Resort and Campground, 3520 N. Fort Wilderness Trail. Tel. W-DISNEY.

Fort Wilderness's rustic log-beamed Pioneer Hall is the setting for this two-hour foot-stompin', hand-clappin' down-home musical revue. It's a high-energy show, with 1890s costumes, corny vaudeville jokes, rousing songs, and lots of good-natured audience participation. During the show, the audience chows down on an all-you-can-eat barbecue dinner including chips and salsa, salad, smoked ribs, country-fried chicken, corn on the cob, baked beans, loaves of fresh-baked bread with honey butter, and a big slab of strawberry shortcake for dessert. Beverages (coffee, tea, beer, sangría, and soda) are included. Reservations required. If you catch an early show stick around for the Electrical Water Pageant at 9:45pm, which can be viewed from the Fort Wilderness Beach.

Prices: $34 adults 21 and over, $25 ages 12–20, $17 children 3–11. Taxes and gratuities are extra.

Show Times: 5, 7:15, and 9:30pm nightly. **Parking:** Free self-parking.

POLYNESIAN LUAU DINNER SHOW, Disney's Polynesian Resort, 1600 Seven Seas Dr. Tel. W-DISNEY.

This delightful two-hour dinner show features a colorfully costumed cast of exotic South Pacific entertainers (from New Zealand, Tahiti, Hawaii, and Samoa) performing authentic hula, warrior, ceremonial, love, and fire dances on a flower-bedecked stage. The show also includes a Hawaiian/Polynesian fashion show. It all takes place in an open-air theater (dress for the weather) with candlelit tables, red-flame lanterns suggesting torchiers, and tapa-bark paintings adorning the walls. The all-you-can-eat meal includes a marvelous tropical fruit and greens salad with creamy ranch dressing, coconut-almond bread, fried rice with vegetables, seafood stir-fry, barbecued ribs, chicken teriyaki, fresh fruit with chocolate dipping sauce and coconut haupia (pudding) for dessert, and beverages (mai-tais, melon coladas, beer, soft drinks, and tea or coffee; nonalcoholic specialty cocktails are available for kids). Everyone is presented with a shell lei on entering, and if the weather's chilly, hot cocoa is served while you're waiting for the show to begin. Reservations required. There is also a 4:30pm version daily (see character meal listings in Chapter 6).

Prices: $32 adults 21 and over, $24.50 ages 12–20, $16.50 children 3–11. Taxes and gratuities are extra.

Show Times: 6:45 and 9:30pm nightly. **Parking:** Free self- and valet parking.

3. ENTERTAINMENT COMPLEXES

PLEASURE ISLAND, in Walt Disney World, adjacent to Walt Disney World Village. Tel. 934-7781.

Opened in 1989, this Walt Disney World theme park is a rollicking six-acre complex of nightclubs, restaurants (a branch of Planet Hollywood is opening shortly after presstime), shops, and movie theaters (details below) where, for a single admission price, you can enjoy a night of club-hopping till the wee hours. The park is designed to evoke an abandoned waterfront industrial district with clubs in "converted" ramshackle lofts, factories, and warehouses, but the streets are festive with brightly colored lights and balloons. Dozens of searchlights play overhead, and rock music emanates from the bushes. You'll be given a map and show schedule when you enter the park; take a look at it, and plan your evening around shows that interest you. The mood here is always festive. For one thing, every night at Pleasure Island is New Year's Eve, celebrated on the stroke of midnight with a high-energy street party, live entertainment, a barrage of fireworks, and showers of confetti. You can feel perfectly secure sending your teenage kids here for the evening, though they must be 18 to get in unless accompanied by a parent or legal guardian. The on-premises clubs do come and go. At this writing they include:

Mannequins Dance Palace: Housed in a vast dance hall with a small-town movie-house facade, Mannequins is supposed to be a converted theatrical mannequin warehouse (remember, you're still in Disney World). It's a high-energy club with a large rotating dance floor. Three levels of bars and hangout space are festooned with elaborately costumed mannequins and moving scenery suspended from overhead rigging. A DJ plays contemporary tunes at ear-splitting decibel level, high-tech lighting effects—with laser shows taking place twice nightly—are part of the excitement, and occasionally bubbles or snowflakes drift down from above the dance floor. You must be 21 to get in, and they're very serious about it. They even carded me, and I learned to dance to the Platters.

Neon Armadillo Music Saloon: You guessed. This tri-level club is country—with neon beer signs, rustic tables mounted on beer barrels, walls hung with spurs and saddles, and a spur-shaped neon chandelier. Live country bands play nightly, and dancers whirl around the floor doing the Texas two-step or cotton-eyed Joe (lessons are given from 7 to 8pm). Sometimes name stars come in and take the stage, and one night actor John Goodman belted out a few songs. The staff is in cowboy/cowgirl garb. A specialty at the bar is jello shooters—jello cubes laced with rum, vodka, and other alcoholic beverages. You can also order southwestern fare here such as chili and fajitas.

The **Island Jazz Company:** This big barnlike club— purported to be an abandoned waterfront carousel factory (pine walls are adorned with merry-go-round horses)—features contemporary and traditional live jazz. Performers are mostly locals, but about once a month there are big names such as Kenny Rankin, Lionel Hampton, Maynard Ferguson, the Rippingtons, and Manfredo Best. Light fare, international coffees, and a variety of foreign and domestic wines are available.

Adventurers Club: The most unique—and my personal favorite—of Pleasure Island's clubs occupies a multistory building that, according to Disney legend, was designed to house the vast library and archeological trophy collection of island founder and compulsive explorer Merriweather Adam Pleasure. It's also headquarters for the Adventure Club, which Pleasure headed up until he vanished at sea in 1941. The plushly furnished club is chock-full of artifacts—early aviation photos, hunting trophies, shrunken heads, Buddhas, Indian goddesses, spears, and a mounted "yakoose" (half yak, half moose) who occasionally speaks. He's not the only one. In the eerie Mask Room, strange sounds are often heard, and more than 100 masks move their eyes, jeer, and make odd pronouncements. Also on hand are Pleasure's zany band of globe-trotting friends and club servants. Played by skilled actors who interact with guests and always stay in character, these include: the Colonel (a British pukka sahib), Pamelia Perkins (the stuffy upper-class club president), Otis T. Wren (a curmudgeonly ichthyologist, oft seen racing up the stairs muttering about being forced to mix with riffraff), Hathaway Brown (dashing aviator; "the earth was no magnet for him, the skies beckoned"), Fletcher Hodges (club curator and absentminded scientist), Emile Bleehall (pigeon trainer and country hick from the Sandusky, Ohio, chapter of the club), Mandora (leopardskin-clad adventuress), Dusty (sexy parlor maid), and Graves (the lugubrious butler). Improvisational comedy shows take place throughout the evening in the main salon, diverse 20-minute cabaret shows in the library (during which "volunteers" are dragooned from the audience). You could easily hang out here all night imbibing potent tropical drinks in the library and at the bar—where elephant-foot barstools rise and sink mysteriously!

Comedy Warehouse: Housed in the island's former power plant, the Comedy Warehouse—another favorite of mine—has a rustic interior with tiered seating. A very talented troupe performs improvisational comedy based on audience suggestions. There are five shows a night, and bar drinks are available. Arrive early. Tickets are distributed 30 minutes before show time, and lines soon form.

Rock & Roll Beach Club: Once the laboratory in which Pleasure developed a unique flying machine, this three-story structure today houses a dance club where live bands play oldies and Top 40 tunes nightly. There are bars on all three floors. The first level contains the dance floor. The second and third levels offers air hockey, pool tables, basketball machines, pinball, video games, blackjack tables, foosball, a bowling machine, and a pizza and beer stand.

8 TRAX: This 1970s-style club, with about 50 TV monitors airing diverse shows and videos over the dance floor, occupies three levels, all with bars. Period movie posters (*Bananas, Star Wars*) adorn the walls, and the top-floor lounge is vaguely psychedelic in decor. A DJ plays disco music, and guests engage in games of Twister.

In addition, live bands—including occasional big-name groups—play the **West End Plaza** outdoor stage and the **Hub Stage;** check your schedule for show times. You can star in your own music video at **SuperStar Studios.** And there are carnival games, a video-game arcade, a Velcro wall (don a jumpsuit over your clothes, bounce on a trampoline, and stick yourself on), and an Orbitron (a "21st-century workout machine," originally developed for NASA, that lets you experience weightlessness). Shops and eateries (with outdoor umbrella tables) are found throughout the park. A jazz club is in the works.

Admission: $15.85. Admission is included in the Five-Day Super Duper Pass. There's no admission prior to 7pm, but you have to pay after that.

Hours: Clubs 8pm–2am, shops 10am–1am. **Parking:** Free self-parking, valet parking $4.

CHURCH STREET STATION, 129 W. Church St., off I-4, between Garland and Orange aves. in downtown Orlando. Tel. 422-2434.

Though not part of Walt Disney World, Church Street Station in downtown Orlando operates on a similar principle to Pleasure Island (in fact, it innovated the concept). Occupying a cobblestoned city block lined with turn-of-the-century buildings (real ones), it, too, is a shopping/dining/nightclub complex offering a diverse evening of entertainment for a single admission price. There are 20 live shows nightly; consult your show schedule on entering. Stunning interiors are the rule here. It's worth coming by just to check out the magnificent woodwork, stained glass, and thousands of authentic antiques. And capitalizing on the traffic Church Street generates, many other clubs have opened in the immediate area, further enlarging your bar-hopping potential. Entry to restaurants, the Exchange Shopping Emporium, and the Midway game area is free. Highlights include:

Rosie O'Grady's Good Time Emporium: This 1890s-style gambling hall–cum-saloon, with beveled- and leaded-glass panels, etched mirrors, and vast globe chandeliers suspended from a high pressed-tin ceiling, is filled with interesting antiques. The train benches came from an old Florida rail station, backbar mirrors from a Glasgow pub, and bank teller's cages from a 19th-century Pittsburgh bank. Dixieland bands, banjo players, singing waiters, and cancan dancers (who enter the room via a shiny brass firepole) entertain nightly. Light fare (deli sandwiches, chili dogs) is available. The house specialty drink is a rum and fruit concoction called the Flaming Hurricane (served in a souvenir glass).

Apple Annie's Courtyard: Adjoining Rosie's, this brick-floored establishment, domed by arched pine and cypress trusses from an early 19th-century New Orleans church, evokes a Victorian tropical garden. The room is further embellished by 12-foot hand-carved filigree mirrors created in Vienna circa 1740 and magnificent 1,000-pound chandeliers suspended from an ornate vaulted cherrywood ceiling. An 18th-century French communion rail serves as the front bar. Seating is in wicker peacock chairs at English pub tables. Patrons sip potent tropical fresh fruit and ice-cream drinks while listening to folk and bluegrass music.

Lili Marlene's Aviator's Pub & Restaurant: Its plush oak-paneled interior is embellished with World War I memorabilia, stained-glass transoms, burnished brass railings, and accoutrements from an 1850 Rothschild town house in Paris, the latter including a walnut fireplace and wine cabinets. Eclectic seating ranges from hand-carved oak pews that came from a French church to a place at a large drop-leaf mahogany table where Al Capone once dined. Model airplanes and marvelous Victorian chandeliers are suspended from a beamed pine ceiling with a stained-glass skylight. The menu features premium aged steaks, prime rib, and fresh seafood.

Phineas Phogg's Balloon Works: This whimsical bar, with hot-air balloons and airplanes over the dance floor, is a high-energy club playing loud, pulsating music. It doubles as a virtual ballooning museum housing photographs and artifacts from historic flights, including Orlando native Joe Kittinger—first man to cross the Atlantic in a gas balloon. Every Wednesday from 6:30 to 7:30pm, beers cost just 5¢ here. No one under 21 is admitted.

Cheyenne Saloon and Opera House: This stunning tri-level balconied saloon, crowned by a lofty stained-glass skylight, is constructed of golden oak lumber from a century-old Ohio barn. Quality western art is displayed throughout, including many oil paintings and 11 Remington sculptures. An 1885 solid rosewood pool table from San Francisco is on the upper tier, the three central chandeliers are from the home of St. Louis beer baron Joseph Schlitz, and six others (circa 1895) came from the Philadelphia Mint. Balcony seating, in restored church pews, overlooks the stage—setting for entertainment ranging from country bands (some big names) to clogging exhibitions—and the dance floor. The menu features steaks, barbecued chicken and ribs, and hickory-smoked brisket, served with buttermilk biscuits and honey and bourbon baked beans.

The Orchid Garden Ballroom: This stunning space, with ornate white wrought-iron arches and Victorian lighting fixtures suspended from an elaborate oak-paneled ceiling, is the setting for an oldies dance club. A DJ plays rock 'n' roll classics like "Great Balls of Fire" and "Let's Go to the Hop" interspersed with live bands. As the evening progresses, so do the musical decades.

Crackers Oyster Bar: Brick columns, oak paneling, and a gorgeous antique oak and mahogany bar, characterize this cozy late 1800s-style dining room. A glass section of the Saltillo-tile floor provides a view of the wine cellar below. Fresh Florida seafood is featured, along with more than 50 imported beers. You can nibble on appetizers such as oysters Rockefeller, smoked fish dip served with carrot and celery sticks, and steamed mussels. Or opt for more serious entrées ranging from crabcakes rémoulade to paella.

In addition, the 87,000-square-foot Exchange houses the carnival-like **Commander Ragtime's Midway of Fun, Food and Games** (including an enormous video-game arcade), a food court, and more than 50 specialty shops. You can rent a horse-drawn carriage out front for a drive around the downtown area and Lake Eola. And hot-air balloon flights can be arranged (tel. 841-8787).

Admission: $16.90; free prior to 5pm, after which you have to pay.

Hours: Clubs are open nightly until 2am, shops until 11pm.

Directions: Take I-4 east to Exit 38 (Anderson St.), stay in the left lane, and follow the blue signs. Most hotels offer transportation to and from Church St., and, since you'll probably be drinking, I advise it. **Parking:** There are several lots nearby (call for specifics). Valet parking, at Church St. and Garland Ave., is $5.

4. MORE ENTERTAINMENT

LITTLE HOUSE OF HORRORS

TERROR ON CHURCH STREET, 135 S. Orange Ave., at Church St. in downtown Orlando, a block from Church Street Station. Tel. 649-FEAR or 649-1912.

This is definitely a weird and spooky entertainment, but it is fun. Terror on Church Street is a multimedia, high-tech house of horrors incorporating innovative special effects and 23 highly theatrical sets on two floors. On a labyrinthine 25-minute tour of the darkened premises, guests are menaced by cleaver- and chain-saw-wielding maniacs, deranged mental patients, ghoulish monks, hunchbacks, assorted cadavers, vicious dogs, Freddie Kreuger, and Dracula, among others—all convincingly portrayed by actors. Children under 8 are not admitted without an adult. A gift shop on the premises sells stick-on warts and burn scars, coffin banks, and the like.

Admission: $10 adults, $8 children under 13.

Hours: Tues–Thurs and Sun 7pm–midnight, Fri–Sat 7pm–1am. **Closed:** Mon. **Directions:** Take I-4 east to Exit 38 (Anderson St.), stay in the left lane, and follow the blue signs to Church Street Station parking. Most hotels offer transportation to the area. **Parking:** There are several lots nearby (call for specifics). You can use Church Street Station's valet parking, at Church St. and Garland Ave. ($5).

A SPORTS BAR

CHAMPIONS, Marriott's Orlando World Center, 8701 World Center Dr. Tel. 239-4200.

Champions is a sports-bar chain—one so appealing it's easy to see why the concept has succeeded. Its interior is chockablock with $25,000 worth of signed sports photos, posters, and artifacts such as Lou Gehrig's baseball bat, a golf bag autographed by Dallas Cowboys coach Jimmy Johnson, and (of local interest) a wet suit belonging to Cypress Gardens' famed barefoot waterski star, Banana George. In addition, thousands of baseball cards are laminated under the bartop. Some nights a DJ plays music (mostly Motown and oldies) for dancing. Otherwise, entertainments include three pool tables, video games, foosball, air hockey, darts, coin-op football and basketball, an indoor putting green, and blackjack tables. In addition, sporting events are aired on a large-screen TV and on smaller monitors around the room (a calendar at the entrance lists all game times). Champions offers a fairly extensive bar-food menu featuring chicken wings, stuffed potato skins, salads, pizza, burgers, and cheese steak sandwiches. *Note to single women:* Men outnumber women about five to one, so this is a good place to meet guys—if you can distract them from the sports action on the screen.

Admission: Free.

Open: Nightly until 2am. **Parking:** Free self-parking, valet parking $5.

A DINNER SHOW

WILD BILL'S WILD WEST DINNER SHOW, 5260 U.S. 192, just east of I-4. Tel. 351-5151, or toll free 800/883-8282.

Located at Fort Liberty, a 22-acre western-themed shopping/dining/entertainment complex, this rambunctious dinner show takes place in a big barnlike wooden building. You'll be given a cardboard cowboy hat and vest when you sit down, which identifies you as a shepherd or cowherd for audience-participation activities (there are a lot of these). The show includes rousing song-and-dance numbers ("Annie Get Your Gun," "Oklahoma," "Back in the Saddle Again"); rodeo roping, knife-throwing, and archery demonstrations; singalongs; a cancan; and Comanche ceremonial and war dances. All the children in the audience get to go up on the stage. Dinner—served on pewterware—is a hearty four-course meal consisting of salad, soup, beef stew, fried chicken, barbecued pork ribs, biscuits with honey butter, corn on the cob, beans, a baked potato, hot apple pie, and ice cream. Beer, wine, or Coca-Cola are included.

Admission: $29.95 adults, $19.95 children 3–11, under 3 free.

Hours: Shows take place nightly at 7pm, with 9:30pm shows on selected nights.

MOVIES

PLEASURE ISLAND AMC THEATER, in Walt Disney World adjacent to the Pleasure Island nightclub complex. Tel. 827-1300.

This 10-screen AMC theater complex—equipped with state-of-the-art Dolby-digital sound systems and 70mm-projection capability—extends the variety of nighttime entertainment available to Disney World guests. A bridge connects the theater complex with Pleasure Island clubs. New Disney films premiere here, and first-run films are shown.

Admission: Matinees $4.50 adults, $3.75 seniors and children 2–13, under 2 free; twilight shows (4:30–6pm) $3.25 for all seats; evening shows $6.50 adults, $4.50 students, $3.75 seniors (over 55) and children 2–13, under 2 free.

Hours: Check the *Orlando Sentinel* for show times. **Parking:** Free self-parking.

CHAPTER 10

EASY EXCURSIONS FROM ORLANDO

1. CYPRESS GARDENS
2. KENNEDY SPACE CENTER
3. WINTER PARK
4. DAYTONA BEACH

Get away from the thrill-a-minute glitter and glitz that characterizes most Orlando attractions to Cypress Gardens —a serene botanical paradise that was central Florida's first major tourist draw; to find out what NASA is up to over at the Kennedy Space Center; to Winter Park, a charming upscale town with some uniquely exquisite attractions; or to the self-proclaimed "World's Most Famous Beach" and "World Center of Racing"— Daytona Beach.

1. CYPRESS GARDENS

40 miles SW of Walt Disney World, 45 miles SW of Orlando

GETTING THERE   By Car Take I-4 west to U.S. 27 south, and proceed west on to FL 540. (If you don't have a car, inquire about public transportation at your hotel.)

Founded in 1936 when Dick and Julie Pope hired a crew of laborers to dig canals and drain swamps, Cypress Gardens, located on FL 540 at Cypress Gardens Boulevard in Winter Haven (tel. 813/324-2111, or toll free 800/237-4826, 800/282-2123 in Florida), came into being as a 16-acre public garden along the banks of Lake Eloise with cypress-wood-block pathways and thousands of tropical and subtropical plants. Today it has grown to over 200 acres, with ponds and lagoons, waterfalls, classic Italian fountains, topiary, bronze sculptures, manicured lawns, and—most notably—ancient cypress trees shrouded in Spanish moss forming a backdrop to ever-changing floral displays of 8,000 varieties of plants from 75 countries. Southern belles in Scarlett O'Hara costumes stroll the grounds or sit on benches under parasols in idyllic tree-shaded nooks. They symbolize Florida's old-fashioned southern hospitality. In the late winter and early spring, more than 40 varieties of bougainvillea, 60 of azalea, and 500 of roses burst into bloom. Crape myrtles, magnolias, and gardenias perfume the late-spring air, while brilliant birds of paradise, hibiscus, and jasmine brighten the summer landscape. And in winter, the golden rain trees, floss silk trees, and camellias of autumn give way to millions of colorful chrysanthemums and red, white, and pink poinsettias.

WHAT TO SEE & DO   Strolling the grounds is, of course, the main attraction (there are over two miles of winding botanical paths, and half of the park's acreage is devoted to floral displays), but this being central Florida it's not the only one. Four shows are scheduled several times each day. The world-famous **Greatest American Ski Team** performs daring freestyle jumps, swivel skiing, barefooting, ski ballet, and slalom exhibitions on Lake Eloise in a show augmented by an awesome hang-gliding display. **Feathered Follies,** a bird show, features trained cockatoos, macaws, and other exotic members of the parrot family roller-skating, playing basketball, and otherwise mimicking humans. **Variété Internationale** features specialty acts from all over the world, at this writing Russian acrobats. And since visitors can't be here to observe all seasonal changes, a slide show called **Seasons of Cypress Gardens** provides an overview of the year's blooms; it also takes visitors behind the scenes to learn how floral exhibits are created and maintained.

And there's still more. An enchanting exhibit called **Wings of Wonder** surrounds visitors with hundreds of brightly colored free-flying butterflies (representing more than 50 species) in a 5,500-square-foot Victorian-style glass conservatory filled with tropical plantings, orchids, and waterfalls. **Electric boats** navigate a maze of lushly landscaped canals in the original botanical gardens area. You can ascend 153 feet to **Kodak's™ Island in the Sky** for a panoramic vista of the gardens and a beautiful chain of central Florida lakes. **Carousel Cove,** with eight kiddie rides and arcade games, centers on an ornate turn-of-the-century-style carousel. It adjoins another kid pleaser, **Cypress Junction™**, an elaborately landscaped model railroad (scenery includes everything from a burning house to Mount Rushmore) that travels 1,100 feet of track with up to 20 trains moving at one time. **Cypress Roots,** a museum of park memorabilia, displays photographs of famous visitors (Elvis on waterskis, Tiny Tim tiptoeing through the roses) and airs ongoing showings of *Easy to Love* starring Esther Williams (it was filmed here). Another museum commemorates the **age of radio** with a display of hundreds of vintage radios, radio memorabilia, and recordings of radio shows and music from the 1920s to the 1950s. Wind up your visit with a relaxing 30-minute narrated **pontoon cruise** on scenic Lake Eloise, past virgin forest, bulrushes, and beautiful shoreline homes. En route, you're likely to observe cormorants, osprey, ducks—maybe even an alligator or two. There's a $3.50 per-person charge.

Admission to Cypress Gardens is $24.95 for ages 10 and over, $16.45 for children 3 to 9; ages 2 and under, free. There are discounts for seniors. Discounted admissions in conjunction with Sea World (see Chapter 7) and Busch Gardens in Tampa are also available; call for details or inquire at the gate. Cypress Gardens is open 365 days a year, from 9:30am to 5:30pm, with extended hours during peak seasons. Parking is free.

WHERE TO DINE   Your options range from a food court to the Crossroads Restaurant, a cheerful full-service facility serving American fare; the latter also offers al fresco seating at umbrella tables on a terrace. I also like the more casual Lakeview Terrace, a cafeteria with covered outdoor seating overlooking Lake Eloise; it offers great views of the ski show. Fresh strawberries are sold throughout the park in season. And if you care to pack a basket, there are picnic tables. Over a dozen shops sell everything from quaint country-store merchandise (bayberry candles, herb wreaths) to gardening books and paraphernalia.

---

2. KENNEDY SPACE CENTER

60 miles E of Walt Disney World, 45 miles E of Orlando

GETTING THERE   By Car   Take the Beeline Expressway (Hwy. 528) east, where the road divides go left on FL 407, make a right on FL 405 and follow signs. (If you don't have a car, inquire about public transportation at your hotel.)

Operated by NASA, the John F. Kennedy Space Center (tel. 407/452-2121) has been the launch site for all United States manned space missions since 1968. Astronauts departed earth at this site en route to the most famous "small step" in history—man's first voyage to the moon. All space shuttle launches have also been staged from this site.

Nonoperational areas of the Kennedy Space Center are part of the 140,000-acre **Merritt Island National Wildlife Refuge** (tel. 407/861-0667). This pristine wilderness of dense woods, unspoiled beaches, fish-filled waterways, marshlands, and mud flats provides refuge for bald eagles, great egrets, ibis, wood storks, owls, falcons, hawks, brown pelicans, deer, bobcats, otters, sea turtles, manatees, alligators, and other native Florida wildlife—more than 500 species in total. There are more threatened and endangered species here than at any other national wildlife refuge. To find out about guided nature walks and interpretative programs (November through March only), sea turtle watches in June and July, and year-round wildlife drives and self-guided hikes (trails range from half a mile to five miles) call or visit the Visitor Information Center, which is four miles east of Titusville on FL 402. It is open Monday to Friday from 8am to 4:30pm, Saturday from 9am to 5pm; closed all major holidays. (*Note:* You won't have time to tour nature trails and see the Space Center in the same day.)

WHAT TO SEE & DO   At Spaceport USA, the visitor facility of the Kennedy Space Center, the past, present, and future of space exploration are explored on bus tours of the facility and in movie presentations and numerous exhibits. It takes at least a full day to see and do everything. Arrive early and make your first stop at **Information Central** (it opens at 9am) to pick up a schedule of events/map and for help in planning your day. Nearby, there are space-related exhibits and interactive computers at which you can access information about all 10 U.S. NASA centers.

On the two-hour **Red Tour** you'll board a double-decker bus to explore the complex. En route, your driver will point out significant buildings such as the laboratories where instruments are calibrated and maintained; the headquarters building, administrative hub for all Space Center activities; astronauts' living quarters during training; and the building where hardware bound for the launch pad is inspected and tested prior to use. At the first stop—in a simulated launch control firing room of the Flight Crew Training Building—visitors view a film about the *Apollo 11* mission. The countdown, launch, and planting of a flag on the moon are thrilling even at second hand. In the adjoining room related exhibits include an *Apollo 11* command service module (home for the three crew members during their round-trip) and a lunar module (their home on the lunar surface). The tour continues to Complex 39 Space Shuttle launch pads (where a stop is made for exploration) and the massive Vehicle Assembly Building where space shuttles are assembled. In volume, the VAB is the world's second-largest building, with doors 456 feet high. Nearby, visitors get a close-up look at an actual *Apollo/Saturn V* moon rocket—America's largest and most powerful launch vehicle. Also on view are massive six-million pound Crawler Transporters that carry space shuttles to their launch pads. There are many photo opportunities, both on the tour and throughout the Spaceport complex. Tours depart at regular intervals beginning at 9:45am, with the last tour leaving two hours before dusk. Purchase tickets at the Ticket Pavilion as soon as you arrive. *Note:* Itinerary variations may occur subject to launch schedules.

Though most visitors are sated by the Red Tour, a second two-hour **Blue Bus Tour** (same hours) visits Cape Canaveral Air Force Station. On this tour, you'll see where America's first satellites and astronauts were launched in the Mercury and Gemini programs, view launch pads currently being used for unmanned launches, visit the original site of Mission Control, and stop at the Air Force Space Museum, which houses a unique collection of missiles and space memorabilia.

Satellites and You is a 50-minute voyage through a simulated future space station. In Disneyesque fashion, the attraction combines Audio-Animatronic™ characters with innovative audiovisual techniques to explain satellites and their uses. Passing through futuristic airlock spacecraft doors à la *Star Trek,* visitors enter work chambers with names like Central Module Alpha 1 and 2. In each chamber you'll learn something new about today's satellite technology and its uses in such diverse areas as environmental studies, weather prediction, crop harvesting, forest management, fishing, medicine, even locating new oil fields. Farther along, the role of satellites in creating a global village focuses on the rapid dissemination of information via teleconferencing; live coverage of news, entertainment, and sporting events; and clear telephone communication worldwide. The final program explains how the space program is involved in improving the quality of life on earth and securing a future threatened by overpopulation, hunger, drought, and air and water pollution.

In the **Galaxy Center building,** two spectacular IMAX films projected on 5½-story screens are shown continually throughout the day in twin theaters. In *The Dream is Alive*—featuring in-flight footage from three space shuttle missions—viewers join astronauts in preflight training, aboard the space shuttle in orbit, and on a breathtaking launch and landing. The second film, *Blue Planet,* is an environmentally themed look at Spaceship Earth from the vantage point of outer space.

The Galaxy Center also houses: a NASA Art Exhibit; a walk-through replica of the future space station *Freedom,* a manned research laboratory that will be orbiting the earth by 1999; and an exhibit called "Spinoffs From Space." The latter—which is hosted by hologram characters—displays some of the 30,000 spin-offs that have resulted from space-program research, including improved consumer products ranging from football helmets to cordless tools, and advances in medicine, computer sciences, energy, public safety, transportation, agriculture, and the environment.

The **Gallery of Spaceflight,** a large museum, houses hardware and models relating to significant space projects such as the *Mercury* missions (1958–63), *Gemini 9* (a two-man mission in 1966), the *Apollo-Soyuz* Test Project (the world's first international space venture), Skylab, and the *Saturn V* moon rocket. It also contains interesting exhibits on lunar exploration and geology. You can view a moon rock and have a photograph taken of yourself in a lunar rover.

Spaceport Theater presents films on a variety of space-related subjects such as what astronauts do inside the space shuttle, the evolution of the space program, and the history of Kennedy Space Center.

The **Astronauts Memorial**—a 42.5-by-50-foot black granite "Space Mirror" dedicated May 9, 1991—honors the 16 American astronauts who have lost their lives in the line of duty.

Aboard *Explorer,* a full-size replica of a space shuttle orbiter, visitors can experience the working environment of NASA astronauts.

And the **Rocket Garden** displays eight actual U.S. rockets.

There are two **cafeterias**—the Orbit and the Lunch Pad—on the premises, though an organization capable of sending men to the moon should be able to create better food and a more pleasant dining environment. The gift shop carries a wide array of innovative space-related books, toys, games, videotapes, astronaut flight suits, NASA and space logo clothing, and more.

Seeing a Launch   Today a rocket soaring skyward is not an uncommon sight, but it's still one that fills most observers with awe. If you'd like to see a launch, call **Spaceport USA** (tel. 407/452-2121 for current launch information, 407/452-2121, ext. 260 to make reservations). Tickets for viewing cost $7 for adults, $4 for children 3 to 11; under 3 free. You can reserve tickets up to seven days before a launch, but they must be picked up at least two days before the launch. A special bus takes observers to a site just six miles from the launch pad.

Admission to the Kennedy Space Center is free. Tickets for either bus tour cost $7 for adults, $4 for children 3 to 11 and free to children under 3. IMAX film tickets are $4 for adults, $2 for children 3 to 11, and free to children under 3. The Kennedy Space Center is open daily from 9am to dusk; it's closed on Christmas. Parking is free.

---

3. WINTER PARK

20 miles N of Walt Disney World, 5 miles N of Orlando

GETTING THERE   By Car   Take I-4 east to Fairbanks Avenue (Exit 45), exit right and proceed east for about a mile, turn left on Park Avenue and follow signs to public parking.

By Bus   Take LYNX bus no. 4 from the Osceola Square Mall at Columbia Street and Hoagland Avenue in Kissimmee. It will take you to the Orlando downtown terminal where you can transfer to bus no. 1 or 9, either of which makes several stops along Park Avenue in Winter Park. Call 841-8240 for schedule.

By Train   Amtrak service (tel. toll free 800/USA-RAIL) is available from Orlando and Kissimmee (see Chapter 2 for locations). The Winter Park station is located at 150 W. Morse Blvd. (tel. 645-5055).

The beautiful lakefront community of Winter Park was created in the early 1880s as "a first class place" for "men and women of intelligence, culture, character, taste and means." Developers Loring A. Chase and Oliver E. Chapman priced their lots accordingly. The town was incorporated in 1887. To this day it remains an affluent haven—Florida's answer to Greenwich, Connecticut. You can visit on a day-trip, or spend a relaxing night or two here away from theme park hubbub. Its attractions include a lovely Beverly Hills–like shopping strip (Park Avenue) lined with posh boutiques and art galleries; golf courses; fine old homes along winding, tree-shaded streets; shimmering lakes and canals (Winter Park has been called the "Venice of America"); Central Park, a large village green with lush lawns, stately oaks, and rose gardens; and a museum housing a treasure trove of Tiffany windows, lamps, and objets d'art. And though (actually because) refined Winter Park takes no official notice of the fact, the town attracts numerous celebrities looking for a quaint and quiet retreat. Don't be surprised if you run into former president Gerald Ford or Paul Newman in a local shop.

For further information about Winter Park contact the **Chamber of Commerce,** 150 N. New York Ave., at Morse Boulevard (P.O. Box 280), Winter Park, FL 32790 (tel. 407/644-8281). Hours are 9am to 4pm Monday through Friday. *Note:* Street parking is sometimes difficult. There's a convenient city lot on South New York Avenue between Morse Boulevard and New England Avenue.

WHAT TO SEE & DO

Stroll Winter Park's main street, browse its boutiques, visit its museums, play a few rounds of golf, and take a leisurely lake cruise.

THE CHARLES HOSMER MORSE MUSEUM OF AMERICAN ART, 133 E. Welbourne Ave., at Center St. Tel. 644-3686.

Anyone who loves the sinuous, nature-inspired art nouveau genre (and who doesn't) will be amazed and thrilled by this gem of a gallery. It was founded by Hugh and Jeanette McKean in 1942 to display their peerless collection (more than 4,000 pieces), including 40 magnificent windows and 21 paintings created by Louis Comfort Tiffany! In addition, there are non-Tiffany windows by William Morris, Frank Lloyd Wright, Frederick Stymetz Lamb, and 15th- and 16th-century German masters; leaded lamps by Tiffany and Emile Gallé; a display of carnival glass; paintings by John Singer Sargent, Samuel F. B. Morse, Maxfield Parrish, Thomas Hart Benton, and Arthur B. Davies; jewelry designed by Tiffany, Lalique, and Fabergé; sculptures by Hiram Powers and Daniel Chester French (of Lincoln Memorial fame); prints by Cézanne, Childe Hassam, Rembrandt, Whistler, Winslow Homer, and Grant Wood; photographic works by Tiffany and other 19th-century artists; and art nouveau furnishings by Tiffany, Gallé, and others. The collection also includes Tiffany memorabilia—letters, furnishings, personal effects, and photographs used by his studio as source materials. Due to space limitations, only a small portion of the above can be shown at any given time; however, the works on display are wonderfully impressive, and plans are underway for expansion. Be sure to peek into the gift shop, where unique items include art nouveau gift wraps, Tiffany coloring books, beautiful reproduction vases and goblets, Maxfield Parrish stationery, and much more.

Admission: $2.50 adults, $1 students of any age.

Open: Tues–Sat 9:30am–4pm, Sun 1–4pm. **Closed:** Memorial Day, July 4th, Labor Day, Thanksgiving, Christmas, and New Year's Day.

THE CORNELL FINE ARTS MUSEUM, at the eastern end of Holt Ave., on the campus of Rollins College at Lake Virginia. Tel. 646-2526.

Rollins College began its art collection in 1935 with several Italian

Renaissance paintings. It was also the first home of Hugh and Jeanette McKean's (see listing above) Tiffany glass. Today, with close to 4,000 square feet of exhibition space, it houses an impressive century-spanning collection that includes works by Hiram Powers, Childe Hassam, Tiffany, Thomas Sully, William Glackens, Reginald Marsh, Leonard Baskin, and the studio of Peter Paul Rubens. Also displayed here: 19th-century silver, 17th-century Dutch Delftware, French rococo decorative panels, and Chippendale furniture. Traveling exhibits supplement the collection.

Admission: Free.

Open: Tues–Fri 10am–5pm, Sat–Sun 1–5pm. **Closed:** July 4th, Thanksgiving, the Friday after Thanksgiving, Christmas Eve, Christmas Day, New Year's Eve, and New Year's Day. **Parking:** Free in adjacent lot "H."

SCENIC BOAT TOUR, at the eastern end of Morse Blvd. on the lake. Tel. 644-4056.

For over half a century, tourists have been boarding pontoons at this location for leisurely hour-long cruises on Winter Park's beautiful chain of natural lakes. The ride traverses Lake Osceola (which flows north into the St. John's River), Lake Virginia, and Lake Maitland, winding through canals built by loggers at the turn of the century and tree-shaded fern gullies lined with bamboo and lush tropical foliage. You'll view magnificent lakeside mansions and villas (Margaret Mitchell used to winter on Lake Maitland), pristine beaches, cypress swamps, ancient trees draped with Spanish moss, and dozens of marsh birds—white herons, grackle, cormorants, osprey, and gallinule, possibly even an American bald eagle. The captain regales passengers with local lore. It's an utterly delightful trip. You can also rent canoes and small fishing boats here.

Admission: $5.50 adults, $2.75 children 2–11, under 2 free.

Open: Tours depart daily between 10am and 4pm, every hour on the hour (more often Dec 26–early June). **Closed:** Christmas.

WHERE TO STAY

Though you could visit Winter Park on a day excursion from Orlando, do consider an overnight stay at one of the following properties.

THE LANGFORD RESORT HOTEL, 300 E. New England Ave., at Interlachen Ave., Winter Park, FL 32789. Tel. 407/644-3400. Fax 407/628-1952. 209 rms, 9 suites. A/C TV TEL

$ Rates: $65–$75 single; $75–$85 double; from $180 suite. Extra person $10. Children 17 and under stay free. Rooms with kitchenettes $10 additional. AE, DC, MC, V. **Parking:** Free self-parking.

In pre-Disney days, Winter Park was one of central Florida's most-visited resorts, and the Langford was the place to stay. Vaughn Monroe entertained in the lounge, and the guest roster listed people like Eleanor Roosevelt, Mamie Eisenhower, Lillian Gish, Vincent Price, and Dina Merrill. Ronald and Nancy Reagan celebrated their 25th wedding anniversary here. This friendly resort, run by the Langford family for four decades, still draws the occasional celebrity guest, but, more importantly, it offers extensive resort facilities at very reasonable rates. And its location, on a lovely street shaded by tall oaks draped with Spanish moss, is just a block from Park Avenue, Winter Park's ritzy shopping street. Rooms in the main building, all with balconies and large walk-in closets, are each uniquely decorated. Those in the seven-story East Wing are done up in soft resort colors (mauve, peach, and powder blue), with rattan and bamboo furnishings. All accommodations offer remote-control cable TVs with free HBO; many have balconies and/or fully equipped kitchenettes with two-burner stoves and small refrigerators.

Dining/Entertainment: The nautical/tropical **Bamboo Room,** with large windows overlooking the pool, offers a reasonably priced American menu at all meals; steak and seafood are featured at dinner. The adjoining **Del Prado** bar/lounge provides piano bar entertainment and complimentary hors d'oeuvres from 5 to 8pm nightly and dancing to live band music Tuesday through Saturday from 8pm to midnight.

Services: Concierge (sells tickets, many of them discounted, to Walt Disney World and other Orlando attractions), room service from 7am to 10pm, *Orlando Sentinel* delivered to your room daily, babysitters.

Facilities: Olympic-size swimming pool, kiddie pool, car-rental desk, small video-game arcade, unisex hair salon. A full on-premises spa, heralded by a waterfall that cascades into a stream, offers sauna, steam, massage (shiatsu, Swedish, and deep athletic), body wraps, seaweed wraps, salt glows, facials, manicures, and pedicures. A full day of beauty is $125, including lunch. Golf and tennis are close by.

PARK PLAZA HOTEL, S. 307 Park Ave., at New England Ave., Winter Park, FL 32789. Tel. 407/647-1072, or toll free 800/228-7220. Fax 407/647-4081. 16 rms, 11 suites. A/C TV TEL

$ Rates (including continental breakfast): $80–$125 single; $90–$135 double; $150–$185 suite. During special events rates may be higher. AE, DC, MC, V. **Parking:** Free self- and valet parking.

Centrally located in the heart of the Park Avenue shopping and restaurant district, this small elegant hotel dates to 1921. In 1975, John and Sandra Spang bought the property and did an exquisite renovation, fitting out rooms bed-and-breakfast style with antique furnishings (handsome walnut armoires and headboards, brass beds, chaise longues, and wicker rockers, among other pieces), Persian rugs, patchwork quilts, and beautiful floral-print bedspreads. Wide wooden Bermuda shutters on the windows and wood-bladed ceiling fans overhead add tropical ambience, and homey touches include live plants in white wicker baskets and magazines in the rooms. Exposed-brick walls are hung with fine art posters. Most rooms open onto a wicker-furnished, plant-filled balcony, and many have cozy parlor areas. Especially lovely is the Balcony Suite, which has Victorian-reproduction wallpaper and a brass bed made up with a Ralph Lauren spread, throw pillows, and white dust ruffle. There are also four luxurious honeymoon suites with oversized oak beds and private balconies. In-room amenities include remote-control cable TVs with free HBO, AM/FM alarm-clock radios, and complimentary fruit baskets at check-in.

The hotel's Park Plaza Gardens restaurant (see "Where to Dine," below) adjoins. The front desk offers conciergelike service. Other amenities here include room service during restaurant hours, the newspaper of your choice delivered to your door each morning, and nightly bed turndown; transport to/from Disney parks and Orlando airport can be arranged. A beauty shop is just behind the property, and, for a fee, guests can use the nearby Winter Park Wellness Center, a health club offering a full line of Nautilus equipment, steam, sauna, indoor track, and an Olympic-size lap pool. A complimentary continental breakfast of fresh-squeezed orange juice, fresh-baked muffins, and coffee or tea is served daily in the European-style oak- and birch-paneled lobby (or in your room). Golf and tennis are close by.

WHERE TO DINE

There are so many fine restaurants in Winter Park that Orlandoans often drive over just to dine and stroll the tree-lined streets. My first listing is in Altamonte Springs, a few minutes' drive from Winter Park.

MAISON & JARDIN, 430 S. Wymore Rd., off I-4 Exit 48 between FL 436 and Maitland Blvd., in nearby Altamonte Springs. Tel. 862-4410.
  Cuisine: CLASSIC EUROPEAN. **Reservations:** Recommended. **Parking:** Free self-parking.
$ **Prices:** Brunch $18.50 prix-fixe; dinner appetizers $6.25–$8.75 (more for caviar-filled blinis); dinner main courses $17.95–$26.50. AE, CB, DC, ER, MC, V.
  Open: Brunch Sun (Oct to mid-June only) 11am–2pm; dinner Mon–Sat 6–10pm, Sun (Oct to mid-June only) 6–9pm.

One of Florida's most highly acclaimed restaurants, Maison & Jardin was architecturally inspired by a mansion in southern France that dates to Roman times. Hence the pedimented neoclassic exterior, manicured formal gardens, and imposing doors with brass-lion knockers. The exquisite interior is furnished with museum-quality pieces and objets d'art—Oriental rugs strewn on marble and terrazzo floors, Austrian crystal chandeliers, Venetian and French chinoiserie cabinets, and mirrors in gilt frames from a 17th-century Venetian palazzo. I especially like the Gazebo Room, evocative of a 17th-century Mediterranean château, with hand-painted blue and white tile walls and balloon-curtained windows looking out on a tiered *putti* fountain, waterfall, and goldfish pond. Equally delightful is the airy canvas-roofed and brick-floored Patio Room. Elegantly appointed tables are candlelit throughout, and a strolling guitarist entertains at dinner.

A featured appetizer is blinis à la Russe filled with sour cream and your choice of caviars (Icelandic, Spanish, or Russian beluga), flamed tableside in brandy and served with chopped egg and onion, radishes, and frosted vodka. Other very recommendable choices are broiled sea scallops on a bed of papaya salsa (flavored with lime juice and cilantro) served with a small mound of wild rice and baked escargots en croûte topped with spinach, Boursin cheese, and garlic cream sauce. The chef does a beautiful job with frequent game specials, such as elk sautéed with morel mushrooms in a brandy cream sauce and served over pasta. I also recommend seafood entrées here— perhaps poached Norwegian salmon in a basil beurre blanc sauce served with an array of fresh vegetables, boiled red potato, and a red, green, and yellow pepper compote. The menu changes seasonally, so your options may vary from the above. A very extensive, award-winning wine list is international in scope, with many selections available by the glass or half bottle. Hence you can experience different wines with each course. Desserts range from fresh raspberries with whipped cream to elaborate flaming finales such as bananas Foster, crêpes Suzette, and cherries jubilee; there are also more than 40 postprandial cognacs and brandies. The prix-fixe Sunday brunch, including free-flowing complimentary champagne, is comprised of an appetizer (perhaps chilled smoked Norwegian salmon), a choice of entrées ranging from eggs Benedict to New Zealand rack of lamb, salad, and dessert. A Dixieland band entertains the first Sunday of every month.

PARK PLAZA GARDENS, 319 S. Park Ave., between Lyman and New England aves., in Winter Park. Tel. 645-2475.

Cuisine: FRENCH. **Reservations:** Recommended. **Parking:** Free at city lot at New England and S. New York aves.

$ Prices: Brunch $17.95 prix-fixe; appetizers $3.95–$7.95 at lunch, $7.95–$10.95 at dinner; main courses $8.95–$12.95 at lunch (sandwiches and salads $5.95–$9.95), $17.95–$27.95 at dinner. AE, CB, DC, DISC, MC, Optima, V.

Open: Brunch Sun 11am–3pm; lunch Mon–Sat 11:30am–3pm; dinner Mon–Thurs 6–10pm, Fri–Sat 6–11pm, Sun 6–9pm.

This charming patio garden restaurant—with white-linened tables shaded by a striped canvas awning and a small forest of ficus trees—offers the feeling of outdoor dining in air-conditioned comfort. During the day sunlight streams in through a skylit ceiling; at night tables are romantically candlelit. Big planters of greenery enhance the airy al fresco ambience, and exposed-brick walls hung with changing exhibits serve as gallery space for local artists. Service is deft and gracious.

Chef Derby Weston III's culinary creations—served on large white platters—are as exquisitely presented as they are delicious. There are many good beginnings here—an herbed escargot strudel layered with blue cheese and finely chopped shiitake mushrooms served over tomato coulis; carpaccio of smoked venison served with pickled beet salad and fried parsnip chips; and velvety lobster bisque beautifully marbleized with crème fraîche among them. Do opt for a salad course—the warm Montrachet goat cheese—tossed with frisé, toasted pine nuts, cracked black peppercorns, and pernod in lemon/olive oil dressing. Entrées include fresh red snapper in a crisp thin-sliced potato crust served on beet sauce *parfumée* with cinnamon and nutmeg. Also excellent is breast of duck Szechuan style, garnished with plum confit and served in a crisp potato basket with Oriental vegetables. For dessert ebony and ivory is a sweet dream—espresso chocolate mousse and thin semisweet chocolate leaves on a mirror of marbleized white chocolate sauce with blackberry garnish. On the other hand, there's crème brûlée. And flamed bananas Foster. And page after page of after-dinner cordials, cognacs, ports, sherries, and brandies. The well-chosen wine list offers many by-the-glass selections. The lunch menu adds pasta, sandwich, and salad options. And brunch—including complimentary champagne, mimosa, or Kir royale—offers the above-mentioned appetizers, a soup or salad course, and entrées ranging from eggs Florentine to angelhair pasta tossed with sautéed shrimp in pesto chive cream sauce with salmon caviar garnish.

---

4. DAYTONA BEACH

73 miles NE of Walt Disney World, 50 miles NE of Orlando

GETTING THERE   By Plane   American, Continental, Delta, and USAir fly into **Daytona Beach International Airport** (tel. 904/248-8030). A taxi from the airport to most beach hotels runs between $8 and $12.

By Train   Closest **Amtrak** station (tel. toll free 800/USA-RAIL) is in De Land, 23 miles southwest of Daytona.

By Bus   Greyhound buses connect Daytona with most of the United States. They pull into a very centrally located terminal at 138 S. Ridgewood Ave. (U.S. 1) between International Speedway Boulevard and Magnolia Avenue (tel. 904/255-7076, or toll free 800/231-2222).

From Orlando, **Daytona-Orlando Transit Service (DOTS)** (tel. 904/257-5411, or toll free 800/231-1965) provides van transport between the two cities. They offer 12 round-trips daily. One-way fare is $26 for adults, round-trip $46; children under 12 pay half price. The service brings passengers to the company's terminal at 1598 N. Nova Rd., at 11th Street, or, for an $8 to $21 fee, to beach hotels. In Orlando the vans depart from the airport.

By Car   If you're coming from north or south, take I-95 and head east on International Speedway Boulevard (U.S. Hwy. 92). From

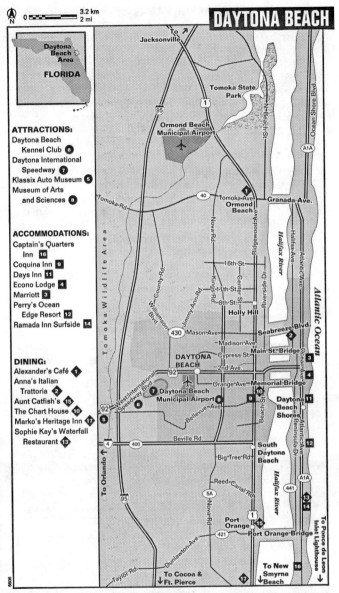

Tampa or Orlando take I-4 east and follow Daytona Beach signs to I-95 north to U.S. Hwy. 92. From northwest Florida take I-10 east to I-95 south to U.S. Hwy. 92.

The self-proclaimed "World's Most Famous Beach" is even more celebrated as "The Birthplace of Speed" and "World Center of Racing." It has been a mecca for car-racing enthusiasts since the days when automobiles were called horseless carriages. Early automobile magnates Ransom E. Olds, Henry Ford, the Stanley brothers (of steamer fame), and Louis Chevrolet—along with motor-mad millionaires like the Vanderbilts, Astors, and Rockefellers—wintered in Florida and raced their vehicles on the hard-packed sand beach. The first competition, in 1902, was between Olds and gentleman racer Alexander Winton; they worked up to the then-impressive speed of 57 miles an hour. By 1904, a Daytona Beach event called the Winter Speed Carnival was drawing participants from all over the world, most of them wealthy sportsmen and financiers. Three years later, Fred Marriott wrapped a mile of piano wire around the boiler of his souped-up Stanley Steamer (to keep it from blowing up) and raced the course at a spectacular 197 m.p.h.! At the end of the stretch he crashed, just as spectacularly, into the pounding surf. He emerged uninjured, but after the accident the Stanley brothers quit racing their steam-driven cars, and gas engines became more prominent. People erroneously believed that Marriott's steam-powered boiler had blown up.

Many men who were to become famous for their skill with machinery first tested their ideas on the sands of Daytona Beach. Glenn Curtiss, the father of naval aviation, raced motorcycles here. And Sir Malcolm Campbell, a millionaire English sportsman, raced a car powered by an aircraft engine in 1928, reaching a speed of over 206 m.p.h.; in later years he set the ultimate beach speed record of 276.8 m.p.h. Most of these early beach events, by the way, were individual speed trials rather than actual races. The final speed trials were held in 1935.

Nineteen-thirty-six ushered in the era of stock-car racing with a new beach racecourse, a host of daredevil drivers, and thousands of cheering fans. In 1947, driver and race promoter Bill France founded the National Association for Stock Car Auto Racing (NASCAR), headquartered at Daytona Beach. Today it is the world's largest motorsports authority, sanctioning the Daytona 500 and other major races at the International Speedway and tracks throughout the United States. The final stock-car race on the beach took place in 1958. A year later, France's dream of a multimotorsports facility, the Daytona International Speedway, was realized.

Of course you don't have to be a racing aficionado to enjoy Daytona. It has 23 miles of sandy beach 500 feet wide at low tide (you can still drive and park—but not race—on the sand; maximum speed allowed is 10 m.p.h.). The town is mobbed with college students during spring break—the annual beach blanket Babylon—and during Bike Week in February thousands of leather-clad motorcycle buffs make the scene. But barring spring break and major speedway events, Daytona is a laid-back beach resort, offering boating, tennis, golf, water sports, and the opportunity to stroll the sands, swim, and soak up some sunshine.

ORIENTATION

TOURIST INFORMATION The **Daytona Beach Area Convention & Visitors Bureau,** 126 E. Orange Ave., just west of the Silver Beach Bridge (P.O. Box 910 if you're writing), Daytona Beach, FL 32115 (tel. 904/255-0415, or toll free 800/854-1234), can help you with information on attractions, accommodations, dining, and events. Call in advance for maps and brochures. Or visit their office when in town. They also maintain a branch at the speedway.

CITY LAYOUT Daytona Beach is surrounded by water. The Atlantic Ocean borders its east coast, and the Halifax River flows north to south through the middle of the city. There are actually four little towns along its beach—**Ormond Beach** to the north, the centrally located **Daytona Beach** and **Daytona Beach Shores,** and **Ponce Inlet** at the southern tip just above New Smyrna Beach. FL A1A (Atlantic Avenue) runs along the beach north to south. U.S. 1 runs inland paralleling the west side of the Halifax River, and I-95 vaguely parallels it still farther west. International Speedway Boulevard is the main east-west artery.

GETTING AROUND

BY CAR You can drive and park directly on the beach here. There is a $3 access fee between February 1 and Labor Day, the rest of the year it's free.

BY TROLLEY & BUS **VOTRAN,** Volusia County's public transit system, runs buses throughout major areas of town between 6am and 7pm, Monday through Saturday. Adults pay 75¢, children under 17 and seniors pay 35¢, and children under 6 accompanied by an adult ride free.

SPECIAL EVENTS

The below-listed are Daytona's *major* annual events. Also check with The Daytona Beach Area Convention & Visitors Bureau (see above) to find out what else is happening in town during your stay.

FEBRUARY Sixteen days of **Speedweeks** events (taking place the first three weeks of February) get underway with the **Rolex 24** (a 24-hour endurance road race for sports cars), which draws international entries. Following that, top names in NASCAR stock-car racing compete in the **Busch Clash, Arca 200, Gatorade Twin 125-mile Qualifying Races, International Race of Champions (IROC), Florida 200,** and **Goody's 300,** culminating in the **Daytona 500** by STP, which is always held on the Sunday prior to the third Monday in February. All events take place at the Daytona International Speedway. Call 904/253-7223 for ticket information. For the Daytona 500, especially, tickets must be purchased far—even as much as a year—in advance. They go on sale January 1 of the prior year.

MARCH   Bike Week/Camel Motorcycle Week is the rallying point for an international gathering of motorcycle enthusiasts for 10 days early in the month. Major races (featuring the world's best road racers, motocrossers, and dirt trackers) at the speedway include the **Daytona 200 by Arai Motorcycle Classic,** the **Daytona Supercross by Honda,** and the **Camel Pro Grand National Kickoff.** There are many other races as well as motorcycle shows, beach parties, and festivities. The last day of Bike Week, after the early morning Blessing of the Bikes at St. Paul's Church, the Annual Motorcycle Parade with thousands of riders leaves Bellair Plaza and continues to the speedway. Call 904/253-7223 for details.

Spring Break. For three weeks in March college students from all over the United States and Canada flock to Daytona Beach for fun in the sun—endless partying, wet T-shirt and bikini contests, free concerts, volleyball tournaments and other games on the beach, hotel pool deck parties, etc. Call 904/255-0981 for details.

Late in the month (sometimes early April), the **Spring Speedway Spectacular,** a car show and swap meet at the Daytona International Speedway, features a wide variety of collector vehicles. In addition, displays include automotive toys and memorabilia, auto-themed art, and a crafts sale. Admission is charged. Call 904/255-7355 for details.

MAY   During the Greater Daytona Beach Striking Fish Tournament on Memorial Day weekend, some 250 boats from all over the southeast compete for more than $75,000 in cash and prizes in seven fishing categories. Call 904/255-0415 for details.

JULY   The Pepsi 400 race, marking the halfway point in the NASCAR Winston Cup Series for stock cars, is held the first Saturday in July at 11am at the Daytona International Speedway. Call 904/253-7223 for details.

The **Florida International Festival,** a week-long musical event taking place every other year (in odd-numbered years), features concerts by major classical and pop musicians from all over the world—everything from the London Symphony Orchestra to Skitch Henderson, as well as preconcert lectures, jazz bands, ballet, and special concerts for children. Events are scheduled at the Peabody Auditorium, Ocean Center, and other local performance places in late July, possibly early August. Call 904/257-7790 for details and ticket information.

SEPTEMBER   The King of the Beach Volleyball Tournament takes place in front of the Marriott Hotel in late September or early October. The top eight male players in the world compete, and a 3,000-seat stadium is erected on the beach. Admission is charged. Call 904/255-0981 for details.

OCTOBER AMA/CCS Motorcycle Championship. During three days in mid-October, road-racing stars of tomorrow compete at the Daytona International Speedway. Events include a program of AMA/CCS "Races of Champions" National Championship Sprints for a variety of road-racing classes, as well as the season-ending U.S. Endurance Championship event and the season finales for the Honda CBR 900RR Series and the Harley-Davidson Twin Sports Series. Other activities for motorcycle enthusiasts take place in the area. Call 904/253-7223 for ticket information.

NOVEMBER The **Daytona Beach Fall Speedway Spectacular,** featuring the Annual Turkey Rod Run, is the southeast's largest combined car show and swap meet, with thousands of street rods and classic vehicles on display and for sale. It takes place at the International Speedway Thanksgiving weekend. Events include an auto-parts swap meet, a collector vehicle auction, and a nonautomotive crafts show. Admission is charged. Call 904/255-7355 for details.

DECEMBER World Karting Association Enduro World Championships, the biggest karting event in the country, takes place between Christmas and New Year's at the Daytona International Speedway. Call 904/253-7223 for details.

WHAT TO SEE & DO

The speedway and the beach are, of course, Daytona's major attractions. In addition, if you're interested in deep-sea fishing and/or whale watching, contact **Critter Fleet,** 4950 S. Peninsula Dr., Ponce Inlet (tel. 904/767-7676), or **Sea Love Marina,** 4884 Front St., Ponce Inlet (tel. 904/767-3406). There are a dozen golf courses within 25 minutes of the beach, and most hotels can arrange starting times for you. The **Daytona Beach Golf Club,** 600 Wilder Blvd. (tel. 904/258-3119), is the city's largest, with 36 holes. **Shenandoah Stables,** 1759 Tomoka Farms Rd., off U.S. Hwy. 92 (tel. 904/257-1444), offers daily trail rides and horseback-riding lessons between 10am and 5pm. For jet ski rentals contact **Daytona High Performance—MBI,** 925 Sickler Dr., at the Seabreeze Bridge (tel. 904/257-5276). Additional water-sports equipment, as well as bicycles, beach buggies, and mopeds, can be rented along the beach in front of major hotels. A good place to look is in front of the Marriott at 100 N. Atlantic Ave. The **Daytona Flea Market** is one of the world's largest with 1,000 covered outdoor booths and 100 vendors in an air-conditioned building. Located on Tomoka Farms Road, a mile west of the speedway at the junction of I-95 and U.S. Hwy. 92 (tel. 904/252-1999), it is open year-round, Friday to Sunday from 8am to 5pm (parking is free). And the **Dixie Queen Riverboat Company** (tel. 904/255-1997, or toll free 800/329-6225) offers year-round lunch, Sunday brunch, and dinner cruises—all with entertainment—as well as full-day trips to St. Augustine aboard a 150-passenger paddlewheeler.

DAYTONA BEACH KENNEL CLUB, 2201 W. International Speedway Blvd., just west of Fentress Blvd. Tel. 904/ 252-6484.

This is a pleasant way to spend a day or evening, especially if you opt to watch the races over lunch or dinner in the upstairs restaurant. There are a variety of ways to bet on the greyhounds; if you've never done it before, pick up a free brochure that explains them all. You can also buy tip sheets recommending computer and expert picks. Each meet includes 14 races. You must be at least 18 years old to enter the betting area.

The moderately priced Pavilion Clubhouse Restaurant (lunch entrées are $5.95 to $9.95; dinner entrées, $11.95 to $17.95) has tiered seating, with big picture windows overlooking the track and TV monitors enhancing your view at higher tables. Tables are elegantly appointed with peach linen napery. At lunch you might order a Caesar salad, or a Reuben sandwich. A typical dinner might consist of French onion soup and an entrée of prime rib or shrimp scampi. There's a full bar. Reservations are suggested; request a window seat.

Admission: $1 adults (seniors 55 and over free at matinees); grandstand seating, 50¢–$1.75; restaurant, $2. Parking is free on the premises; preferred parking (closer to entrance) is $1, and valet parking, $2.

Open: Night races usually Mon–Sat at 7:45pm (call before you go); matinees Mon, Wed, and Sat at 1pm. Doors and restaurant open an hour before post time.

DAYTONA INTERNATIONAL SPEEDWAY, 1801 W. International Speedway Blvd. (U.S. 92), at Bill France Blvd. Tel. 904/253-RACE for tickets, 254-2700 for information.

Opened in 1959 with the first Daytona 500, this 450-acre "World Center of Racing" is practically the raison d'être for Daytona Beach—certainly the keynote of the city's fame. It presents about eight weekends of major racing events annually, featuring stock cars, sports cars, motorcycles, and go-karts, and is also used for automobile testing. Its grandstand, a mile long, seats over 100,000.

Major annual races here include Speedweeks (16 days of stock- and sports-car racing in February, culminating in the Daytona 500 by STP), Bike Week (10 days of motorcycle events in early March), Daytona Beach Spring Speedway Spectacular (car show and swap meet featuring collector vehicles, late March or early April), the Pepsi 400 (stock cars, in July), the AMA/CCS Motorcycle Championship (on a three-day weekend in mid-October), and the Daytona Beach Fall Speedway Spectacular (a car show and swap meet Thanksgiving weekend). For further information, write to Daytona International Speedway, P.O. Box 2801, Daytona Beach, FL 32120-2801.

To learn more about racing, head for the **Visitors' Center** at the west end of the Speedway and NASCAR office complex. Open daily from 9am to 5pm, the center is also the departure site for entertainingly narrated 25-minute guided van tours of the facility that provide a close look at the high-banked 2.5-mile trioval and 3.56-mile road courses, the Winston Tower, the pit, and the garage area. Admission is $3 for adults, free for children 7 and under. Tours depart daily every 10 to 20 minutes between 9:10am and 4:10pm, except during races, special events, or car testing. Also at the Visitors' Center are a large gift shop; a snack bar; the Gallery of Legends, where the history of motorsports in the Daytona Beach area is documented through photographs and memorabilia; and the Budweiser Video Wall, presenting a continuous showing of racing in the Daytona Beach area, tracing its history from the "Birthplace of Speed" to the "World Center of Racing." You can "feel the thunder" while listening to a 20-minute Surround-Sound audio presentation called *The Daytona 500: From Dawn to Determination*. The center also stocks information on area accommodations, restaurants, attractions, and nightlife.

Admission: Auto events, $30–$80; motorcycle events, $10–$35; go-kart events, under $10. Big events sell out months in advance (the Daytona 500 at least a year in advance), so plan far ahead and also reserve accommodations well before your trip. Parking is free for grandstand seating; infield parking charges vary with the event.

Open: Daily. **Closed:** New Year's Day, Thanksgiving, and Christmas Day.

KLASSIX AUTO MUSEUM, 2909 W. International Speedway Blvd., at Tomoka Farms Rd., just west of I-95. Tel. 904/252-3800.

Opened with appropriate fanfare during 1994 Speedweeks—complete with special events at the Speedway and a parade of antique race cars, classic cars, and modern show cars on Ormond Beach—this exciting new museum showcases every Corvette model manufactured from 1953 to the present. Also on display are collector cars (including the car from the movie *Days of Thunder*), special-interest Corvettes (such as the Mako Shark, a mid-'60s prototype), historic Daytona race cars from all motorsports, motorcycles, and racing memorabilia, along with exhibits on the same. Interactive videos allow visitors to vicariously experience the thrills of car racing—an activity that will be further enhanced in the near future via virtual reality. A 1950s-style soda shop and gift shop are on the premises.

Admission: $8.50 adults, $4.25 children 7–12, 6 and under free.
Open: Daily 9am–9pm. **Closed:** Christmas Day.

MUSEUM OF ARTS AND SCIENCES, 1040 Museum Blvd., off Nova Rd. Tel. 904/255-0285.

Housing both art and natural science exhibits, this eclectic museum dates to 1956, when Cuban dictator Fulgencio Batista donated his vacation home and art collection to the city. In 1971 the museum relocated to its present building, and, over the years, its holdings have increased in volume and scope. The Cuban collection—mostly paintings—spans two centuries from 1759 to 1959. "Masterworks of American Art: 300 Years of American Culture" includes art and furnishings from the Pilgrim period, Abolitionist paintings, works by Gilbert Stuart and Samuel Morse, Federalist furnishings, and Tiffany silver. In the Karshan Center of Graphic Arts you'll view 18th- and 19th-century European prints, turn-of-the-century art nouveau posters, and lithographs by artists ranging from William Blake to Degas. A lobby gallery highlights "Fine and Decorative Arts from the Age of Napoleon." A "Pre-History of Florida" section contains such artifacts as a million-year-old mammoth tooth and the skeleton of a Pleistocene giant ground sloth that roamed the Daytona coast 130,000 years ago. And the museum's most recent permanent installation, "Africa: Life and Ritual," documents African peoples from over 30 cultures in 15 countries. A contemporary sculpture garden and a one-mile nature trail are on the grounds. Permanent exhibits are complemented by an ongoing schedule of concerts, lectures, and changing shows. Planetarium shows take place at 1 and 3pm daily.

Admission: $3 for adults, $1 for children and students with ID, under 6 free. Planetarium shows $1.

Open: Tues–Fri 9am–4pm, Sat–Sun noon–5pm. **Closed:** Mon, Thanksgiving, Christmas Day, and New Year's Day. **Directions:** Take International Speedway Blvd. west, make a left on Nova Rd., and look for a sign on your right.

WHERE TO STAY

Daytona Beach hotels fill to the bursting point during major races at the speedway, whenever college students are on break, and during other special events. At these times room rates skyrocket, if you can find a room at all, and there's often a minimum-stay requirement. If you're planning to be in town at one of these busy times (see "Special Events," above, in this section), reserve far in advance. All of the accommodations listed below are on or near the beach and close to the speedway.

AT THE BEACH

Expensive

MARRIOTT, 100 N. Atlantic Ave., between Earl St. and Auditorium Blvd., Daytona Beach, FL 32118. Tel. 904/254-8200, or toll free 800/228-9290. Fax 904/253-8841. 377 rms, 25 suites. A/C MINIBAR TV TEL

$ Rates: $149 single or double ($235–$250 during special events when there's also a seven-night minimum stay); Executive Level, $198 single or double ($250–$265 during special events); $250–$750 suite. Children under 18 stay free. Extra person $20. AE, CB, DC, DISC, MC, V. **Parking:** Free in lot across the street, valet parking $8 per night.

★ This is Daytona's most luxurious—and most central—beachfront hotel, designed so that every room offers a gorgeous ocean view. It is right at the clock tower and bandshell, and, in season, its beach and boardwalk are the site of concessions offering parasailing, bicycle rentals, motorized four-wheelers, pedal carts, surfboards, boogie boards, cabanas, and umbrellas. Accommodations are decorated in pleasing resort colors—mauve, peach, and light turquoise—with bleached-oak furnishings. In-room amenities include alarm-clock radios and remote-control cable TVs with Spectravision movie stations. Rooms on the Executive Level (16th floor) feature upgraded amenities such as king-size beds, pullout sofas and armchairs, ceiling fans, VCRs, and, in the baths, black-and-white TVs, hairdryers, and extra phones. Executive Level guests have use of a gorgeous private ocean-view lounge with a console TV and games.

Dining/Entertainment: The Marriott has two full-service restaurants. **Coquinas** is the hotel's plush premier dining room, with candlelit, peach-clothed tables amid massive oak columns, Louis XV–style chairs, and mirrored walls embellished with frosted-glass swans. Gourmet steak and seafood dinners are featured, and there's an extensive wine list. The very pretty plant-filled **Parkside Oceanfront Café,** with picture windows overlooking the beach, serves moderately priced breakfasts, lunches, and dinners daily. Weather permitting, you can sit outside at umbrella tables. Early-bird dinners here, served from 5 to 7pm daily, are a great bargain. **Splash,** an attractive poolside bar with Saltillo-tile floors, pots of ferns, and palm trees, serves light fare and specialty drinks; it has indoor and outdoor seating. Also on the beach is a complex of small restaurants with outdoor café seating, serving international fare—everything from tacos to souvlaki. There's a lively on-premises sports bar called **Waves,** and the sophisticated **Clock Tower Lounge** offers live jazz (see "Evening Entertainment," below).

Services: Concierge, room service from 7am to 11pm, gratis newspapers at bell desk.

Facilities: Indoor/outdoor swimming pool, two whirlpools, steam and sauna, kiddie pool, vast palm-fringed sun deck, sand volleyball court, playground, video-game arcade, full-service unisex hair and beauty salon (also offers massage), coin-op washers/dryers, complete health club (admission of $5 per visit or $10 per length of stay is charged), business services, florist, camera shop offering photographic supplies and one-hour developing, arcade of shops (selling hats, gifts, beach and resort wear for the whole family, and equipment for surfing and other beach sports). Memorial Day through Labor Day there are free activities for children 5 to 12—arts and crafts, sports, etc. A small amusement park adjoins the hotel, and there are cable-car rides on the pier.

Moderate

PERRY'S OCEAN EDGE RESORT, 2209 S. Atlantic Ave., between Moore and Bonner aves., Daytona Beach, FL

32118. Tel. 904/255-0581 or toll free 800/447-0002. Fax 904/258-7315. 204 rms. A/C TV TEL

$ Rates (including continental breakfast): $50–$120 single or double, $108–$242 suite (formed by combining rooms). Two children under 12 stay free. Additional person $10. Rate range reflects view and season; rates may be even higher during major events when there's also a four- to five-night minimum stay. Inquire about packages/weekly rates. AE, CB, DC, DISC, MC, V.
Parking: Free on the premises.

Some people say the secret of this family-run property's popularity is the fresh-baked doughnuts served with your coffee, fresh fruit, and juice each morning. They certainly are a treat, but Perry's has more going for it than free frosted bear claws. Entered via an attractive knotty pine-paneled lobby, it has a grassy palm-fringed garden beachfront—the prettiest in Daytona. The staff is extremely friendly and helpful. And spacious rooms (75% of them with ocean views and private balconies or patios) are equipped with remote-control cable TVs, AM/FM alarm-clock radios, microwave ovens, coffee makers, and small refrigerators. Many units have full kitchens, living rooms, and dining areas, and most have hairdryers in the bath. Some rooms are furnished in wicker, others in knotty pine. A supermarket and 7-11 store are directly across the street.

Dining/Entertainment: The **Smoke House Restaurant,** a homey little coffee shop with curtained windows and hanging copper pots is open for full American breakfasts and lunches daily. The above-mentioned doughnuts are served in two comfortable on-premises lounges equipped with pianos and large TVs. Guests gather for Monday night football in the lodgelike South Tower lounge.

Services: Year-round activities (Bingo, movies, tournaments, Monte Carlo nights, and more) for adults and children.

Facilities: A large free-form indoor pool with retractable roof, surrounded by a lushly planted garden sun deck; 2 large outdoor swimming pools; kiddie pool; whirlpool; shuffleboard; 9-hole putting green; horseshoes; bocci ball court; beach volleyball; coin-op washers/dryers; video-game arcade; car-rental desk; gift shop.

RAMADA INN SURFSIDE, 3125 S. Atlantic Ave., between Van and Atares aves., Daytona Beach, FL 32118. Tel. 904/788-1000, or toll free 800/255-3838. Fax 904/756-9906. 102 rms, 17 suites. A/C TV TEL

$ Rates: $60–$90 single or double; $70–$100 efficiency with kitchen; $85–$145 suite. Children under 19 stay free. Additional person $10. Rate range reflects low and high seasons; rates may be even higher during major events when there's also a five-night minimum stay. Inquire about packages. AE, CB, DC, DISC, ER, JCB, MC, V. **Parking:** Free on the premises.

This Ramada boasts a prime beachfront location, and all of its rooms offer ocean views and balconies. Accommodations are attractively decorated with oak furnishings, grasspaper-like textured wall coverings, burgundy carpets, and mauve shell-motif bedspreads and curtains. All offer remote-control cable TVs with free HBO and Showtime movies and visitor-information channels, AM/FM alarm-clock radios, and in-room safes; most have sofas. Families will appreciate the units with fully equipped eat-in kitchens and, in summer, the full schedule of free children's activities.

Dining/Entertainment: The very pleasant **Sandcastle Restaurant,** serving all meals and specializing in steak and seafood, has windowed walls overlooking the ocean and swimming pool. Kids under 12 eat free. The adjoining **Sundancer Lounge**—which features complimentary happy hour hors d'oeuvres, live bands for dancing weekends (Wednesday to Saturday in high season), and a blackjack machine at the bar—has the same beach view. It airs sporting events on a large-screen TV and serves a free halftime buffet during Monday-night football. A pool bar with umbrella tables on an awninged wooden deck serves food and drinks from the restaurant and bar.

Services: Room service during restaurant hours; guest services can arrange tours, transportation, fishing excursions, trips to Walt Disney World, and more.

Facilities: Large oceanfront swimming pool and sun deck, kiddie pool, oceanfront picnic tables, sand volleyball court, shuffleboard, video-game arcade, coin-op washers/dryers, snack machines, gift shop, activities for seniors Oct–Feb and Apr–May.

Inexpensive

DAYS INN, 1909 S. Atlantic Ave., at Flamingo Ave., Daytona Beach, FL 32118. Tel. 904/255-4492, or toll free 800/224-5056 or 800/329-7466. Fax 904/238-0632. 188 rms. 8 efficiency units. A/C TV TEL

$ Rates: $35–$50 single; $45–$60 double; $55–$75 efficiency unit for one or two. During special events $100–$125 single or double; $120–$145 efficiency unit. Children under 12 stay free. Additional person $6 extra. AE, CB, DC, DISC, MC, V. **Parking:** Free on the premises.

At this recently renovated nine-story beachfront hotel, every room provides an ocean view. Pretty peach-and-teal rooms with oak furnishings offer remote-control cable TVs with HBO and visitor-information channels, in-room safes, and bed massagers. All have balconies, and some contain small refrigerators and microwave ovens. Large oceanfront efficiencies with fully equipped kitchens are ideal for families.

Facilities include a swimming pool/kiddie pool/sun deck overlooking the beach, an on-premises restaurant called the Tropical Tree serving breakfast only, and a video-game arcade. During summer, light fare is offered at a pool bar.

Days Inns nationwide offer a Super Saver rate of just $29 to $49 single or double if you reserve 30 days in advance via the second-listed toll-free phone number. This deal is, of course, subject to availability, but it's worth a try. If you can't get in here, there are three other Days Inns in town, all conveniently located beachfront properties.

ECONO LODGE, 301 S. Atlantic Ave., at Broadway, Daytona Beach, FL 32018. Tel. 904/255-6421, or toll free 800/76-LODGE. Fax 904/252-6195. 100 rms. A/C TV TEL

$ Rates: $38–$78 single or double, $90–$150 during special events. Children under 15 stay free. Additional person $5 extra, $10 during special events. AE, CB, DC, DISC, MC, V. **Parking:** Free on the premises.

This very centrally located Econo Lodge occupies a beachfront five-story building, with half of its rooms overlooking the ocean. Accommodations—standard motel units attractively decorated in peach and mauve—are equipped with cable TVs that offer visitor-information channels. A good deal for families are the reasonably priced suites (at the higher end of the rates quoted above) offering sizable living room areas with sofas in addition to bedrooms, plus small refrigerators and microwave ovens; some of these have private balconies.

Facilities include a very large swimming pool with a sun deck overlooking the beach (there's a pool bar in season, and a concession called the Tiki Hut vends beach accessories), a coin-op laundry, and a small video-game arcade. A casual hotel coffee shop called Time Out serves breakfast and lunch. Room service is available during restaurant hours (6am to 2pm daily). And a cozy on-premises pub called the Hole Bar is a popular local hangout featuring music (live or DJ) nightly, pool tables, dart boards, foosball, and video games; sporting events—including Monday-night football—are aired on a large-screen TV.

BED & BREAKFASTS

CAPTAIN'S QUARTERS INN, 3711 S. Atlantic Ave. (about a quarter mile south of Dunlawton Ave.), Daytona Beach, FL 32127. Tel. 904/767-3119, or toll free 800/332-3119. Fax 904/760-7712. 26 suites. A/C TV TEL

$ Rates (including full breakfast): $75–$95 single or double, $110–$145 oceanfront penthouse suite. During special events, $90–$140 single or double; $130–$195 oceanfront penthouse suite. Additional adult $5, free for children under 17. Lower rates available for weekly and monthly stays. AE, DISC, MC, V. **Parking:** Free.

This five-story beachfront inn offers large and lovely suites, most with ocean or river views. They have living/dining room areas, fully equipped kitchens, and country-look bedrooms furnished in oak antique reproductions. Residential decorator schemes utilize charming floral-print wall coverings and fabrics, balloon curtains, dried-flower wreaths, and framed botanical prints. French doors open onto balconies or patios furnished with wooden rockers.

Accommodations are equipped with clock radios, remote-control cable TVs (two per unit) offering HBO and another free movie station, and VCRs (movies can be rented). Penthouse suites have fireplaces, spa tubs, and big picture windows overlooking the ocean. On-premises facilities include a country crafts/gift shop off the lobby, a heated swimming pool, coin-op washer/dryers, and the Galley Restaurant, which has an outdoor deck overlooking the ocean. Open for breakfast and lunch daily, it serves scrumptious fresh-baked cakes, cinnamon buns, and danish, as well as homemade soups, salads, and sandwiches on homemade breads. It's worth stopping by even if you're staying elsewhere. Other pluses: free transport to and from the airport, complimentary daily newspapers, wine and cheese at check-in, chocolate mints on your night table, and a full breakfast of eggs, bacon, grits or home-fries, juice, and coffee served each morning in your room or the Galley. Owner Becky Sue Morgan provides warm hospitality.

COQUINA INN, 544 S. Palmetto Ave. (at Cedar St.), Daytona Beach, FL 32114. Tel. 904/254-4969, or toll free 800/727-0678. 4 rms (all with bath). A/C
$ Rates (including full breakfast): $75–$105 single or double, $115–$140 during special events; $195 suite. Additional person $10 extra, $30 during special events. No children under 12 accepted. MC, V. **Parking:** Free on the premises.

This charming terra-cotta–roofed coquina and cream stucco house sits on a tranquil tree-shaded street half a block west of the Halifax River and Harbor Marina. Guests can relax before a working fireplace in a lovely parlor furnished with leather wing chairs, a comfortable sofa, and a baby grand piano. Baskets of magazines, books, games, and a TV are in the adjoining sunroom, which has terra-cotta–tile floors and cheerfully upholstered white wicker furnishings. An Oriental rug graces the highly polished oak floor of the dining room, which also features French doors, casement windows, and a crystal chandelier. Breakfast—elegantly served on Lenox and Rosenthal china—includes an entrée such as eggs Benedict or French toast stuffed with cream cheese, bananas, and pecans; fresh fruit; fresh-ground coffee; and homemade breads and muffins. Classical music is played in public areas.

Each room is exquisitely decorated, most with area rugs strewn on oak floors and ceiling fans overhead. The Jasmine Room, painted adobe peach, features a working coquina fireplace and a canopied mahogany bed. In the Hibiscus Room, decorated in soft greens and pinks, a black iron bed embellished with gold leaf is made up with a pretty floral chintz spread. French doors lead to a private plant-filled balcony (pots of geraniums, hibiscus, gardenias, and hydrangeas) overlooking an ancient live oak draped with Spanish moss. Painted in raspberry with a floral frieze, the sunny Azalea Room has light streaming in from corner windows. Overlooking the patio garden, it's furnished with a mahogany waterfall bed (a Victorian teddy bear sits amid its throw pillows), white wicker chairs, and an antique Governor Winthrop desk. And the Magnolia Room, its mint stucco walls hung with framed botanical prints, contains a shell-shaped sink and a hand-carved mahogany four-poster bed and white iron day bed, both made up with beautiful floral chintz bedspreads and ruffled pillows. The Jasmine and Hibiscus rooms can be combined to create a two-bedroom/two-bath suite. All rooms have clock radios and are provided with bubble bath and candles. Portable phones and TVs are available on request. Complimentary tea and sherry are served in the parlor throughout the day. Also gratis—10-speed bicycles and use of an Olympic-size pool at the nearby YWCA. During busy seasons, a two-night minimum stay is required.

WHERE TO DINE
EXPENSIVE

ALEXANDER'S CAFE, 123 W. Granada Blvd., between N. Ridgewood Ave. and U.S. 1 in Ormond Beach. Tel. 904/673-5312.
  Cuisine: FRENCH/CONTINENTAL. **Reservations:** Suggested.
$ **Prices:** Appetizers $3.75–$5.50 at lunch, $6.75–$7.75 at dinner; main courses $5.20–$6.95 at lunch, $18.95–$23.95 at dinner; prix-fixe Sun brunch $18.95. AE, MC, V.
  Open: Lunch Mon–Sat 11:30am–4pm, Sun brunch 11:30am–3pm, dinner Mon–Sat 5–9:30pm.

This charming innlike restaurant has a dark wood-beamed ceiling, multipaned windows, glossy pine floors, and seating in comfortable upholstered armchairs at tables clothed in white linen and lit (at night) by shaded candle lamps. Soft lighting also emanates from hunting-horn motif brass chandeliers and sconces. The War Room—with green- and sienna-striped wallpaper above pine wainscoting—is decorated with framed photographs of Civil War generals, a painting of Napoleon, battle scenes, and recruitment posters. The Bacchus Room offers a view of the wine cellar via a glass door. And in the third dining room a pianist plays standards (Cole Porter et al.) on a baby grand during dinner.

Though the menu changes frequently (owner John Cunningham likes to try new things), you can always count on French chef Christian Drouin for a superb meal. If it's available, do order his tangy Cheddar soup spiked with sherry. On other visits, I've enjoyed appetizers of baked mushrooms stuffed with mild Italian sausage and spinach tortellini served atop fresh spinach in a light Alfredo sauce. Thick oven-baked pork chops in a cranberry-orange-Dijon sauce was a memorable entrée. Also excellent were large grilled sea scallops in a beurre blanc citrus cream sauce and a classic steak au poivre in brandy cream sauce. All entrées are accompanied by a delicious salad, fresh vegetables, potatoes or rice du jour, and sorbets between courses; appropriate wines are recommended. Don't skip the desserts, which might include a very rich black velvet chocolate cake or a raspberry torte topped with butter-cream frosting and toasted almonds. The lunch menu lists sandwiches, salads, and a few entrées, and brunch is an elaborate seven-course feast including a glass of champagne. Alexander's offers an extensive wine list, several dozen single-malt scotches, and 14 draft beers. The adjoining bar/lounge is deservedly popular (details in "Evening Entertainment," below).

MODERATE

ANNA'S ITALIAN TRATTORIA, 304 Seabreeze Blvd., at Peninsula Dr. Tel. 904/239-9624.
   Cuisine: ITALIAN. **Reservations:** Recommended.
$ Prices: Appetizers $4.25–$8; main courses mostly $8.50–$14; early-bird dinners (served 5–6:30pm) $5–$8. AE, MC, V. **Parking:** Free in a lot on Seabreeze Blvd. across Peninsula Dr.
   Open: Dinner only, daily 5–10pm.

At this charming little trattoria, the Triani family, from Sicily, have created a homelike atmosphere enhanced by cheerful Italian music. Soft lighting emanates from brass oil lamps and sconces. Everything here is homemade—from the creamy Italian dressing on your house salad to the basket of hot crusty bread that accompanies all entrées. That bread comes in handy for soaking up the dressing (extra-virgin olive oil with pieces of celery, slivers of fresh garlic, lemon, parsley, and oregano) of a scungilli salad appetizer. An order of lightly breaded fried calamari with a piquant marinara sauce is also a good starter. Two irresistible pasta dishes are the *fettuccine alla campagniola* (pasta tossed with strips of sautéed eggplant and chunks of sausage in tomato cream sauce flavored with a soupçon of crushed red pepper and romano cheese) and rigatoni Siciliana (tubular pasta with sautéed broccoli, garlic, and pine nuts in a fresh tomato sauce). Non-pasta recommendables include salmon scampi (sautéed in garlic butter, mushrooms, sherry wine, and lemon); and risotto alla Anna, similar to a Spanish paella—a rice dish cooked with chunks of chicken, shrimp, green peas, and onions in a light tomato sauce.

Portions are hearty. If you like a heavy hand with garlic, as I do, tell your waiter. Entrées come with soup or salad and a side dish of angelhair pasta or a vegetable. Take the pasta and order a vegetable side dish as well, perhaps asparagus, escarole, or broccoli rabe sautéed in oil and garlic. There's a nice selection of Italian wines to complement your meal. Both the tiramisu and the homemade ricotta cheesecake make for excellent desserts.

AUNT CATFISH'S, 4009 Halifax Dr., at the west end of the Port Orange Bridge. Tel. 904/767-4768.
   Cuisine: SOUTHERN/SEAFOOD. **Reservations:** Not accepted, but you can—and should—call ahead for priority seating (that means you get the first table available when you arrive).
$ Prices: Appetizers $2.90–$4.95; main courses $3.99–$8 at lunch, mostly $8–$13.50 at dinner; early-bird dinners $7–$10.50. Reduced prices for children and seniors. Sun brunch $9 for adults, $5.50 for children 4–12, free for kids under 4. AE, DC, DISC, MC, V.

Open: Mon–Sat 11:30am–9:30pm, Sun 9am–9:30pm (brunch Sun 9am–2pm; early-bird dinners daily noon–6:30pm). **Closed:** Christmas.

S Aunt Catfish was the nickname of a gruff-voiced local character whom owner Jim Galbreath knew as a kid. She fished all day, drove around in a black Cadillac, and ate dinner every night in a restaurant owned by Jim's parents. Her namesake restaurant abounds in cozy southern-cracker ambience. Tables are topped with laminated horse-feed sacks, weathered-looking rough-hewn wood-paneled walls are hung with historic photographs of the Daytona Beach area, and decorative elements include antique clothes wringers and corn huskers. During the day, ask for a window seat overlooking the Halifax River.

The food is great, and there's plenty of it. No way will you finish everything you order. For one thing, all entrées include hush puppies, a chunk of watermelon, unbelievable yummy hot cinnamon rolls, a side dish (perhaps baked Mexican potato skins with melted Cheddar, salsa, and sour cream), and unlimited helpings from an extensive salad bar, which in addition to salads is laden with such down-home fare as cheese grits, cinnamon apples, fresh-baked cornbread, and hominy. A great entrée choice is the Florida cracker sampler platter—a spit-roasted quarter chicken with cranberry-orange relish, crabcakes served in hollandaise sauce, fried shrimp, and fried catfish fingerlings. Lightly breaded fried oysters here are also highly recommendable. Beverage options include house wines, bar drinks, bottomless pitchers of iced tea, and fresh-squeezed lemonade. For dessert, split a boatsinker fudge pie with Häagen-Dazs coffee ice cream dipped in a coat of hardened chocolate and topped with whipped cream. Aunt Catfish's key lime and raspberry pies are also excellent.

Sunday brunch provides an opportunity for overindulgence. A buffet meal, it includes all the above-mentioned salad bar items, plus an omelet station, pancakes, French toast, hot entrées, a carving station, fresh-baked muffins and pastries (even bananas Foster), and more—all for under $10! Lunch choices include burgers, sandwiches, and a soup and salad buffet in addition to ribs, chicken, and seafood entrées.

THE CHART HOUSE, 1100 Marina Point Dr., off Beach St. Tel. 904/255-9022.

Cuisine: CONTINENTAL/STEAK/SEAFOOD. **Reservations:** Suggested.

$ Prices: Appetizers $4.50–$8.95; main courses mostly $14.95–$21.95. AE, CB, DC, DISC, MC, V.

Open: Sun–Thurs 5–10pm, Fri–Sat 5–11pm.

The lushly plant-filled Chart House is of octagonal design, with palm trees growing towards a lofty skylit bamboo ceiling. Oak tables topped with laminated world maps, ship models, palm-frond-motif carpeting, and a waitstaff in Hawaiian shirts enhance the restaurant's tropical/marine ambience. And windowed walls overlooking the

Halifax River and a boat-filled marina insure every diner a water view. Consider having dessert or after-dinner drinks in the plush bar/lounge downstairs or on an open-air riverside deck with umbrella tables.

You might want to bypass appetizers here, since your entrée price includes a very extensive salad bar (including items such as caviar, artichoke hearts, and an array of fresh fruits), a basket of hot sourdough and seven-grain squaw bread (it's made with molasses), and a baked potato or Chart House wild rice cooked in chicken broth and tossed with slivered almonds, pineapple, pimento, and chives. For your main course select shrimp or chicken Santa Fe dusted with cumin, paprika, and cayenne, grilled in butter, and served with tangy bleu cheese dip. Steak, prime rib au jus with creamed horseradish sauce, and surf-and-turf combinations are also options. Mud pie is the dessert of choice—coffee ice cream on an Oreo cookie crust.

SOPHIE KAY'S WATERFALL RESTAURANT, 3516 S. Atlantic Ave., at Raymond Ave. Tel. 904/756-4444.
Cuisine: CONTINENTAL/STEAK/SEAFOOD/PASTA. **Reservations:** Suggested.
$ Prices: Appetizers $3.95–$5.95; main courses $8.95–$23.95 (most under $15). AE, DC, DISC, MC, V.
Open: Sun–Thurs 4–10pm, Fri–Sat 4–11pm, bar (serving light fare) Sun–Thurs to midnight, Fri–Sat to 1am.

Long-time Daytona restaurateur, cookbook author, and local television personality Sophie Kay has entertained dozens of celebrities—everyone from John Travolta (he celebrated his mom's birthday at Sophie's) to Carol Channing. Her newest restaurant venture—designed by talented son Dean, who also serves as maitre d'—has an elegant plant-filled interior. The room centers on a rock waterfall that cascades into a goldfish pond. Stark white stucco walls are hung with attractive abstract paintings and tapestries, while pottery and plants are displayed on rough stone ledges. Arched mirrors enhance the feeling of spaciousness, and full-size palm trees, candles aglow in peach frosted-glass holders, and soft piano music add romantic tropical nuance.

An order of half a dozen oysters Rockefeller bubbling with cheese, or lightly breaded crisp-fried shrimp scampi (the latter also available as an entrée), makes an excellent beginning. Sophie is a great hand with pasta (she's written an entire book on the subject), and her primavera pasta tossed with al dente chunks of broccoli, onions, carrots, yellow squash, zucchini, mushrooms, and sun-dried tomatoes in a delicate white sauce is perfection. Also very good: baked seafood (shrimp, scallops, and filet of orange roughly) served en papillote in a creamy lobster béchamel sauce. And many people come here for items such as filet mignon, roast prime rib au jus with creamy horseradish sauce, or surf-and-turf combinations. Entrées include soup or salad, wild rice or baked potato, and a basket of fresh-baked bread and muffins. For dessert, don't pass up Sophie's delicious twice-baked cheesecake on a buttery graham-cracker crust—one of the best of its genre. After dinner adjourn to the sophisticated piano bar for cocktails.

INEXPENSIVE

DOWN THE HATCH, 4894 Front St., Ponce Inlet. Tel. 904/761-4831.
   Cuisine: SEAFOOD. **Reservations:** Not accepted, but call ahead for priority seating (that means you get the first table available when you arrive). **Directions:** Take Fla. A1A south, make a right on Beach St., and follow the signs.
$ Prices: Appetizers $2.75–$5.95; main courses $7.95–$12.95; sandwiches $3.25–$5.25. Reduced prices for children. AE, MC, V.
   Open: Daily 11:30am–10pm. **Closed:** Thanksgiving and Christmas.

Occupying a half-century-old fish camp on the Halifax River, Down the Hatch is a cozy, candlelit restaurant serving up fresh fish and seafood (note their shrimp boat docked outside). During the day, picture windows provide scenic views of a passing parade of boats and shore birds—blue herons, egrets, pelicans, and cormorants—and you might even see dolphins frolicking. At night, arrive early to catch the sunset over the river, and also to beat the crowd at this very popular place. Inside, rough-hewn cypress walls are hung with hundreds of photographs of the Daytona Speedway and the old fish camp, and the nautical ambience is enhanced by a clutter of mounted fish trophies, ship models, harpoons, hurricane lamps, and antique bottles. In summer, light fare is served outside on an awninged wooden deck.

Start your meal with an order of buffalo shrimp—tiny shrimp quick-fried in hot oil, finished with a piquant Louisiana hot sauce, and served with chunky homemade bleu cheese dressing. Lightly breaded, deep-fried grouper fingers, served with tartar sauce, are also tasty. Ditto the raw oysters served with cocktail sauce and horseradish. Entrées include fried or broiled fresh fish such as red snapper or grouper, and there's an excellent crab Imperial—crabmeat broiled in a tarragon-mayonnaise sauce and garnished with chopped green peppers. If seafood isn't your thing, filet mignon and prime rib are aged on the premises. All entrées are served with hush puppies and a choice of baked potato, salad, cole slaw, or fries. There's a full bar; desserts include mud pie, key lime pie, and cheesecake.

MARKO'S HERITAGE INN, 5420 S. Ridgewood Ave., at Niver St. Tel. 904/761-9520.
   Cuisine: SOUTHERN/SEAFOOD. **Reservations:** Not accepted, but you can—and should—call ahead for priority seating (that means you get the first table available when you arrive).
$ Prices: Appetizers $2.95–$6.95; main courses mostly $8–$13; early-bird dinners $5.95–$9.95. Reduced prices for children and

seniors. Sun breakfast/brunch buffet $5.95 for adults, $3.50 for children 4–12, under 4 free. AE, DC, DISC, MC, V.

Open: Mon–Sat 4:30–9:30pm; Sun 8am–2pm for buffet breakfast/brunch, 11:30am–9pm for dinner. Early-bird dinners served daily until 6pm. **Closed:** Christmas.

S Like Aunt Catfish's (see above) Marko's is owned by Jim Galbreath. In fact, its 17,000-square-foot warren of cozy dining rooms encompasses the house in which he grew up and his parents' original Daytona Beach restaurant. Off the entrance you'll see large photographs of its 1950s interior, with Jim as a young lad tending the counter. It's all very southern and homelike. Overflow crowds wait for tables on a porch or in an antique-filled Victorian parlor, and there's an old-fashioned candy counter and bakery up front. Dining areas have windows with shutters or ruffled café curtains, walls paneled in knotty pine or whitewashed cypress lapsiding, hutches and shelves filled with display china, tables covered in pretty floral-print cotton cloths, and many hanging plants. One room even has a working fireplace.

Don't eat a big lunch the day you dine here. Your entrée price includes a complimentary bowl of Florida cracker-style clam chowder, salad (go for the fruit with creamy poppyseed dressing), an array of vegetables served family style (cole slaw, stewed apples, stringbeans, a jar of pickled beets), potato or scrumptious broccoli casserole, tangerine sherbet between courses, and a basket of fresh-baked oatmeal and cinnamon rolls. All of this bounty precludes the need for appetizers, but there are some great ones nevertheless: blackened mahi mahi with hollandaise, buffalo shrimp with hot sauce, and buttery-garlicky chicken tenders prepared like escargots and served in mushroom caps. My favorite entrée is the grouper Hemingway, sautéed in a crisp sesame crust. Other good choices include smoky barbecued baby back ribs and fried Maryland-style crabcakes. And desserts—such as a first-rate key lime pie, chocolate peanut-butter pie, and funnel cake topped with macadamia-nut ice cream and hot fudge—are not to be missed. There's a full bar. After dinner browse in the gift shop filled with charming country crafts.

EVENING ENTERTAINMENT
THE PERFORMING ARTS

At the 2,552-seat **Peabody Auditorium,** 600 Auditorium Blvd., between Noble Street and Wild Olive Avenue (tel. 904/255-1314), Daytona Beach's Civic Ballet performs *The Nutcracker* every Christmas and sponsors another ballet every spring. The Daytona Beach Symphony Society arranges a series of six classical concerts between December and April. During the same season, Concert Showcase features pop artists such as Liza Minnelli, Tony Bennett, Steve Lawrence and Eydie Gorme, and Frank Sinatra, as well as full Broadway-cast stage shows like *Cats* and *City of Angels*. And the London Symphony Orchestra has been performing here for over 25 years during the semiannual Florida International Festival.

Under the same city auspices is the **Oceanfront Bandshell** (tel. 904/258-3169), on the boardwalk next to the Marriott Hotel. The city hosts a series of free big-band concerts at the Bandshell every Sunday night from early June through Labor Day. It is also the scene of spring-break concerts.

Prices at the Peabody vary with performances. Bandshell concerts are usually free. Parking is $3 in a lot adjacent to the Peabody.

THE CLUB & BAR SCENE

In addition to the following, the piano bar at **Sophie Kay's Waterfall Restaurant,** which offers a special bar menu (pizzas, potato skins, steak sandwiches), and **The Chart House** downstairs bar are elegant and simpatico nighttime settings. See details in restaurant listings above.

ALEXANDER'S CAFE, 123 W. Granada Blvd., between N. Ridgewood Ave. and U.S. 1 in Ormond Beach. Tel. 904/673-5312.

The convivial bar/lounge of this upscale restaurant has a ski-lodgey ambience comprised of exposed-brick and pine-paneled walls and a cathedral ceiling. A sled called Rosebud behind the bar and a painting of Batman are among its whimsical adornments. The crowd comes for the music (live guitarists play oldies, and there's a primo jukebox stocked with Otis Redding, Bob Marley, Joe Cocker, and Springsteen tunes). Sporting events (most notably Monday-night football) are aired on three TV monitors. You can order from the extensive wine list, have an appetizer or dessert, try one of the café's many single-malt scotches (I recommend the smoky Lagavulin) or draft beers, even order up a fine cigar. The bar is cigar-friendly, but open windows keep the smoke-level down. Open Monday through Saturday till between midnight and 2am, depending on the crowd. No cover charge.

CLOCK TOWER LOUNGE, in the Marriott hotel, 100 N. Atlantic Ave., between Earl St. and Auditorium Blvd. Tel. 904/254-8200.

This sophisticated bar/lounge, with bamboo furnishings and palm trees growing towards a skylight ceiling, offers piano-bar music or live jazz Tuesday through Saturday from 8pm to midnight. There's a small dance floor, and, in addition to drinks, you can order interesting light fare items such as smoked-salmon mousse with crackers or black lobster ravioli in a light cream sauce. This is one of Daytona's most romantic settings. Make a night of it, and dine earlier in Coquinas, the Marriott's elegant steak and seafood restaurant. It's open from 8pm to midnight nightly. There is no cover charge; parking is free in a lot across the street; valet parking is $3. See also "Waves," below.

COLISEUM, 176 N. Beach St., at Bay St. Tel. 904/257-9982.

Heralded by a pedimented Doric colonnade, this upscale Roman-themed dance club occupies a converted movie theater. Inside, a raised dance floor is flanked by Ionic columns, and Roman-style bas-reliefs and sculpture adorn the walls. A DJ plays alternative progressive dance music, with lapses into Top 40 tunes; four big movie screens project music and ambience videos; and nightly laser shows are high-tech, utilizing 3-D and sophisticated graphic-arts effects. The crowd is mostly twentysomething with occasional glitterati (Tom Cruise partied here during the filming of *Days of Thunder*), rock musicians, and local athletes in attendance. During spring break there are live concerts and special events. The Coliseum is open from 10pm to 3am nightly from February to October, from 11pm to 3am Thursday through Sunday the rest of the year. The cover charge is $5 to $6. Parking is free behind the club on Bay Street; usually there's ample street parking as well.

RAZZLES, 611 Seabreeze Blvd., between Grandview and S. Atlantic aves. Tel. 904/257-6236.

At this large and popular dance club, a DJ plays Top 40 tunes and high-energy music till 3am nightly. The setting is archetypical, with lots of neon tubing, the requisite monitors flashing music videos, and sophisticated lighting effects over the dance floor. A magician frequently entertains in the lobby, there are four pool tables, a blackjack table, and a few video games. An awninged patio out front provides a place for quiet conversation. The crowd is young—early 20s. There's free parking behind the club on Grandview Avenue between Seabreeze and Oakridge boulevards. The cover charge is $6 to $8 before 10pm and includes free drinks; after 10pm, 18- to 20-year-olds pay $5, those 21 and over pay $3.

701 SOUTH, in the South Beach Resort, 701 S. Atlantic Ave., at Revilo Blvd. Tel. 904/255-8431.

This is a high-energy club, with a big dance floor, two giant matrix (multi-screen) video walls, 13 bartenders (overseeing 8,000 square feet of bar area), and "shooter" girls in leotards proffering shots of a drink called Sex on the Beach—a mix of cranberry and orange juices, peach schnapps, and vodka—to willing customers. Monday through Saturday a DJ and live bands alternate playing progressive music and rock 'n' roll, Sunday there's a DJ only. Big-name acts have played here, among them Paula Abdul, Samantha Fox, Red Hot Chile Peppers, Marky Mark, and Naughty by Nature. When you weary of dancing, you can play pool, darts, foosball, or air hockey. Light fare is available. Open nightly till 3am. The cover charge is $6 for ages 18–20, $4 for those 21 and over; covers are higher when big-name bands play. Parking is free on the premises.

THE SPOT, 176 N. Beach St., at Bay St. Tel. 904/257-9982.

Under the same ownership as the above-mentioned Coliseum, The Spot shares its address and phone as well. Billing itself as a "premier sports bar," it has large-screen TVs in every corner, which, along with over 30 smaller monitors, air major worldwide sporting events via satellite. This cavernous club centers on a U-shaped Formica-topped bar trimmed in turquoise neon. Walls are decorated in a painterly collage of baseball cards, car-racing photos, sports para-phernalia, and American flags. And there's a comfortable seating area on a fire-engine-red vinyl sofa in front of a large TV. Less passive amusements include foosball, air hockey, video games, pinball machines, a one-on-one basketball court, eight regulation pool tables, dart boards, and bar games. Light fare is available. The Spot sponsors local rugby and pool teams. Monday-night football parties include raffles for tickets to local sporting events, and a DJ is on hand Tuesday nights. The Spot is open nightly until 3am and does not charge a cover. Parking is free behind the club on Bay Street; there's usually ample street parking as well.

WAVES, in the Marriott hotel, 100 N. Atlantic Ave., be-tween Earl St. and Auditorium Blvd. Tel. 904/254-8200.

An elegant sports bar on the hotel's boardwalk level, Waves airs continuous sporting events (via a four-dish satellite system) on two large screens and 23 additional monitors. Its main bar centers on a large aquarium of tropical fish. In addition to upholstered bamboo furnishings, there are comfy sofas in a quiet alcove with a large-screen TV. Bartenders and servers are dressed as referees. A DJ plays music for dancing nightly from 9pm. Other activities here include backgam-mon, QB1 interactive sports and trivia games, and electronic darts. There is no cover charge except during special events, and the bar is open nightly till 3am. Parking is free in the lot across the street; valet parking is $3.

INDEX

ACCOMMODATIONS

Excursion Areas

KEY TO ABBREVIATIONS: *B* = Budget; *B&B* = Bed & Breakfast; *CG* = Campground; *E* = Expensive; *I* = Inexpensive; *M* = Moderately priced; *VE* = Very expensive.

Please Send Me the Books Checked Below:

FROMMER'S COMPREHENSIVE GUIDES
(Guides listing facilities from budget to deluxe, with emphasis on the medium-priced)

	Retail Price	Code		Retail Price	Code
☐ Acapulco/Ixtapa/Taxco 1993–94	$15.00	C120	☐ Morocco 1992–93	$18.00	C021
☐ Alaska 1994–95	$17.00	C131	☐ Nepal 1994–95	$18.00	C126
☐ Arizona 1993–94	$18.00	C101	☐ New England 1994 (Avail. 1/94)	$16.00	C137
☐ Australia 1992–93	$18.00	C002	☐ New Mexico 1993–94	$15.00	C117
☐ Austria 1993–94	$19.00	C119	☐ New York State 1994–95	$19.00	C133
☐ Bahamas 1994–95	$17.00	C121	☐ Northwest 1994–95 (Avail. 2/94)	$17.00	C140
☐ Belgium/Holland/ Luxembourg 1993–94	$18.00	C106	☐ Portugal 1994–95 (Avail. 2/94)	$17.00	C141
☐ Bermuda 1994–95	$15.00	C122	☐ Puerto Rico 1993–94	$15.00	C103
☐ Brazil 1993–94	$20.00	C111	☐ Puerto Vallarta/ Manzanillo/Guadalajara 1994–95 (Avail. 1/94)	$14.00	C028
☐ California 1994	$15.00	C134	☐ Scandinavia 1993–94	$19.00	C135
☐ Canada 1994–95 (Avail. 4/94)	$19.00	C145	☐ Scotland 1994–95 (Avail. 4/94)	$17.00	C146
☐ Caribbean 1994	$18.00	C123	☐ South Pacific 1994–95 (Avail. 1/94)	$20.00	C138
☐ Carolinas/Georgia 1994–95	$17.00	C128	☐ Spain 1993–94	$19.00	C115
☐ Colorado 1994–95 (Avail. 3/94)	$16.00	C143	☐ Switzerland/ Liechtenstein 1994–95 (Avail. 1/94)	$19.00	C139
☐ Cruises 1993–94	$19.00	C107	☐ Thailand 1992–93	$20.00	C033
☐ Delaware/Maryland 1994–95 (Avail. 1/94)	$15.00	C136	☐ U.S.A. 1993–94	$19.00	C116
☐ England 1994	$18.00	C129	☐ Virgin Islands 1994–95	$13.00	C127
☐ Florida 1994	$18.00	C124	☐ Virginia 1994–95 (Avail. 2/94)	$14.00	C142
☐ France 1994–95	$20.00	C132	☐ Yucatán 1993–94	$18.00	C110
☐ Germany 1994	$19.00	C125			
☐ Italy 1994	$19.00	C130			
☐ Jamaica/Barbados 1993–94	$15.00	C105			
☐ Japan 1994–95 (Avail. 3/94)	$19.00	C144			

FROMMER'S $-A-DAY GUIDES
(Guides to low-cost tourist accommodations and facilities)

	Retail Price	Code		Retail Price	Code
☐ Australia on $45 1993–94	$18.00	D102	☐ Israel on $45 1993–94	$18.00	D101
☐ Costa Rica/Guatemala/ Belize on $35 1993–94	$17.00	D108	☐ Mexico on $45 1994	$19.00	D116
☐ Eastern Europe on $30 1993–94	$18.00	D110	☐ New York on $70 1994–95	$16.00	D120
☐ England on $60 1994	$18.00	D112	☐ New Zealand on $45 1993–94	$18.00	D103
☐ Europe on $50 1994	$19.00	D115	☐ Scotland/Wales on $50 1992–93	$18.00	D019
☐ Greece on $45 1993–94	$19.00	D100	☐ South America on $40 1993–94	$19.00	D109
☐ Hawaii on $75 1994	$19.00	D113	☐ Turkey on $40 1992–93	$22.00	D023
☐ India on $40 1992–93	$20.00	D010	☐ Washington, D.C. on $40 1994–95 (Avail. 2/94)	$17.00	D119
☐ Ireland on $45 1994–95 (Avail. 1/94)	$17.00	D117			

FROMMER'S CITY $-A-DAY GUIDES
(Pocket-size guides to low-cost tourist accommodations and facilities)

	Retail Price	Code		Retail Price	Code
☐ Berlin on $40 1994–95	$12.00	D111	☐ Madrid on $50 1994–95 (Avail. 1/94)	$13.00	D118
☐ Copenhagen on $50 1992–93	$12.00	D003	☐ Paris on $50 1994–95	$12.00	D117
☐ London on $45 1994–95	$12.00	D114	☐ Stockholm on $50 1992–93	$13.00	D022

FROMMER'S WALKING TOURS
(With routes and detailed maps, these companion guides point out the places and pleasures that make a city unique)

	Retail Price	Code		Retail Price	Code
☐ Berlin	$12.00	W100	☐ Paris	$12.00	W103
☐ London	$12.00	W101	☐ San Francisco	$12.00	W104
☐ New York	$12.00	W102	☐ Washington, D.C.	$12.00	W105

FROMMER'S TOURING GUIDES
(Color-illustrated guides that include walking tours, cultural and historic sights, and practical information)

	Retail Price	Code		Retail Price	Code
☐ Amsterdam	$11.00	T001	☐ New York	$11.00	T008
☐ Barcelona	$14.00	T015	☐ Rome	$11.00	T010
☐ Brazil	$11.00	T003	☐ Scotland	$10.00	T011
☐ Florence	$ 9.00	T005	☐ Sicily	$15.00	T017
☐ Hong Kong/Singapore/ Macau	$11.00	T006	☐ Tokyo	$15.00	T016
☐ Kenya	$14.00	T018	☐ Turkey	$11.00	T013
☐ London	$13.00	T007	☐ Venice	$ 9.00	T014

FROMMER'S FAMILY GUIDES

	Retail Price	Code		Retail Price	Code
☐ California with Kids	$18.00	F100	☐ San Francisco with Kids (Avail. 4/94)	$17.00	F104
☐ Los Angeles with Kids (Avail. 4/94)	$17.00	F103	☐ Washington, D.C. with Kids (Avail. 2/94)	$17.00	F102
☐ New York City with Kids (Avail. 2/94)	$18.00	F101			

FROMMER'S CITY GUIDES
(Pocket-size guides to sightseeing and tourist accommodations and facilities in all price ranges)

	Retail Price	Code		Retail Price	Code
☐ Amsterdam 1993–94	$13.00	S110	☐ Montréal/Québec City 1993–94	$13.00	S125
☐ Athens 1993–94	$13.00	S114	☐ Nashville/Memphis 1994–95 (Avail. 4/94)	$13.00	S141
☐ Atlanta 1993–94	$13.00	S112	☐ New Orleans 1993–94	$13.00	S103
☐ Atlantic City/Cape May 1993–94	$13.00	S130	☐ New York 1994 (Avail. 1/94)	$13.00	S138
☐ Bangkok 1992–93	$13.00	S005	☐ Orlando 1994	$13.00	S135
☐ Barcelona/Majorca/ Minorca/Ibiza 1993–94	$13.00	S115	☐ Paris 1993–94	$13.00	S109
☐ Berlin 1993–94	$13.00	S116	☐ Philadelphia 1993–94	$13.00	S113
☐ Boston 1993–94	$13.00	S117	☐ San Diego 1993–94	$13.00	S107
☐ Budapest 1994–95 (Avail. 2/94)	$13.00	S139	☐ San Francisco 1994	$13.00	S133
☐ Chicago 1993–94	$13.00	S122	☐ Santa Fe/Taos/ Albuquerque 1993–94	$13.00	S108
☐ Denver/Boulder/ Colorado Springs 1993–94	$13.00	S131	☐ Seattle/Portland 1994–95	$13.00	S137
☐ Dublin 1993–94	$13.00	S128	☐ St. Louis/Kansas City 1993–94	$13.00	S127
☐ Hong Kong 1994–95 (Avail. 4/94)	$13.00	S140	☐ Sydney 1993–94	$13.00	S129
☐ Honolulu/Oahu 1994	$13.00	S134	☐ Tampa/St. Petersburg 1993–94	$13.00	S105
☐ Las Vegas 1993–94	$13.00	S121	☐ Tokyo 1992–93	$13.00	S039
☐ London 1994	$13.00	S132	☐ Toronto 1993–94	$13.00	S126
☐ Los Angeles 1993–94	$13.00	S123	☐ Vancouver/Victoria 1994–95 (Avail. 1/94)	$13.00	S142
☐ Madrid/Costa del Sol 1993–94	$13.00	S124	☐ Washington, D.C. 1994 (Avail. 1/94)	$13.00	S136
☐ Miami 1993–94	$13.00	S118			
☐ Minneapolis/St. Paul 1993–94	$13.00	S119			

SPECIAL EDITIONS

	Retail Price	Code		Retail Price	Code
☐ Bed & Breakfast Southwest	$16.00	P100	☐ Caribbean Hideaways	$16.00	P103
☐ Bed & Breakfast Great American Cities (Avail. 1/94	$16.00	P104	☐ National Park Guide 1994 (Avail. 3/94)	$16.00	P105
			☐ Where to Stay U.S.A.	$15.00	P102

Please note: if the availability of a book is several months away, we may have back issues of guides to that particular destination. Call customer service at (815) 734-1104.